Springer Japan KK

H. Horaguchi
K. Shimokawa (Eds.)

Japanese Foreign Direct Investment and the East Asian Industrial System

Case Studies from the Automobile and Electronics Industries

With 30 Figures

Springer

Haruo Horaguchi
Professor, Faculty of Business Administration
Hosei University
2-17-1 Fujimi, Chiyoda-ku, Tokyo 102-8160, Japan

Koichi Shimokawa
Professor, Department of Business Administration
Tokai Gakuen University
21-233 Nishinohora, Ukigai, Miyoshi-cho, Nishikamo-gun, Aichi 470-0207, Japan

ISBN 978-4-431-66992-0 ISBN 978-4-431-66990-6 (eBook)
DOI 10.1007/978-4-431-66990-6

Printed on acid-free paper

Originally published by Springer-Verlag Tokyo in 2002

Typesetting: Camera-ready by the editors
SPIN: 10867739

Preface

This volume is the final output of the 19th Hosei University International Conference, "Japanese Foreign Direct Investment and Structural Change in the East Asian Industrial System: Global Restructuring for the 21st Century." The conference was held from the 30th of October to the 1st of November 2000 in the Boissonade Tower at Hosei University in Tokyo. Hosei University sponsored the entire project, which was started in order to evaluate economic aspects of Japanese foreign direct investment and its consequences after the Asian economic crisis in 1997. The conference brought together prominent scholars from China, France, Germany, Hong Kong, Japan, Korea, Malaysia, Singapore, Taiwan, Thailand, and the U.S.A. All of them are specialists in field studies of manufacturing industries in which Japanese multinational corporations (MNCs) operate outside their home country.

A research project which aimed to study the manufacturing sector in the East Asian region started when one of the organizing members obtained a Grant-in-Aid for International Scientific Research from the Ministry of Education (now, the Ministry of Education and Science) in Japan. The research was classified as university-to-university corporate research, and was based on an agreement between Hosei University and Université Jean Moulin-Lyon 3. The research title was "Strategic Alliance and Industrial Location of Japanese and French Multinationals (Research No. 32675-3801)" from 1999 to 2000. Haruo Horaguchi of Hosei University represented the project, and Françoise Guelle of Université Jean Moulin-Lyon 3 was his collaborator. Professor Koichi Shimokawa of Tokai Gakuen University and Professor Yveline Lecler of Université Lumiere-Lyon 2 supported the project. The Hosei International Fund also gave financial support to encourage this international research.

This collection gives the reader a detailed overview and analysis of the key management issues associated with the East Asian industrial system. It is almost a decade since a World Bank policy research report, *The East Asian Miracle: Economic Growth and Public Policy,* was published in 1993. The report amazed scholars in East Asia, not because of its clarity in analysis, but because of its excessive simplicity with regard to economic reality and its lack of managerial insights. Four years later, the devaluation of the Thai baht in July 1997 caused a contagion of currency devaluation in East Asian countries. Their economies suffered shrinking domestic demand and falling asset prices. Restructuring of production capacity became one of the global issues for these economies, since multinational corporations linked their production networks among these countries.

The process of recovery from the Asian economic crisis has been associated with three international players. The first is the creation of the ASEAN Free Trade Area (AFTA), whereby the ten ASEAN nations cooperate in regional liberalization of trade and investment. The second is the growing influence of China. China now exceeds Japan in exports of certain products, and will continue to penetrate World markets. AFTA will not be effective in protecting against Chinese products in the arena of cost competitiveness. The third is European multinationals. As we will see in this book, Japanese and U.S. MNCs are dominant players in the region, whereas European multinationals entered Asian markets and took on an active role only in the 1990s. European MNCs entered Asian markets creating alliances with Japanese multinationals and gaining market share. We can see a detailed study in the main body of this book.

We are grateful to the chairpersons and discussants of the three-day conference, as well as to the contributors to this volume: Yukiko Fukagawa, Norio Gomi, Shigeki Higashi, Momoko Kawakami, Kazuo Koike, Jochen Legewie, Akira Suehiro, Shigeru Takayanagi, Mariko Watanabe, and Fumio Yoshino. The Center for Business and Industrial Research at Hosei University played an active role in organizing the conference. The undergraduate students of the Horaguchi seminar at Hosei University helped in welcoming foreign scholars and participants to the Ichigaya campus. Ayako Miyazawa prepared the camera-ready manuscript, and the staff of Springer-Verlag Tokyo contributed by publishing this volume.

Haruo Horaguchi

Contents

Introduction: East Asian Industrial Dynamics and International Business

Haruo Horaguchi
Hosei University

1 Foreign Direct Investment and the East Asian Industrial System

Most observers are agreed upon the growth potential of East Asian countries. One must admit, however, that their growth potential was put into doubt by the impact of the East Asian Currency Crisis starting in July 1997. The recovery process progressed in parallel with political reforms in some countries, and the financial sector has been restructured in others. This volume focuses on two industries, which represent the real side of the economy and undoubtedly act as engines of growth, the electronics industry and the automobile industry.

In this volume the realities of East Asian business are assessed by two groups of researchers. The researchers from Korea, Taiwan, Hong Kong, Singapore, China, Malaysia and Thailand trace the evolution of the two industries after the currency crisis. Their contributed chapters ask to what extent the manufacturing businesses in this region call for new challenges. We also see the issues of indigenous growth of local corporations in relation to global market networks. This is a particular arena which was once called the East Asian Miracle but which is now facing new realities in the early twenty-first century.

Multinational corporations (MNCs) are undoubtedly one of the most important players in this age of globalization. MNCs are studied both from the home and local country perspectives. The scholars in France, Japan and the United States trace the corporate strategies of foreign MNCs in East Asian countries. As the market place shrank after the crisis, MNCs had to restructure their business in this region, and had to adapt to Asian regional integration, where appropriate.

This volume consists of four parts and fifteen chapters. I would like to briefly explain the structure of the book and the contribution of each chapter.

2 Overview after the Asian Economic Crisis in 1997

Part one, on the impact of the East Asian Currency Crisis in 1997 and the recovery process, has two chapters. In chapter one, Simon and Lecler focus on country analysis and present an optimistic view on the period after the Crisis. They see the period after the Crisis, from 1997 to 2000, as the "recovery process," and say that it did not evolve into a full scale recession, and nor did it develop a "fusion syndrome," with a new chain reaction triggered, for example, by a currency devaluation in China. Simon and Lecler diagnose that in the electronics industry, the impact of consumption shrinkage and the credit squeeze was largely offset by the recovery in world markets. These are evidenced by various published statistics, and by their field survey in Thailand and Japan.

In chapter two, Enright discusses the raison d'être of large MNCs operating in East Asian countries. Enright conducted a two-year questionnaire survey in 1998-99, from which he received around 1,100 usable responses. He also interviewed 350 managers to obtain detailed information. The most important reason for MNCs operating in this region is to access market opportunities. Developing relationships, brand names, and distribution networks are keys to sustain MNCs' competitive advantages. Enright points out how MNCs make their location choices. The Chinese Mainland and Japan are the leading sales locations for more than 80 percent of respondents. More than 70 percent reported significant sales in Korea, Singapore, Taiwan, and Hong Kong. The Chinese Mainland is the most popular location for production purposes by Western MNCs, with distant second and third positions held by Japan and Australia respectively. Japanese MNCs favor the Chinese Mainland as a production site. Thailand, Taiwan and Malaysia follow as significant production locations. With regard to cities in the region, Hong Kong and Singapore are the two most important locations for Asia-Pacific regional headquarters or regional offices, Enright concludes.

3 Electronics Industry: Singapore, Malaysia, and Hong Kong in the Age of AFTA

Part two, Regional Integration and Changing Industrial Organization in the Electronics Industry, consists of four chapters. In chapter three, Horaguchi surveys the economic theories of regional integration. Horaguchi interviewed seven major Japanese MNCs in the electronics industry and concludes that the ASEAN Industry Cooperation (AICO) scheme of AFTA does not have a significant impact on Japanese Electronics MNCs. The reasons are two-fold. One is that the administrative procedure of each AFTA member country is lengthy when it concerns admitting increased import from the counterpart country. The other is that the Japanese MNCs are operating for markets outside ASEAN, using the American dollar. The currency depreciation in 1997 did not affect Japanese MNCs and they have no incentive to integrate their production sites for ASEAN internal markets.

In chapter four, Sieh traces the Malaysian economy through the recovery process after the 1997 currency crisis. Malaysia was conspicuous in avoiding the contagion of currency depreciation by introducing currency controls and pegging the Malaysian ringgit at 3.80 to 1 U.S. dollar. Short-term capital flows were also limited to suppress speculation. The electronics industry in Malaysia has "double-linkage," Sieh writes. Double-linkage are created as backward integration of worldwide procurement by subsidiaries of MNCs, as well as forward networks of international marketing. Intra-firm and inter-firm networks provide linkages both forward and backward for the worldwide electronics industry. Although per capita income in Malaysia fell from US $4,496 in 1996 to US $3,255 in 1999, the electronics industry absorbed the largest share of employment in the manufacturing sector with an average growth of 10.8 per cent between 1991 and 1998. Policy recommendations are also summarized in this chapter.

It is interesting that chapter five by Wong focuses on backward linkage by Singapore firms, whereas chapter six by Chan discusses forward linkage through the Hong Kong electronics industry.

In chapter five, Wong focuses on the backward linkage of the electronics industry in Singapore, namely Contract Manufacturers (CMs). Wong explains that the contract manufacturing industry had its origin in the 1970s when IBM contracted SCI Systems to produce computer parts on their behalf. SCM System was a contractor for the US National Aeronautical and Space Administration. Although it has been a common practice for Japanese and Korean manufacturers to utilize subcontractors, it is a new phenomenon for the Singaporean economy. Wong gives detailed evidence on the mushrooming of electronic manufacturing service (EMS) companies, or CMs. CMs have sophisticated capabilities of design, product idea, and high-speed surface mounting technology on multi-layer circuit boards.

In chapter six, Chan illustrates an interesting observation. Based upon his questionnaire survey to Hong Kong electronics MNCs, he shows that Hong Kong electronics MNCs have expanded from establishing overseas sales and marketing subsidiaries to operating international production sites. Hong Kong MNCs are horizontally integrated to pursue their foreign operations. The respondents are classified in three categories. The first group represents those firms which established production facilities in China only. The second group has production facilities in China and other LDCs. The third group has production sites in LDCs and also in Developed Countries (DCs). The third group answered that "country experience" is the priority to invest in DCs, whereas the first and the second answered that "lower labor cost" is important.

4 Automobile Industry: Korea, Taiwan, Thailand and Global Trends

Part three of this volume deals with the global restructuring process of the automobile industry. From the 1980s to the first half of the 1990s, the automobile industry seemed to prosper in Korea, Taiwan and Thailand. Local companies, with technological alliances with Japanese and Western multinationals, took a lion's share in the local market, and they started to seek international markets and foreign direct investment opportunities. Korean automobile companies were seeking emerging markets in Eastern Europe. Taiwan makers started to invest in Mainland China. Thailand played an important role in the ASEAN market. Japanese automobile manufacturers as well as European and American manufacturers have been responding to the changing market environment.

Kim portrays a striking feature of the Korean automobile industry in chapter seven. As of September 2000, there were only four automobile companies; Hyundai/Kia, Daewoo, Renault-Samsung, and Samsung Commercial Vehicles. One should notice that before the Korean financial crisis of 1997, there had been nine automobile makers. Daimler-Chrysler invested capital of 430.9 billion won in Hyundai Motors, to become the largest shareholder having 9 percent of the equity. General Motors took over a suspension plant from Daewoo in 1998, and successive investment in Korea made Delphi the largest auto manufacturer in Korea in terms of sales. The Korean automobile industry has allowed the integration by Western MNCs, although it had carefully controlled Japanese investment. Kim analyses this as a necessary process for the world automobile industry. Kim argues that historically the top eight automobile companies have shared 80 percent of the world automobile market. There was tremendous overcapacity in every country. Kim questions, however, whether the automobile industry is a "strategic asset" to any nation, as the idiosyncratic nature and cultural diversity must also be incorporated in the management of automobile production.

In chapter eight, Lynch contrasts the growth of the Taiwan automobile industry with other East Asian nations. Although industry observers envisage that the number of assemblers in Taiwan will decrease to four or five in the first decade after 2000, there are currently ten assemblers, five of which account for most of Taiwan's vehicle production. Four of them have accepted Japanese equity holdings and technical assistance, and one is 70 percent owned by Ford. Mitsubishi owns 21 percent of China Motors Corporation; Nissan owns 25 percent of Yulon; Toyota and Hino own 49 percent of Kuozui; and Honda owns 13.5 percent of San Yang. Taiwanese assemblers are operating in two different economic environments. Firstly, Taiwan may well join the WTO, when import taxes on vehicles will be reduced from their current 30 percent to 17.5 percent by 2007, and import quotas will also be phased out. Secondly, the Taiwanese assemblers started foreign operations in the mid-1990s, and Mainland China became the target region to acquire new market opportunities. Lynch describes this strategy as a type of "insurance" for Taiwanese assemblers, whereby they can pursue cost reduction and market penetration at the same time. As we will see in the chapter thirteen and fourteen, Lynch also assesses the lack of technological competence among foreign operations of Taiwanese assemblers in Mainland China.

In chapter nine, Thamavit, Kreingkrai, and Peera study the changing character of the automobile industry in Thailand. After the 1997 economic crisis, the automobile industry in Thailand also changed drastically. The major automobile assemblers were long dominated by foreign, especially Japanese, manufacturers. After the crisis, there was huge excess capacity in automobile assembly plants, and so the assemblers increased exports to Europe, New Zealand, Australia, Singapore, and Brunei. It is important to notice the new strategy of GM and Auto Alliance Thailand (Ford and Mazda). Along with the modularization of auto parts, a competitive bidding system for part outsourcing has been introduced. Thamavit, Kreingkrai, and Peera are concerned about the negative effect of this global sourcing strategy. Since the bidding is held in Japan, so-called 'open sourcing' may become an entry barrier for local Thai manufacturers. After the crisis, many local suppliers have withdrawn from the auto parts industry, while Japanese assemblers increased their equity in local joint ventures.

In chapter ten, Shimokawa surveys various secondary data on Japanese MNCs in ASEAN. Shimokawa concludes that "AICO is presently not functional" for the automobile industry in ASEAN, and that the Common Effective Preferential Tariff (CEPT) will accelerate a full-scale international division of labor. This network will include Japan, Taiwan, and ASEAN nations. Based upon his interview survey in Malaysia and Thailand, Shimokawa also reports that Toyota and Denso practiced various employment adjustment techniques after the Asian Economic Crisis in 1997. Voluntary retirement, dispatching employees to other countries, and providing off-the-job training in Japan are examples, which are basically a replica of Japanese practices for adjusting labor force to an economic downturn.

In chapter eleven, Guelle compares the internationalization strategy of three tire makers: Michelin, Bridgestone, and Goodyear. Guelle summarizes that the CEO of each company has a similar business policy to win leadership in the tire industry. Their presences in Asian nations are, however, different. Mainland China, Thailand and Japan are the destinations where all three big MNCs have already acquired some local companies, or invested to operate subsidiaries. Joint ventures are a common form of foreign entry for this industry. The alliance between Goodyear and Sumitomo Rubber is an interesting case, because Sumitomo Rubber transferred its Dunlop tire business in the U.S. and Europe to Goodyear in September 1999. Bridgestone -Firestone recalled around 6.5 million tires in the U.S market from August 2000. This is the major reason for Bridgestone's discontent with its global business. Michelin supplies tires for Renault, which is now actively increasing its market share in Asia. In 2000, Toyo, which is the second tire maker in Japan, made an alliance with Michelin. Since Toyo is the major supplier for Nissan, which is now owned by Renault, Toyo is aiming to supply vibration-absorbing rubber components for use with new engines being developed jointly by Nissan and Renault.

5 New Challenges: Product Development and Technology Transfer

The final part of this volume deals with the new challenges of the early 21st century in the Asian market. Product development and technology transfer are the major issues for the automobile manufacturing industry.

In chapter twelve, Fujimoto and Sugiyama focus on the product development strategy of Asia Car. Across the ASEAN countries, consumer preferences of vehicle types differ immensely. In Malaysia, 80 percent of total sales are passenger car sales, while in Thailand it is about 30 percent, and in Indonesia only about 10 percent of total sales. Japanese automobile assemblers are thus taking an "Old Platform Derivative" strategy for the Indonesian market. (A vehicle platform refers to the main frame of the car.) In one Indonesian case, the suspension and transmission were reused unchanged from a first generation car, although the frame was remodeled. In another case, an Indonesian model was developed using an old platform from Japan without any change, although this model is quite different in its physical structure. This strategy helps to reduce the equipment cost and development cost.

In chapter thirteen, Chen presents a case study of Fujian Southeast Motor Co.(SEM). Since the Taiwanese "China Motor Corporation (CMC)" was not allowed to invest directly in Mainland China, CMC established a 100 percent subsidiary, the "Hwa-Wai Co." in the U.K. Virgin Islands in 1995. Hwa-Wai Co. and a Mainland Chinese company, "Fuzhou Motors Co." agreed upon establishing a joint venture company in September 1995. This is the Fujian Southeast Motor Co.(SEM). The fifty-fifty ownership is agreed and the Board of Directors of SEM are also half and half, six each. In order to meet a requirement of the localization policy of Mainland China, SEM virtually invited thirty Taiwanese suppliers, which are located nearby SEM in Fujian province. These Taiwanese suppliers follow SEM's directions to assure quality, minimize cost, and deliver on time. Chen points out that these suppliers are loyal to SEM, having long-term business contacts. It is important to note that the Japanese Mitsubishi Motor Corporation transferred its technology to the Taiwanese "China Motor Corporation (CMC)," and CMC transferred its technology to the Fujian Southeast Motor Co.(SEM). Thus, a hybrid technology between Japanese and Taiwanese is now transferred to generate another generation of 'triple hybridization.' In chapter fifteen, we will see that Kumon describes the process of technology transfer between Mitsubishi and its Asian plants including the Taiwanese CMC.

In chapter fourteen, Lee traces the historical process of technology transfer from Japan to Mainland China. The "First Automotive Works (FAW)" in Changchun city, China, is a case where the Toyota production system was introduced in the late 1970s. Lee gathers evidence that Taiichi Ohno, a legendary technical manager of the Toyota production system, visited FAW in 1977 and gave his technical guidance to the management of FAW. In 1978, FAW sent twenty of its top management team to Japan. They spent five months visiting plants at Toyota, Nissan, Mitsubishi, Hino and other companies in Japan. The team internally published instruction booklets, called "Yellow Books," based upon their field research notes. The "Yellow Books" were used in seminars for all the executives and technicians in the company. The Toyota production system was fully implemented when a new plant started operation in August 1990. Hino, one of the biggest truck manufacturers having a close relationship with Toyota, sent 23 technicians, and 49 FAW technicians were also sent to Hino. As the Toyota production system encouraged multiprocess handling and increased work intensity, the workers opposed it. Although the work intensity was being increased, wages did not keep pace. Then a "management bonus" system was introduced, which was a visible form of scoring system, based on inspection criteria points. The publication of *The Machine that Changed the World* by the MIT group was another driving force to spread the 'lean production system' around 1993-95. Japanese production system had such a big repercussion across the pacific.

In chapter fifteen, Kumon describes the international strategy of Mitsubishi Motors Corporation(MMC). Kumon summarizes the history and degree of managerial characteristics. MMC has its roots in Mitsubishi Heavy Industries Ltd, and it inherited a high level of engine design and production technology. In 1970, Mitsubishi Motors tied up with Chrysler Corporation. Thus the sale of Mitsubishi cars in the US and Mexican markets had to be conducted through the Chrysler sales network. The only countries where MMC had the right to market its own cars were 17 countries in Asia including Korea, Taiwan, the Philippines, Thailand and Indonesia. MMC operates eight assembly plants and two engine plants in Asian countries. Kumon concludes that the Joint venture in Taiwan, China Motor has the highest ratio of similarity to the Japanese style management, which are characterized by multi-skilled workers, 'kaizen' activity and just-in-time parts delivery. Kumon also points out a conspicuous difference between two Philippine plants: whereas the assembly plant has inertia from the American style labor management, the Japanese management style was successfully implemented in the transmission plant.

I hope that this volume, as a whole, will give two messages to the readers. One is the importance of manufacturing industry in Asian nations and elsewhere. The other is academic enthusiasm that a number of researchers are involved in fieldwork through which the real dynamics of an economic system is described.

1 Post-Crisis Asian Economies: Some New Industrial Prospects

Yveline Lecler
University Lumière Lyon2

Jean-Christophe Simon
University Pierre Mendès France Grenoble

1 Introduction

Asian economies are back on growth tracks, or so it seems. Whereas various comments in mid-1998 questioned the future of Asian economies – particularly Newly Industrialized Economies of East and Southeast Asia, a year later amazed comments applauded the resurgence of growth[1]. As for the year 2000, the rosy mood based on overall growth performance in Asian emerging countries. The so-called Asian crisis vanished in early 1999 although some major structural issues such as bad loans, companies restructuring and stock exchange instability are still at the forefront of economic life. The Asian crisis was indeed a multi-faceted crisis in a new context of globalization: monetary (as a consequence of weak currency management in Thailand and other ASEAN countries), financial (partly derived from asset speculative bubbles), industrial (evidence of this is clear in the case of chaebol conglomerates failures in Korea, and also in the competitiveness issues in some ASEAN-4 countries in the years preceding the crisis), political (cronyism aggravating the structural failures, inefficiencies in State institutions, supervision and legal capabilities) and social (affecting the new middle class consumers).

In countries that were most affected (ASEAN-4 and Korea), consumption declined because of rising prices of imported manufactured goods, falling of income due to rising unemployment, loss of confidence in the future. The breakdown of the financial system making loan both scarce and very expensive also contributed to the consumption and investment shrinkage. For a couple of years, mostly 1997–98, but up to now in some emerging economies, small and medium sized firms which cannot finance activities by issuing bonds and therefore

[1] Among many other titles form leading economic magazines : "Can Asia be revived" Far Eastern Economic Review, June 18,2000 ; "Asia's astonishing bounce back,"The Economist, 21 August 1999.

are highly depending on banks borrowing found it particularly difficult to raise the necessary funds to continue production, lacking of the means to import raw material or parts and components. All together this lead to a broader deterioration of the economic climate.

The crisis revealed the urgent need for structural reforms. Governments generally acted in that direction taking measures to reform their financial system, to deregulate and review the grouping structure or diversification strategies of them like in Korea, to liberalized exchanges (or accelerate its pace) and to attract new investors, through taxes exemptions or easing of M&A. But the crisis did not promote strong regional collective reaction, or institution building that could capitalize on the experience and implement corrective measures to prevent a future similar crisis.

What is left of the crisis ? Which issues keep a strong relevance for firms strategies? In this paper we will try to identify new trends in major industrial powers in Asia and recent NIEs[2], and introduce some fundamental elements related to industrial dynamics.

2 From Crisis to Recovery: a Tentative Diagnosis

The regional spread of economic recovery followed the regional diffusion of the crisis. Statistical data, whatever optimistic or not, all confirm this recovery trend. This should not obscure the fact that national situations differ a lot. Beyond figures, some qualitative elements have also to be considered to explain these differences and the challenges countries in the region are facing.

2.1 A New Impetus: is New Growth Taking Roots in Asia ?

Since late 1999, only two years after currency collapsed, recovery is confirmed. The recovery – with performances better than expected – lead to upward growth figure revision by the beginning of 2000. It was suggested that growth was reaching a sustainable pace, avoiding overheating.

Depending of sources, the return to growth seems to be more or less optimistic. The FMI considers that Korea, China, Hong Kong, Taiwan and Malaysia could achieve a 6–7% growth in 2000 while the Philippines, Vietnam, Thailand and Indonesia would register only a 3–4.5% of GDP growth. The World bank for its part, estimates that all major Asian economies – Japan excepted (credited by a 0.7%) – are back on tracks with a growth rate for year 2000 and even for year 2001 being robust in several countries. The GDP growth rate of each countries is

[2] We refer to Japan, China, first generation NIEs – Korea,Taiwan, Hong-Kong, Singapore, and second generation Asian NIEs – or so called ASEAN-4, namely Malaysia, Thailand, Philippines, Indonesia. A more thourough analysis in a global context,should take into account South Asia, particularly India.

evaluated to between 3.8 for the Philippines and 6.5 for Korea and China in 2000; between 4.2 for the Philippines and 6.2 for Singapore and Taiwan in 2001 (see Table 1–1 in the statistical annex).

This optimism can be explained by two factors : on the side of world demand, the export led growth accelerated, based on consumption in North America and revival in Europe. On the domestic front most emerging economies have succeeded in maintaining budgetary and fiscal discipline and monetary stability. In recent months though, several governments, particularly in ASEAN-4 countries have been subjected to pressure from private sector for more subsidies for industrial restructuring and development, and from popular demands for social budget and less taxation.

However, even with the more optimistic estimates, the growth rate remains generally lower than in mid 90's with rates ranging from 5 to 9% (Table 1–1). Production volume as well as domestic or regional sales are also far behind pre-crisis levels in most industries. Consumption is increasing again in most countries covered by this study, and firms too, are resuming investment again, even at a rather low pace. The signs of health that we just mentioned could be counterbalanced by the remaining large amount of bad loans that some of the concerned countries still have to absorb and by the structural and institutional reforms that ought to be carried out.

The speed and extend of recovery are (and will be further) related to the capability of each country to cope with the restructuring issue. They also differ from one industry to another: there are for example great differences between industries turned to domestic demand and industries highly turned towards exports as we shall see in points 2 and 3. So if generally speaking, the recovery is faster and broader than expected during the first years of the crisis, the question remains: is the present recovery trend a long lasting one?

Table 1–1. Evolution of GDP in Asian Countries

unit:%	1996	1997	1998	1999	2000	2001
Malaysia	8.6	7.5	- 7.5	5.4	6.0	6.1
Thailand	5.5	-1.3	-10.0	4.1	4.5	4.6
Indonesia	8.0	4.5	-13.7	0.2	4.0	5.0
Philippines	5.8	5.2	-0.04	3.2	3.8	4.3
Singapore	7.5	9.0	0.3	5.4	5.9	6.2
Vietnam	9.3	8.2	5.8	4.4	5.0	6.0
Japan	5.0	1.4	-2.8	0.7	0.7	**
Korea	6.8	5.0	-5.8	10.7	6.5	6.0
China	9.6	8.8	7.8	7.1	6.5	6.0
HongKong	4.5	5.3	-5.1	2.9	5.0	5.5
Taiwan	5.7	6.8	4.8	5.7	6.3	6.2

Source: World bank, until 1999 = actual, 2000 and 2001= estimated

In fact, the future prospects are not only subject to the crisis and its impact, but also to a lot of other interrelated factors including American (or European) and Japanese growth, foreign investors behavior, and national and regional regulation.

2.2 Middle Term Prospects in Selected Asian Countries

In most emerging countries, large scars are left, although issues tend to be diluted in current optimism, or to belong to a not so distant past.

This on one hand can be explained because of the outcome of the crisis: it did not evolve into a full scale recession, neither did it develop a "fusion syndrome" with a new drastic chain reaction triggered, for example by a currency devaluation in China.

On the other hand, although a common feeling was shared about the crisis among most countries in Asia, there was much complacency about the lessons to be drawn and the measures to be implemented to facilitate recovery. This is even more an handicap now that recovery does not seem to be just a one country issue. Given the higher level of interdependence, the question should be much more addressed at the regional level, including the heavyweights countries that could be expected to act as engine for regional growth.

Japan representing about half of Asian GDP, the recovery of this heavyweight country constitutes a major expectation for its Asian neighbors. Unfortunately, although it recovered since early 1999, the pace is still low and unstable, generating apprehensions. In fact, growth is largely driven by government measures to sustain activity through public demand, taxes exemptions and also measures favoring SMEs and employment. Successive government plans result in higher growth for first term of 1999. Public investments increased by 10.3% and even private demand peaked again (family consumption, property investments, and firms investments). Thanks to these plans, the growth rate of Japan for fiscal year 2000 was re-estimated (Dourille 2000).

Public expenditures can be stimulus for growth in the short term, but the limit of this process seems in view by late 2000 and the long term remains uncertain. To recover effectively, Japan still has several issues to address: reduce excess production capacities (keeping low private investment), stop the increasing unemployment rate which is partly responsible for lack of confidence of Japanese household/consumers, and most of all further the restructuring of its capitalistic pattern.

Admittedly, deregulation progressed in the telecommunication or financial sectors, but there is still a lot to do to cope with needed changes in the employment system and in the firm governance structure. As long as Japan does not progress enough in these direction, confidence will not come back and consumption will stay at too low a pace to allow recovery. This is even more true because exports to the Asian region are lagging behind and do not fuel recovery.

Table 1–2. Fundamentals

2000 – latest as 1 sept	CPI Yoy %	Interbank rate	Current Accnt 12mnth $bln
China	0.5	2.55	15.6*
Hong Kong	2.1	6.56	13.2
Indonesia	4.4	14	-5.8
Japan	0.5	0.396	121.6
Korea	2.0	6.75	14.5
Malaysia	1.4	3.08	19.3
Philippines	4.6	9.25	14.3
Singapore	1.1	2.5	24.3
Taiwan	0.3	4.97	5.6
Thailand	5.2	2.765	10.6
United States	5.5	6.62	-393
Euro-11	2.3	4.62	-4.7

Source : JP Morgan – The Economist.

Table 1–3. Trade and industrial activity

mid 2000	Trade balance	Industrial Production % chge yoy
China	29.6	12.8
Hong Kong	-8.7	-0.2
Indonesia	30.5	4.1
Japan	110	4.2
Korea	17.7	19.3
Malaysia	17.3	19.4
Philippines	5.9	14.3
Singapore	3.2	11.3
Taiwan	7.9	9.3
Thailand	6.5	-0.8
United States	-330	5.8
Euro-11	37	3.9

Source : Asian Development Bank and Far Eastern Economic Review

A new springboard could be found through the "new economy" and Information technology related activities – recent investment by firms or new firms creation are strongly linked to telecommunication, and information related services. But if the evolution of the new economy seems interesting, it is necessary to keep in mind that the Japanese government does not have a lot of resource left to promote this new promising sector.

In **China**, fiscal policy aims at maintaining stable economic growth – the country displays probably the strongest growth in 2000 – public incentives are a major element to incite domestic consumption and defuse social crisis at sectoral or regional level. Exports are a key driver of current expansion. Considering the last step of WTO negotiation, prospects are quite rosy too. This explains most assumption on stability of the Renmibi – particularly as inflationary pressure fail to materialize (estimation of 0.5% year on year, see Table 1–2 and 1–3). The low interbank rate is a poor reflection of the state of financial institutions, and much restructuring is to be expected on that front. A major remaining issue is restructuring of some public assets and their social consequences, to be felt well into the future. As for Hong Kong, external demand and fixed investment are strong drivers of the economy, and recovery is also confirmed to accelerate (5 to 5.5%), with a strong current account surplus.

Korea growth accelerated in 1999 and remains sustained, with macro-economic consolidation – stable currency and balance of payment surplus – which will contribute to limit inflation. Major remaining problems are reform of financial institution and chaebol structure – which is lagging behind for political reasons.

Taiwan too shows impressive growth. Exports remaining strong, largely because of world electronics demand. Post election public policy is unlikely to change – therefore strategic ties with China could increase steadily.

The **ASEAN-4** countries show strongest unstable elements : weak monetary situation, shaky financial restructuring, and political pressure on top at various degrees of magnitude. In Thailand and Malaysia the recovery momentum continues – largely export led. Thailand shows rapid growth but slow restructuring and disappointing recovery of domestic consumption. Malaysia, despite political problems, seems in healthier situation – although the financial sector has yet to recover from its restructuring. Philippines enjoys good economic fundamentals but political issues increase the local uncertainties. This is even more so for Indonesia – where political issues are paramount – the only positive point being the current benefits from the oil price hike.

2.3 The Outcome of the Crisis and Structural Issues for Industries

Beyond the short term figures that outline the current context, other elements contribute to shaping firms' strategies in the coming decade. We would like to mention just a few, the pattern of which the crisis years have decisively affected both in terms of financial and public policy. Some elements can be considered as assets for future industrial expansion – nevertheless, inadequate policies, lack of resources or structural changes derived from the crisis will determine evolution in the coming decade – either to generate improvement or to generate bottlenecks or deficiencies that will bear upon industrial activities.

Education: East Asia was, and is even more than before a region with a well educated population. The widespread literacy and education was said to be an ingredient to the "Asian miracle" – referring both to educated steelworkers in Japan in the late 70's or to high school and university graduates in the car or electronic industries. In that respect Japan remains ahead, followed closely by some NIEs such as Korea, Taiwan or Singapore. The crisis struck at a time of transition for the educational system (particularly the new private institutions in Southeast Asia). One issue is the continuing mobilization of private capital and public fund to improve the development of education to higher levels in emerging countries (e.g. Thailand extended its compulsory education to 16 years but like other Asian-4 still show deficiencies in technical and engineering education, China showing a tremendous potential, and flexibility to adapt educational institutions with active foreign partnership still has a long way to go for mass technical education).

Networking infrastructure: The region is endowed with a powerful communication network, especially when compared to lower densities or grades in South America or Africa. The crisis years have delayed some investment, but all in all, in an area ranging from Singapore to Seoul, industrialists can take a regional view regarding transport infrastructure and services. The situation is marred though with local congestion, inadequate network management or even corrupt and inefficient institutions. Most industrialists (and investment agencies) would agree, there is still room for improvement. The issue of financing further development is an acute one, though, at a time of tightening government budgets. There is also a tough constraint on operation of some infrastructure – particularly mass transit systems – when purchasing power of private consumers is kept low.

Innovation: this is a crucial aspect of industrial dynamics for the coming decade. On the public side, there are clear achievements in many institutions of the NIEs whereas ASEAN-4 countries need to beef up their technology oriented policies. Regarding first generation NIEs, the challenge is to maintain technological capability of public research center and put oil in networks that make use of brain resource (reverse brain drain, regional cooperation...). Considering firms strategies, resource endowment – particularly educational levels – do play the key role in location decision for R&D centers or technology-based facilities – but the picture is being blurred by the intense restructuring following the crisis.

Market: Asia was labeled the most promising regional market at the end of the 90's, when emerging countries where fostering new consumer societies, with increasing number of so-called "middle class" consumers, plus very substantial potential for rural consumption increase. The crisis struck hard on consumers, altering patterns and strategies (such as loan seeking). Therefore, it remains to be seen whether mild growth can restore pre-crisis habits, or else new elements have to be put to revive a strong consumption pattern (such as e-commerce, new forms of loan allocation). This thinking also applies to the 'mammoth market' of China –

the magnitude of which will excite the appetite of industrialists for the next half century.

Governing the markets was identified as one of the key ingredients of Asia's emerging economies (Wade 1993) – some questions remain concerns the identification and implementation of policies to capitalize on these assets – at a time when developmental states are weakened and public budgets strained. Public institution improvement is a matter not only of increasing efficiency but also restoring legitimacy of State to intervene for progress and equity.

2.4 Asian Markets Recovery in Car and Electronic Industries

Almost Asian countries are on the track to recovery. Admittedly the diverse recovery paces of are also to be found at sector level: depending on industry the situations show substantial differences. Car industry which production was mostly dedicated to local markets strongly suffered of the crisis, while electronic industry much more export-based founded it easier to adjust.

2.4.1 Car Industry: Markets Shrinkage and Recovery Path

Car industry was at the center of new consumption patterns in emerging economies (see the late opening of the Korean market in the 90', and the rapid transport congestion of ASEAN-4 capitals as early as the 80's). In the context of the economic crisis of 1997–99, domestic markets were affected by a strong contraction derived from the domestic personal income and credit crunch.

With 218,330 vehicles sold on the Thai market in 1999, it is higher than the 144 065 of 1998, but compared to the 589,126 sold in 1996 (peak year), the pre-crisis level is still far behind. Future demand forecasts show that in 2003 the markets recovery will bring the sales around the 1994 level. It is the case for Thailand with 490,000 vehicles or for Indonesia with 359,000. Malaysia could recover a little faster with the 2003 estimated 363,000 vehicles being close below the 1996 level (Table 1–4).

Production numbers are following the same trend: with 327,233 vehicles produced in 1999 in Thailand for example, the recovery is noticeable compared to the 158,130 of 1998, but if compared to the 559,428 vehicles produced in 1996, the difference is still important (Table 1–5).

The Chinese market is the only one registering a permanent growth during the crisis years, confirming that the country was not hit directly by the crisis.

Comparing sales and production numbers shows that except Korea, the vehicles produced in each countries were almost dedicated to the local markets (see Table 1–4 and 1–5). In the case of Thailand for example, production reached 559 428 vehicles in 1996, short below the number of vehicles sold: 589 126 vehicles.

Table 1–4. Car industry (truck and buses excluded): Real sales and *demand forecast* in main Asian countries (unit: vehicles number)

	93	94	95	96	97	98	99	*00*	*01*	*02*	*03*
Thai	456,468	485,678	571,580	589,126	363,156	144,065	218,330	*283,000*	*348,000*	*417,000*	*490,000*
Philippines	83,811	103,471	128,162	162,011	144,435	80,231	74,414	*81,000*	*85,000*	*98,000*	*117,000*
Malaysia	167,928	200,435	285,792	364,788	404,837	163,851	288,547	*307,000*	*334,000*	*342,000*	*363,000*
Indonesia	210,679	321,760	378,694	332,035	386,691	58,303	93,814	*195,000*	*252,000*	*302,000*	*359,000*
Korea	1,435,967	1,555,602	1,555,902	1,644,132	1,512,935	779,905	1,273,079				
Taiwan	557,183	575,499	546,634	470,636	481,567	474,069	423,540				
China	1,470,151	1,451,696	1,564,000	1,458,666	1,565,904	1,604,480	1,832,470				

Source: Sakurasogo kenkyujo, 2000 for 1993 to 1999 real numbers and Mitsubishi 2000 (Ajia jidosha kenkyukai, May 30th) for ASEAN–4 forecast.

Table 1–5. Annual production of car and LCV in Asian countries

	1996	1997	1998	1999
Korea	2,812,714	2,818,275	1,954,494	2,843,114
Taiwan	389,417	381,103	404,545	350,273
Thai	559,428	360,303	158,130	327,233
Malaysia	398,936	457,144	164,238	269,103
Indonesia	325,495	389,279	58,079	123,244
Philippines	136,556	110,983	45,040	n.a.
China	1,474,905	1,582,628	1,627,829	1,830,323

Source: Sakura sogo kenkyujo 2000

2.4.2 The Electronic Industry: Weathering a Market Cycle

On the eve of the Asian crisis, the world electronic industry was larger in gross turnover terms than all activities related to car industry. Major producers were the largest industrial nations – USA, Japan, United Kingdom and Germany, but the total consolidated production of emerging Asia was ranked just after. In terms of exports, Asia and Japan controlled a 50% share (emerging countries about 35%), before Europe (30%) and United States (15%). It was already global to a large extent – which means that major companies located their facilities in various regions – particularly in Asia.

Among Asian producers Japan had the lead, and still has to a large extent ; In 1997 Japan production surpassed $250 billions, followed by Korea, Singapore and China (producing about $US40–50 billions). Asia was also a major market for electronic products – similar in size to the US market – half of it being in Japan though. The prospects for expansion were considered very bright – taking into account the rapid integration of China in the network of world electronics and as a rapidly growing market.

The world electronics industry weathered a downturn as early as 1994 – for activities ranging from telecom to computers and Integrated Circuits (Ics). This was largely due to new product cycle, over-investment followed by drastic price cuts for products that could almost be labeled "world commodities" (standard Ics or chips, lower range of PCs).

This market stagnation was followed by the storm of the Asian crisis – in that respect deterioration of profitability was followed by actual market shrinkage in emerging Asia and Japan, which in turn resulted in excess capacity at some major production sites – in Korea, Malaysia, Taiwan, but also Scotland or other sites in Europe. Therefore, the electronics – and the electrical goods sectors too – in Asia were to a certain extent subject to instability during the "Asian crisis" – but not so much to the turmoil that struck the automotive industry. Indeed due to specific condition, these sectors adjusted quickly since 1997 and weathered the storm after 1998.

Several reasons can be put forward to explain this specific feature.

In the electronics industry (comprising both equipment components and consumers goods), where production was largely dedicated to exports, the impact of the consumption shrinkage, credit squeeze... was largely offset by the recovery on world markets. The market for general consumer products collapsed in NIEs, and has not fully recovered in most of them though.

Regarding the specifically electronic components and particularly the integrated circuits, the export crisis actually preceded the currency and monetary crisis. A cycle downturn was observed before, as said above, concerning demand of ICs on major markets. The crisis was unprecedented as the market glut led to sales contraction of up to 30% for some segments, and the effect was particularly hard felt by companies that invested heavily in the preceding years. Regarding standard integrated circuits, the crisis was an internal one – largely due to a product cycle and over capacity built in Korea and Taiwan.

Production of electrical goods suffered much more because of shrinkage of domestic markets in emerging countries. There was a drastic reduction of both industrial and public investment – mostly concerning facilities maintenance and extension, or electrical networks.

To put it in a nutshell, production took off again due mostly to external factors – and this trend was backed up by new organization changes of firms to answer demand with more flexibility. As Table 1–6 illustrates, the good situation for production of some major items brightened over the past years ;

(1) Most segments of production have recovered since 1998. The increase in production is largely export led. (2) At the same time, some reshuffle of production site took place among NIEs – particularly between ASEAN-4 countries as firms maximized their procurement and subcontractors network. (3) The quantitative recovery does not tell the whole picture though – as profitability of many companies suffered over the past years from heavy financial costs, intense competition in the region and expensive capacity investment.

The recovery might be faster or more or less stable depending on industry or production segments. The future prospects in both car and electronic industries are subject to several elements which combination can lead to further growth and to further restructuring.

Table 1–6. Trends in production of selected electronic consumer goods for major countries

Annual production of selected items				
Unit : thousand				Increase
	1998	**1999**	**2000**	2000/1998
Thailand				
Color TV	7,500	6,840	6,000	-20%
car stereo	3,780	6,010	6,000	59%
Electronic lens	3,000	3,600	4,000	33%
Portable phone	0	0	0	
HDD	21,000	25,800	30,000	43%
Fax	2,930	2,630	2,500	-15%
Malaysia				
Color TV	6,000	5,350	5,520	-8%
car stereo	8,370	8,230	8,640	3%
Electronic lens	620	650	650	5%
Portable phone	1,210	3,520	2,600	115%
HDD	10,000	18,000	18,000	80%
Fax	2,340	2,420	2,400	3%
Taiwan				
Color TV	610	600	600	-2%
car stereo	800	650	500	-38%
Electronic lens	240	250	250	4%
Portable phone	30	820	2,200	7233%
HDD	0	0	0	
Fax	1,330	1,760	1,850	39%
China				
Color TV	33,000	29,000	32,000	-3%
car stereo	16,800	16,300	17,500	4%
Electronic lens	2,600	2,700	2,800	8%
Portable phone	9,300	17,000	30,000	223%
HDD	6,800	11,700	16,000	135%
Fax	2,200	2,300	2,400	9%
Korea				
Color TV	10,600	10,700	10,700	1%
car stereo	4,640	5,400	5,500	19%
Electronic lens	8,060	9,200	9,500	18%
Portable phone	17,980	43,000	50,000	178%
HDD	8,210	6,000	12,000	46%
Fax	720	600	630	-13%
Singapore				
Color TV	1,030	1,080	1,000	-3%
car stereo	2,200	1,090	1,080	-51%
Electronic lens	960	960	960	0%
Portable phone	1,500	4,800	4,900	227%
HDD	60,960	74,640	80,600	32%
Fax	300	250	250	-17%

Source: from Sakura sogo kenkyujo 2000: I–1 to I–3

3 New Challenge for Car Industry in Asian Emerging Countries

The car industry is a symbol of both a particular industrial organization for which Japanese companies have played an increasing role over the past three decades and a national activity that used to be promoted and protected in some emerging economies for reasons of national strategy (Humphrey, Lecler, Salerno 2000). Changes in industries could be monitored in terms of ownership, restructuring of network and division of labor (at national and regional scale). The transformation that firms are implementing derives from several interacting factors. The crisis plaid its part for example in bringing ASEAN plants to serve as exports bases to some extend and in favoring concentration through mergers and acquisitions. But the present WTO membership of most of the Asian countries is probably a factor of more importance in the long term.

3.1 From National Markets to Exports Oriented Production

Japanese car manufacturers, which presence is quite high (except in China) with more than 90% of production volume and market share in the ASEAN for example, were not concerned by exporting from these countries until the crisis. They all focussed on the national markets which growth potentiality was high and exports of CBU[3] prohibitive, developing their Asian car concept, aiming at coping with local regulations in terms of local content and so on (Lecler Guiheux, 2000). Korean car makers followed the same strategy while opening plants in the ASEAN area in the 1990's to challenge Japanese domination on these attractive markets. European and American car makers, which presence was quite limited in the ASEAN area, are playing the same part in China where they are more involved, dedicating their production to the national market only.

In fact, in all these countries, multinational car makers are producing vehicles locally because they cannot secure the markets and/or take position on these growing markets by exporting from their home production basis. Concerned national governments aim at developing a national car industry or at least a national component industry. Therefore they implemented regulation to avoid CBU imports (taxes and/or quotas) and limit components imports too (local content ratios).

But considering :

(1) the high production costs, even if the manpower is cheap, due to low production volumes (markets are growing but still small, fragmented...) avoiding economy of scale. (2) the lack of supporting industries, leading to re-location of parts makers which production costs are high for the same reasons than car makers. (3) the poor technological capabilities making necessary to import a rather

[3] CBU = Completely Build Up vehicles.

high number of 'sophisticated' components, a majority of which are manufactured in Japan (thus became quite expensive with the yen increase of the 90s). (4) the difficulties, in the ASEAN, of implementation of regional exchange liberalization through scheme like BBC or AICO. (5) and finally, related to all this, the difficulty of achieving production at the international quality requirement, car makers, and to a rather large extend parts makers, generally think there is no competitive advantage for producing locally. Worldwide exports from these countries, were therefore not on the agenda until the markets shrinkage that resulted from crisis.

3.1.1 Increasing Exports as a Strategy Derived from Crisis

The market shrinkage due to crisis struck all car and parts manufacturers. The impact was stronger than in electronic industry as we shall see later, as automotive firms were only producing for local markets (Korea excepted). Amongst the survival strategies they developed (most of them being short term ones), the use of ASEAN production plants as export basis is probably the most important for future prospects.

Before the crisis, exports from ASEAN countries in the car industry were limited to some labor intensive and simple parts. But to maintain production levels as high as possible, exports of vehicles were envisaged by all car makers at the very beginning of the crisis, and it was quite a new attitude. This explains why Toyota could start production of the Hilux again (with only one shift instead of two however) after stopping it completely in November 1997. Mitsubishi decided to concentrate its production of one ton pick-up trucks in its new Thai plant. Production was progressively stopped in Japan, and pick-up trucks are now exported from Thailand to 80 different countries (Mitsubishi data 2000). Isuzu is thinking to do the same as far as pick-up are concerned (firm interview in July 1999). Other examples were related by newspapers almost everyday. In 1999, Thailand exported more than 150 000 vehicles, most of which being one ton pick-up trucks. Car manufacturers made every effort to export vehicles to ensure the survival of their ASEAN plants.

It is however not likely to see this trend increase drastically in the coming years, with the exception of pick-up trucks. In fact, the "Asian car strategy" that leads Japanese car makers to develop vehicles adapted to each Asian country, is showing its limit. These vehicles cannot easily be sold on other markets because of quality standards, lack of sophistication or simply because of different climatic conditions (e.g. no heating required). This "Asian car strategy" might not last any longer, but the situation cannot be changed so fast in the car industry. Therefore, export of vehicles will not increase substantially – at least until new models are introduced. These new model will not be specific to one or another country. It seems that to avoid the risk of market shrinkage, car makers are now considering to take, as basis for production everywhere, models developed for Japan. These models would be adapted to each market by suppression of the most sophisticated options like airbag, cooler, or heating depending on climatic conditions. This confirms that exports of car from ASEAN countries targeted mainly a short term survival strategy. But at the same time it also reveals that if local/regional market, probably extended to peripheral countries like Australia, New Zealand, remains the main focus of Japanese car manufacturers, they also intend to integrate markets risk in their future behavior – keeping exports as a lifejacket in case of new market shock.

As far as parts and components are concerned, the situation might be quite different. It is in that area that exports increase is the most substantial and that potential for growth is highest. Already before crisis, exports from ASEAN-4 countries (Thailand, Malaysia, Indonesia, Philippines) were significant, even if concerned amounts involved were still low. Unlike the case of CBU cars, the dynamics that resulted from the crisis and from the necessity to maintain plants in activity seems to be an irreversible one.

It is still difficult to measure statistically to what extend the export strategy is successful, but if production shift, or purchasing from ASEAN plants, announced almost daily since the very beginning of the crisis until now, are to be taken into account, there is no doubt that changes are underway, especially as far as re-importation to Japan are concerned.

But question remains if growth of exports will favor intra-ASEAN trade. Car and parts makers, not only Japanese but also western ones – which are now more involved in the area than before – are demanding procedural simplifications and a greater liberalization so that their international division of labor can be extended, not only within the ASEAN area but also to include Japan (as re-imports growth show), Asia-Pacific neighboring countries, and later possibly other countries outside Asia.

To increase exports further, parts manufactured in ASEAN countries still have to be improved in quality, and technology mastering has to be increased to make it possible to produce sub-systems instead of simple parts. In the case of Thailand or Malaysia for example, this seems achievable on a long term perspective. Supporting industries in Thailand improved tremendously in the past decade due to relocation of numerous Japanese parts makers. Concerning Malaysia, the development of the electronic industry implies that a specialization in transmission and electronic related parts and components is possible.

The need for economies of scale – by increasing production volume – lead to focus not only on local markets but also consider production for exports. Consequently, production of one component reference will be located in the country having the best comparative advantage to produce it. This implies a reviewing of the international division of labor by car and parts makers and a kind of specialization by country and by product. Such a trend was already underway before the crisis but firms had difficulties to actually implement it because of national regulations. Presently, expecting the liberalization of trade under the WTO requirement, some companies are acting in that direction at a faster pace than before. The entrance of non Japanese new comers on the market (for example

GM, Ford in Thailand) and the increasing number of M&A in the sector leading to broader supplying opportunities for local or relocated Japanese/Western suppliers should contribute to decisive changes in supplying networks – on a more global level.

3.2 The Issue of Trade Liberalization (Revision/Suppression of Local Contents, Integration in the WTO)

The trade liberalization which is on the agenda is not only related to crisis, at least directly. To some extent, the crisis acted as an accelerator of the liberalization move, to another extent, it acted on the contrary as a brake. The situation is contrasted depending on countries or areas. In the case of ASEAN countries, the liberalization move which was scheduled through the implementation of CEPT (AFTA) was somehow slowed down, with most countries delaying the date of implementation, while others maintained it. Also, existing regional scheme, like AICO seems to be used on a broader scale than before. In China, the liberalization is more concerned by the entrance in the WTO and by the related 1999 agreement with the United States of America.

For example, through this agreement, **China** will have to revise constraints on car and parts imports to promote national production. Taxes on CBU imports are still prohibitive even if they were reduced several times recently. They are supposed to be significantly lowered at the 2006 horizon. But, even if the rate for 2006 is not yet announced, it is estimated that it will remains higher in the case of cars (around 25%) than it will probably be for industrial products as a whole (around 10%) (French Embassy in China 1999). This shows how strategic car industry is for China. Also a licensing system as well as quotas aim at strongly controlling the market. The suppression of quotas will be progressive until 2005.

As far as parts and components are concerned, the level of import taxes (28 to 30%) is not the only one difficulty. A reduced rate is applicable on parts for assembly on car produced in China. But the reduction level depends on the amount invested in the plant and on the local content ratio achieved. The measure of these gives a lot of room to negotiation with the authorities, the result of which being more related to bargaining power of the firm than to standards fixed by regulation. The agreement says that the rate should be the same than for all industrial products (10%) in 2006 giving an end to the preferential tariff system.

Finally, the minority ownership required on car and strategic components foreign assembling plants, the special agreement needed for each new model production are limiting the adaptation capabilities of firms making international competitiveness rather low. These points are not clearly addressed in the agreement with the States but some exception to the rule already exists (benefiting to Volkswagen Honda or GM) leading to expect an announcement of loosening of the regulation.

If these liberalization measures are effectively implemented (there is often a gap in China between official national government regulation and their real application especially at the local level), the question of competitiveness of vehicles produced in China will be at stake. For the moment, competitiveness is low and without import taxes, cars produced in China are more expensive than could imported CBU cars be. This is especially true for middle and higher class passengers cars and less for light trucks. Car makers having facilities in China could benefit of the opening measures on other segments like distribution or finance, they could take this opportunity to reinforce their distribution networks not only for models produced in China but also for models produced outside China to be sold on the Chinese market (some easing measures for imports of CBU are granted to manufacturers producing in China through the agreement of 1999). Also the possibility given to non-Chinese to operate on the market of financial services related to car distribution and sales allow them to propose directly credits to consumers. But, there is also a need for restructuring. Economy of scale have to be achieved to increase competitiveness towards imports. It means first that further concentration of the sector is absolutely needed at the car assembling level but also at the component manufacturing level. The loosening of local content request (preferential tariff according to local content rate will be eliminated), will make it quite necessary for parts makers to merge and/or diversify their buyer to survive in China. Facing competition of imported parts and probably request for cost reduction from buyers they need to increase order volume, achieve economy of scale and cut production costs.

No doubt that international competition on the Chinese market will be one of the big issue for the coming year. Depending partly on how regulation and law will evolve and be implemented in and after the transition period, and particularly on how the local protectionism will react, the choice between producing in China or importing from abroad will constitute a big challenge for both car and parts makers.

In the **ASEAN area** too, prohibitive taxes on CBU imports are the common rule while local content ratio tend to promote a national car or parts industry. But measures to favor intra-area trade were taken rather early even if their effectiveness can be questioned at least until recently.

A regional complementation system in the ASEAN was at stake as early as 1969 but it is only in 1988 that the first real scheme was undersigned under the name of Brand to Brand Complementation Scheme (for more details see, Legewie 1998, Guiheux, Lecler 2000). Even if most Japanese car makers (parts makers were not involved) adopted this scheme, the intra-ASEAN components exports remained quite low in comparison to exports outside the area. For example in 1995, Thailand was exporting 6% of the total exported components to other countries of the ASEAN 4 (Indonesia, Philippines and Malaysia). If we add the 19.5% exported to Singapour, it is more than the 15.7% to Japan but still far behind the 57.9% exported to other areas.

Table 1–7. Components exports from the ASEAN-4 countries – by destination (1995, per cent of total component exports)

Exports to:	Exports from:			
	Thailand	*Indonesia*	*Malaysia**	*Philippines*
Thailand	x	1.2	2.9	9.2
Indonesia	1.1	x	1.9	1.8
Malaysia	3.5	2.1	X	0.7
Philippines	1.4	3.0	1.9	x
Singapore	19.5	31.2	17.4	0.4
Vietnam	0.9	0.8	0.1	0.2
Japan	15.7	11.7	8.4	31.8
Others	57.9	50.1	67.5	55.9
Total	100	100	100	100

* Data refers to 1994

Source: elaborated from LTCBR (1997: 70–3).

For the Philippines, the more exporting country to the ASEAN 4, the respective numbers are 11.3 (Singapore account only for 0.4) 31.8 and 55.9% (Table 1–7 in statistical annex).

In 1996, a new scheme, broader in scope (not restricted to car industry, thus allowing parts makers to use it), was implemented (AICO: ASEAN Industrial Cooperation Organization) as a transition to the Common Effective Preferential Tariff Scheme (CEPT) which is schedule for a full application in 2003. Under AICO scheme, tariffs were lowered to between 0 to 5%. At least 30 per cent of the capital of any participating firm had to be owned locally (a condition that will disappear with CEPT), but the local manufacturing ratio for the whole of the ASEAN region could drop to 40 per cent, compared to 50% for BBC. However, no single local content requirement prevailed throughout the entire zone, as each member state remained free to make its own decisions. Procedural complexity remains, as trade reciprocity must still be proven. The pace of signature was slow at the beginning because both of firms attitude (complexity of procedure, late taxes refunding under former BBC) and governments reluctance (fear of trade imbalance). The crisis-related market shrinkage gave a new impetus to the scheme as government saw in the easing of AICO procedure, a mean to increase exports and therefore production volumes. The first agreements within AICO were signed in 1998, between such car makers as Volvo, Toyota, Isuzu, and parts makers such as Sanden, Denso, and Nihon Cable (Fourin, 1999: 14). At the end of 1999, 29 agreements were signed under this scheme (SIR 2000/3:58). But if it seems that involvement in AICO scheme is higher than before, this does not mean that liberalization is higher. In fact, the situation is quite different from one country to another. Arguing of the crisis impact on car industries, some of the ASEAN countries decided to delay the implementation of some of the transition policies.

For example, Malaysia decided to extend the national local content ratio rules which were supposed to be abolished in January 2000, to deferred the transfer of items from the list of those which cannot benefit of reduce import taxes to 'the CEPT inclusion list', while Thailand continue to favor liberalization, shifting every year components from one list to another.

But, if liberalization is delayed to some extent, foreign manufacturers and parts makers are getting prepared to the opening of the markets. The situation derived from crisis as lack of liquidity by local partner firms or difficulties of local suppliers gave them an opportunity to restructure their networks, to contract new alliances through increase of capital or mergers and acquisitions.

3.3 The Increasing M&A and Business Tie-up, with a Correlative Restructuring of Groups

In most emerging countries, public regulations regarding foreign ownership in financial and industrial companies were strongly reformed. In ASEAN-4, and Korea, restrictions of majority foreign ownership for non-exporting companies were strongly disputed before and waived during the crisis. This enabled foreign shareholder to reinforce companies threatened by shrinking domestic markets and drastic local financing conditions. One could assume that national prejudices towards foreign long term capital is steadily decreasing (as opposed reinforced aversion to hot money and short term stock exchange oriented funds). If that holds true joint-venture creation and shareholding transparency will have been definitely reinforced by the crisis.

During the crisis, due to difficulties faced by local joint-ventures or partners, Japanese car or parts makers had to support them financially. They used to pay their orders in advance enabling local suppliers to purchase raw material or parts. But it is mostly by increasing their share in capital that they contributed to financial recovery of their partners. For example, Daihatsu rose its part in PT Astra of Indonesia from 20 to 40%, while Showa Corporation, a parts maker affiliated to Honda, doubled its share in its Thai joint-venture. Of course, these moves were emergency measures aimed first at facing both the credit crunch and credit cost problems, but they finally participated to the present concentration trend.

This trend is visible in Japan too where the taboo of foreign ownership is no longer widespread. The increasing number of mergers and acquisitions taking place in Japan – thanks to the easing of procedures through changes of corporate law since the Yamaichi failure – will bring Japanese and Foreign firms even closer. While the acquisition of Japanese firms by foreign ones in Japan were limited to 20–30 cases a year (2.5% of the total in 1990) in the first half of the 1990s, the number grew to 86 (12.2%) of the total in 1999 (Etienne 1999).

Japanese firms are also merging together to a larger extent than before: 429 cases in 1999, representing 60.7% of the total instead of 35.5% in 1990 (Etienne

1999). Most of these mergers concern the financial sector, but mergers of industrial firms are also on the agenda. For example, Bosch took the control of Zexel, Delphi acquired 6% of Akebono assets, without speaking of the Nissan-Renault case. Two of the main suppliers of Nissan (Calsonic and Kansei) also merged to better compete on the globalized market.

Facing changes of the international context and stagnation of national markets, big car makers intend to become more global. Business tie up are seen as means:

(1) to reinforce competitiveness at the global level through economy of scale, namely by common purchasing of parts. (2) to penetrate new markets and especially emerging ones without taking too much risk. (3) to diversify model range and benefit from advances in the new technologies related to environment, security, assisted navigation systems.

All these reasons are particularly true in the case of tie-up between Western and Japanese car makers.

The former are expecting an opportunity to penetrate Asian markets on which their presence was low and to acquire technologies in which Japanese have an advance. For example, Renault is expecting to benefit from the alliance with Nissan to increase its sales (mainly of light truck vehicles) on the Asian emerging markets. The firm created a structure in Japan to work in that direction. For the later, the business tie-up or mergers allow to share risks on emerging markets, the importance of which was clearly revealed by crisis and/or to reinforce their competitiveness on the global market.

This concentration trend at the car makers level leads to a broad restructuring of groups and networks. To better compete on their core business line, some are selling 'peripheral' activities (Renault selling its truck activity to Volvo). To achieve cost cutting through economy of scale, some plants are closed and production is shifted to other plants or relocated in emerging countries. Japanese parts makers too are starting to concentrate their production in some units while closing other plants in Japan. For example, Akebono announced that in the coming two years the firm will concentrate production of both drum braking and disk braking system in the same unit in Saitama prefecture. Futaba is gathering the production of exhaust pipe in its Fukushima unit and will close its Nagoya plant in 2004. Also they tend to specialize on their most performing components, progressively stopping production of less efficient ones.

All the recent business tie-up, M & A, will also have an impact in terms of firm governance. While Toyota is more concerned by reinforcing internal consistency of the group, taking a majority holding in Daihatsu, Hino and increasing its share in 11 other firms of its group (Nikkei 13/6/98), most of other car makers are experiencing bi-cultural or multi-cultural equity and management, the efficiency of which still has to be proved on the long term.

This concentration trend at the car makers level is followed by a concentration trend at the part makers level too. Business tie-up and M & A are usually accompanied by purchasing networks restructuring on a more globalized scale.

Parts makers have to adapt to this new situation by cutting production costs and also becoming more global. To do so, they need partnership to make economy of scale (by increasing orders volume), to share risks of investments in emerging countries and of R & D. This leads to business tie-up, M & A, between Japanese firms or Japanese-Western ones on the parts segments too. Thus, networks are changing enhancing a transformation of the division of labor between the center and the periphery, but also between the peripheral countries themselves. The move is still at its beginning stage and further changes have to be expected on that matter.

3.4 From National to Regional/Global Based Activities: Reviewing the Division of Labor

The Japanese car makers invested the ASEAN region quite early to supply local market. During the 1970s, as the ASEAN countries began to adopt policies that favored localization, Japanese parts makers also began to set up operations in the region. Japanese firms were for a long time the only ones to have established operation in the region for CKD[4] vehicles.At that time, Japanese car makers were able to charge high prices for the vehicles they offered. Parts makers also could deliver components at higher price than in Japan. Thus, despite the small size of markets, and the high production costs, the ASEAN located firms were profitable.

In the 1990s, because of increasing competition on the markets, with growing demand from middle class consumers, Japanese car makers had to implement a new strategy aiming at cutting cost by increasing local procurements and achieving economies of scale by concentrating orders. Parts makers had to follow in the same direction.

Increasing local procurements and reducing imports from Japan was not so easy because the technological level of ASEAN countries and capability building is a long lasting process. A new wave of penetration by Japanese suppliers, on the request of their buyers or because of new opportunities of markets, took place in the mid-1990s.

Achieving economy of scale was not easy too. ASEAN markets for vehicles were fast growing in the 1990s and cumulative annual sales volumes would have justify mass production. However, strongly fragmented, markets remained limited in size for both vehicles and parts (see Lecler and Guiheux 2000).

Japanese firms that oriented production to local markets could not reproduce an organization of purchasing like in Japan. It was quite impossible for suppliers to follow the affiliated car maker in Thailand or Indonesia just to supply him. Opening a production unit could not be profitable without supplying several car makers in the region. The borders of industrial keiretsu had to be crossed to make local production possible at a reasonable cost. The distinctive feature of markets in a context of increased competition and high yen led Japanese firms to adapt their

[4]CKD = Completely Knock Down.

purchasing strategies to the regional environment. Car makers experimented joint production and joint procurement from parts makers belonging to different keiretsu. Parts makers had the opportunity to experiment new relations with customers they were not supplying in Japan and also concluded agreement for joint production without keiretsu parts makers. This, tending to networks restructuring, also constituted a learning to change relations in Japan.

The ASEAN complementation scheme (BBC, AICO) does not seem to be the main factor why an Asian division of labor finally progressed, but they can be seen as an easing policy. From the moment where cost became the core element to secure market domination in the region, an Asian division of labor was the only mean to reach the goal, leading to a specialization of each country in one or several type of components[5].

This move was already engaged when the crisis started and cannot be hold for responsible of the purchasing networks restructuring. But, the crisis acted as an accelerator of this move, making it more urgent and probably also more accurate if M & A and business tie-up are taken into account. Therefore, the revision of the division of labor and correlatively of purchasing networks (now including Western parts makers) and practices (Japanese and Western practices being mixted) is now a big issue of the globalization path of firms.

This division of labor of Japanese car makers which was still rather national even if some assembling plants and components purchasing were carried out of Japan (often because of regulation) is becoming much more regional for the time being and will probably become more globalized in the future. From a general point of view, it appears that buyers are locating their parts and components production or procurement in the country having the better advantage to produce it, leading to a kind of specialization by products and by countries.This division of labor is implemented between Japan and other Asian countries taken as a whole, and also between Asian countries themselves. Different patterns exist, depending on firms, but it is clear that parts with few value-added and low technology will increasingly be reserved to production in Asian emerging countries while high value-added one will remain produced in Japan or be purchase from Western countries. The location country will be chosen depending on the technological complexity of the product and on the local capabilities: less complex and less value-added parts or process in ASEAN countries, more complex and more value-added ones in the NIEs and high complexity/high value-added one in Japan (mostly), in the USA or Europe (with the development of e-commerce for some components bought on catalogue). Also it appears that mass production is shifting progressively to Asian emerging countries, with Japanese suppliers (in Japan) specializing on small lot production of highly specialized products. Commercial activities are also often transferred abroad but design of parts is still scarce. Eventually adaptation of products may be transferred (in the case of Taiwan, Korea) but original design remains anyway in Japan.

---

[5] For more details on this matter, see Lecler 1999 and Guiheux/Lecler 2000.

4 The Electronics/Electrical Products Industries in Asia: Becoming Even More Global

Electronics and electrical products industries are at the core of the industrial revolution in East Asia – Japan caught the first wave, as a leader for light consumer goods and equipment production in the 1960 and 70's, and the "gang of 4" conquered several segments of the market since the late 80's.

Several countries among the first and second generation of NIEs developed their electrical and electronics sector largely thanks to foreign direct investment and promotion of export oriented industries. The "Asian crisis", in a context of slow market growth (even downturn for Integrated Circuits) struck directly in the form of disruption of production circuits in some countries (because of credit crunch and currency fluctuations) and contraction of domestic and regional sales. It also affected the image of the region as a stable production base and the fast growing market area for electronics and electrical products industries. In spite of this, it is assumed that these activities will remain a strong pillar of the NIEs industry in the coming decade.

4.1 Electronics and Electrical Products Industries Beyond the Asian Crisis.

This group of industries show quite diversified structure, products and dynamics, but exemplify the challenge of competitiveness of industries in Asia in the age of globalization. We derive our analysis from observations of recent trends in three sectors.

Semi-conductors/Integrated circuits, which is a global industry producing a "high tech commodity" supplying both equipment and consumers industries. For integrated circuits, several Asian companies have acquired and maintained a competitive hedge on selected segments – particularly in Singapore, Taiwan and Korea. This sector is characterized by rapid innovation, expensive capacity building (high entry costs) and periodical cycle of price fall/market renewal.

The market glut issue lasted until late 1998. The decisive factor for recovery was the sharp increase of demand in G6 countries for both Ics and electronic products (based on Ics too). It is well known that Asian exports (from countries such as Malaysia, Singapore, Taiwan, and to a lesser extent Korea, Thailand and Philippines) are strongly correlated to world demand – particularly USA. The increase of about 40% through the year 1999 in purchase by U.S based firms of major electronic components from suppliers located in Asia accounted for about 1.5% additional growth for producing countries (SG Securities estimate – with a similar figure for 1st semester 2000). This cycle is expected to last until beginning of 2001. The current technological cycle – related to maturity of large scale production memories such as 64 M Dram – is expected to last until 2003.

As some large new facilities in Korea and Taiwan are still far from recouping their investment, and restructuring is not completed in Korea, future expansion is marred with uncertainties for some companies. The major issue for emerging countries is to maintain their position among leading producing countries, while avoiding excess capacity and strengthening innovative and research capacity.

Consumer electronic products. They are characterized by oligopolies for some products, and a relatively strong position of Asian based firms – particularly Japanese, Taiwanese and Korean – for production of both mass produced component and standardized consumer products. Markets are expanding, very flexible with strong price elasticity, and innovations are flowing at lower pace – with a substantial proportion designed in Asia, and Japan retaining a leadership.

The squeeze of local markets in Asia was more than offset by the improving conditions for exports to North America and Europe. Consequently, product design is becoming more flexible to suit a wider range of markets, and production networks, division of labor are further adjusted to respond to market fluctuations and to trade liberalization (see some case study in 3.2). Japanese companies have managed well to retain their high grade image, particularly vis à vis firms from Korea and Taiwan. But things are expecting to change in the coming decade: innovation is getting more difficult and costly for the former and less sophisticated product in Eastern Europe, China will offer increasing opportunities for the latter. In addition the technological proximity between some consumer products and the personal computer system will increase the strategic conflicts between Asian companies.

Considering the position of Japanese subsidiaries, the production cost structure and the innovation pattern, last generation NIEs – i.e ASEAN-4 – can certainly improve further their position on regional and world markets for consumer electronics, but they face the formidable challenge of China.

Electrical equipment and consumer products – where a few companies of advanced industrial nations (USA, Japan, Europe) constitute a strong oligopoly, together with a very limited numbers of firms from emerging countries. Markets are determined by private and public investment programs and innovation is relatively steady.

4.2 The Asian Division of Labor: the Example of Some Consumer Electronic Products

The diversified structure and the broad product range of the industry does not allow to give a general picture of it like in the case of car production. Nevertheless, considering one product range through case studies of firms, we shall try to introduce what is at stake as far as changes in the division of labor and production networking is concerned.

In the case of electric/electronic appliances industry, relocation of activities in emerging Asian countries began rather early. Already in the 1970s, after the Nixon shock ending the fixed currency system of 360 yens for a dollar, some companies decided to relocate labor intensive production to cheap labor countries to cut production cost and stay competitive. For example, Sharp opened its first foreign plants in Korea in 1973 and the second one in Malaysia in 1974. These plants only aimed at exporting products to the US and Europe. At the end of the 70s and during the 80s, Japan had to cope with commercial frictions with advanced economies and firms started to invest in the US and Europe. The strategy was of course to secure market by substituting local production to exports. In the case of Sharp, in the early 80s for example, half of the products sold in Europe was produced in Europe and the other half exported from Asian countries.

Japanese firms implemented two different FDI strategies which coexisted at least until the mid-1980s: plants in advanced economies being dedicated to local markets while plants in Asian countries, whatever NIEs or ASEAN, export-oriented. After the mid-80s, the economic growth in Asian countries, NIES first then ASEAN, making it possible to sell product on these markets too (Audio, TV, white goods), production volume increased and new plants were opened both for exports and for local demand – the two strategies became less differentiated. The re-appreciation of the yen after the Plaza agreement, and its increase in the following years contributed to the relocation of more activities in cheap labor countries (ASEAN but also China). Production of some product was completely transferred to these countries, and completely cut off in Japan.

Firms structured their networks within the host country purchasing as much as possible in the country of location because of import taxes. When this was impossible, components were procured from neighbor countries or from Japan – with most components supplied from Japan because of quality problem. Thus, local procurement is the common rule but the suppliers are mainly Japanese relocated firms, or local/Japanese joint-venture. For example, on the 80% local procurement that Sharp achieves in Malaysia for the TV production, about 60% is delivered by Japanese affiliated firms[6]. Contrasting with car industry, in the case of electric/electronic appliances, the production units being also dedicated to exports the production volume are high enough to make investment by suppliers profitable. For this reason firms of this sector suffered less of the Asian crisis than firms engaged in the car industry. Local procurement ratios being high, exports became cheaper because of fall in currencies. Even when local markets shrank, the reduction of sales was compensated by better competitiveness of exports.

Matsushita is an interesting example of change in the international division of labor. The firm originally developed a strategy to supply each market through local production creating 'mini-Matsushitas' in each country that offered a sufficient market in sales volume. These mini-Matsushita philosophy aimed at avoiding imports of components from other countries. It can be considered as a reproduction of the Japanese purchasing organization in each country of

[6] Case studied by author in June 1999.

localization. In the mid-90s, Matsushita decided to change this organization[7] and began to implement an organization where each country would be specialized in one product to be exported to other countries in the region. The mini-Matsushitas constituted an embarrassment to develop the new strategy and the evolution was therefore slow. But the firm was quite decided to act in this direction not only in Asian region but also in the US and in Europe. In each region, a network coordinator firm is charged of importing and exporting components and products for the whole network.

Sharp also thinks of such an organization for the coming years, but taxes are still high even between ASEAN countries and according to the firm, complementation scheme like AICO is not suitable. First, only firms having 30% of local capital may use the AICO scheme. It is not the case in most of the Sharp plants. Second, the exchange reciprocity is a condition that Sharp cannot satisfy. According to Sharp managers, AICO is dedicated to car industry and is not adapted to other ones. But with the AFTA, the possibility is coming, so the firm is rethinking its organization. For the moment, in the ASEAN countries, the firm manufactures in each country. For example, TV are produced in Malaysia, in Thailand and in Indonesia. The firm recognizes that it could achieve better economies of scale by producing the TV in one country only and exporting to the others. The same can be said for video and so on. The case of copying machines by Sharp is interesting in this regard. In 1993, Sharp opened a plant in China. The choice of China was related to the cheap labor force, the possibility to procure components locally and to the incentives of the Chinese government. The plants is selling 80% of its production to the US, 10% is exported to other foreign markets and the 10% remaining are sold on the Chinese market. Final assembly is made in China but parts are coming from Japan, Taiwan, Hong Kong and ASEAN countries, depending on their sophistication level.

Thus, the division of labor, which is rather advanced in the consumer electronic products where relocation of firms in the Asian area was drastic and concerned a whole range of products (which production completely disappeared in Japan), could become even more globalized through the impact of crisis and the liberalization of trade associated to the WTO.

4.3 Global Activities Strengthening Their Asian Base

At present the dynamics of electronics and electrical products industries in Asia is characterized by three factors : oligopolies and increased foreign intervention; requirement for technology acquisition, and strengthening of global dimension.

[7] Case studied by the author in September 1995.

4.3.1 The IC and Electronic Component Producers Restructuring Their Production

Through several waves of industrial investment the electronics industry created a complex production structure. It can be based on pluri-located network of production sites (the case of ICs) or specialized product dedicated sites (such as various types of consumer electronics in Southeast Asia). Some companies, particularly from Japan and Korea are still very specialized on standard components or mass production consumer goods. This strategy does not yield fat returns and is a handicap to both further investment and strong R&D.

The era of fully integrated firms is probably over and many companies in Korea and Japan (particularly in consumer electronics, IC and component manufacturing) still have to increase their ability to subcontract, organize outsourcing and network production.

4.3.2 *Consumer Electronics and PC : Networks to Face a New Technological Wave*

The crisis gave some impetus to a certain extent in these networks: production costs fell as a result of currency variation in emerging economies. At present the cost competitiveness is considered very satisfactory for consumer electronics and ICs although the rising US$ (and uncertainty concerning future trends) makes things difficult in the short term (Problems of comparison to the Euro zone – which UK sites are not part of but Irish are – for multi-site assembly and sourcing in the specialized circuits production for example). It is very likely that stronger networking will be preferred to increasing M&A strategies. The expansion of high tech subcontracting in a strong Asian but USD denominated production area is also an emerging feature.

Markets do not show drastic changes, but channels to reach them do change e.g. NAFTA regulations will change access rules by 2003 for IC and TV parts, justifying more relocation of Asian firms to Mexico.

Firms form emerging Asia have not sought formal alliances with major world partners even if informal cooperation agreements have flourished. A sort of wait and see attitude seems to prevail. This could be a weakness at a time of increased oligopolies. Indeed "Major league" producers from industrial countries prospered: Thomson Consumer Electronics or Siemens are good cases of this. Increased competition between Asian based and world leading firms is already felt – particularly for computers, flat screens. It is increasingly harder to select product niches with moderate entry cost and easy world market channel.

Location strategies can be selected by firms depending on local competitiveness but also heavily influenced by local market potential. In that respect China is a very special case: on one hand it accepted low-tech relocation of consumer electronics and standard circuit manufacturing, particularly from Taiwan, Japan – this explains that export share of China among Asian countries increased steadily since the beginning of 90's. On the other hand, because of potential local market major world class companies settled in China to manufacture for local needs with increasing technological content such as portable phone and telecommunication, and professional electrical equipment. The tendency to create strategic partnership between local and foreign actors seems to have been more decisive here than elsewhere throughout emerging Asia. This makes China a strong world competitor for the coming decade.

4.3.3 Beyond the Short Term Context, Some Major Challenges Are Facing Industries in Asia:

Innovation is heavily dependant on adequate financing – this is the Achilles heel for many Asia electronics companies, following crisis years. An option to maximize leverage of R&D funding is seeking private partnership – as the source of public fund is getting scarce in most countries (with the exception of Taiwan).

Market cycle effects such as for integrated circuits ICs – are still a parameter difficult to anticipate. They create costly excess capacity and handicap for product reorientation.

The regional relocation of assembly plants such as for consumer electronics (TV, CD, DVD) suggests there is a similar position of ASEAN-4 regarding location and competitiveness – which emphasize the question of cooperation/competition between countries in the region to attract and keep substantial share of activity in these sectors.

5 Conclusion : Prospects for Industrial Organization and Competitiveness in Asia

To sum up we consider that the post crisis years have resulted in a greater degree of volatility and diversity of growth patterns in the Asia region so called "soft divergence". In that context, we assume that firms and States having shown resiliency and adaptive capacities through the "Asian crisis" years, will need to further strengthen their strategies to address both the issue of regional unstable integration, and the demands of the global economic environment.

5.1 Renewal of Industrial Dynamics ?

Selected major features in post-crisis firms'strategies, are derived from sector analysis; obviously their relevance and magnitude varies depending on products or companies strategies.

Sector restructuring – meaning more mergers and concentration – is one of the consequences of crisis years. Changes in structures and organisational patterns gained momentum since 1998, and new forms slowly emerged in spite of pressure to resist increased foreign ownership or reduction of protection for national industries. This was exemplified in the car industry, but also illustrated by other sectors.

Some leading world companies have snapped up opportunities for acquisition, taking advantage of weakened situation of potential Asian partners. This gave access to some closed markets, or strenghtened position of foreign firms vis-à-vis local oligopolies. Future prospects for M&A will probably be more determined by the need for strategic alliances to access or control technologies markets. Other forms of inter-firms relation, with less formal control, are likely to spread in Asia, being well suited to business climate and to the regional market. Evidence of this can be found in the electronics industry where various grades of subcontracting, informal technological control or cooperation agreements contribute to the flexibility of a global network base.

Market strategies – In the current Asian context, more firms have learned to envisage both local and external markets. This does not mean learning global competitiveness, but developing an awareness of production and marketing beyond national niches.

At present, some industries do show a strengthening of their regional production base at the expense of their national dimension sectors; it will required futher research to monitor how this translate into new marketing channels, together with claims for freer trade in the Asian region.

5.2 New Regional Context for Firms' Operation

The regional volatility is a major consequence of the crisis – the acute political conflicts in some NIEs, the depth of institutional reform make the regional scene full of contrasts, with a widening of differences between nations, at a time of increased regional trade.

We refer below to an expert assessment of institutional and system risk in countries under the scope of this study. Admitedly ranking is always debatable, but major criteria are relevant to understand major remaining issues: they refer to regulations and institutions, market mechanisms, role of States.

The Table 1–8 offers a framework to sketch some contrasted features and challenges for emerging Asian economies. Strikingly China remains at the top, when it comes to concerns and uncertainties. The second position is attributed to Malaysia – which comes as a surprise but give food for thought regarding systemic risk. Two neighboring second generation NIEs, Philippines and Thailand – although showing different recovery patterns face similar issues. A final surprise is the marking concerning Indonesia which might some actual recent changes well accepted by the international business community.

Considering the frail recovery, the degradation of the position of "developmental states", questions remain regarding new policies to shape the future for Asian economies and their industries:

Table 1–8. Risk and industrial systems in Emerging Asian Economies

	Financial regulation transparency	Pricing ability for risk and credits	Joint venture acceptability	Labour mobility	appropriate mix labour– capital	State crony capitalism	Reform and restructuring capability	rating
China	**Strong**	**strong**	Medium	**strong**	**strong**	**Strong**	medium	**79**
Hong–Kong	Low	**strong**	Low	low	low	Low	medium	**21**
Indonesia	**Strong**	low	Medium	medium	medium	Medium	**strong**	**50**
Korea	**Strong**	low	Low	low	**strong**	Medium	low	**46**
Malaysia	Medium	**strong**	Low	medium	**strong**	**Strong**	**strong**	**71**
Philippines	Moderate	low	**Strong**	low	low	**Strong**	**strong**	**54**
Singapore	Low	medium	Low	low	low	**Strong**	low	**25**
Taiwan	Moderate	low	Low	low	low	**Strong**	medium	**33**
Thailand	Low	medium	Medium	medium	medium	Medium	**strong**	**54**

Risk: scaled from low / medium / strong

Source :adapted from French trade office "Asie–strategie"

- Can a regional political impetus for regional integration flourish at the age of globalisation ?
- Which are the required elements for new competitive advantages enabling Asian countries to benchmark each other?

How will these issues be addressed when companies have less financial resource, more temptation to tap the scores of unemployed workers and States have to face social unrest and budget constraints – thus limiting their promotion capacity?

References

Asia Pacific Journal of Management (1998) *Special Issue : The Asia MNC.* National University of Singapore. Ed John Wiley.

Asian Development Bank (2000) *Asian Develoment Outlook 2000.* Oxford University Press.

Bank of Thailand (1999) *Asian Corporate Recovery: Corporate Governance, Role of Governements.* Bangkok

Chiratiwat S. (1998) *Crisis and its Impact on ASEAN Economic Iintegration.* Workshop paper, EU consortium programme, Chulalongkorn University, Bangkok.

Dourille Evelyne (2000) La difficile reprise japonaise (the difficult Japanese Recovery), in *Mutations Asiatiques* n° 15/16, avril, pp.:2–4.

Etienne Gilles (1999) Les fusions-acquisitions au Japon, in *Notes Economiques du Japon,* note n°14, PEE de Tokyo.

Fourin (1999) Ajia Jidosha Sangyo (The Asian Car Industry), *Sekai Jidosha Sangyo* Vol. 9, No. 1. Nagoya: Fourin Inc.

Foy C. Harrigan F. O'Connor D. (1998) *L'avenir de l'Asie dans l'économie mondiale.* OCDE.

Humphrey John, Lecler Yveline, Salerno Mario, (2000) *Global Strategies and Local Realities: the Auto Industry in Emerging Markets,* London: Macmillan.

Institute of Developing Economies (1998) *The Study onTtrade and Investment Policies in Developing Countries – Thailand.* I.D.E, Tokyo.

JETRO–IDE Joint Symposium (1998) *Can Asia Recover Its Vitality? Globalization and the Roles of Japanese and U.S Corporations.* IDE,Tokyo.

LTCBR (ed.) (1997) ASEAN Jidosha Sangyo – Buhinsangyo no Kyosoryoku to Nikkei Buhinmeka no Shinshutsu – (The ASEAN Car Industry – the Competitiveness of the Parts Industry and the Penetration of the Japanese Transplants' Parts Makers). *Sokenchosa,* No. 72.

LVMH Conference (2000) *The XXI Century in Asia – Scenarios for the Next Millenium.* INSEAD Euro Asia Centre, Fontainebleau.

Lasserre P., Schütte H. (1999) Strategies for Asia Pacific – Beyond the crisis. Mac Millan Business.

Lecler Yveline (1999) Recession and Globalisation: What Future for Japanese Industrial Keiretsu, in Dirks, Huchet, Ribault eds, *Japanese Management in the Low Growth Era: Between External Shocks and Internal Evolution,* Springer Verlag, pp. 183–205.

Lecler Yveline, Guiheux Gilles (2000) Japanese Car Manufacturers and Parts Makers in the ASEAN Region: A case of Expatriation under Duress – or Regionally Integrated Production ? in Humphrey J., Lecler Y., Salerno M. *Global Strategies and Local Realities: the Auto Industry in Emerging Markets*, London: Macmillan.

Legewie J. (1998) Driving Industrial Integration: Japanese Firms and the Automobile Industry in Southeast Asia. Paper presented at the DIJ-Conference, *Regional Co-operation in Asia. Will Japan Stand up to a Leadership Role*, Tokyo, October.

Mori Minako (1999) New trends in ASEAN Strategies of Japanese–affiliated Automobile Parts Manufacturers – the Role of Exporting and Priorities for the Future –. *RIM Pacific Business and Industries*, Vol. 1, No. 43, 12–27.

PEE Chine, French Embassy China (1999) *L'accord sino-américain sur l'accès de la Chine à l'Organisation Mondiale du Commerce: dispositions particulières au secteur automobile*, 29 novembre.

Rexecode Forecast and Analysis on Emerging Countries – Verious Issues. Paris.

Sakura Institute of Research (2000) *1999/2000nen; Ajia Shuyosangyono Kaito toTtenbo* (Revovery and Perspectives of Most Important Industries in Asia), Sakura Sogo Kenkyujo, 2000, March.

Sakura Institute of Research: *Pacific Business and Industries*. Various Issues. Tokyo.

Simon Jean-Christophe (2000) Outcome of the Crisis for Emerging Countries in Asia and Renewal of Industrial Strategies of Foreign Firms: the Case of Thailand. Mc Millan, forthcoming.

Wade R. (1993) *Governing the Market. Economic Theory and the Role of Govenment in East Asian Industrialization*. Princeton University Press.

Williamson P. J. (1997) Asias's New Competitive Game. *Harvard Business Review* – September–October.,

World Bank (2000) *East Asia Recovery and Beyond*. IBRD/The World Bank.

2 Trends in Multinational Strategies and Organizations in the Asia-Pacific

Michael J. Enright
The University of Hong Kong

1 Introduction

Multinational companies face a variety of forces that are shaping their strategies and organizations. The globalization of competition, the localization of competitive advantage, and technological change, are affecting multinationals all over the world. For some traditional multinational companies, and for many new firms, modern developments will provide opportunities for them to develop and exploit competitive advantages across wider and wider markets. For others, the speed and scope of the challenge will be too much to handle. Today, rapid changes in the world economy present unprecedented challenges and opportunities. The interaction of product markets, service markets, financial markets, macroeconomics, public policy, and business strategy is reshaping firms, industries, cities, and entire economies.

Nowhere are the challenges faced by multinational firms more acute than in the Asia-Pacific region (East Asia plus Australia and New Zealand). The emergence of the economies of the Asia-Pacific was one of the most important stories in the world economy in the last quarter of the 20th century. The growing importance of the Asia-Pacific economies and the fact that multinational positions tend to be less entrenched and less stable than in North America and Europe mean that the Asia-Pacific may well be the main battleground for multinationals in the 21st century. Compounding the challenges will be additional features that set the Asia-Pacific apart from North America and Western Europe, namely greater volatility, vaster distances, wider cultural variation, more substantial differences in government and governance structures, and greater variety in development and development potential. Taken together, these features make the choices of strategies, organizations, and locations necessary to succeed in the Asia-Pacific among the most important choices multinational firms will face for decades.

This chapter summarizes some of the results of a two year project on the activities of major multinational companies in the Asia-Pacific region. Over 8,000 firms were surveyed in 1998–1999 about the nature of their activities in the Asia-Pacific, their organization and management structures in the region, the locations of their regional headquarters, and related issues. Some 1,100 usable responses were received, making the resulting database probably the largest for any study of this nature. In addition, 350 managers were interviewed to obtain detailed information about the management and organization of their companies' activities in the region. A complete discussion of this project is the subject of a book presently in process. This chapter will focus on the relative importance of the Asia-Pacific to multinational firms, the placement and management of multinational activities in the region, and the roles of some of the region's major city centers in the strategies of multinational companies.

2 Importance of the Asia-Pacific for Multinational Firms

Overall, the Asia-Pacific's economic importance has increased greatly in the last two decades. Between 1980 and 1998, the Asia-Pacific's (East Asia plus Australia and New Zealand) share of world output went from 16 percent to over 22 percent. Correcting for purchasing power parities, the Asia-Pacific's share of world output in 1998 was 25 percent (calculated from data in World Bank, various years). During the 1980s and 1990s, economic growth in the region was roughly twice that of the rest of the world. While some of economies of the Asia-Pacific have grown from a low base, this is no longer true for economies such as Japan, Hong Kong, and Singapore, which are now among the wealthiest economies in the world on a per capita basis.

The Asia-Pacific is growing in importance for major multinational firms. Foreign direct investment flows into the Asia-Pacific rose from nearly US$54 billion in 1993 to nearly US$83 billion in 1998 (see Table 2–1). Despite this growth, however, the region's share of inbound foreign direct investment fell from nearly 25 percent in 1993 to approximately 13 percent in 1998. According to our interviewees, the fall in the Asia-Pacific's share of inbound FDI largely was due to the Asian crisis combined with massive increases in cross-border mergers in the industrialized countries and a sharp rise in investment into the United States. The Asia-Pacific's share of inbound foreign investment stock stood at 19 percent in 1998.

Despite the Asian crisis, multinationals plan to expand their Asia-Pacific activities substantially. In our survey, we asked managers of Western multinationals who are based in the Asia Pacific about the importance of their activities in the region (Figure 2-1). The vast majority of managers who responded indicated that the Asia Pacific accounted for only a small portion of the sales, production, assets, or employment of their companies. The bulk of the respondents indicated that the Asia Pacific accounted for ten percent or less of worldwide corporate sales (52 percent of the respondents), production (74 percent of respondents), assets (72 percent), and employment (66 percent) in 1998–1999. Only a small percentage of respondents indicated that the Asia Pacific accounted

Table 2–1. Foreign Investment Inflows, Selected Host Economies

Host Economy	FDI inflows (US$ millions)			FDI inward stocks (US$ millions)
	1993	1995	1998	1998
World	219,421	328,862	643,879	4,088,068
Australia	4,003	12,735	6,568	104,977
China	27,515	35,849	45,460	261,117
Hong Kong	3,657	3,279	1,600	96,158
Indonesia	2,004	4,346	-356	61,116
Japan	119	41	3,192	30,272
Malaysia	5,006	4,178	3,727	41,005
New Zealand	2,350	3,744	1,160	34,093
Philippines	1,238	1,478	1,713	10,133
Singapore	4,686	7,206	7,218	85,885
South Korea	588	1,776	5,143	20,478
Taiwan	917	1,559	222	20,070
Thailand	1,805	2,068	6,969	19,978
Total of these economies	53,888	78,259	82,616	785,282

Source: UNCTAD (1999)

for more than 20 percent of sales (26 percent of respondents), production (17 percent), assets (14 percent), or employment (18 percent). The overall picture, at least among Western multinationals, is one of relatively low levels of engagement in the region to date.

There are many reasons for this low level of engagement on the part of Western firms. The most obvious one is distance. However, there also are economic, cultural, and strategic reasons. Until recently, most markets in Asia were relatively small, not particularly open, or both. Many Western companies have faced cultural and language issues that have made it difficult for them to penetrate Asian markets. In addition, given the development of NAFTA, the expansion of the EU, the advent of large cross-border mergers, and the opening of Eastern European economies, many Western companies have had their attention elsewhere.

When the same managers were asked about the future plans of their companies, the picture changes dramatically (Figure 2-2). Nearly all the respondents indicated that their companies planned to have a much more extensive presence in the region. Far fewer respondents indicated that their companies planned to have the Asia Pacific account for ten percent or less of worldwide corporate sales (22 percent of the respondents), production (51 percent of respondents), assets (50 percent), and employment (47 percent) by 2005. Far more respondents than before indicated that their companies planned to have the Asia Pacific account for more than 20 percent of sales (48 percent of respondents), production (26 percent), assets (25 percent), or employment (30 percent).

Clearly, the Western multinationals hope to expand their presence in the region. When asked why, the managers almost invariably mentioned the region's growth potential. Many expected that the markets of North America and Western Europe would not grow as fast and that the markets of Latin America, Eastern Europe, and Africa would not develop as quickly or be as important.

Figure 2–1. What percentage, roughly, of your parent firm's total world-wide sales, production, assets, and employment are currently (1998–99) in the Asia-Pacific region? (Responses from Western MNCs)

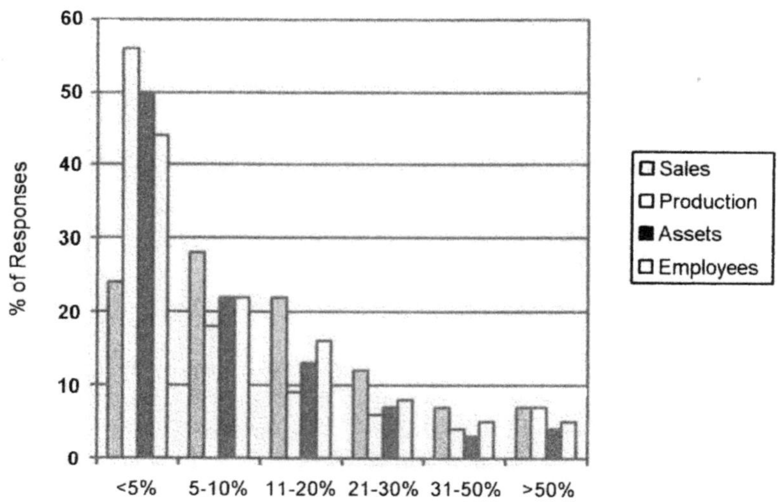

Source: Author's survey

Figure 2–2. By the year 2005, roughly what percentage of total world-wide sales, production, assets, and employment do you think your parent firm intends to have in the Asia-Pacific region? (Responses from Western MNCs)

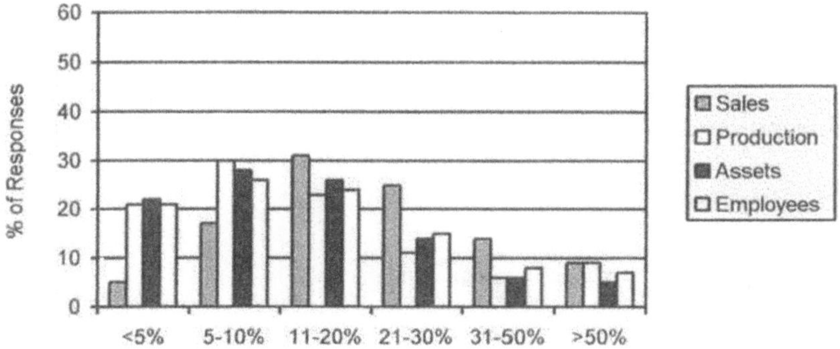

Source: Author's survey

3 Why in the Asia-Pacific?

The literature on multinational firms recognizes several rationales for multinational investment. These include market access, access to resources, access to strategic assets, exploitation of intangible assets, competitive dynamics, access to information, and access to particular marketplaces (Dunning 2000, Enright 2000c). When we asked the managers of major multinational companies why their companies were active in the Asia-Pacific region, the vast majority indicated that the most important reason is to access market opportunities. Contrary to popular perceptions in the West, market opportunities are viewed as far more important than raw materials availability, low cost production, or the activities of competitors. To put it simply, most multinationals set up in the Asia-Pacific to sell into the region.

Figure 2–3. In deciding to have or maintain a presence in the Asia-Pacific region, how important are the following for your parent company?

1 = Very Unimportant, 2 = Slightly Unimportant, 3 = Neutral, 4 = Slightly Important, 5 = Very Important

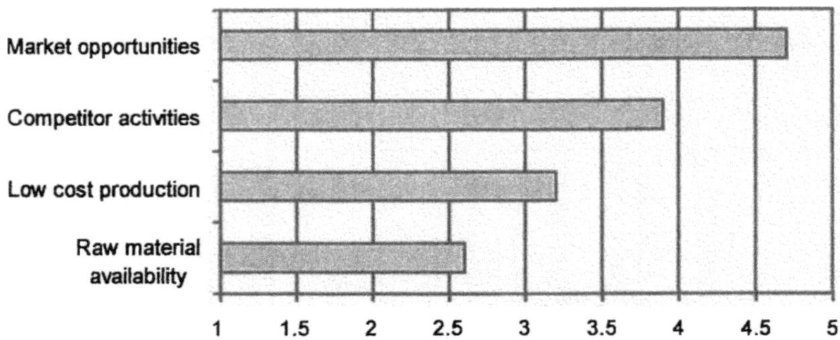

Source: Author's survey

The second most important reason for a presence in the region shown in Figure 2–3. involves competitor activities. The perhaps surprising strength of responses citing competitor activities as an important motivation for a presence in the region also can be understood in market terms. When asked to explain such answers, managers replied that they did not wish to be foreclosed from markets by competitors who might obtain advantages in developing relationships, brand names, and distribution networks in key economies in the region. This focus on market opportunities and competitive interaction is likely to continue in the medium and long term as incomes in several Asian economies rise to levels that make them more attractive markets for multinational firms.

4 Corporate Activities in the Asia-Pacific

Multinational firms must decide how to locate and coordinate their international activities (Porter 1986, Yip 1999). In general, such decisions will be influenced by the nature of the activity, the characteristics of each location, the nationality of the firm, and the firm's own competitive position and strategy. We asked managers from multinationals active in the region about the location of their significant sales, production, service provision, internal corporate support activities, and research and development in the region.

4.1 Western Manufacturing MNCs

Western manufacturing firms have a distinct pattern of activity locations in the region. Table 2–2 shows a relatively wide range of locations. Each of the economies was the home of significant *sales activities* for at least half of the responding firms. The exact pattern appears closely linked to the size and affluence of the individual economies. The Chinese Mainland (84 percent of responding firms) and Japan (80 percent), the two largest economies in the region, were the leading sales locations. More than seventy percent reported significant sales in Korea, Singapore, Taiwan, and Hong Kong. Next came the medium sized economies of Australia, Thailand, and Malaysia. Finally, fewer companies reported significant sales in some of the lesser developed (Indonesia and the Philippines) or smaller (New Zealand) economies. China's position is rather startling, given the fact that it was essentially closed to foreign investment until recently.

The Chinese Mainland was by far the most popular location for *production* in the region (54 percent of respondents in the category reporting significant production in China), with Japan (34 percent) and Australia (30 percent) distant second and third. China's position is due to the importance of the economy, policies that have promoted investment rather than imports, and increasing openness. Japan's position is related to the importance and affluence of its economy, as well as the difficulties that some foreign firms have had penetrating the Japanese market. Australia's probably is due to its geographic isolation, a long manufacturing history, and past protectionist policies. Malaysia was a more popular production location than Singapore, while Hong Kong (whose own production activities largely have migrated to the Chinese Mainland) and New Zealand were the least popular production locations. On the whole, far fewer of the multinationals produced in the Asia Pacific than sold there.

Service provision to customers appears to be closely related to sales activities, as one would expect. The most popular locations for *internal support activities* are the large markets, which have local demand for support, and the business service centers of Hong Kong and Singapore, which tend to provide support on a regional or subregional level. Very few Western manufacturing multinationals do significant *research and development* anywhere in the region. Japan ranked first as an R&D location with just over a quarter of the responding firms indicating they did significant research and development in the country. Australia, Singapore, and the Chinese Mainland were homes for significant research and development for more than 10 percent of responding firms. The rest of the locations received only minimal mention.

Table 2–2. In which locations does your company have significant activities?
(Western Manufacturing Firms, Percentage of Response, n=352)

Country	Sales	Production	Service Provision to Customers	Internal Support Activities	R&D
Japan	80	34	51	41	26
Korea	74	22	38	23	4
Mainland China	84	54	52	40	11
Taiwan	72	20	37	23	9
Hong Kong	71	11	43	36	8
Philippines	56	15	27	14	4
Thailand	65	21	35	15	4
Malaysia	65	25	36	20	7
Singapore	74	23	51	46	13
Indonesia	58	21	30	18	3
Australia	68	30	41	33	13
New Zealand	50	10	24	12	3

Source: Author's survey

4.2 Western Service MNCs

The most striking feature of the Asia Pacific locations of activities of Western service multinationals is the leading position of Hong Kong. Hong Kong ranked first as a location for sales (67 percent of respondents), service provision (69 percent), internal support activities (45 percent), and research and development (15 percent), by a wide margin in the first three cases (Table 2–3). This reflects Hong Kong's role as a major service center for Greater China and for the region as a whole. Singapore, second in each of the categories, plays a similar role, mostly for ASEAN economies. Japan, the Chinese Mainland, Australia, and Taiwan are the next most popular locations for the activities of the service multinationals. On average, Western service multinationals have less sales coverage in the region than their manufacturing counterparts. The service multinationals seem to concentrate their activities in the large and/or affluent economies of the region. Sales and service provision for these firms are closely linked, as one would expect. Again relatively few of the Western service multinationals do any research and development in the region that they consider important.

Table 2–3. In which locations does your company have significant activities? (Western Service Firms, Percentages of Responses, n=499)

Country	Sales	Service Provision to Customers	Internal Support Activities	R&D
Japan	58	57	32	11
Korea	47	44	18	5
Mainland China	54	57	28	11
Taiwan	52	49	23	7
Hong Kong	67	69	45	15
Philippines	45	43	18	4
Thailand	50	46	18	5
Malaysia	50	48	19	5
Singapore	60	60	40	14
Indonesia	44	41	18	4
Australia	54	49	31	13
New Zealand	36	33	13	3

Source: Author's survey

4.3 Japanese Manufacturing MNCs

Japanese firms in our sample are distinctive in that they have a home base in the region. Japan itself also has different legacies in the region than Western economies, which translates into a distinct network of pre-existing business partners, contacts, cultural affinities, and some antagonisms. Japanese manufacturing multinationals exhibit less of a *sales* presence in many of the economies of the region than their Western counterparts (see Table 2–4). Perhaps this reflects the fact that Western firms active in the region already are far from home. Therefore it might not be more challenging for such firms to set up in many markets than in one. Some Japanese firms, on the other hand, may be sequentially expanding by focusing on near neighbors first. Among the Japanese manufacturing multinationals, Hong Kong (64 percent), Singapore (64 percent), the Chinese Mainland (63 percent), and Taiwan (61 percent) were the most popular sales locations after Japan. The relatively limited presence in Korea (46 percent), Australia (33 percent), and New Zealand (22 percent) is quite striking. The first might be due to historical circumstances and the direct competition between Japanese and Korean firms in a number of industries. The last two might be due to geographic and cultural distance.

The Chinese Mainland (59 percent) is the most popular non-Japanese location in the Asia-Pacific for *production* among the Japanese manufacturing multinationals. Thailand (50 percent), Taiwan (41 percent), and Malaysia (41 percent) also are significant production locations. Singapore appears to be losing out to its ASEAN neighbors and once again Korea (22 percent), Australia (11 percent), and New Zealand (4 percent) show a low presence of Japanese firms. Japanese manufacturing multinationals appear to *provide services* in far fewer locations than their Western counterparts, with Hong Kong and Singapore being the primary locations, and the Chinese Mainland roughly on par with ASEAN economies. Singapore is by far the leading location for non-Japanese based *research and development* in the region for these firms, though only 20 percent of respondents indicated their company had significant R&D there. All of the other locations were mentioned by fewer than 10 percent of the respondents for research and development.

Table 2–4. In which locations does your company have significant activities? (Japanese Manufacturing Firms, Percentages of Responses, n=98)

Country	Sales	Production	Service Provision to Customers	Internal Support Activities	R&D
Korea	46	22	21	9	2
Mainland China	63	59	31	20	9
Taiwan	61	41	29	15	6
Hong Kong	64	15	34	28	4
Philippines	46	26	20	8	3
Thailand	58	50	24	11	8
Malaysia	56	41	27	15	8
Singapore	64	30	38	32	20
Indonesia	45	32	18	11	4
Australia	33	11	15	6	5
New Zealand	22	4	12	3	3

Source: Author's survey

4.4 Japanese Service MNCs

The Japanese service multinationals in the sample tend to operate in even fewer locations in the region than their manufacturing counterparts (see Table 2–5). Only Hong Kong and Singapore are the locations for significant *sales* for more than half the relevant firms. These two are followed by several locations, the Chinese Mainland, Taiwan, Thailand, Malaysia, and Indonesia, in which around 40 percent of the Japanese service multinationals have significant sales. Again the lack of presence in Korea (only 27 percent), Australia (29 percent), and New Zealand (14 percent) is striking. A similar pattern, at somewhat lower level of activity, is found for *service provision*. Hong Kong and Singapore are by far the most important locations *for internal support activities* of the Japanese service multinationals, but these locations were significant for only a little over a fifth of the relevant firms. Interviewees claim that this is due to support activities that are provided by corporate headquarters in Japan. Very few Japanese service multinationals due appreciable *research and development* in the region. Again, Hong Kong and Singapore are the leading locations for what does get done.

Table 2–5. In which locations does your company have significant activities? (Japanese Service Firms, Percentages of Responses, n=92)

Country	Sales	Service Provision to Customers	Internal Support Activities	R&D
Korea	27	16	7	1
Mainland China	40	26	10	9
Taiwan	39	23	9	9
Hong Kong	55	34	21	11
Philippines	33	16	2	2
Thailand	41	23	8	8
Malaysia	40	28	10	6
Singapore	54	33	23	12
Indonesia	39	22	9	7
Australia	29	15	7	4
New Zealand	14	9	0	0

Source: Author's survey

4.5 Activity Location

There are distinct asymmetries in the location patterns for the activities of multinational firms in the Asia-Pacific. While sales are relatively dispersed to many economies around the region, especially for Western multinationals in our sample, other activities are more concentrated in particular economies. Production activities tend to be located in large markets and in economies where low cost labor is present. Servicing activities are linked to markets and to specific locations, most notably Hong Kong and Singapore, that tend to act as regional service centers. The Japanese firms in the sample tend to have fewer locations for their activities. This is perhaps due to a process of sequential expansion. Western firms active in the region by definition are operating far from home, while some Japanese firms in the sample have not developed extensive international networks as of yet.

5 Factors Likely to Shift Activity Locations in the Future

Managers of multinational firms have indicated three major factors that are likely to shift the location of their investments in the region in the future. The first involves the ongoing fallout from the Asian crisis, particularly in Southeast Asian countries. The second involves a shift in the geographic focus of investment in the region. The third involves the rise of China as an investment location.

5.1 The Asian Crisis

The Asian economic crisis, generally dated from the floating of the Thai baht on 2 July 1998, soon spread through ASEAN, to South Korea, and beyond. Although several of the economies that were hardest hit by the crisis have since started to recover, its impact on the investment decisions of multinational companies has been substantial. In the short term, infrastructure and construction projects have been put on hold in several places, affecting overseas contractors and suppliers. The wholesale departure of Western portfolio capital from the region precipitated cutbacks by several financial service companies. Some other multinationals have shelved planned investments in manufacturing, distribution, and sales facilities designed to serve economies where purchasing power has fallen dramatically.

However, despite the crisis, multinationals as a whole continue to look positively toward Asia in the medium term. More than 50 percent of the CEOs of major corporations surveyed by the World Economic Forum in 1998 indicated that Asia would be their major growth market in the coming years. In a March 1998 UNCTAD survey, 26 percent of the multinational firm respondents indicated that as a result of the current economic crisis they plan to increase their investments in Asia in the short to medium term; 62 percent planned to keep their investments unchanged; and only 12 percent planned to reduce investments. Some 13 percent of the UNCTAD respondents indicated that their view of the longer term prospects of Asia as a destination for investment had improved; 81 percent reported no change; and just 6 percent reported diminished prospects (UNCTAD 1998).

Our own interviews and surveys indicate a similar picture. Most of the managers we interviewed said that the fundamentals of the Asian economies are still strong, that there is a potential benefit of improved regulation, and that the economies, as well as the multinational companies, eventually will benefit from more transparency and open competition. Several multinational firms reported that the crisis actually presented them with opportunities to buy cheap assets, to buy out ailing local partners, to create new partnerships on better terms, to obtain greater leverage over governments in the region, or to achieve entry into markets that have been closed to them.

Although it varies by industry, economy, and company, firms tending now to avoid Asia are smaller, younger, less experienced in the region, less international overall, more leveraged, and more oriented toward the short term. Companies that look at the Asian economic crisis and its aftermath as an opportunity tend to be larger, older, more experienced in the Asia-Pacific region, more international, consumer or distribution oriented, cash rich, and oriented toward the medium to longer term. In other words, multinationals that have been through ups and downs in Asia and elsewhere before have been focusing on the opportunities. Experienced firms like GM, Ford, Renault, Daimler–Chrysler, GE, Merrill–Lynch, Citicorp, HSBC, and others have been moving to expand their activities in the region.

In order to check on the generality of the interview information, in late 1998 and early 1999, we asked the managers of multinational firms active in the region about their views on the Asian crisis (Table 2-6). The results show that Japanese firms believe that after an initial two year decline in the attractiveness of the rest of Asia as a market and a production location, in subsequent years, the crisis actually will make the region a more attractive place. The Western firms show a similar pattern of attitudes in terms of Asia as a market, although they place the benefits as coming further into the future than did the Japanese companies. The Western firms did not believe that the crisis will result in a significant increase or decrease in Asia's attractiveness as a production location over the next three to ten years. The reason for this might be that Asia (excluding Japan) is far less important to Western firms than to Japanese firms as a production location.

The crisis has placed managers in the region under increased pressure from their corporate headquarters. Firms that were willing to put up with limited profitability in growing markets have been less willing to do so in markets that are perceived to be stagnant or declining. Managers in the Asia-Pacific have found themselves under pressure to reduce costs and to provide additional justification for investment programs. In some cases, managers with mandates for growth have been replaced by managers with cost cutting mandates.

Table 2–6. Will the Asian crisis make the region generally more or less attractive as a location for sales and production for firms like yours over the following periods of time? (asked in 1998–1999)

1 = Much Less Attractive, 2 = Less Attractive, 3 = Neutral, 4 = More Attractive, 5 = Much More Attractive

	Japanese Firms MEAN	Western Firms MEAN
Next one to two years	2.5	2.0
Next three to five years	3.5	3.0
Next six to ten years	3.9	3.5
For production over the		
Next one to two years	3.0	2.7
Next three to five years	3.6	3.2
Next six to ten years	3.9	3.2

Source: Author's survey

5.2 Shifting Weight of Investment

In general, there has been a strong shift in interest away from ASEAN economies and toward the economies of the Northern Asia-Pacific. Japan's economy, though not growing rapidly, has become significantly more open to foreign investment in a number of sectors. The "Big Bang" in the financial sector has provided an impetus toward further opening and reform. The sale of financial institutions, such as Long Term Credit Bank, and other interests, such as those in some of the major auto companies, to foreign players would have been unthinkable just a few years ago. Given the size of Japan's economy and the wealth of Japanese consumers, any signs of additional opening will bring substantial new inward investment.

South Korea's economy has rebounded much more strongly than the other crisis economies. Its economic weight and increasing openness has made it an attractive investment location. Although the process of selling off assets and reforming the chaebol and financial institutions have been slow and painful, the size and potential of the South Korean economy make it an attractive destination for multinational firms who largely have been shut out of the market to date.

In contrast, many managers of multinational companies foresee continued difficulties in the ASEAN economies. Indonesia, the most troubled, suffers from political and social tensions as well as economic and financial systems in need of the type of overhaul that might be beyond the capabilities of the Indonesian leadership to carry out. Thailand has suffered from a series of setbacks in its own reform process that recently have set the Thai baht to its lowest levels in two years. The Philippines is suffering from a leadership vacuum and the seeming inability to move beyond crony capitalism. While Malaysia's economy has been rebounding nicely, statements by the Prime Minister and fears about arbitrary opening and closing of Malaysian markets have caused investors to look elsewhere. Even Singapore, whose government has been widely credited for its performance since the middle of 1998, increasingly is viewed as "a good house in a bad neighborhood." ASEAN economies, in general, are viewed as poor prospects for the next several years as economic difficulties, political uncertainties, and social instability limit growth. Increases in FDI in some of these nations are best understood as foreign firms taking advantage of the ability to buy relatively inexpensive assets (Enright 2000a, 2000b).

5.3 The Rise of China

At the same time, China's growth, its imminent accession into the Word Trade Organization, its ongoing reform program, and the size of China's economy are likely to make it even more attractive in the future than in the past. In recent years, China has become the world's second leading destination for foreign direct investment behind the United States. Much of this investment is linked to export processing activities which account for roughly half of China's total trade. China occupies a specific position in what has become an Asian production system. For a vast range of light manufactured goods, China has become the location of choice for assembly and final production involving capital and knowledge-intensive components, inputs, and capital goods imported from elsewhere in the region. In the process, it has displaced Asian economies, largely the Newly Industrializing Economies of Hong Kong, Singapore, South Korea, and Taiwan, in the final steps in the production process in competition with other developing economies in ASEAN.

This shift in final production to China has allowed companies from the NIEs and Japan to retain or improve their cost competitiveness and expand their total output and reach in international markets. In 1986 and 1987, for example, approximately 60 percent of the United States imports of footwear were from Taiwan and South Korea. By 1998, the share of Taiwan and South Korea was 4 percent and that of China 60 percent. In toys and sporting goods, approximately 60 percent of US imports came from Hong Kong, Taiwan, and South Korea in 1987. China was the source of only 7 percent. By the late 1990s, China supplied 60 percent of the US imports and the rest of Asia only 10 percent (Lardy 2000).

China also is a competitor for some Asian economies as an investment location. It will increasingly attract investment for manufacturing activities in preference to Southeast Asia due to low labor costs and high productivity. China also will benefit from a shift in economic weight from Southeast Asia to Northeast Asia. The Asian crisis left Southeast Asian economies weak, while greater openness in China, South Korea, and Japan, combined with strong growth in the former two economies and the economic weight of the latter, make Northeast Asia a far more attractive investment option. Increases in the technology content of import demand from major economies would favor the more technologically sophisticated economies of the North. North Asia's ability to benefits from growing global demand will be further enhanced by China's accession to the WTO (and Taiwan's subsequent accession), which will result in an upsurge of investment from North Asian neighbors to China and an increase in North Asian trade. In the past, the stock of foreign investment of major investor economies in ASEAN economies has been larger than their investments in either Greater China or Japan and Korea. The new trends represent a sharp departure from this past situation.

6 Potential Impact in Electronics

The combination of factors listed above is likely to have a profound impact on investment patterns in particular industries. One of the most important impacts is likely to be on the electronics industry. China's electronic industry grew at an annual rate of more than 34 per cent from 1995 to 1999. In electronics, the rise of China's exports has been the result of a division of labor in which Chinese facilities have specialized in the labor intensive assembly stages of the production process, while other economies in the region have supplied key components, subassemblies, and other inputs. China has emerged as a major player in the dispersed Asian production chain which has come to characterize electronics manufacturing, particularly for consumer electronics.

In one sense, electronics assembly in the Chinese Mainland has been complementary with the component, subassembly, and other input production of ASEAN, Japan, Korea, and Taiwan. In another sense, it has displaced the assembly activities that used to take place in Singapore, Korea, Taiwan, and Hong Kong and competes directly with ASEAN economies such as Thailand, Malaysia, Indonesia, and the Philippines. By 1999, roughly 30 percent of the computer related output of Taiwanese firms came from the Chinese Mainland. This percentage was expected to double in just a few years. For some products, such as monitors (over 70 percent), keyboards (approximately 90 percent), and power supplies (approximately 90 percent), the Chinese Mainland already is the dominant production location. Taiwanese firms are attracted by wages one-tenth those of Taiwan, a common language, the hope of entering the Mainland market, and worker productivity that some managers claim is 30 to 40 percent higher than in Taiwan (Baum 1999).

According to the *Asian Wall Street Journal*, "Japan's biggest factory these days is a country called China. Japanese companies in China are pumping out more and more goods aimed for exports back to Japan, with trade booming as a result" (Kanabayashi 2000). According to Jetro, 73 percent of the Japanese companies operating facilities in China export more than half of their main products back to Japan. Some 60 percent obtain more than half of their inputs from outside of China (mostly from Japan and other Asian economies) (Jetro 2000). For some Japanese companies, China has become their dominant production location. Citizen, a leading Japanese watch company, produces 78 percent of its watches in China and expects the figure to be 100 percent by 2002. The rapid growth in trade between Japan and China in 1999 and the first half of 2000 has been due to sharp increases in trade in electronic components (to China) and finished electronics goods (to Japan).

China will soon be a major competitor for trade and investment in components with countries such as Thailand and Malaysia, which largely rely on foreign investment and technology for component production. China's electronics assemblers have relied almost exclusively on imports for advanced components (ENews 2000). In the short run, this creates a complementary situation with component producers in other Asian economies, but eventually economic pressures to produce components close to assembly sites, China's increasing technological sophistication, and government policy to push China up the value-added ladder will have an impact. Major multinational companies already are placing facilities for advanced components in China. In August 2000, for example, Motorola announced a US$1.9 billion semiconductor facility to be built in China. The single investment represented more capital than the company's total cumulative investment of US$1.1 billion in Malaysia (Goad 2000).

As China moves up the technology ladder, its vast army of lesser skilled workers is still going to provide it with advantages in labor intensive assembly activities. There is a good chance that, instead of remaining as the last destination in a pan-Asian production chain, the Chinese electronics industry will attract complete production chains from ASEAN with low cost assembly labor, local component capabilities, and immediate access to one of the world's largest markets. Though such competition will not occur overnight, given the capital and technology required for advanced component production and the embedded electronics production chains in ASEAN economies, the pressures will be very real. Asian economies with the technology, capabilities, and designs to continue to develop new products ahead of China will benefit. Asian economies that rely on foreign technology, capabilities, and designs, and who cannot find defensible niches, will find their positions threatened. For companies, it will be increasingly difficult to compete in world markets without a strong production base in China.

7 Organization in the Asia-Pacific

Multinational firms must locate their operations in the region, but they also must manage and coordinate these operations. Many companies have adopted regional management structures for their Asia-Pacific operations. Regional organizations have received relatively little attention in the literature on multinationals. Much of this literature focuses on the tradeoffs between global organizations, in which key decisions are made on a centralized basis, and country based organizations, where major decisions are far more decentralized. The tension the literature focuses on is that between potential efficiency and clarity of a globally integrated strategy and the ability to respond to specific local conditions of a country focused organization (Martinez and Jarillo 1989, 1991). Proposed solutions to this tension have included "multifocal multinationals" (Prahalad and Doz 1987), the "transnational" corporation (Bartlett and Ghoshal 1989) and the "heterarchical multinational" (Hedlund 1986). More recently, there was increased attention on achieving the right tradeoff through alliances (Parkhe 1993), human resource practices (Tayler, Beecher, and Napier 1996), and organizational flexibility (Buckley and Casson 1998).

As early as the 1970s, however, some researchers noted the trend toward regional integration as an important force influencing multinational organizations (Heenan and Perlmutter 1979). However, many have viewed regional strategies as "second best" or "compromise" options when global strategies cannot be employed (Morrison and Roth 1992; Morrison, Ricks, and Roth 1991). Reasons given for the development of regional strategies and organizations include limits to economies of scale, the creation of trade blocs, difficulties in implementing global strategies, regional differences in markets and employees, and the need to preserve region-based organizational capabilities (Lehrer and Saskawa 1999). With respect to the Asia-Pacific, additional reasons include the physical and psychic distances between the region and the corporate headquarters of Western multinationals, the need for concerted regional strategy to penetrate the Asia-Pacific, the importance of government relations, and the heterogeneity of economies (Lasserre 1996 and Schütte 1997).

8 Geographic Structures

Most of the managers we interviewed indicated that their primary structure for managing in the Asia-Pacific was geographic. By far the most common structure involved an Asia-Pacific regional headquarters or regional office, a Northern Asia-Pacific subregional headquarters or office, a Southern Asia-Pacific subregional headquarters or office, a Japan-Korea office, and an Australia-New Zealand office, with the last four each reporting directly to the Asia-Pacific regional headquarters or office. Country organizations (except those of Japan-Korea and Australia-New Zealand) reported into either the Northern and Southern Asia-Pacific offices. In this type of structure, Hong Kong was the location of most of the Northern Asia-Pacific headquarters or offices and Singapore the location of most of the Southern Asia-Pacific headquarters or offices. Hong Kong and

Figure 2–4. Most Common MNC Organizational Structure in the Asia-Pacific

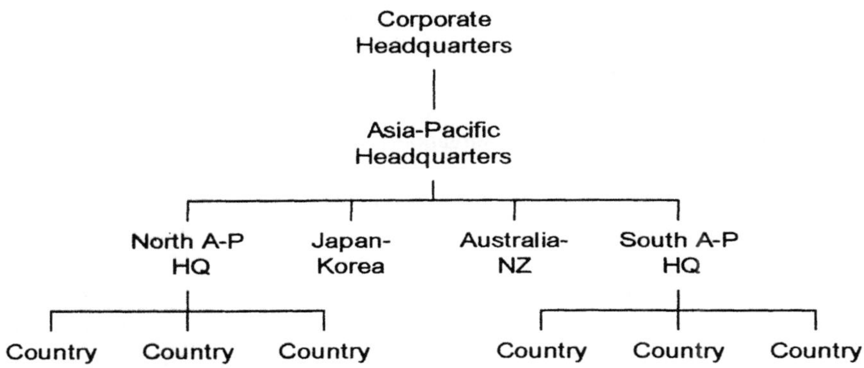

Source: Author's interviews

Singapore were the two most popular locations for the Asia-Pacific regional headquarters or regional office (see Figure 2–4).

The most common alternatives were, in order of importance: a greater China office instead of a Northern Asia-Pacific office, Japan-Korea reporting into the Northern Asia-Pacific subregional headquarters and Australia-New Zealand reporting into the Southern Asia-Pacific headquarters, and a series of country offices reporting directly into the Asia-Pacific regional headquarters. The trends mentioned above indicate that the Northern Asia-Pacific and Japan-Korea regions are likely to have much greater weight in the future, indicating that these parts of the organization are likely to receive a disproportionate amount of attention going forward.

The dominant organizational structures indicate that multinational companies increasingly are thinking of the Asia-Pacific not as a single entity, but as distinct markets and sources of supply. Although most multinationals organize their Asia-Pacific operations on a geographic basis, the segmentation scheme actually is far more complex. *Geographic segmentation* is reinforced by differences in purchasing power, market potential, and culture. Segmentation by *purchasing power* divides the region into the relatively rich developed economies (including Japan, Hong Kong, Singapore, Australia, and New Zealand), the not quite so developed economies (Korea and Taiwan), lower income developing economies (Malaysia, Thailand, the Philippines, and Indonesia), and poorer emerging economies (including China and Vietnam). Such segmentation does not correlate precisely with per capita income, but with what might be called effective purchasing power, which is related to the presence of a significant number of people with substantial purchasing power combined with markets open enough to be accessible for multinational firms.

Market potential is related to future potential purchasing power. Population, economic growth rates, and the opening of previously closed economies are all important determinants of market potential. High-potential markets tend to include the Chinese Mainland, Japan, and Korea. Medium potential markets include Australasia, Thailand, Taiwan, Malaysia, Indonesia, and sometimes Hong Kong. Lower potential markets include Singapore, the Philippines, Myanmar, and Indochina. China and Indonesia tend to get more attention than present income and market size would warrant given the major potential for growth that is seen by major multinational companies.

Segmentation by *culture* tends to divide the region into Greater China, ASEAN, Australia and New Zealand, and Japan-Korea. Although the ASEAN nations have different cultures, none is considered large enough a market to merit its own category, except for the firms that are organized solely on a country basis. Japan and Korea tend to be lumped together despite cultural differences as do Hong Kong, Taiwan, and the Chinese Mainland, despite the fact that these economies are at different stages in development. Many multinationals have found that people who perform well in one subregion often do not perform as well in another subregion, particularly in sales and marketing positions.

9 MNC Business Relationships

Although the dominant form of organization in the region is geographic, many managers emphasized that this often was mostly for reporting purposes and coordination. Interview data suggests that multinationals are increasingly shifting responsibility away from country managers and even heads of Asia-Pacific toward regional function and region product line managers. In many companies, figures and results are aggregated and communicated to corporate headquarters on a geographic basis, but the "way the business actually gets done" in functional terms is rather different.

With each passing year, multinationals are placing each corporate activity under a more powerful microscope, and are assessing the optimal location of the management of each activity more carefully. Many companies have dispersed the regional management of specific activities or product lines to different locations around the region. One package delivery company recently completed its assessment of where to place its regional headquarters, it decided to split the relevant activities into three pieces, one in Hong Kong, one in Singapore, and one in Malaysia. A UK food packaged goods company carries out strategy formulation for the Asia-Pacific region in London, creates local marketing strategies in each local market, has its regional accounting and financial consolidation activities in Hong Kong, manages its marketing data processing in Sydney, co-ordinates its sales in three locations (Hong Kong, Singapore, and Tokyo), and co-ordinates manufacturing operations in two location (Shanghai and Singapore). Another Western MNC has a regional headquarters in Hong Kong, but the product managers for its major product lines are located in Hong Kong, Singapore, Taipei, and Tokyo. In this company, the critical communications within each of the company's major product lines tends to be between the product manager and dedicated product line personnel in the different markets, rather than between the regional headquarters and national subsidiaries.

Despite the distribution of the management of various activities we observed, we found only a few companies that have developed truly transnational networked organizations in which key individuals and expertise are dispersed around the region. In such cases, the regional headquarters or office acts less as a control center and more as a co-ordination center for activities within the region and a communication center for information flows between the region and the parent company's worldwide headquarters. It seems that the disadvantages in terms of lack of a clear locus of decision making and lack of a clear responsibility for relaying the needs of the regional organization to corporate management outweigh the potential benefits of such networks.

10 Importance of City Centers

It is impossible to separate a discussion of how multinational companies spread the management of their operations around the region from a discussion of the roles of the major city centers in the region. The globalization of economic activity, the rise of multinational companies, and the corresponding increase in importance of producer services have vastly increased the importance of city centers in the world economy (Sassen 1994, Beaverstock et al. 2000). Cities are the crucial nodes for international coordination and servicing of firms, markets, and economies. Some researchers have gone so far as to claim that the "work of globalization" goes on in cities (Sassen 1994). A literature has emerged on "systems of cities" that postulates that different cities play different economic roles, with so-called "world cities", cities that provide coordination, management, servicing, finance, and information functions for wide areas, at the apex of a hierarchy of metropolitan locations (Friedman 1995).

Much of the work in this vein uses indirect measures, such as visitor flows or locations of major offices of professional services firms, to identify "world cities" (Beaverstock et al. 2000). Our survey data allows for a direct measure of the roles that major city centers in the Asia-Pacific play for multinational firms. We asked managers from Japanese and Western multinationals how important six different city centers (Hong Kong, Shanghai, Singapore, Sydney, Taipei, and Tokyo) were to their parent companies' performance in several management related activities.

Table 2–7. How important are these cities for your parent company's performance of the following business related activities? (Mean response)

1 = Very Unimportant, 2 = Slightly Unimportant, 3 = Neutral, 4 = Slightly Important, 5 = Very Important

Business activity	Hong Kong	Shanghai	Singapore	Sydney	Taipei	Tokyo *
Regional co-ordination activities	3.85	2.79	3.84	2.42	2.15	2.79
Supporting regional operations	3.79	2.72	3.86	2.45	2.18	2.75
Corporate media relations	3.31	2.34	3.18	2.28	2.01	2.49
Finance and Accounting	3.46	2.27	3.31	2.35	1.99	2.49
New product/service development	2.93	2.40	2.87	2.27	2.11	2.63
Business process development	3.12	2.40	3.09	2.30	2.11	2.51
Purchasing management	2.86	2.30	2.77	1.97	2.02	2.16
Logistics management	3.12	2.41	3.02	2.08	2.02	2.30
Marketing management	3.53	2.77	3.56	2.55	2.39	2.92
Sales management	3.56	2.93	3.54	2.62	2.53	3.03
Goods distribution	3.07	2.63	3.07	2.19	2.21	2.51
Service provision to clients	3.71	3.23	3.68	2.87	2.84	3.30
Import / export	3.22	2.71	3.04	2.16	2.26	2.50
Manufacturing management	2.32	2.42	2.39	1.86	1.97	2.13
Customer relations and service	3.77	3.33	3.67	2.98	2.91	3.38

Note: * Tokyo numbers refer to responses of Western companies

Source: Author's survey

The results show that Hong Kong and Singapore have emerged as the most important locations for most of the corporate activities found in Table 2–7. These two cities clearly are the leading management centers for multinationals in the region, far ahead of Tokyo, Shanghai, Sydney, and Taipei. This was even true when responses from Japanese firms were included in the results (Table 2–7 lists only the mean response for Western firms in the Tokyo column).

The results imply that Hong Kong and Singapore have major regional roles, while the other cities have essentially national or local roles. This was confirmed in interviews with managers in the cities in question. These managers confirmed that for foreign multinationals, Tokyo is primarily a center from which to manage Japan operations, Sydney primarily a place to manage Australia operations, Shanghai primarily a place to manage operations in the Yangzi Delta area, and Taipei primarily a place to manage Taiwan operations. Hong Kong on the other hand, primarily was viewed as a pan-Asia-Pacific management center, and secondarily as a North Asia-Pacific center. Singapore was viewed primarily as a South Asia-Pacific center, and secondarily as a pan-Asia-Pacific management center (see also Enright, Scott, and Dodwell 1997). The trends identified above indicate that Hong Kong, Shanghai, and Tokyo may become significantly more important going forward, while Singapore and Sydney may become less significant, as the weight of investment moves northward.

11 Regional Headquarters in the Asia-Pacific

The most important management activities that multinational companies place in the Asia-Pacific region are their regional headquarters activities. Although the days of the "corporate battleship" regional headquarters, in which each function is managed from the same location and the regional headquarters acts as a command and control center, are numbered, the regional headquarters still is the locus of a distinct set of activities. These include regional strategy development, regional coordination, supporting regional operations, consolidation and reporting of results, and liaison with corporate headquarters (see Lasserre 1996, Hungenberg 1993).

There is a great deal of consistency in the views of managers of multinational firms as to the most important criteria for locating regional headquarters and regional offices in the Asia-Pacific region. The primary consideration is proximity to existing and potential buyers. This is followed by consistency and stability of government policy and worldclass legal and regulatory regimes. These features were considered far more important than government inducements, which were considered relatively unimportant. Next in importance tends to be communications and transportation infrastructure, which makes sense given the need to manage over dispersed geographies in the region. This is followed closely by the presence of high quality support and financial services.

Table 2–8. Where are your regional headquarters in the Asia-Pacific region? (Percentage of Responses)

RHQ Locations	Total	Western Manu	Western Service	Japanese Manu	Japanese Service
Hong Kong	35	28	42	27	22
Shanghai	3	3	2	4	0
Singapore	30	34	29	38	18
Sydney	5	3	8	1	1
Tokyo *	9	10	8	NA	NA
N	1,041	352	499	98	92

Note: * Tokyo numbers refer to the percentage of Western companies

Source: Author's survey

Although quality of life for executives ranked as only middling in importance in our survey of multinational companies, this might actually understate the importance of quality of life features in actual location decisions. Many managers indicated that the "place the regional manager wanted to live" was the ultimate factor that determined the location choice after it had been narrowed down to two or three choices based on other criteria. Given the fact that many regional managers are constantly travelling, they consider the quality of life for spouses and family as a more important factor than for the executive himself or herself.

To date, observers have found it difficult to compare the incidence of regional headquarters across different cities because of an absence of data that would permit cross-comparisons among cities. In our survey, we asked the managers of multinationals active in the region to indicate where their regional headquarters are located. A regional headquarters was defined as an organization which has control over the operation of one or more other offices and subsidiaries in other economies or countries in the region and which does not need to make frequent referrals to the overseas parent companies. Respondents also were reminded that Hong Kong, Taiwan, and the Chinese Mainland were to be considered as separate economies. With 1,041 responses to this question, we are able to tabulate the distribution of regional headquarters across regional centers by nationality, industry, size of firm, and "multinationalness" (defined as number of countries in which the firm is active). Table 2–8 contains an extremely abbreviated abstract of the results.

Overall, Hong Kong is the leading choice among the multinational firms in our database as a location for regional headquarters. Some 35 percent of firms in our sample have a regional headquarters in Hong Kong. Singapore, with 30 percent, holds a strong second place. Hong Kong and Singapore are far and away the leading regional headquarters locations in the region. After these two leaders,

Tokyo is in distant third place, serving as regional headquarters location for 9 percent of the Western firms in our database. (Japanese firms were excluded from the calculation for Tokyo because Tokyo is often their home, rather than regional, base.) Sydney is home to regional headquarters of 5 percent of the multinationals. Shanghai serves as regional headquarters location for a mere 3 percent of the multinationals. In fact, the percentage is likely to be even lower, since it seems that some managers mistakenly equated Shanghai being an "East Chinese Mainland" headquarters with being a "regional" headquarters, which was a misreading of the question.

We also obtained detailed data on regional headquarters locations by nationality and industry of the multinational firm. Space considerations preclude going into the detailed data. As can be seen in Table 2–8, however, Hong Kong's lead position is due to its dominance of regional headquarters locations for service sector firms, while Singapore leads as a regional headquarters for manufacturing firms. This is true among Western and Japanese firms. Western firms on the whole show a preference for Hong Kong, due in part to the prominence of service sector firms as well as Hong Kong's position as a major center for China and the whole region. Japanese firms as a whole show a slight preference for Singapore, probably due to the larger proportion of manufacturing firms among the Japanese multinationals in the sample, and the fact that many Japanese firms manage the northern part of the region from Japan and so really only look for another location to act as a headquarters for the Southern Asia-Pacific. Again, trends in the region suggest an increase in the importance of Hong Kong, Shanghai, and Tokyo and a potential relative decline for Singapore and Sydney.

These results provide further confirmation for the conclusion that different city centers in the region play different roles in the strategies of multinational companies. Some are regional management and coordination centers, others are focused more on linking particular countries or economies into larger regional or global networks.

12 Conclusion

Despite the Asian crisis, major multinational firms still view the Asia-Pacific region as their primary area for growth in the future. This is due to the market opportunities that they perceive will be available in the region. Although some firms have cut back for the time being, in general, the multinationals believe that a return to growth plus greater openness on the part of the region's economies, particularly in Japan, South Korea, and China, will dominate the region's shortcomings.

The pattern of activity location in the region shows that multinational companies do not treat the various economies the same. Most have widespread sales operations and customer service activities, while far fewer manufacture or produce in the region, and even fewer do significant research and development in the region (other than Japanese firms who do substantial research and development in their home country). Trends among the multinational companies indicate that the northern part of the Asia-Pacific is likely to become much more important than the southern part of the region due to the effects of the Asian crisis, greater openness in Japan and Korea, and the rise of China. These trends might well result in sharp changes in existing patterns of investment in particular industries, such as electronics.

In order to manage their operations in the Asia-Pacific, many firms have set up distinct regional organizations in which the major reporting relationships are geographic, but in which management increasingly is dispersed on an activity our product line basis. The major city centers of the region take on distinct roles in the strategies of the multinational companies. Hong Kong and Singapore tend to be used as regional coordination and management centers, while Tokyo, Shanghai, and Sydney are viewed more as national than regional centers.

Companies are becoming more and more precise in the siting of activities and management centers. One striking theme that ran through our interviews with the managers of the multinationals in the region, is that few of them were completely happy with the way their company was organized in the region. Many of the companies had reorganized in the region not to long ago and many claimed to be likely to do so again in the not too distant future. This trend could be accelerated by the shift in investment priorities within the region. These results imply that the structure and organization of multinational firms in the Asia-Pacific will important issues for years to come.

References

Bartlett, C. and S. Ghoshal (1989) *Managing Across Borders: The Transnational Solution.* (Cambridge, MA Harvard Business School Press).

Baum, J. (1999) "Dangerous Liaisons," *Far Eastern Economic Review*, 25 March 1999, pp. 10–15.

Beaverstock, J. V.; R. G. Smith; P. J. Taylor, D. R. F. Walker; and H. Lorimer (2000) "Globalization and World Cities: Some Measurement Methodologies," *Applied Geography*, *20*, 43–63.

Buckley, P. J. and M. C. Casson (1998) "Models of the Multinational Enterprise," *Journal of International Business Studies*, *29* (1) 21–44.

Dunning, J. H. (2000) "Globalization and the Theory of MNE Activity," in N. Hood and S. Young (eds.), *The Globalization of Multinational Enterprise Activity and Economic Development*, (London: Macmillan).

ENews (2000) "China and the Global Economy," *ENews*, 28 February 2000, p. 42.

Enright, M. J. (2000a) "China and Its Neighbors: The Economic Interaction," Paper prepared for Wilton Park Conference WP621, "China and Its Neighbors," 20–23 November 2000.

Enright, M. J. (2000b) "China's Future Economic Roles in the Asian Region," Paper prepared for Wilton Park Conference WP621, "China and its Neighbors," 20–23 November 2000.

Enright, M. J. (2000c) "Regional Clusters and Multinational Enterprise: Independence, Dependence, or Interdependence?," *International Studies of Management and Organization, 30* (2), 114–138.

Enright, M. J.; E. E. Scott; and D. Dodwell (1997) *The Hong Kong Advantage*, (Hong Kong: Oxford University Press).

Friedmann, J. (1995) "Where We Stand: a Decade of World City Research," in P. L. Knox and P. J. Taylor (eds.), *World Cities in a World System*, (Cambridge: Cambridge University Press), pp. 21–47.

Goad, G. P. (2000) "Anaemic Asean," *Far Eastern Economic Review*, 7 September 2000, pp. 65–66.

Hedlund, G. (1986) "The Hypermodern MNC—A Heterachy?," *Human Resource Management, 25* (1), 9–35.

Heenan, D. A. and H. V. Perlmutter (1979) *Multinational Organization Development*, (Reading, MA: Addison–Wesley).

Hungenberg, H. (1993) "How to Ensure that Headquarters Add Value," *Long Range Planning, 26* (6), 62–73.

Jetro (2000) "Japanese Firms in China Foresee Better Sales this Year," Press Release, Jetro, 2 May 2000

Kanabayashi, M. (2000) "Japan and Asia: China Toils to Meet Consumers' Demand for Japanese Goods," *Asian Wall Street Journal*, 17 February 2000, p.12.

Lardy, N. R. (2000) "Is China a 'Closed' Economy?," Prepared statement for a Public Hearing of the United States Trade Deficit Review Commission, 24 February 2000.

Lasserre, P. (1996) "Regional Headquarters: The Spearhead for Asia Pacific Markets," *Long Range Planning, 29* (1), 30–37.

Lehrer, M. and K. Asakawa (1999) "Unbundling European Operations: Regional Management and Corporate Flexibility in American and Japanese MNCs," *Journal of World Business, 34* (3), p.267–286.

Martinez, J. I. and J. C. Jarillo (1989) "The Evolution of Research on Coordination Mechanisms in Multinational Corporations," *Journal of International Business Studies, 20* (3), 489–514.

Martinez, J. I. and J. C. Jarillo (1991) "Coordination Demands of International Strategies," *Journal of International Business Studies, 22* (3), 429–444.

Morrison, A. J.; D. A. Ricks; and K. Roth (1991) "Globalization Versus Regionalization: Which Way for the Multinational?," *Organizational Dynamics*, Winter, 17–29.

Morrison A. J. and K. Roth (1992) "The Regional Solution: An Alternative to Globalization," *Transnational Corporations, 1* (2), 42–52.

Parkhe, A. (1993) "Messy Research, Methodological Predispositions, and Theory Development in International Joint Ventures," *Academy of Management Review, 19*, 227–268.

Porter, M. E. (ed.) (1986) *Competition in Global Industries*, (Boston: Harvard Business School Press).

Prahalad, C. K. and Y. Doz (1987) *The Multinational Mission: Balancing Local Demands and Global Vision*, (New York: The Free Press).

Sassen, S. (1994) *Cities in a World Economy*, (Thousand Oaks, California: Pine Forge Press).

Schütte, H. (1997) "Strategy and Organisation: Challenges for European MNCs in Asia," *European Management Journal, 15* (4), 436–445.

Taylor, S.; S. Beechler; and N. Napier (1996) "Towards an Integrative Model of Strategic International Human Resource Management, " *Academy of Management Review, 17* (4), 959–985.

UNCTAD (1998) "The Financial Crisis in Asia and Foreign Direct Investment," 20 March 1998.

UNCTAD (1999) *World Investment Report*, (Geneva: UNCTD).

World Bank (various years), *World Development Indicators*, (Washington, DC: World Bank).

Yip, G. S. (1998) *Asian Advantage*, (Reading, MA: Addison–Wesley).

3 Japanese Multinational Enterprises and AFTA: Restructuring and Market Segmentation

Haruo Horaguchi
Hosei University

1 Functions of AFTA

The 6th ASEAN summit meeting was held at Hanoi in December 1998. It set the target year for realization of AFTA (ASEAN Free Trade Area) in January 1, 2002. As Cambodia joined ASEAN in April 1999, the membership of ASEAN became 10 countries, namely Singapore, Indonesia, Malaysia, the Philippines, Thailand, Brunei, Vietnam, Laos, Myanmar, and Cambodia[1].

AFTA has mainly three functions[2]. The first is the Common Effective Preferential Tariff (CEPT). CEPT is a policy to lower tariff rates in ASEAN countries for targeted trade items, and six nations, Indonesia, Malaysia, the Philippines, Singapore, Thailand, and Brunei, reduced their tariff rates to 0–5% for about 85% of total targeted items by 2000. The six nations then ought to reduce the tariff rates of all targeted items by January 1, 2002. Vietnam will reduce its tariff rates by 2003, and Laos and Myanmar will lower their tariff rates by 2005. Although 40% of "ASEAN Content," is required, CEPT items can be uniquely determined by each country. The concept of "ASEAN Contents" means that CEPT is applied to items which are produced in ASEAN using more than 40% local materials or components.

---

[1] See, for example, Shimizu (1999) as it outlines how Cambodia was affiliated to ASEAN. Shimizu (1999) also explains the notion of "the regional economic cooperation" in ASEAN. One must be careful, however, that Shimizu (1999) differs from the description of Ueda (1999) in explaining AFTA. Shimizu (1999) conceptualizes "regional economic cooperation," which is supposed by the policy of AFTA, AICO, and AIA. Ueda (1999), on the other hand, does not use the concept of "regional economic cooperation" and explains that AFTA has three components of CEPT, AICO, and AIA. This paper is based on the latter understanding.

[2] Tan(1996) , Aoki(1997) and Shimizu (1998) (1999) are tracing the formation of regional economy and the history of AFTA. Ministry of International Trade and Industry (1996) presents the economic analysis of the regional association including AFTA. Policy implications of AFTA in this paper are also based on these researches.

The second policy in AFTA is the ASEAN Industrial Cooperation (AICO) scheme. It waives customs duties for the mutual exportation and importation of parts or finished goods between subsidiaries of a multinational corporation. In order to apply for the AICO scheme, a company must satisfy two conditions. One is that the company needs to have a part or a finished good which can be mutually traded among two or more subsidiaries within ASEAN countries. The other is that the subsidiaries must have at least 30% of local equity. Thus the applicant company must be a multinational company with local partnership. During 1999 and 2000, the requirement of local equity was waived, however.

The third is a plan to create the ASEAN Investment Area (AIA). When AFTA was agreed in 1993, liberalization of regional investment was targeted for 2010 and foreign investment outside of ASEAN was also to be liberalized by 2020.

The Asian currency crisis in July 1997 had an impact on these three policies. CEPT became an agenda item to be enacted earlier than originally envisaged. Deregulating the local equity requirement for the AICO scheme was another example. The Hanoi meeting in December 1998 determined that AIA would be enacted for regional investors in 2003.

Two classes of questions are discussed in this paper. (a) What is the economic rationale behind the AFTA? Which member nations benefited from AFTA as a free trade area? (b) How do Japanese multinational enterprises respond to AFTA policies?

Do they concentrate their production locations in a single ASEAN country?

Or, do they pursue international division of labor among their subsidiaries ?

In Section 1, basic concepts such as regional association, customs union, free trade area, and economic integration are defined. Theories about formation of a regional association, and empirical researches on trade creation effect in relation to AFTA are surveyed. In Section 2, the results of an interview survey of Japanese multinational enterprises (MNEs) are summarized. The questions are about how Japanese MNEs have reacted to the creation of AFTA, or how they operate Southeast Asian subsidiaries under the regional policy imposed by AFTA. The final section summarizes the implications of the interview survey and discusses the future research agenda.

2 Economic Models of Regional Association

2.1 Definitions and the Classic Research

Regional associations[3] are classified into various forms such as a customs union, free trade area, and economic integration. A customs union sets a tariff rate, which is common to countries both inside and outside of the customs union. The customs union lowers the tariff rate of the member countries and sets a common tariff rate for the outside of the region. The member countries of a free trade area are allowed to set a tariff rate only outside the free trade area, when a regional tariff rate of the FTA is lowered. Economic integration is a state where free movement of factors of production, such as capital and labor, are ensured. At the same time, it sets a common tariff rate between the inside and outside of the zone of integration. Economic integration also includes a policy of issuing a common currency for the member countries.

Regional association has been a traditional theme in international trade theory. And contemporary researchers are also actively tackling this issue. The formation of the EEC, EC market integration and creation of the EU were occasions to attract theoretical and empirical attention. NAFTA (North American Free Trade Agreement) , AFTA and MERCOSUR (Mercado Comun del Sur) were created during the 1990s, and the idea of "opening regionalism" in APEC (Asia Pacific Economic Cooperation) has been advocated[4]. The proliferation of regional associations has stimulated theoretical and positive research.

There are many survey articles on regional economic associations. Yotopoulos and Nugent (1976), Tokunaga (1994), and Shimizu (1998) are a few examples. All three articles refer to Viner (1950) as a classic research. The partial equilibrium model of Viner (1950) assumes that a regional market price exists somewhere between the world price after tariffs levied and the domestic production price. If the domestic market is exposed to world imports, the domestic industry cannot survive the world competition. However, supply countries in the regional market under the regime of a customs union lowers the domestic market price which is protected by the higher tariff rate. Yotopoulos and Nugent (1976) point out that the Viner model has limitations as it employs a partial equilibrium analysis.

Economic analysis of regional associations has been developing remarkably since the second half of the 1980s through the 1990s. I would like to classify this work into three categories, i.e., models of strategic foreign trade policy,

---

[3] The term "regional association" is based on Ito (1996) (p.386). A regional association is the concept which includes (1) a free trade zone, (2) a customs union, (3) a single market, and (4) economic integration. Some authors define "economic integration" to include (1) to (4), in which there are gradations of integration.

[4] For example, please refer to Takachi (1987), Eguchi(1991), Okada(1991), and Komiya (1999).

endogenous growth theory, and computational general equilibrium (CGE) models. Some of the major researches is surveyed below.

2.2 Models of Strategic Foreign Trade Policy

Gatsios and Karp (1991) use a model in which the production cost for two countries A and B is not identical. The two countries are facing a decision whether to create a regional association. Since production costs of the two countries differ, one of the countries may not benefit from the creation of a regional association. This is a situation where potential conflict may occur. Gatsios and Karp (1991) further assume that "another part of the world" has a different cost condition to the two countries. If country A is able to compete with "another part of the world," while country B is unable to compete, the tariff rate for the regional association would not be uniquely defined.

The structure of the Gatsios and Karp (1991) model is essentially the same as Cournot competition but the players are not firms but nations. In order to attain an agreement to sustain the regional association, Gatsios and Karp (1991) argue that country A and country B must abide by either one of the following: 1)One of the countries must delegate the right to represent the regional association. 2)The two nations must make a trustworthy commitment. 3)The creation of a regional association may work as a strategic complement in the region.

Krugman (1991) supposes a CES type utility function to measure the welfare of one country such that:

$$U = [N(1-B^{-1})(c^{w})^{\theta} + N B^{-1}(c^{D})^{\theta}]^{1/\theta}$$

where, c^{w} is consumption level of an imported product from outside of the trade block for a country which has welfare function U. c^{D} is the amount of consumed product which is produced within the trade block. The elasticity of substitution of these goods is shown by θ and the elasticity of substitution of arbitrary 2 goods becomes $\sigma = 1/(1-\theta)$. N is the number of countries that carry on trade, and B is the number of trade blocks. Since each country is assumed to produce one good for 1 unit at common price, respectively, the production quantity in the whole world becomes N unit.

If N is 120 countries and B is defined as three trade blocks, one trade block consists of N/B=40 countries. The countries which belong to the other trade blocks account for $N(1-1/B) = N - N/B = 80$ countries. And the production volume of one trade block is 40 units (N/B=40). In Eq.1, welfare function has $N(1-B^{-1})$ and NB^{-1} because it is assumed that identical countries exist for the consumption of c^{w} and c^{D} respectively. A share in world trade for a trade block is defined as $s = m^{w}/y^{w}$, where w is a superscript to indicate "world." Since it is assumed that each trade block is identical, the quantity of imports from outside the trade block m^{w} is now rewritten as m, so that $s = m/y^{w}$. For example, three trade blocks means that one trade block produces 33.3% of a product within the region, while it imports 33.3% from another trade block, which sums up to 66.6% from outside the trade block. Since the number of countries which belongs to a trade block is expressed as N/B, the amount of imports for one country is given by s/(N/B). In this example, one country imports c^w=33.3%/40 countries.

The budget constraint for the representative trading block is m + d = y, where m is the volume of imports from outside the trading block, and d is the volume of domestic consumption within the trading block. If one unit is produced by each country symmetrically, we see that m/d = B–1 holds. According to our example, y = N/B, or 40 = 120/3. In addition, y=m+d and m/d=B–1 must hold. In such a case, 40 = 26.7 + 13.3 and 26.7/13.3 = 3–1. If we normalize the import volume of a trading block, m / d = B–1 is the volume of imports, which is affected by an import tariff rate and the elasticity of substitution. Therefore the m/d is redefined as $m/d = (1+t)^{-\sigma}(B-1)$. Three equations in this discussion, y=N/B, m+d=y, and $m/d = (1+t)^{-\sigma}(B-1)$, can be rewritten as

$$m = (N/B)/(1+t)^{\sigma}(B-1)^{-1}$$

and,

$$s = m/N(1-B^{-1}) = [(1+t)^{\sigma}+(B-1)]^{-1}$$

Now, the following two equations are plugged into the utility function of the trading block. These are:

$$c^w = s/(N/B) = (B/N)/[(1+t)^{\sigma}+(B-1)]$$

$$c^D = s/(N/B)(1+t)^{\sigma} = [B(1+t)^{\sigma}/N]/[(1+t)^{\sigma}+(B-1)]$$

It is now possible to substitute c^w and c^D into equation (1), and the welfare function of country U becomes a function of the number of trade blocks B in the world.

Krugman (1991) shows the result of a simulation based upon the above-mentioned function. He concludes that the welfare level is highest when B=1, which is the state of free trade throughout the world. When the world is divided into three trade blocks, B=3, the welfare level becomes the lowest. Krugman argues that this result of the simulation gives a theoretical basis for concern that the world's recent tripolarization to North America, Europe, and Asia may have the effect of shrinking trade.

Yi (1996) supposes a welfare function of quadratic form for identical countries and discusses the case where some of the countries form a regional association. He draws a conclusion that Nash equilibrium is attained when the whole world is integrated into a single regional association, i.e., world free trade gives the highest welfare to a country. The logic is as follows. Now there exist n nations in the world and m nations (m<n) form a regional association. Several regional associations are going to be formed in the world as long as economic welfare of a member nation is increased. If such a regional association increases the public welfare because of additional national interest, regional associations are merged into a bigger regional association to have higher public welfare. The process ends when all nations merge entirety to cover the whole world, where the welfare of

each nation will be the highest. Yi (1996) suggests that "opening regionalism," i.e., the inter-regional association which may be expanded, will increase public welfare, bearing APEC in mind.

2.3 Endogenous Growth Theory

Rivera-Batiz and Romer (1991) discuss the merit of regional integration by endogenous growth theory. One can say that endogenous growth theory enables economic modeling to show the benefit of regional integration without assuming a classic Ricardian trade theory of comparative advantage. According to Ricardian trade theory, two nations with completely identical production function and factor price of endowment cannot obtain trade profits by specializing in "garments" or "wines" as in Ricardo's illustration. Endogenous growth theory captures the reality that the rate of changing technical stock and therefore of technical progress are an increasing function of human resources. As long as regional integration facilitates the accumulation of human resources in a production location, the rate of technical growth will also be accelerated.

Rivera-Batiz and Romer (1991) derive a function of technological growth,

$$\dot{A} = \delta\,(H + H^*)\,A$$

where A is a state of technology, δ is a coefficient to induce technological progress, H is the human resources in the home country and H^* is the foreign human resources. $\dot{A}$ is the time rate of change of the technical stock A. It is clear that the locus of the solution for this differential equation shows a steeper slope if H^* is added to H[5]. That is, if regional economic integration is completed and capital and labor movement become free, the rate of technical progress in the region will increase. However, Rivera-Batiz and Romer (1991) do not address the issue about "who" is in possession of the technical progress. I would like to

[5] It is shown that the equation, $dA/dt = \delta\,(H+H^*)\,A$
is transformed into, $(1/A)(dA/dt) = \delta\,(H+H^*)$, which is directly integrated by t.

$$\int \frac{1}{A}\,\frac{dA}{dt}\,dt = \int \delta\,(H+H^*)\,dt$$

then, $\ln|A| = \delta\,(H+H^*)\,t + c$ is obtained. Here, c is a constant of integration. Supposing A is always positive, both sides of the equation can be transformed into a form with exponential functions.

$$A = e^{c} \cdot e^{\delta (H+H^*)\,t} = B\,e^{\delta (H+H^*)\,t}$$

Initial value is defined as $A(0) = B$ when $t = 0$,

$$A(t) = A(0)\,e^{\delta (H+H^*)\,t}$$

shows the locus of the growth. Here, the effect of regional integration is shown as $H + H^* > H$, which means the speed of growth in accumulation is higher as long as $H+H^*$ is larger than H point out the possibility that the most technologically advanced company will possess the power to monopolize the fruits of technical progress.

Bearing the EU integrated market in mind, Baldwin (1989) draws the conclusion that the dynamic effect of scale economies makes the growth rate shift upward. Dynamic effect is caused by regional economic integration. For the sake of simplicity, ignoring labor input, Baldwin (1989) uses a production function of Yt=AKt, and defines growth of capital stock,

$$Kt{+}1 = (1-d)\,Kt + sYt$$

where d is a depreciation rate and s is a saving rate. The capital stock of the next term (Kt+1) becomes equal to the level of the capital stock for this term (Kt) and saving from the total output (sYt) and to subtract depreciation of capital stock (dKt). Now, we can see a growth rate (1+g).

$$1{+}g = \frac{Yt{+}1}{Yt} = \frac{AKt{+}1}{AKt} = (1-d) + s\,(Yt\,/\,Kt)$$

Although the increase in the capital output ratio (Yt/Kt) is expected when production efficiency improves by trade liberalization or creation of a regional single market, some variables have additional effect on the growth rate (1+g). The savings ratio (s) accelerates the growth rate combined with the capital output ratio (Yt/Kt). If the capital output ratio (Yt/Kt) increases 5% and the savings ratio increases 20%, the growth rate will increases 1%.

Iwata (1998) summarizes the model of Baldwin (1989) with some empirical evidence. Based on the above mentioned model, Iwata (1998) estimates the dynamic effect of real income growth in AFTA. According to the model, it is estimated that the dynamic effect of income growth exceeds the static effect in real earnings increase. However, one must notice that the static increase in real earnings here is derived from the fact that regional trade expands by the amount of the tariff reduction for import.

2.4 Computational General Equilibrium Model

A large number of researchers collaborate to quantitatively evaluate the influence of regional integration in the world economy by constructing econometric models. Although there are various names for this class of analysis, it is in many cases called Computational General Equilibrium Model (CGE model) .

Economic Planning Agency (EPA), Economic Research Institute (EPA 1988) builds a trade model of the whole world, and assumes the foreign trade policy of various Asian countries to evaluate the effects in quantitatively. It is interesting to see three cases of simulations here: (Case–1) The free trade area is limited to six

ASEAN member nations. (Case–2) The "closed APEC," which limits the reduction of import duties to APEC member nations, (Case–3) The "open APEC," which applies a low rate customs duty to APEC non-member nations, when APEC member nations reduce import duties. The following interesting conclusions are drawn.

According to EPA (1998), the tariff reduction is advantageous for Malaysia if the free trade area is limited to ASEAN member countries (Case–1). One can recall that the EAEG planned by Prime Minister Mahathir of Malaysia was designed for East Asian nations to participate in a regional trade area. The CGE model of the Japanese EPA coincides with the intuition of this politician in so far as the free trade area is advantageous to Malaysia if it is limited to East Asia, although the EPA (1998) does not tell much about its interpretation of the simulation result.

EPA (1998) also draws the conclusion that the case of "open APEC" (Case–2), can increase trade benefit for Thailand. Ikemoto (1996) claims that the formation of NAFTA accelerated the process of forming AFTA. Thailand was pressured by the formation of NAFTA because Thailand was forced to compete with Mexico for exports to the United States. In order to be competitive in price for exports to the United States, the cost of parts procurement within ASEAN had to be reduced. Thus the exporting companies in Thailand also benefited from the reduction of regional customs duty among ASEAN nations. According to Ikemoto(1996), more than 20% of exports were destined for the U.S. from Thailand while 17% were going to Japan in the early 1990s. The conclusion given by EPA (1998) is that "open APEC" is advantageous to Thailand. This coincides with the importance of the American market for Thai firms.

EPA (1998) shows that "open APEC" (Case–3) is advantageous to Indonesia and the Philippines. Since the tariff rate is close to zero, there is no big influence from Singapore.

Ballard and Cheong (1997) report the result of econometric analysis of inter-regional association bearing APEC in mind. According to them, when a regional customs duty falls, public welfare increases for every participating nation. In addition, even if only South East Asian countries form the free trade area, excluding major powers like the United States and Japan among APEC, the participating nations' welfare level goes up. This econometric result is interpreted to support the implementation of AFTA policy.

Kawasaki, Kushima, and Mitsufuji (1997) report a simulation result by CGE model. They focus on liberalization of trade and investment envisaged in the "Bogor Declaration" of APEC in 1994, although the member nations differ greatly from the countries affiliated to APEC and AFTA. The simulation result shows the features of a CGE model clearly, and is interesting. That is, if simulation using a CGE model is performed, the trade expansion effect will be large, the larger the country, the area, and the industrial section in which the liberalizing measure is carried out. This is because the fall in import prices enables the efficient use of factors of production, and the falling prices contribute to expand exports. Kawasaki, Kushima, and Mitsufuji (1997) take into account that trade and investment liberalization of developing countries among APEC countries scheduled for 2020. It is predicted that the trade expansion effect is largest for China, and the ASEAN countries follow. The trade benefit is higher in the order of Indonesia, Malaysia, Philippines, and Thailand.

2.5 Summary of Literature Survey

There are four main conclusions drawn from the above literature survey. First, economic welfare will increase through the trade creation effect of regional association when the tariff rate is reduced. This is a common conclusion with the simulation results of CGE models. Second, national interest may be contradictory among the participating nations in a regional association. A national interest in this context means protection of a domestic industry, and such a policy may distort the actual conditions of regional association. It is suggested by the simulation result of EPA(1988) that improvement of economic welfare is different in accordance with which countries are participating in the regional association. And the model of Gatsios and Karp (1991) also suggests the existence of friction between the participating nations in the regional association. Third, Krugman (1991) asserts a very different proposition. Based upon the model and its simulation result, an tripolarized regional associations have a possibility of worsening economic welfare. This may be an alarm bell concerning so-called "economic regionalism" in the world. Fourth, endogenous growth theory asserts that concentration of production location in the region has the possibility of raising the rate of economic growth through accelerating technical progress.

The following section focuses on the existence of multinational enterprises (MNEs) tacitly assumed in the economic analyses surveyed above. The policy of AFTA greatly affects the MNEs' production activities in the region. The trade creation effect may mean that the MNEs have to restructure there production capacity. Local capital requirements and local contents regulations, for example, are constraints on applying for the incentives in AFTA.

3 International Coordination of Multinational Production

National interest does not necessarily accord with the interest of MNEs. Hence, the foreign trade policy, which is sometimes designed for a state cannot be supportive to the international production organization of MNEs. In this section, some results of interview surveys from 1998 to 2000 are summarized. It shows how Japanese MNE's activities correspond to the formation of AFTA. One can see, however, the trade policy of AFTA does not affect the production strategy of Japanese MNEs so much.

The questions are whether or not formation of AFTA makes the business environment for Japanese MNEs advantageous. This is related to the question whether export and import within AFTA nations are an important business for them. Is there any change in parts procurement policy between subsidiaries? Is there a move towards concentrating production bases in one place? The results of the interview survey of major Japanese MNEs and some materials about AFTA are summarized below.

3.1 The Feature of AICO Application: The Case of Thailand and Philippines

The data on AICO applications was available for Thailand and the Philippines. Some features are summarized below.

Table 3–1 shows the list of applications to the AICO scheme by the ministry of industry in Thailand[6]. The total number of applications is 36 as of July 1999. Among 36 applications, 26 applications are submitted by eight groups of companies to get multiple approval. That is, (1)Toyota occupies the first place with eight applications, and (2)Nissan, (3)Nihon–Denso, (4)Honda and (5)Volvo follow with three applications, and two applications were submitted by (6)Isuzu and (7)Auto Alliance Thailand, Ford Motor Company Philippine and AMIM Malaysia, in the automobile industry. In the electrical industry (8)Matsushita and (9)Mitsubishi Electric have made two applications each.

Eight groups of companies are listed as applying for AICO scheme as a single group to the Thai government, and one group is listed on the application list of the Philippine government. The eight groups are: (10) Sanden–Kayama, (11)Sony, (12)Thai Steel Cables–Armstrong Cycle Parts, (13)Yanmar, (14)Mitsubishi Motor, (15) Kayaba, (16)Nestle, and (17)Summit Showa Manufacturing and P.T. Showa Indonesia Manufacturing. One group of companies, (18) Kraft Foods in the Philippines, Indonesia and Thailand, is listed on the Philippine government application list. Therefore the number of applications are 18 for AICO scheme to Thai and Philippine government.

Japanese MNEs made the majority of AICO applications, although the famous European and American multinationals such as Volvo, Ford, Nestle and Kraft Foods are found on the list. Twelve groups are in the automobile industry whereas Nestle and Kraft Foods are in the food industry, Matsushita, Mitsubishi Electric and Sony are in the electrical industry, and Yanmar is producing diesel engines of "sideways water-cooled type" by parts complementation[7]. As is shown later in the result of the interview survey, Mistubishi Electric is involved in electrical parts production for automobiles.

---

[6] Data was kindly offered through JETRO Bangkok center. I appreciate Mr. Hiroshi Yoneya's cooperation.

[7] See Kokusai Boueki Toushi Kenkyusho, Kousei Boueki Senta (International Trade and Investment Research Institute, Fair-Trade Center) (1999) Chapter 9.

Table 3–1 shows the partner countries for the 36 applications to Thailand. That is, 13 Malaysia, 12 Philippines, 9 Indonesia, 2 Singapore. However, about the 27th application by Volvo and the 29th application by Kayaba, it is annotated that "Malaysia has rejected the importation of some components from Thailand" (Appendix: Table 3–1). On the other hand, about the 28th application by Ford Motor, it is mentioned that "Thailand has approved only parts which are not located" in the Thai government approval list.

There are many cases in which "Date of Acceptance" and "Date of Decision" remained blank in Table 3–1. This may indicate that the formal approval from a counterpart country has not been given as of the listing date. Six cases about Indonesia are shown in Table 3–1. In other words, among nine applications relating to Thailand and Indonesia, only three of the applications on the list are approved — Nihon–Denso, Honda and Yanmar .

I calculated the number of months from the application to approval. In the case of having approval, the average duration is 4.6 months. One must be cautious, however, that many cases have not been approved and thus do not have a number of months calculated for the average. Many business people point out that approval of the exporting country is quick but the importing country takes time to approve.

3.2 AICO and Japanese Multinationals

The result of the interview survey toward the main Japanese multinational companies is summarized below. There are seven companies in the list. Two of them, Matsushita and Sony have applied and have been approved by the AICO scheme from the local governments. Four companies, Hitachi, Mitsubishi, Toshiba and Sharp have applied but not yet approved by the time of the interview. Those applications are now substituted by CEPT scheme for tariff reduction. One company, NEC, has never applied and Fujitsu was unable to accept the interview survey since there was no appropriate person to answer the AFTA related questions.

The conclusion of the interview survey is summarized here in advance, that the AICO scheme does not have significant impact on the production organization of Japanese electrical MNEs. When there is export capability, import duties for the parts in production do not play an important role. Most of the Japanese MNEs export from ASEAN to the Middle East, Europe and American markets, and their electrical parts and materials are exempted from the import duty for reexport. This is the main difference between electrical and automobile industries. As automobile MNEs supply the domestic market where they locate, exemption of import duties by AICO sheme is not negligible. The duration from AICO application to approval is said to be a reason why many Japanese MNEs are reluctant to construct international production organizations.

3.2.1 Matsushita[8]

Matsushita's application to the AICO scheme was approved by the ASEAN secretariat in October 1999. It was three months before CEPT scheme would be enacted in January 2000. About 85% of electrical machinery products was targeted under CEPT scheme to be zero to five percent import duty, which nullifies the tariff reduction by AICO approval. Thailand and Indonesia took six months to permit the application but the Philippine took two years and four months. This is because the Philippine government was anxious about trade imbalance, which means imports from outside of the Philippines exceed the exports from the Philippines Matsushita subsidiary.

Matsushta planned the AICO scheme as follows (Figure 3–1). They export injection molding parts and ventilation fans from Thailand. From Malaysia, the circuit control, motors, and remote controlled fan are exported. "The special parts" and a baby fan are exported from Indonesia, and the press parts, stand fan and the box fan from the Philippines. This complementation scheme seemed to be possible because Matsushita had subsidiaries in each country, which satisfy the local equity requirement for AICO application. This contrasts with the fact that most of the Japanese MNEs do not own joint-venture subsidiaries in the electrical industry in ASEAN countries. Matsushita once pursued a business policy to establish a so-called "Mini-Matsushita" in each ASEAN country, so that the "Mini-Matsushita" could supply multi-kind products for local small-lot production. The headquarters of Matsushita in Japan coordinated the parts for mutual complementation plan by AICO scheme. It is estimated that the total amount of exempted customs duty reached 10 million yen (about 0.1 million dollars).

CEPT has been enforced since January 2000 for most of the electrical parts and products relating to Matsushita, and many of the subsidiaries of Matsushita with 100% investment from Japan have been involved in exporting production. Headquarters in Japan does not have the intention to make additional AICO applications.

In 2000, Matsushita has been starting restructuring its fan and ventilator production in Asian countries and in Japan. The production of fans and ventilators may be suspended in some Asian countries in the near future, the AICO scheme will be void entirely. The fundamental reason for the restructuring is fierce competition in the region, a Matsushita spokesman said[9].

---

[8] Based on interview in the Tokyo head office of Matsushita Electric Industrial Co. on October 8, 1999.

[9] Based on an e-mail correspondence with Matsushita Tokyo Head Office, International Relations Department, July 21, 2000.

Figure 3–1. Planned Organization of AICO by Matsushita

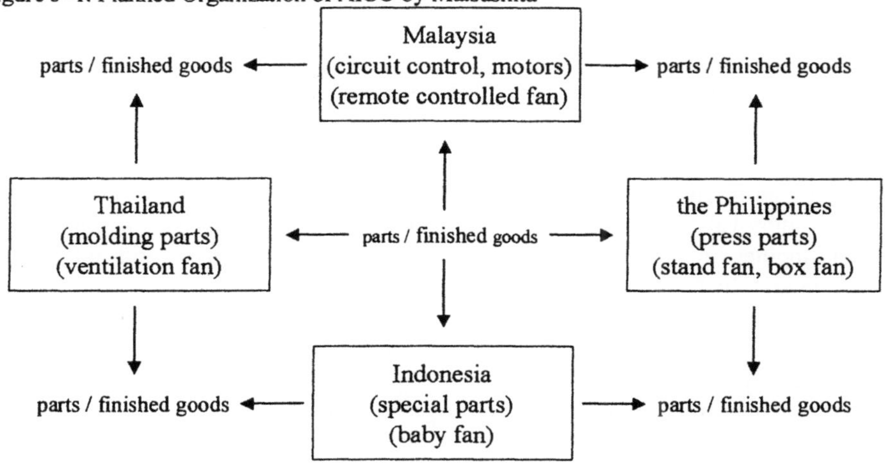

Source: Kokusai Boueki Toushi Kenkyusho–Kousei Boueki Senta (International Trade and Investment Research Institute and Fair–trade Center) [1999].

3.2.2 Sony[10]

Sony uses the AICO scheme between its subsidiaries in Thailand and in Singapore. Color televisions as finished goods are exported from Thailand and cathode-ray tubes are exported from Singapore. An application to Thailand was made in June 1998, and it took only one month to be approved in July 1998. In July 1998 Sony applied for AICO to Singapore, and Singapore approved in the same month.

Sony had established international division of labor between Singapore, Malaysia, Thailand and Vietnam before the AICO scheme was enacted. After equipping the cathode-ray tubes in Singapore with parts made in Malaysia, they were exported to Thailand and Vietnam. AICO scheme was only applicable to Singapore and Thailand. In Thailand the color television for domestic sales uses the cathode-ray tube from Singapore, hence a part of a customs duty is saved. CEPT was enforced for about 85% of listed products in January 2000, then the product of Sony corresponded to the category in CEPT. Then, the need for AICO

[10] Interview is done in the Tokyo head office of Sony on October 9, 1999. In addition, JETRO Bangkok Center offered data on October 14.

application was reduced. Moreover, a customs duty is not levied on the imported parts for re-export, thus the importance of AICO has never been so important for the Sony subsidiaries for exporting products.

3.2.3 Mitsubishi Electric[11]

Mitsubishi Electric constructed mutual parts complementation organization for electric auto-parts such as starter and alternator among Thailand, Indonesia and the Philippines. Mitsubishi applied to Indonesia in November 1997 and was approved in July 1998, and applied to Thailand in February and April 1999 and got approval in June 1999. However, although Mitsubishi applied to the Philippines in November 1998, the Philippine government and the ASEAN secretariat have not yet given approval to it as of October 1999[12].

The on-going application of AICO will have no use, and additional application for AICO is not considered, since the application items of CEPT will include household electric applications currently produced in Thailand, such as air-conditioner, washing machine, refrigerator, and electric fan. Although there are some production bases for elevator and escalator production, mutual parts complementation organization is not planned. In Malaysia and Singapore, import duties of parts are exempted since the product is exported. Therefore, there is no problem of tariff barriers.

3.2.4 Hitachi[13]

Hitachi applied for AICO in Thailand and in Malaysia from July to August 1999. Hitachi planned to export washing machines, electric fans, and color televisions from Thailand to Malaysia, and VTRs were scheduled to be exported from Malaysia to Thailand. The local dealer and the sales branch of Hitachi applied. This application became possible after the ASEAN working group about industrial cooperation met in Jakarta in February 1999 and decided that mutual supply of finished goods of the same brand was included in AICO scheme. There was no reaction from the Malaysian and Thai governments to Hitachi as of October 1999.

The compressor of an air-conditioner is manufactured in Malaysia, and is exported to Thailand to manufacture finished air-conditioners. Since these are set as the object of CEPT, the application of AICO is not made for the air-conditioner.

---

[11] At the Tokyo head office of Mitsubishi Electric on October 19, 1999.

[12] The date of application is given by JETRO Bangkok Center.

[13] The author conducted interview in the Hitachi head office on October 9, 1999.

3.2.5 Toshiba[14]

Toshiba applied for AICO to barter finished goods of refrigerators made in Thailand and large-size televisions from Singapore in September1999. As mentioned above, this application became possible after the Hanoi meeting in December 1998. That is, the requirements for the application of 30% of local equity was suspended from 1999 to 2000. And AICO applications about finished goods have been accepted since February 1999. Approval was not yet received as of October 1999.

Toshiba examined the possibility of another application to AICO among production items such as refrigerators from Thailand, televisions from Singapore, and cathode-ray tubes from Indonesia. But Toshiba gave up planning. It was because this complementation would cause an excess of imports for Thailand. These products will be covered as the object items of CEPT. The semiconductors from Malaysia and televisions from Singapore were also examined, but Toshiba gave up because of the local equity requirement.

3.2.6 Sharp[15]

Although the sales subsidiary of Singapore took the lead to apply for AICO in 1997, there has been no progress since then in its mutual complementation plan between Thailand and Malaysia. Since most of the Sharp subsidiaries were operating for export, import duties for parts were exempted. Thus the urgency for AICO application was low. Although the Thai subsidiary produces color televisions for the domestic market, exporting is considered of primary importance rather than importing parts from ASEAN countries.

3.2.7 NEC[16]

No application to AICO has ever been made. There are two reasons.

First, there is no local subsidiary where local equity exceeds 30%. The production subsidiaries of NEC in ASEAN countries correspond to the local governments' regulations. That is, the investment purpose of NEC is installation of communication systems. After winning a competitive bid, NEC is required to establish a local subsidiary by the local government. This local subsidiary has the monopolistic right to construct a communication system. Maintenance of the network after construction is also a management objective.

Second, NEC in Japan supplies the main parts from Japan, so parts dealings are not conducted in two or more ASEAN countries. Investment in the domestic

---

[14] At the Toshiba head office on October 14, 1999.

[15] At Sharp Tokyo head office on October 21, 1999.

[16] At NEC head office on October 21, 1999.

market of each country is operated independently between Japanese headquarters and the local subsidiary. Therefore, a mutual complementation plan within ASEAN cannot be envisaged. Since the local content ratio of parts is low in general, the operation will not have consequences with CEPT, either.

3.3 Concentration of Production Capacity

Some Japanese MNEs of the electrical machinery and electronic industry have integrated their production capacities in one place during the second half of the 1990s. This corresponds to market segmentation for profitable products. However, it is difficult to conclude that concentration of production capacity corresponds to the formation of AFTA. It has been a long period of time from the announcement of AFTA to realization, so the MNEs have independently pursued economies of scale whenever possible and necessary. The Asian economic crisis made it necessary for MNEs to streamline over-capacity in the ASEAN region. Moreover, production in China had an impact on production in South East Asia. Price competitiveness of Chinese parts and products urged Japanese MNEs in ASEAN to focus on a specific profitable segment in each market.

The 4th ASEAN Summit Meeting in January 1992 agreed the ground design of AFTA, cutting the customs duty of industrial and agricultural processed products to 0 – 5% by 2008. The tariff reduction was planned within 15 years after the first accord of AFTA. The early 1990s was a period when the "Asian Miracle" occurred. Japanese MNEs augmented production capacities as well as foreign direct investment in ASEAN countries. Then, at the 6th Economic Cabinet meeting in 1994, the year of enforcement was shortened five years and set to 2003, and raw agricultural products were included as CEPT objects. And as this paper described, after the Asian economic crisis, which started in July 1997, the 6th Summit Meeting in December 1998 further shortened the commencement of CEPT one year to 2002. Also customs duties were to be reduced for about 85% of items from January, 2000.

Concentration of production capacity may be a strategic option for a Japanese MNE. Economic turmoil after the Asian economic crisis is one reason, and upgrading the technological level in the production base is the second. It is difficult to explain the corporate activity over a long period of time from the point of view of AFTA policy. AFTA was officially agreed in 1993, and the process continues on. As long as the Japanese MNEs involve export production, they do not need to correspond with enforcement of CEPT.

Although a clear reply or presentation of data was not obtained from all of the companies for interview survey, some trends are evident, which are summarized below for Matsushita, Hitachi, Sony, and Mitsubishi Electric.

3.3.1 Matsushita

Matsushita stopped its production of electric products in the Philippines in 1995 and air-conditioner production in Thailand in 1996. Air compressors in Taiwan had been produced until 1997 and then stopped. All this production was changed to supply from a parts production company in Malaysia. Matsushita in the Philippines changed its procurement of electronic products from the parts company in Malaysia to that in China. According to an article written by a Matsushita spokesman, this is positioned as "the selection and concentration" of production items before CEPT enactment[17].

Matsushita Air-conditioning Corporation Sdn. Bhd. (MAICO) is the Malaysia subsidiary of Matsushita Electric Industrial Corporation[18]. It is the manufacturer of an air-conditioner and is performing as design and development department. There are five companies at the same location. MCM (1987 operation start) produces finished parts, MAICO produces air-conditioner (1990 establishment), MACRAD designs, develops, and researches air-conditioner finished goods (1991 establishment), MACC produces an indoor and outdoor split type air-conditioner (1993 establishment), and MACOMRAD (1997 establishment) is involved in research and development. MACOMRAD is transferred from Kusatsu city, Shiga prefecture and Takeo city, Fukui prefecture, where the research and development department of the household-electric-appliances division performs research and development of motors. These companies have been extended one by one, which also corresponds with the pulling out of air-conditioner parts production in Thailand and Taiwan. In addition to the five companies, MACTEC, which is a division inside the company, produces metallic molds.

MAICO exports to 120 or more nations of the world, and the United States, China, and Europe are the main export markets. The number of employees in 1998 were 7,328 regular employees. In addition to this number there were part-time workers. It broke the record of accumulated production of 10 million units in 1994. The production processes include press, injection molding, manufacture of heating board, printed circuit board, and remote controller. Design and development are connected to Shiga Kusatsu using CAD in real-time on-line. Local parts suppliers consist of 59 Japanese companies and 51 local companies. Almost all local companies are concentrating on Shah Alam and Rawang, and are not in Pulau Pinang, Ipoh, or Johore. Technical levels of local companies in Malaysia are generally low, they produce products like thermal insulation materials, printed matter, and a power supply code.

---

[17] See Kokusai Boueki Toushi Kenkyusho, Kousei Boueki Senta (International Trade and Investment Research Institute, Fair-Trade Center) (1999) p.108. It is written by a business person in Matsushita, International Division.

[18] November 5, 1998 visit. For details, please refer to Horaguchi (1999).

3.3.2 Hitachi

A large number of production subsidiaries of Hitachi are located in ASEAN countries. In Indonesia and Thailand small size color televisions are produced, in Singapore large size are produced, and projection TVs and televideos are made in Malaysia. Thus Hitachi's production sites are segmented according to the type of products. Moreover, Hitachi produces color televisions also in Taiwan and China. Although Hitachi may concentrate these production sites into one location in the future, there has been no discussion of this possibility in the present condition. The management of air-conditioner production in Thailand, however, was transferred to Malaysia, and that of electric cleaner production in Singapore was to be transferred to Thailand[19].

The Malaysian subsidiary of Hitachi, namely Hitachi Air Conditioning Products (M) Sdn. Bhd (HAPM) was established in 1989, and started its operation on November 2, 1990[20]. The invested capital was about 2,400 million yen, or 68 million ringgits. About 450,000 room type air–conditioners are manufactured per year, and 650,000 rotary type compressors are produced in three shifts or two shifts. About 100,000 scroll type compressors are produced. The markets are Hong Kong, Europe, and Australia, and those for Malaysia are about 10%. The final destinations are 24–25% to Asia, 15% to Europe, and 4% to the Middle East. The demand for air-conditioners in 1998 fell off by one eighth of the peak year 1996.

Since HAPM of air-conditioner manufacture, HEPM of television parts manufacture, and HCPM of television manufacture have been closely located, the workers of HAPM were helping television parts and television manufacture in November 1999. For example, six out of 18 air-conditioner employees at one line were sent to help TV production. And, at another line, nine workers out of 32 total were aiding television parts or television manufacture, and ten workers were temporarily moved to the other lines of an air-conditioner factory, and one had maternity leave.

The total number of employees was 1,024 persons, and Japanese employees were 13 persons or 1.2%. The average age is 25.7 years old and female employees account for 23%. The total number of employees has been changing over time: i.e., March 1996, 1,725 persons, March 1997, 1,428 persons, and March 1998, 1,100 persons. This is due to shifting the production to China and the economic downturn after the peak year of 1996. HAPM stopped new recruitment and is producing in only one shift. Sending for on-the-job training to Japan was carried out 14 times, and a total of 520 staff was sent to Tochigi, Japan[21].

About 70 percent of parts can be procured in Malaysia for HAPM. Many are supplied by Japanese parts makers in Malaysia. Only eight companies are

---

[19] It is based on my interview on October 9, 1999.

[20] November 4, 1998 visit.

[21] August 31, 1998 visit.

considered as local companies. 74 companies are owned 100% by Japanese interests, 54 are joint ventures with local and Japanese partnership. Ten or more local parts suppliers are in Bangi, Shah Alam, and Pulau Pinang. There is no local company supplying in Johore. In addition, at the Tochigi factory in Japan, cast production was ended in September 1998, so castings have been purchased from Matsushita Foundry Industry (MFI) in Malacca. The maintenance of dies for resin injection molding is done by a Japanese company in Malaysia.

HAPM is shipping its compressors to Taiwan and China, and the Funai Electrical Machinery Co. is the customer there. Moreover, Funai is a customer in Italy for which HAPM procures OEM production. 400,000 sets were produced in 1996, and 330,000 sets were produced in 1997. The compressor of the reciprocal type for refrigerators is manufactured in Thailand. The scroll type compressor for air-conditioners is manufactured at the Shimizu factory in Japan, and the rotary type is not manufactured any longer at the Shimizu factory. At the Tochigi factory, the rotary type compressor for air-conditioners and the small scroll type compressor are manufactured.

As mentioned above, a feature of the management of the manufacturing subsidiary of Matsushita and Hitachi is that the subsidiaries have been in operation over a long period of time as an export base for world markets. There is no necessity of considering the balance of exports and imports and the parts supply ratio from local companies and Japanese local companies is high. In Malaysia, the formation of industrial agglomeration in Shah Alam, Bangi, and Pulau Pinang is seen.

3.3.3 Sony[22]

Sony has been restructuring its international production bases and is not especially conscious of AFTA. It precedes with enactment of CEPT and the factories have been reorganized. Specifically, three factories in Pinang, Malaysia are made into one company organization from February to March, 1999. It is not aimed at streamlining personnel. The television factory in Indonesia was closed and the staff moved to the audio factory, a domestic market center. In Singapore, the qualification of regional headquarters is returned to the Singapore government. In Thailand, there are factories for (1) television and audio, (2) car audio, (3)the latter process of semiconductor, and (4) video tape. Thus reorganization may become a future subject there. Moreover, in Kuala Lumpur, television and video are produced at one factory and as a 'Mother Factory' the designers are sent into other factories in Southeast Asia.

---

[22] Based on Tokyo head office visit on October 9, 1999.

3.3.4 Mitsubishi Electric[23]

Mitsubishi is considering that its three production subsidiaries in Thailand may change the equity ratios. Although Mitsubishi may take over the equity which a local partner holds, the equity which Mitsubishi is going to hold may be sold off simultaneously. This is not a reaction to AFTA, but rather the consequence of restructuring Mitsubishi Electric in Japan. According to the announcement by Mitsubishi headquarters on the 8th of October 1999, although Mitsubishi Electric had made sales of about 4 trillion yen, the target of reducing interest–bearing liabilities to 1.4 trillion yen was made as a management objective. Therefore, new investment will become much more difficult under these circumstances.

4 Conclusions

4.1 Validity of Economic Policy

The AICO scheme plays the role of political advertisement symbolizing AFTA. So far as the electrical machinery industry is concerned, however, the trade creation effect is quite low. The number of applications for AICO to the Thai government was only 36, and the number of companies was only 18 in 1999. Japanese MNEs considered that the time from application to approval took a very long time, and sometimes approval has been suspended without explanation. This is regarded as due to the conflict of national interests between an exporting country and an importing country among ASEAN nations. Even if it applies and receives an approval of AICO, CEPT covers the same product. What is resulting from the AICO policy is a tedious procedure for application and long waiting time for approval.

The reduction in the regional customs duty by the CEPT scheme has probably the largest impact on AFTA economic policy. However, there is also a doubt about the CEPT scheme. For example, regional customs duty for AFTA will be maintained at 30% for the import tariff while it will be reduced to 0% for the AFTA member countries. However, even if imports from China, which is outside AFTA pay 30% customs duty, Chinese products could maintain price competitiveness. The same logic worked in the case of market integration of EU, as to the role of exports from Southeast Asia. Regional integration could not protect local industry, and so international restructuring of the industry may be needed.

On the other hand, in the industry set as the object of CEPT, Japanese MNEs have heavily invested in each ASEAN country to supply the local market. In this

---

[23] Based on Tokyo head office visit on October 19, 1999.

case, can it be said that it is meaningful to discriminatory treat outside of the area and the ASEAN countries? Excess supply pressure may exist in the ASEAN countries already. Some local electrical products like stand fan or ventilator are competitive in this region since they have been exported with low price. In many cases a customs duty is already exempted at the stage of parts import to the company which manufactures the export product for foreign countries, the requirement for the ASEAN contents of 40% for CEPT does not function as an export supporting measure. The Japanese MNEs in electrical machinery industry are mostly export-oriented. As a destination for exports, the ASEAN market does not have priority.

The research in this paper clarified the following point. Japanese electrical MNEs have not greatly changed their international division of labor strategy due to the formation of AFTA, because there was no need to do so. Whether this observation is peculiar to the electrical machinery and electronic industries or is also observed in the auto industry needs further investigation.

4.2 Regional Association and WTO: Constructing Pareto Superior Trade Organization

The Peoples Republic of China decided to be affiliated with the World Trade Organization (WTO) in November, 1999[24]. The WTO Cabinet meeting in Seattle ended on December 3, 1999, without reaching any agreement. It was reported on December 7, 1999 that the Japanese government started discussing the possibility to reach a free trade agreement with Singapore[25]. It has already been said that plans towards free trade agreements between Japan and the Republic of Korea, and Japan and Mexico are under examination[26]. Although it is considered that Japan has received great benefit from tariff reductions by the GATT and WTO, bilateral free trade agreement can be used as steps toward regional association. One can argue whether or not bilateral free trade agreements could be admitted as having a role in the WTO economic policy. How should we understand the relationship between a regional association and the World Trade Organization (WTO)? For example, the 40% local contents regulation in CEPT is said to be breaking the trade-related investment measures (TRIM) in WTO.

In this paper, although it is not possible to develop sufficient argument on this problem, the following principle for policy design is proposed. So long as a "Pareto superior trade organization" is built, regional association has a reason d'être. "Pareto superior" means the following: When there are two resource-allocation systems τ and σ, and if the resource allocation of τ is better than the

[24] Nihon Keizai Shimbun (Nikkei Newspaper), morning edition, November 16, 1999.

[25] Nihon Keizai Shimbun (Nikkei Newspaper), morning edition, December 5, 1999.

[26] Yomiuri Shimbun (Yomiuri Newspaper), morning edition, December 8, 1999.

resource allocation of σ without harming the welfare of any others, it is said that resource-allocation τ is Pareto superior to σ.

That is, it is called Pareto improvement if some individuals' economic conditions are improved without worsening others' economic conditions. Paraphrased along the context of this paper, a regional association is Pareto superior to a trade protection regime if participating nations' economic welfare is improved without spoiling the economic welfare of WTO member nations. This could be a guiding principle for economic policy in relation to a non-discriminatory worldwide trade organization and regional associations.

The Pareto superior trade organization does not put up an external customs duty, at the same time reducing regional customs duty. The basic policy of AFTA is regarded as Pareto superior for trade. However, it can also be concluded that it is discriminatory for the MNEs in AFTA if their operation is accompanied by local contents regulation or local equity ratio regulation. Needless to say, further research is needed to determine whether or not regional associations like EU or NAFTA make the resource allocation of member nations efficient without creating disadvantages for foreign countries.

References

Aoki, T (1997) "AFTA to Nihon Kigyo (AFTA and Japanese Companies)," in T.Aoki and K. Umada eds., *Nihon Kigyo to Chokusetsu Toushi: Tai Ajia Toushi no Aratana Kadai* (Japanese Companies and Foreign Direct Investment: New Challenge for Asian Investment), Keisou publishing Co.

Baldwin. R.(1989) "The Growth Effect of 1992," *Economic Policy*, October.

Ballard C.L. and Cheong, I.(1997) "The Effects of Economic Integration in the Pacific Rim: A Computational General Equilibrium Analysis," *Journal of Asian Economics*, vol.8, no.4, pp.505–524.

Eguchi, Y. (1991) "Chiikishugi no Shinshiten (A New Viewpoint of Regionalism), "*Sekai Keizai Hyouron* (World Economy Review), August.

Gatsios K., and Karp, L.(1991) "Delegation Games in Customs Unions," *Review of Economic Studies*, vol.58, no.2, pp.391–397.

Horaguchi, H. (1999) "Singapore, Malaysia no Denki Denshi Sangyou: 14 Kigyou deno Hiyaringu Kekka (Electrical Machinery and Electronic Industry in Singapore and Malaysia: Hearing Result of the 14 Companies) in T. Maruya ed., *Gaikoku Chokusetsu Toushi to Jiba Kigyou no Hatten*, Chosa Kenkyuu Houkokusho,

Keizai Kyouryoku Kenkyubu (Foreign Direct Investment and Development of Local Company, Research Report an Economic Assistance Research Section), 1998–No.1, Nihon Boueki Shinkoukai–Ajia Keizai Kenkyusho (JETRO and the Institute of Developing Economies).

Ikemoto, Y. (1996) " NAFTA to Tai Keizai (NAFTA and Thai Economy)," T. Taniura ed., *NAFTA to Ajia Keizai: Jiyuuka niyoru Chiikitougou eno Taiou* (NAFTA and Asian Economy: Response to Regional Integration by Liberalization), Chapter 8, Institute of Developing Economies.

Itoh, M. (1996) *Zemiraaru Kokusai Keizaigaku Nyuumon* (Seminar on International Economy), Nihon Keizai Shimbunshya.

Iwata, K. (1998) "Riijonarizumu no Hikari to Kage (Light and Shadow of Regionalism)" T. Kamo, M. Ito, and K. Ishiguro eds., *Riidingusu Kokusai Seiji Keizai Sisutemu 2: Soutaika suru Kokkyou* (Readings, Internaional Political Economy System, vol.2, Relativity in National Border), Yuuhikaku Publishing Co.

Kawasaki, K., Kushima, T., and Mitsufuji, M. (1997) "APEC Jiyuu Boueki no Keizai Bunseki: CGE Moderu niyoru Simyureishon Bunseki (Economic Analysis of APEC Trade Liberalization: Simulation Analysis by CGE Model)," *Kaigai Toushi Kenkyushohou* (Bulletin of Foreign Investment Research Institute), vol.23, no. 12.

Keizai Kikakucho Keizai Kenkyusho Hen, (Economic Planning Agency Economic Research Institute ed.) (1998) "Ouyou Ippan Kinkou Moderu niyoru Boueki Toushi Jiyuuka to Kankyou Seisaku no Hyouka (Evaluation for Trade, Investment Liberalization and Environment by the Applied General Equilibrium Model)," *Keizai Bunseki* (Economic Analysis), no. 156.

Kokusai Boueki Toushi Kenkyusho–Kousei Boueki Senta (International Trade and Investment Research Institute and Fair–trade Center) (1999) *AICO Sukiimu ni Kansuru Chosa Kenkyuu: ASEAN Sangyou Kougyou Kyouryoku Sukiimu* (Research on the AICO Scheme: ASEAN Industrial Cooperation Scheme), Kokusai Boueki Toushi Kenkyusho–Kousei Boueki Senta (International Trade and Investment Research Institute and Fair–trade Center).

Komiya, R. (1999) *Nihon no Sangyou Boueki no Keizai Bunseki* (Economic Analysis of Japanese Industry and Trade), Touyou Keizai publishing Co.

Krugman, P., (1991) "Is Bilateralism Bad?" E. Helpman and A. Razin eds., *International Trade and Policy*, Cambridge, MIT Press.

MacDougall, G.D.A. (1960) "The Benefits and Costs of Private Investment from Abroad: A Theoretical Approach," *Economic Record*, Special Issue, March.

Okada, A. (1991) "Ajia Taiheiyou no 'Keizaiken' Kousou to Sono Yukue (A Perspective and the Future of the "Economic Bloc" of Asia and the Pacific Ocean)," *Sekai Keizai Hyouron* (World Economy Review), October.

Shimizu, K. (1998) *ASEAN Ikinai Keizai Kyouryoku no Seiji Keizaigaku* (Political Economy of ASEAN Regional Economic Cooperation), Minerva Shobou publishing Co.

Shimizu, K. (1999) "Ajia Keizaikiki to ASEAN Ikinai Keizai Kyouryoku (Asian Economic Crisis and ASEAN Regional Economic Cooperation), *Sekai Keizai Hyouron* (World Economy Review), May.

Takachi, Y. (1987) "ASEAN niokeru Ikinai Keizai Kyouryoku no Jittai to Tenbou (Reality and Perspective for the Regional Economic Cooperation in ASEAN), *Kaigai Toushi Kenkyushohou* (Bulletin of Foreign Investment Research Institute), vol.13, no. 12.

Tan, J.L.H.(1996), *AFTA in the Changing International Economy*, Institute of Southeast Asian Studies.

Tokunaga, S. (1994) "Chiiki Tougou ni Kansuru Keizai Bunseki no Saabei (Survey of the Economical Analysis about Regional Integration)," in K. Ono ed., *Keizai Tougou to Hatten Tojoukoku: EC, NAFTA, Higashi Ajia* (Economic Integration and Developing Countries: EC, NAFTA and East Asia) , Chapter 2, Ajia Keizai Kenkyusho (Institute of Developing Economies).

Tsusho Sangyou Shou (The Ministry of International Trade and Industry) ed. (1996) *Heisei Hachinenban Tsusho Hakusho: Souron* (Year of Heisei 8 edition, White Paper on International Trade and Industry: General Survey), Ookurashou Insatsukyoku (Printing Bureau of Ministry of Finance).

Ueda, R. (1999) "AFTA (ASEAN Jiyuu Boueki Ken) Tenbou: Susumu ASEAN no Boueki Toushi no Jiyuuka (Survey on AFTA (ASEAN Free Trade Area): Progressing Liberalizaion of Trade and Investment)," Dai–Ichi Kangin Sougou Kenkyusho ed., (Dai–Ichi Kangyo Bank Research Institutes ed.,) *Chosa Repouto* (Investigation Report), No.13 (May 27).

Viner, J. (1950) *The Customs Union Issue*, New York, Carnegie Endowment for International Peace.

Yi, S. (1996) "Endogenous Formation of Customs Unions Under Imperfect Competition: Open Regionalism is Good," *Journal of International Economics*, vol.41, no.1/2, pp.153–177.

Yotopoulos, P.A., and Nugent, J.B.(1976) *Economics of Development: Empirical Investigations*, Harper & Row

Table 3–1. AICO Applications Monitored by Thailand Ministry of Industry: (July, 1999)

No.	Participating Companies	Countries	Acceptance	Common	Decision	Months No.	Remarks
1	Sanden Int'l(S)Pte.,Ltd.	Singapore	26 May 1997	26 May 1997	24 Jun.1997	1	
	Ka.yama Engineering Co.,Ltd	Thailand	3 Apr 1997	26 May 1997	28 Jul.1997	12	
2	Matsusita Electric Philippines Co. (MEPCO)	Philippines	22 Jul.1998	22 Jul.1998	4 Sep.1998	2	1 of 2
	Matsusita Seiko Co., Ltd.(THAMS)	Thailand	21 Nov.1997	22 Jul.1998	22 Jan.1999	14	
3	Matsusita Electric (M) Bhd.(MELCO)	Malaysia	29 Nov 1997	22 Jul.1998	22 Jan.1999	14	2 of 2
	Matsusita Seiko Co., Ltd.(THAMS)	Thailand	21 Nov.1997	22 Jul.1998	22 Jan.1999	14	
4	Denso (T) Co., Ltd.	Thailand	10 Jul. 1998	10 Jul. 1998	17 Nov.1998	4	1 of 3
	PT.Denso Ind.,Co.	Indonesia			17 Jul. 1998	–	
5	Denso (T) Co., Ltd.	Thailand	10 Jul. 1998	10 Jul. 1998	15 Feb.1999	7	2 of 3
	Denso (M) Co., Ltd. &	Malaysia	1 Jul.1998	10 Jul. 1998	15 Feb.1999	7	
	Nippon Wiper Blade (M) Sdn. Bhd.				10 Dec.1998	5	Air-Conditioner
6	Denso (T) Co., Ltd.	Thailand	22 May 1998	22 May 1998	22 May 1998	0	3 of 3
	Philippines Auto Components, Inc.	Philippines	28 May 1998	28 May 1998	18 Jun. 1998	1	
7	Toyota Motor Thailand Co.,Ltd.	Thailand	9 Feb.1998	9 Feb.1998	15 May 1998	3	1st
	Toyota Motor Philippines Corp.	Philippines	13 Aug.1997	9 Feb.1998	14 May 1998	5	1 of 8
8	Toyota Motor Thailand Co.,Ltd.	Thailand	9 Feb.1998	9 Feb.1998	15 May 1998	3	1st
	Assembly Services Sd. Bhd. (TOYOTA)	Malaysia	14 Jan.1998	9 Feb.1998	3 Mar.1998	1	2 of 8
9	Honda Cars Manufacturing	Thailand	12 Sep.1997	12 Sep.1997	4 Jun.1998	9	1 of 3
	Honda Cars Philippines Inc.	Philippines	11 Jul.1997	12 Sep.1997	11 Jun.1998	11	
10	Honda Cars Manufacturing	Thailand	12 Sep.1997	14 Jan.1998	4 Jun.1998	9	2 of 3
	Oriental Assemblrs Sdn. Bhd.	Malaysia	14 Jan.1998	14 Jan.1998	3 Mar.1998	3	
11	Honda Cars Manufacturing	Thailand	12 Sep.1997	18 Sep.1997	18 Jan.1998	4	3 of 3
	PT.Prospect Motor (HONDA)	Indonesia	18 Sep.1997	18 Sep.1997	27 Oct.1997	1	
12	Thai–Swedish Assembly Co.,Ltd. (VOLVO)	Thailand	17 Sep.1997	17 Sep.1997	13 Jan.1998	4	1st
	Swedish Motor Assemblies Sd.Bhd.	Malaysia	27 Aug.1997	17 Sep.1997	27 Oct 1997	2	1 of 3
					18 Jun.1999		re-issued
13	SONY Siam industries Co., Ltd.	Thailand	13 Jun.1998	17 Jul.1998	6 Aug.1998	2	
	Elevam Precision Engineering						
	SONY Display Devices (S) Pte.,Ltd.	Singapore	17 Jul.1998	17 Jul.1998	8 Sep.1998	2	

14	Thai Steel Cable (TSK) Co., Ltd.	Thailand	17 Fev.1998	17 Fev.1998	22 Mar.1998	1	
	Armstrong Cycle Parts Sdn.Bhd.	Malaysia	11 Fev.1998	17 Fev.1998	3 Mar.1998	1	
15	Isuzu Motors Co., Ltd.	Thailand	17 Apr.1998	4 Apr.1998	30 Jul.1998	3	1 of 2
	Isuzu Philippines Corporation	Philippines	4 Aug.1998	4 Aug.1998	24 Nov.1998	3	
16	Thai–Swedish Assembly Co.,Ltd. (VOLVO)	Thailand	11 Mar.1998	16 Mar.1998	19 May 1998	2	2nd
	Swedish Motor Assemblies Sd.Bhd.	Malaysia	16 Mar.1998	16 Mar.1998	10 Apr.1998	1	2 of 3
17	Yammar SP.Co.,Ltd.	Thailand	26 Jan.1998	26 Jan.1998	15 Feb.1999	13	
	Pt.Yammar Indonesia	Indonesia	8 Dec.1997	26 Jan.1998	18 Sep.1998	10	
18	Toyota Motor Thailand Co.,Ltd.	Thailand	20 Oct.1998	29 Oct.1998	8 Mar.1999	5	2nd
	Toyota Motor Philippines Corp.	Philippines	29 Oct.1998	29 Oct.1998			3 of 8
19	Toyota Motor Thailand Co.,Ltd.	Thailand	20 Oct.1998	29 Oct.1998	8 Mar.1999	5	2nd
	Assembly Services Sd. Bhd. (TOYOTA)	Malaysia	29 Oct.1998	29 Oct.1998	10 Dec.1998	2	4 of 8
20	Toyota Motor Thailand Co.,Ltd.	Thailand	29 Oct.1998		8 Mar.1999	5	2nd
	P.T.TOYOTA Astra Motor	Indonesia					5 of 8
21	Siam Nissan Automobile Co.,Ltd.	Thailand	23 Nov.1998		8 Mar.1999	4	1 of 3
	P.T.Ismac Nissan Manufacturing	Indonesia					
22	Siam Nissan Automobile Co.,Ltd.	Thailand	23 Nov.1998		8 Mar.1999	4	2 of 3
	Tan chong Motor Assemblies Sdn. Bhd. (NISSAN)	Malaysia			10 Jun.1999	–	
23	Siam NISSAN Automobile Co.,Ltd.	Thailand	23 Nov.1998	21 May 1999	8 Mar.1999		3 of 3
	Nissan Motor Philippines, Inc.	Philippines		21 May 1999			
24	Mitsubishi Motor Corporation Sittipol Co.,Ltd.	Thailand	2 Apr.1999		25 Jun.1999	2	
	Mitsubishi Motor Philippines Co.,Ltd.	Philippines	7 Jan.1999				
25	Mitsubishi Electric Thai Auto–Part Co.,Ltd.	Thailand	2 Apr.1999		25 Jun.1999	4	1 of 2
	PT.Lippo MELCO Auto–Part (LMA)	Indonesia					
26	Mitsubishi Electric Thai Auto–Part Co.,Ltd.	Thailand	19 Feb.1999		25 Jun.1999	4	2 of 2
	Laguna Auto parts Manufacturing Co.,Ltd. (LMA)	Philippines					
27	Thai–Swedish Assembly Co.,Ltd. (VOLVO)	Thailand	15 Mar.1999		5 Apr.1999	1	3rd
	Swedish Motor Assemblies Sd.Bhd.	Malaysia			20 Apr.1999		

				Malaysia rejected parts importation from Thailand.			
28	Auto Alliance Thailand	Thailand	15 May 1999		25 Jun.1999	3	
	Ford Motor Company Philippines Inc.	Philippines					
				Thailand approved partially parts importation.			
29	Siam Kayaba Co.,Ltd.	Thailand					
	Kayaba Malaysia Sdn.Bhd.	Malaysia			5 Apr.1999		
				Malaysia rejected partially parts importation from Thailand.			
30	Nestle' Foods (Thailand) Ltd.	Thailand	13 May 1999		25 Jun.1999	1	
	Goya Incorporation	Philippines	5 Feb.1999		13 May 1999	3	
31	Isuzu Motors (Thailand) Co.,Ltd.	Thailand	30 Apr.1999		25 Jun.1999	2	2 of 2
	Isuzu Engine Manufacturing Co.,Ltd.						
	PT Panja Motor	Indonesia					
	PT Mesin Isuzu Indonesia						
	PT Tri Dharma Wisesa						
32	Auto Alliance Thailand	Thailand	25 May 1999				
	AMIM Holding Sdn.Bhd.	Malaysia					
33	Summit Showa Manufacturing Co.,Ltd	Thailand	1 Jun.1999		25 Jun.1999		
	PT Showa Indonesia Manufacturing Co.,Ltd	Indonesia					
34	Toyota Motor Thailand Co.,Ltd.	Thailand	23 Jul.1999				6 of 8
	Siam Toyota Manufacturing Co.,Ltd						
	P.T.Toyota Astra Motor	Indonesia					
35	Toyota Motor Thailand Co.,Ltd.	Thailand	23 Jul.1999				7 of 8
	Assembly Services Sd. Bhd. (TOYOTA)	Malaysia					
36	Toyota Motor Thailand Co.,Ltd.	Thailand	23 Jul.1999				8 of 8
	Siam Toyota Manufacturing Co.,Ltd						3rd
	Toyota Motor Philippines	Philippines					
					Average	4.6	

Source: Thai JETRO, the original data is provided by the Ministry of Industry Thailand.

4 AFTA in the Globalization Process: Perspectives from Industries in Malaysia

Sieh Lee Mei Ling
University of Malaya

1 Introduction

At the dawn of the twenty first century, it is timely for Malaysia to review its economic position and role in Asia, along with fellow member states of the Association of South East Asian Nations (ASEAN) especially in the context of an increasingly globalising world economy. Globalization is forging growing economic interdependencies of countries worldwide through cross-border trade in goods and services, as well as through massive international capital flows either for investment into real production facilities or for short term portfolio holdings, in ways and magnitude that are unprecedented. The process of pan-global extension of business and economic linkages is accelerated by the rapid and widespread diffusion of technology, again through modes that never existed before.

It is becoming clear that any significant business or economic activity will be impacted as structural changes become inevitable as the Malaysian economy continues to search for appropriate paths for economic development partly in response to external global forces and partly in preparation for what is to come. Industries in Malaysia generally realise that with the further liberalisation of trade through the creation of the ASEAN Free Trade Area (AFTA) and with implementation of the World Trade Organization (WTO) agreements, in an already open economy that has always sought and attracted foreign direct investment, workable strategies are needed for long term survival and growth.

Several important phenomena have been introduced as globalization permeates the economies in the ASEAN region to result in structural changes. These changes may originate from world level agreements between and among countries, such as the WTO; or from inter-government arrangements within a region or sub-region, such as APEC or AFTA; or from within a particular economy such as policy adjustments to accommodate the new positions taken by respective governments. Some of the shifts are related to issues concerning intellectual property rights; or from changes within a particular sector, sub-sector or industry such as for financial services; or even adjustments from a firm that dominates a particular industry. In the case of a small developing economy like Malaysia, it is not uncommon to find that the introduction of a single large firm, that may be local or foreign, causing revolutionary changes for the entire industry within the economy. The best example in Malaysia is the formation of the corporation for the national car project about fifteen years ago. Even in the services sector, the entry of a single foreign hypermarket, usually as a joint venture with locals, such as Carrefour or Makro, has resulted in reactions from the retail sub-sector of the distributive trade.

Undoubtedly, intensification of competition has caused the most apprehensions, even fear, among industries and traders alike, notwithstanding the opportunities that come with deregulation and greater market liberalisation. Technological innovations are also bringing both solutions and hardships, while regulatory changes to implement new policy directions in anticipation of the globalized era have also been a source of hope to some and difficulty to others.

1.1 Objectives of Chapter

This chapter attempts to pursue three broad objectives so as to generate discussion and ideas of future strategies for industries that operate in Malaysia as globalization progresses. First, the major structural and operational changes of two selected industries, namely the electronics industry and the automobile industry within Malaysia are reviewed. The changes that are taking place in response to the changing needs of markets, the rising standards and the new expectations of others along the value chain are examined. This chapter tries to understand the changing role of firms within these industries in recent years as regional and global economic agreements are implemented.

Secondly, the business-economic and regulatory effects of the sudden change in scenario caused by the Asian crisis are highlighted for the two selected industries in Malaysia. While some have attributed the crisis to the globalization process, for the longer term the adjustments needed to cope with the crisis may be viewed as severe interruptions in the globalization process itself. Thirdly, as the Malaysian economy together with other Asian economies emerge from the financial and economic crises at a time when globalization pushes on, the strategies that are being taken or will likely be taken by Malaysian businesses and the Malaysian government in anticipation of AFTA and the global forces are also considered.

1.2 Approach Taken

On the basis of recent research on industries in Malaysia, the thoughts that have emerged from a few industries are gathered to take stock of current trends and changes for the purposes of this chapter. Particular interest is paid to the electronics and automobile industries. Section Two of the chapter begins with a contextual overview of the Malaysian economy. Following an update of the Malaysian economy, arrangements within AFTA as a regional agreement for industries and firms will be outlined. AFTA will be briefly compared with developments within the Asia Pacific Economic Cooperation (APEC) arrangement which is more extensive in terms of geographic-economic coverage; as well as with WTO which is even more extensive – because Malaysia is a member of good standing in all three.

The Third Section provides a brief review of the two selected industries, namely, the electronics industry, and secondly the auto industry in Malaysia. The review focuses on the increasingly liberal trends that underlie the development of the industries in recent years despite differences between the two industries. Section Four discusses the business effects, the domestic production effects and the market effects attributable to the Asian crisis within the context of the globalization process, experienced by the two industries.

The last section examines the strategic responses of industries and firms in the fast changing post-crisis environment. Some attention will be paid to the regulatory role of the Malaysian government both in economic recovery and in steadying the economy to regain confidence. As globalization encroaches further into the Malaysian economy in terms of scope and depth and as firms react to global forces, while simultaneously acting as agents of globalization, the integrative role of businesses will be emphasized. This chapter concludes with some recommendations for future paths as Malaysia within AFTA are further integrated into the global economy.

2 AFTA within Regional and Global Frameworks

2.1 Malaysian Economy Update

Discussion of any aspect of Malaysia's economy, for that matter of Asia's economy towards the close of the 1990s and the start of the new century, has to take into account the impact of the financial and economic crisis. The severity of the turbulence in many Asian countries is clearly evident in the fact that the crisis had buckled the trends observable in the earlier part of the decade. Before the crisis erupted in mid-1997, Malaysia recorded very high GDP growth rates of about 8 per cent per annum for nearly ten years. The deflationary impact of the crisis resulted in a negative 7.5 per cent GDP growth for 1998. Such a severe contraction of the economy was unprecedented since the country gained political independence since 1957. However, with prudent economic measures taken by the government and with favourable domestic and external market developments, the Malaysian economy recovered remarkably in 1999. GDP grew 4.3 per cent in 1999 as a result of the remedial actions taken. For 2000, GDP growth has been projected at 5.8 per cent. Based on the first quarter 11.9 per cent growth and second quarter 9 per cent growth, the 2000 rate has been informally revised upwards to 7.8 per cent while some slowing down is expected for 2001, due to projected inflation rate of 3 to 4 per cent attributable to a 30 per cent increase in domestic transportation costs.

Several key measures were adopted by the Malaysian government to overcome the recessionary impact of the crisis. Steps were taken to restructure and re-capitalize the banking and financial system, to restructure corporate debts, to introduce currency controls and to peg the Malaysian ringgit to 3.80 a US dollar. The most controversial was the limitation of short term capital flows at the border. Attempts were also made to suppress speculation of the ringgit and excessive speculation in the capital market. In 1999, Malaysia's population of 22.71 million people had to contend with a per capita income of US $3,255 – a definite decline from the pre-crisis level of US$ 4496 in 1996 (i.e. 11,239 Malaysian ringgit).

Malaysia's future economic development will see expansion in services industries while growth in the manufacturing sector will remain important and relevant. As is expected of a relatively higher income developing economy, Malaysia's services sector commands just over half of the economy accounting for 54.6 per cent of GDP in 1999 (inclusive of construction services), which is definitely larger than the 29.2 per cent share of manufacturing and the 9.4 per cent share of agriculture and mining in the primary sector.

2.2 Major Commitments for the New Millennium

Malaysia has entered into liberalization arrangements at three levels in the past decade. First, as an original member state of the Association of South East Asian Nations, ASEAN, Malaysia is a keen supporter of the ASEAN Free Trade Area or AFTA agreement. Secondly, as one of the major trading economies within the wider Asia Pacific region, Malaysia has a definite role to play in the agreements reached through the Asia Pacific Economic Cooperation, that is APEC arrangements. Thirdly, having signed as a contracting party within the World Trade Organization, Malaysia has another set of trade related commitments to keep at the world level. Before discussing the likely impacts of these arrangements which reinforce each other in propelling the Malaysian economy into the global economy along with others, the fundamental features of each of the three sets of agreements are briefly compared.

2.2.1 In South East Asia

The ASEAN Free Trade Area (AFTA) was established as a result of the adoption of the Common Effective Preferential Tariff scheme (CEPT) in January 1992. After adjustments and changes in time targets, AFTA member countries agreed to reduce their tariffs to between zero to five per cent and to eliminate most non-tariff barriers by 2003. AFTA's objective of guiding ASEAN members to pursue free trade is in line with the APEC agreement among Asia Pacific economies expressed in the Bogor Declaration of November 1994. A distinctive difference between AFTA and APEC is that ASEAN works through consensus among members whereas APEC tends to operate through peer pressure. In addition, AFTA also tries to expand co-operation for cross-border investment through the ASEAN Investment Area (AIA) arrangement and the ASEAN Industrial Co-operation Scheme (AICO).

Endorsed at the ASEAN summit in December 1995, AIA has the objective of drawing more foreign direct investment (FDI) into ASEAN by reducing barriers to the free flow of capital and adopting simpler and more transparent rules on FDI. It aims to encourage foreign investors to perceive ASEAN as a single investment region rather than a collection of different investment destinations. Through AIA, ASEAN will work towards joint investment and intra-ASEAN investment promotions based on market size and credibility.

AICO established in April 1996 and which became operational in November 1996 is to encourage investors and to promote intra-ASEAN trade in line with CEPT and AFTA. It replaces the ASEAN Industrial Joint Venture (AIJV) plan and the brand-to-brand complementation scheme (BBC) that applied to individual companies sourcing automotive components in several ASEAN countries. AICO offers preferential tariff treatment to its participating countries until 2003, by immediately benefiting from the lower tariffs of 0–5 per cent upon approval instead of in 2003.

With the objective of simplifying and harmonising investment procedures so as to promote foreign investment inflow, AICO also aims to increase intra-ASEAN regional industrial co-operation by encouraging investment from ASEAN and from non-ASEAN sources by providing the institutional framework within which companies can collaborate for mutual benefit in the region. With immediate reduction of tariffs, projects under AICO can enjoy lower import tariffs for raw materials and machinery and be subject to the same tax structure as domestic items. Another feature of AICO is that unlike before, approved companies can market industrial products directly to the retail trade or to end-users. To be eligible for AICO concessions, companies must be incorporated and operating in one of the ASEAN countries, undertaking resource-sharing or industrial co-operation activities, and must have a minimum of 30 per cent combined ASEAN equity.

Besides encouraging the sourcing of materials and components from among member countries, as well as to forge trade linkages through the accelerated preferential trading agreements, AFTA will open the possibility of a freer flow of production information among member countries to facilitate partnerships and production linkages among firms of among ASEAN countries. The arrangements for trade and investment will result in greater economic integration, especially through co-operations in areas identified as growth triangles, though relationships built will not be confined to these sub-areas only. ASEAN governments are also expected to enhance policy co-ordination and co-operation with AFTA, which is seen as a concrete step towards the creation of an ASEAN economic community. It is a positive development in ASEAN as it will lead the group to a faster pace consistent with the expectations of global trade liberalization within the WTO.

2.2.2 In Asia Pacific

APEC was formed in 1989 to achieve free trade by the year 2020 by adopting the principles of transparency, national treatment, and the most-favoured-nation treatment within an open multilateral system, particularly for the interests of member economies. To date the 21 members comprise the economies of ASEAN, the USA, Japan, Chile and China. Malaysia, along with other APEC economies, has pledged to progressively liberalise trade within the Asia Pacific region consistent with WTO commitments for goods, services, capital and technology. Without going into the details of APEC arrangements that are already well documented, it is observed that APEC is akin to an intermediate co-operative agreement that can be posited between AFTA and WTO in terms of geographic scope, in terms of breadth of economic activities covered and in terms of *modus operandi*.

2.2.3 At the Global Level

The World Trade Organisation or WTO, which took over the functions of GATT on 1 January 1995, is perhaps the most comprehensive agreement ever that governs the international trading system. The agreement itself consists of a Preamble, 16 Articles and four Annexes where the multilateral trade agreements, including the Multilateral Agreement on Trade in Goods, the General Agreement on Trade in Services and the Agreement on Trade-related Aspects of Intellectual Property Rights, are contained in Annex 1. As a contracting party to WTO, Malaysia is subject to the wide ranging powers of the organisation which in effect, has substantial legislative, executive and judicial authority, including the power to impose sanctions on countries. The system is rule-oriented, strictly institutional and procedural in character. Although Article IX of the Agreement says that the WTO will continue the GATT practice of decision-making by consensus, it is also clear that when a decision cannot be reached by consensus, the matter will be decided by a vote. While rules seem to restrict behaviour, their importance is recognized because they create a degree of certainty for traders, and hence are expected to stimulate investment and growth. The WTO rules are also important in providing a multilateral forum for negotiating reciprocal reductions in trade barriers among the 150 or so contracting parties.

3 Brief Review of Selected Industries

The way increasing liberalization and globalization impinge on industries in Malaysia and the Malaysian economy is examined from the viewpoint of two selected industries: electronics and auto. We shall proceed with a brief review of the industries.

3.1 The Electronics Industry in Malaysia

The electronics industry in Malaysia began with the assembly of consumer electronics for the domestic market under import-substituting industrialisation. In the 1970s, USA firms increased their investment in off-shore assembly of electronics components, particularly semi-conductors. In the 1980s East Asian electronics manufacturers relocated in lower wage ASEAN countries, including in Malaysia which by then had shifted from import substitution to export orientation. A consequence of these developments was the proliferation of small and medium sized industries that supply the electronics industry in ASEAN. Locals supplied plastic materials, packaging, metal parts and some specialized machinery.

The Malaysian electronics industry grew rapidly. By 1992, the industry contributed to 33 per cent (RM40.66billion) of the total manufacturing sector's output, 31 per cent (RM7.96 billion) of the total value added generated from the manufacturing sector, absorbing 30 per cent (RM735,965) of the total labour force and 30 per cent (RM3.34 billion) of the total labour cost within the manufacturing sector, and 23 per cent (RM6.03billion) of the total fixed asset investment within the manufacturing sector. In 1993, a total of 185 establishments operated within the country's electronics industry as compared with 62 in 1985. Exports from the industry amounted to 65 per cent (RM76.65 billion) of the total exports from the manufacturing sector in 1994.

Structural changes have occurred in the electronics industry in Malaysia as the industry itself has undergone transformation necessitated by international competition and threats of growing protectionism and regionalism since the late 1980s. The regional restructuring of the industry is also reflected in the patterns of changing production and of trade, which comprise a mixture of horizontal and vertical integration across national boundaries. Electronics in Malaysia, along with the industry in the ASEAN region have come to assume international prominence as major production centers, not just assemblers, for consumer electronics and for components, with production of both increasing considerably in volume, value and product range.

The Malaysian electronics industry has been foreign dominated, with most companies being wholly-owned subsidiaries of foreign MNCs. In 1994, FDI accounted for 76 per cent of the total investment by the industry in Malaysia amounting to 7.6 billion ringgit or US$2.49 billion. Firms from the USA owned 15.4 per cent of the total FDI in the industry, followed by Japanese MNCs with

14.4 per cent (MITI Report 1995). In general, USA and European firms tend to concentrate on the manufacture of a particular component in Malaysia: semiconductor components for supporting the electronics industry in their home country. Japanese firms adopt a different policy in Malaysia producing a broad range of related products, often consumer electronics. Most FDIs in the industry in Malaysia have maintained well-developed intra-firm trading networks. Trade with parent firms in the home country and with affiliates outside the home country have become increasingly important as production establishments along different sections of the value chain are split among a few countries, usually in neighbouring countries within the region.

The industry is also characterized by a high degree of concentration. The top 18 firms out of 185 firms in 1993 i.e.10 per cent comprising both local and FDIs, accounted for about 41 per cent and 32 per cent of the industry's sales and employment (Sieh and Yew 1997). The electronics industry is the largest employer within the manufacturing sector, having enjoyed an average annual growth of 10.8 per cent between 1991 and 1998. In 1998, the industry accounted for 37.9 per cent of the total employment of the economy. However, Malaysian participation in the industry has been small and linkages to the rest of the economy has remained insignificant. This has prompted the granting of tax incentives for higher local material content and linkages to local suppliers. The weak local backward linkage is because of the dependence on imported inputs while the weak forward linkage is due to the limited domestic market.

The electronics industry comprises three main segments, namely industrial electronics (including telecommunications equipment), electronic components and consumer electronics. In 1985, electronic components such as semiconductors constituted over 80 percent of the industry's output. The Industrial Master Plan of 1986 targeted a reduction of components production to 61 per cent while increasing consumer electronics and industrial electronics output to 24 percent and 15 percent respectively by 1995. These targets were achieved earlier than planned in 1993, when electronic components accounted for 43 per cent, consumer electronics for 27 per cent and industrial electronics for 30 per cent of the industry's output (MIDA 1993). By 1998, the corresponding ratios were 44.6 for components, 14.1 for consumer electronics and 41.3 for industrial electronics. The response of MNCs to the direction deemed desirable by the Malaysian Government was remarkable. Provisions to encourage the development of suppliers and support industries through local vendor linkages, as well as incentives for investment in R&D activities, design capabilities and to shift towards the production of higher value-added products have not gone unheeded.

Undoubtedly, comparative and competitive advantages within the ASEAN region also strongly determined the distribution of production in particular segments and products. Malaysia has one of the more advanced electronics industries in the ASEAN region, although FDI plays a dominant role in determining where Malaysia fits into regional networks and what products are produced. For trade in the electronics industry, the USA was Malaysia's largest trading partner (35.9 per cent), followed by the ASEAN market (26.55 per cent), EU (15.35 per cent) and Japan (7 per cent). Such a pattern of trade supported the earlier proposition that trade with the USA was mainly intra-firm between USA firms in Malaysia and their affiliates and parent companies in the USA.

Besides providing a base for lower cost production for FDIs within a politically friendly, economically attractive and socially acceptable environment, the types of electronics imported into and exported from Malaysia clearly show that Malaysia plays a dual role in the industry's global production system in terms of providing linkages both forward and backward for the world-wide electronics industry. In 1993, export of components fell to 43 percent from 72 percent in 1988; export of consumer electronics rose to 27 percent from 18 percent in 1988, and export of industrial electronics rose to 30 percent from 10 percent in 1988. Imports of electronics into Malaysia had also changed following the product mix adjustments. In 1993, components accounted for 69.6 percent of electronic imports, consumer electronics for 1.6 percent and industrial electronics for 28.8 percent, which was valued at US$ 12.193 billion. The strong global linkages, especially ties with parent firms continue to be strongly maintained. But MNCs were beginning to use Malaysia as a focal point for regional markets, both as a gateway for ASEAN – including for entry into the emerging Indo-China markets and as a human resource training center, especially with Malaysia's policy shift towards liberalization of education and training.

The electronics industry in Malaysia is expected to shift continuously depending on relative developments and costs in neighbouring economies and economies of other regions. The trend towards growing intra-firm and inter-firm networks has been documented elsewhere (Sieh and Yew 1997). Much of the sales of Japanese firms in Malaysia were sent to third countries through intra-firm channels. It has also been observed that there were more vertical integration of US and European firms than of Japanese firms. The reluctance of US firms to source from unrelated firms in third countries could be explained by a combination of intra-firm networking behaviour and value-added chain considerations.

Foreign and local firm linkages are also undergoing changes. Significant changes were seen in the role of domestic partners as some Malaysian joint-venture partners had started to acquire technology over time – although limited to lower technology areas of the electronics industry, such as in plastic parts manufacturing, diode leads, contract manufacturing of consumers electronics products and DC power supply systems. Even in export marketing, Malaysian joint-ventures have started to export directly despite their narrow customer base. Other Malaysian partners in electronics have benefited in terms of human resource development. Generally, locals in the industry have started to experiment with a higher level of autonomy from their foreign partners as they are being increasingly exposed to global transactions.

3.2 The Auto Industry in Malaysia

In the early post-independent economy of the 1960s, Malaysia was mainly a consumer in the automotive industry, relying on imports especially from the UK and Japan. Foreign automotive firms especially from Japan started to set up joint ventures with locals to assemble vehicles using components and parts imported from parent firms. FDI in the automotive industry then, was mainly to leap trade barriers. The bulk of the output bearing the brand names of the parent firms were sold within the country. Local partners in Malaysia were mainly distributors. The auto industry only began developing along a new direction at the initiative of the Malaysian government in the mid-1980s and has since expanded under heavy protection. Manufacturing activities beyond mere assembly work started usually with foreign automotive firms as partners.

The well-known national car project led the way with Japanese joint venture partners providing design, technology and management inputs. Vehicles produced in Malaysia were marketed under local brand-names, initially domestically and subsequently internationally. Specific policies were implemented to nurture the embryonic auto industry, such as tax breaks, financing facilities for purchasers even directive for public sector buyers. Progressive increase in local content was also pushed as parts and component suppliers were encouraged to grow under officially sponsored vendor development programmes. Under programmes for mandatory deletion of imported parts and components, local content targets for passenger and commercial vehicles were met, reaching levels of around 60 per cent.

In 1997, there were 17 motor vehicle assembly and manufacturing plants operating in Malaysia, while over 350 firms produced component parts (MIDA 1998a). Malaysia's auto manufacturing centered on passenger cars as motorcycle and commercial vehicle industries were mainly assembly activities. Production of passenger cars accounted for 84 per cent of the industry. This can be contrasted with the industry in Thailand and Indonesia where commercial vehicles production has been prioritised. Commercial vehicles in Malaysia represented only 12 per cent of the total production of all auto output, manufactured and assembled combined.

By 1997, "assembled" passenger cars accounted for 14 per cent of the industry's output in the category while "manufactured" products constituted 86 per cent. Such achievements would not have been possible without heavy government leadership, protection and intervention. For the national car Proton for instance, over 20 companies were given financial and technical assistance to shift to OEM manufacturing of components and parts. Perodua, the second national car project also had at least five such vendors. The highly preferential import duty at 13 per cent for Proton and 7 per cent for Perodua, compared to 35 to 50 per cent for CKD imports and even higher rates for CBU units, explains the national brands' control of more than 80 per cent of domestic market.

Despite the Government's active participation and commitments in the country's automotive industry, the overall industry has not reached the international level of competitiveness. The fact that Malaysia is still a net importer in the automotive industry reflects its uncompetitive position in the international market. Malaysia's market share in the world automotive industry was only 0.1 per cent in 1993 (MIER and DRI/McGraw–Hill 1996). Trade performances are better in the production of parts and components than in for wholly built vehicles. (See Malaysia's net export to total trade ratio in Table 7.2 Sieh 2000). The bulk of exports of motor vehicles and parts are directed to the European and Asian markets. In 1986, exports to the European market were only 5 per cent of total exports but by the 1990s, more than 60 per cent of total exports of motor vehicles and parts landed in Europe, mainly the UK. Overall, Asia has been the second largest market for Malaysia's motor vehicles and parts. On the other hand imports of motor vehicles and parts came primarily from Japan which supplied about 70 per cent of Malaysia's import needs.

Foreign investment in this industry has been important in the industry's development, accounting for 20 to 30 per cent of total investment. Japan has been the single most important foreign investor, followed by the UK, Singapore, Panama, Germany, USA and Taiwan. But in recent years, the motives and forms of FDI and trade of multinationals in this industry have been changing as global strategic horizons have assumed greater importance. In the past, equity interest was the sole reason of foreign firms investing in Malaysia. However, technical assistance is emerging as a growing important form of investment by foreign firms because local automotive firms have assumed far more active roles in the production process as Malaysian expertise and skills in certain areas have been developed. Nevertheless, local firms continue to rely on technical assistance from their foreign partners.

In the 1990s, there have been attempts in outward investment by Malaysian auto firms, for example to Australia and the UK for distribution purposes. Some larger Malaysian Proton vendors have also formed joint ventures with Japanese interests to produce parts in neighbouring Philippines and Vietnam, as well as in emerging markets such as China.

4 Effects of The Asian Crisis Within The Context of Globalization

It has been clear that Malaysia's commitments for liberalisation overlap and reinforce one another irrespective of the geographic coverage of each of the three agreements discussed earlier. Together the economic agreements signal to players within the economy that changes are definitely needed to adjust to the effects of the global forces some of which are already being felt. However, in the late 1990s, as Malaysian industries were seriously planning strategic directions for the future, the Asian crisis erupted suddenly and swiftly. For instance, some of the attempts by Malaysian businesses to forge strategies with foreign direct investors both within the Malaysian economy and outside Malaysia in preparation of global competition, as already described for electronics and auto industries, had to be suspended. Firms scrambled for tactical steps just to ensure survival. Longer term issues, such as globalization had to be shelved temporarily. We shall briefly discuss some of the business effects, domestic production capability effects, and market effects that firms within the two selected industries had to cope with in a very urgent manner as the crisis erupted.

The Asian crisis that blew up in July 1997 began as a currency crisis which deteriorated into a financial crisis and then an economic crisis. In turn, for several countries, the situation aggravated into a political crisis. Malaysia was spared the last stage, probably because of the political stability that the country has enjoyed over four decades and partly because of stock of assets accumulated as real income rose during the period. One of the earliest impacts of the crisis was the sharp depreciation of the Malaysian ringgit (by 40 per cent by August 1998 compared with 54 per cent for the Thai baht, 48 per cent for the Korean won and 83 per cent for the Indonesian rupiah). Another impact was the massive asset deflation – partly linked to loans backed up stocks that were given out by financial institutions at a time of stock market crash. Following, the Malaysian economy as a whole suffered a sharp and unexpected set back which was evident in the 7.5 per cent decline in GDP for 1998.

The severe economic recession affected almost all sectors of the economy. Industries that depended heavily on imported inputs while selling to the domestic market, such as most fast consumer goods and consumer durables manufactured in Malaysia, including automobiles suffered most. The only exceptions were activities or industries that utilized mainly local inputs but sold to foreign markets, such as resource based industries that produced palm oil, rubber and wood products – because they continued to enjoy export revenue usually denominated in US dollars while costs were incurred in the weaker domestic currency. Electronic firms was in the moderately affected category because despite their reliance on inputs from foreign sources, a substantial proportion of their output was sold internationally, either as electronic components or as industrial or consumer electronic goods. Being an industry that was already operating as a forerunner among global industries and with relatively few restrictions in terms of business strategies in much of ASEAN, the performance of electronic firms in Malaysia were dictated more by business cycles within the global industry than the fortunes of any one of the host economies in which they have links with.

In Malaysia, production and sale of motor vehicles primarily in the domestic market fell dramatically as a result of the crisis. Production of all types of motor vehicles experienced sharp falls in 1998, with commercial vehicles being the worst affected recording a 83 per cent decline, followed by passenger cars at 62 per cent and motorcycles at 36 per cent. The auto industry had to struggle with three serious problems. First, the industry was operating below its optimum scale of production. Secondly, urgent steps had to be taken to arrest the high costs of production, particularly at a time when firms were facing sharp reduction in sales and production. Thirdly, the surge in interest rates following the sudden squeeze in liquidity in the economy, together with other government controls over credit for passenger car purchase aggravated the market situation then.

Nevertheless, the effects of the Asian crisis bear several very important messages for the economic planners and regulators of the Malaysian economy particularly within the context of globalization. First, it is evident that the tide of economic global forces has not only reached Malaysian shores but more importantly, external economic forces has the potential of disrupting the economic and financial system with devastating effects, notwithstanding the state of prosperity and strong economic fundamentals that prevail and irrespective of what domestic regulators try to do to halt the contagion effects from related economies. In effect, the crisis was a wake-up call. The crisis instilled a sense of urgency to prepare for contingencies particularly under globalized conditions.

Secondly, it is becoming apparent that as a very open economy for both trade and investment, Malaysia has to live with the complex interlocking business and economic relationships that are becoming even more complicated. Developments in the international currency and financial markets in ways not envisaged before were causing bewilderment to businesses that had yet to experience the full impact of globalization. Yet these markets are important for transactional purposes and for managing financial risks. The new markets exist not only to support and service trade in real goods and services, but they have developed into exchanges for innovative financial products that are transacted in their own right within financial investment industries that have a life of their own. Such creative products often involve risky speculations.

Thirdly, a comparison of the electronics industry and the auto industry shows that different effects will result from different industry structure, mode of operation, strategies and degree of government regulation and protection. Clearly, the two industries provide an interesting comparative study. In particular, the basically free business behaviour in electronics can be contrasted against the protectionistic strategies and effects of the auto industry, some of which have been alluded to earlier on. The auto industry had fewer options than electronics because of the high degree of regulations designed for the development of the industry itself. While electronics with much fewer restrictions were able to adjust more quickly and in more appropriate ways with assistance from affiliates in regional and global production sites.

Fourthly, the crisis demonstrates that with increasing globalization, policy interventions by governments may not be as effective as before, simply because economies can no longer be kept apart and the effectiveness of one's policies may be reduced even neutralized by the action of other countries. Information technology and new ways of communication are not only forging new ways of conducting business but are causing constant adjustments by businesses in search of the best strategy for themselves. For example, with the fast pace of regional and international liberalization in trade and investment, the automotive industry is no longer seen as an industry within a national boundary but rather a global industry, even from the perspective of the Malaysian industry that originated as a domestic oriented project with numerous policy crutches to rely on till the present time. Both the national car firms had to resort to seeking new external markets more aggressively. Some assemblers of other auto categories e.g. MAA successfully made inroads into previously unexplored export markets, such as in Egypt and elsewhere.

Fifthly, it is interesting to observe the manner in which the electronics industry in Malaysia has managed to continue with its excellent performance notwithstanding the crisis, and to shift gears into higher value-added technology and products while adjusting to the changes in resource availability. The firms' responses after the crisis and in anticipation of global industry demand and supply within the context of regional, sub-regional and international agreements must be further pursued. I strongly suspect that the intra-firm and inter-firm transactions regardless of national boundaries are far more active than before. However, with the changing post-crisis risk profiles of ASEAN economies, the growth of regionalism and the new economic axis that accompany their emergence, and the rapid rise of China and India as two important pool of labour in the global economy, further analysis is needed to understand the structural changes attributable to the globalization process.

5 Post Crisis Implications of AFTA and Globalization for Firms–Industries, the Malaysian Economy and the Government

Generally, the level of economic activity in Malaysia will have effects on the performance of nearly every sector of the economy. Gobalization is expected to impact Malaysia at three main levels, namely the ASEAN sub-regional level, the Asia Pacific regional level and the world or pan-global level. At all levels, firms will certainly become important agents of the globalization process. They include traditional MNCs, newer and more regional based multinationals from the higher income developing economies or the Newly Industrialising Economies (NIEs) of Asia, and from the more advanced among the original ASEAN countries. Firms in various industries, economies and governments will need to seek suitable strategies to cope with the developments as Asia fully recovers from the crisis. Several changes are expected.

5.1 Implications for Firms and Industries

Easier market entry will be accompanied by increased supply and demand for firms in Malaysia, including those in both the industries discussed, assuming that favourable external global economic conditions prevail. MNCs that are long established in the economy, or new comers, will certainly view the role of Malaysia as a host in different light. The extent Malaysian firms can benefit from a sizeable share of the global pie within their respective industries will depend on their ability to move swiftly to strategize by themselves or in alliance with partners from the region and beyond. The trend for domination by a handful of the largest firms within each industry is expected to continue.

Heavier competition will undoubtedly be experienced as freer market access encourages inward as well as outward movement of firms. Globalization will see greater mobility of consumers, suppliers and workers. Cross-cultural management will have to be dealt with on a much larger scale than ever before. As Asian economies pick up steam and as purchasing power gets re-instated, Malaysian industries, including electronics and auto will find competition from many more firms and brands that did not exist before. Innovative strategies using new media and methods of promotion and selling that have yet to reach their peak – partly because many of the plans were aborted with the crisis – will be intensified especially with the opportunities presented by AFTA. For instance, newer information technology (IT) driven modes of business may change the role and jobs of car distributors as middlemen in the auto industry while new formats for B–B transactions coupled with new logistics for physical distribution that amalgamate techniques of JIT, MRP and EDI made possible by liberalised shipping, telecon and banking activities will certainly open strategic windows for firms.

Smaller firms such as those from ASEAN will actively seek linkages with the mega-firms, even to cater to their own national domestic markets, so as not to be left behind. Opportunities for small and medium sized enterprises will be opened although their roles may differ from before. Emphasis on ability to supply the best, at the lowest cost, at the right time and place, to fulfill specialized niche demand for regional or global markets will be made. Higher productivity and greater efficiency though important, will not be sufficient for small and medium Malaysian enterprises to survive. A shift in mindset towards a co-operative attitude is necessary for strategic alliances and shared responsibility, irrespective of nationality, in order to form innovative partnerships and to survive.

5.2 Implication for the Malaysian Economy

Generally, economic policies must take into account the need to cope with expanding investment activities by MNCs and by Malaysians, and the consequences of widening production and trade networks regardless of national boundaries. Economic managers need to anticipate rather than react to new business management modalities and innovative developments. Preparations must be made to face the economic and social impact of globalization that are inevitable and imminent.

The scope for intra-regional trade and investment will enlarge within ASEAN due to AFTA and AIA. As tariffs decline and even removed for thousands for tradable items by 2003, opportunities for new trade directions and channels will present themselves among the ASEAN economies. The reduction of such an important trade barrier will encourage new investments and new patterns of intra-regional investment. Some businesses hampered by investment conditions or restrictions in a particular ASEAN country may invest in a neighbouring country and export from that country. For instance, there are already thoughts of such possibilities for overcoming Malaysian equity conditions by planting up in Thailand. Alternatively, more cross-border investment and trade are expected to take advantage of newer technologies and resource or labour availability, because without trade barriers, more options are open for the siting of production facilities.

More linkages with other economies are expected through firms either in the same industry or otherwise. Investment and trade activities among affiliates within corporate groups will expand significantly. The focus on home–host relations will give way to ties between and among affiliates intra-firm, irrespective of location. The hub and spoke relationships will be overshadowed by the network relationships. Relevant policy and administrative measures will be needed from managers of the economy to facilitate such relationships. Irrelevant policies and measures should be removed.

Also, ties with unrelated firms will grow because new forms of inter-firm co-operation will emerge along on grounds of technology or R&D or even marketing interests. Maintaining conducive economic policies for drawing foreign direct investments must be prioritised. Attracting trade and training activities will be important. Competing through relevant regulatory reforms to cope with such business developments will also be important. For instance, public administration services have to anticipate new demand and needs of the new forms of businesses. The old cliché of reducing red tape is insufficient because competing host economies are pro-actively becoming business friendly and problem solvers. Malaysia surely cannot be left behind as a problem giver as far as government services are concerned.

As Asian economies recover from the crisis to face a rapidly globalising economy, the dynamics of economic development right within Asia will force ASEAN to work seriously towards making AFTA and AIA a real success. Besides the need to strengthen the financial system and the role of the capital market, ASEAN will need to face competition from the changes in the labour market within Asia. Apart from the ready pool of labour from Indonesia within AFTA, the abundant supply of labour from China within APEC as well as from India will impact on trade and investment within the Asia Pacific region. With both the China and Indian economies on strong growth paths, Malaysia will experience effects from the wider Asian region that were not serious threats before. However, with gradually rising income levels in both these Asian economies, ASEAN will also be able to benefit from their development. For instance, Proton is already seriously considering possibilities of penetrating the Indian market whose burgeoning middle class may be a target market.

Steps to correct the technological deficiencies in the economy must be taken seriously so that strategic alliances on various grounds and logic can be promoted. While technical training and technology transfer clauses have long been given attention, faster and more effective approaches must be sought to meet the skilled manpower needs of businesses, especially those in technology driven IT and electronics industries. As with other developing countries, Malaysia has been attempting to draw highly skilled and experienced professionals home. However, obstacles continue to remain for real repatriation of such Malaysians, despite willingness of some to return. For a highly globalised post-crisis environment, political will is needed to overcome reasons that may be economic liabilities for the nation as a whole.

5.3 Implications for the Malaysian Government

The Malaysian government has to recognise the new threats and hardships while exploiting new opportunities and benefits for the nation as the role of Malaysia alters for FDIs and for traders. Already, foreign businesses that landed in Malaysia in the 1990s, such as in electronics, have been increasingly motivated by factors that are different from those in the earlier periods. Before, Malaysia was an important import market for foreign manufactured consumption goods in the sixties. Subsequent local production as a result of the import substitution policy in the 1970s had paved the way for Malaysia as an exporter of those goods in the 1980s. Since early 1990s, Malaysia has been gaining momentum as a regional and sub-regional trader by serving as double-linkage (i.e. forward and backward) gateway to the east Asian and southeast Asian markets. For instance, with global effects on consumer preferences such as uniformity of taste for consumer goods, more cross borders transactions will take place, when tariffs decline with AFTA, APEC and WTO implementation.

Malaysia is increasingly seen as a useful bridge between the less developed economies in the region like Cambodia and Myanmar and the more advanced NIEs of East Asia, for consumer goods as well as industrial materials and components. With the full enforcement of AFTA in 2003, when tariffs will be reduced to between 0 to 5 per cent for most goods traded within the region, the role of Malaysia as a regional focal point for regional and global markets is expected to be further enhanced. The enlargement of the scope of economic activities, including for investment and trade, will give rise to positive business effects, domestic production effects and market effects for Malaysian industries. Positive income effects will also be seen in the economy if macro-economic management is carefully and properly executed, with adequately clear and transparent policy directions and political stability.

The government has to accept that the effectiveness of its future policy prescriptions will be eroded by the porosity of borders due to advancements in information technology that has given rise to new forms of doing business, either among businesses or with final consumers. Currently, e-commerce is the foremost area of such developments. Post-crisis improvements in economic management are expected, particularly in terms of public accountability. Corruption–free processes with new guidelines and codes of conduct for internationally accepted standards of corporate governance will become the norm. Efficiency must be sought through raising productivity on the one hand and cutting costs, including transaction costs on the other. Reduction or elimination of economic rent within the Malaysian economy as the middle-class grows to include a substantial proportion of the population should be stressed. This is possible as income and wealth distribution attains a reasonable spread within the economy. It is envisaged that with the bitter experiences of the crisis still fresh in mind, ASEAN governments will try to put their house in order for the all important reason of rebuilding confidence among investors both among MNCs and locals alike, as well as among consumers.

While trade and investment between ASEAN and other regions will shift because of AFTA, APEC and WTO implementation, Malaysia needs to take meaningful global-oriented positions along with its ASEAN partners, as well with other like-minded economies, at relevant forums so as to ensure its viability in the global economy. There is also the need to enhance the nation's international credibility in various ways. Among the pertinent issues are the manner the government prepares the nation at different levels for the impact of globalization, for coping with the movements and swings to suit the mood of global phenomena, for competing through relevant reforms to ensure a conducive "good-feel" investment and trade environment, for seeking acceptable ways of harnessing the immense corporate power vested in the hands of mega pan-global corporations so that some discipline may be exercised to benefit the nation. Greater effort is needed to catch up with time lost due to the interference of the Asian crisis. Malaysia should avoid shirking from earlier commitments, such as the two-year extension from AFTA's 2003 deadline for auto, especially when the economy is on the path to recovery.

Some degree of confidence has returned after the Asian crisis as borne by recent economic indicators. The interruptions of the depressed period appear are beginning to fade although full recovery will require more time. Economic wounds are expected to take longer to heal and to recover fully. The process of liberalisation is resuming in selected industries such as in telcos, in education and in retail distribution. Reforms have also taken place especially in the worst affected activities. The nation will need to take heed of encroaching international standards, many of which Malaysia and other globally oriented economies will have little option but to adopt.

The financial system, particularly in the banking and securities industries, have undergone a series of improvements after the crisis to unsure a stronger and competitive system to support the real economy. While a period of consolidation and adjustment is needed, active steps must be taken to cater for new modes of business transaction, especially through electronic channels. Regulations though needed, will to some extent be frustrated by the loopholes created by telecommunication and information advancements. New paradigms for regulatory intervention must be sought for ethical and consumer protection reasons so as to achieve the highest level of confidence in the financial system and the underlying economy. Numerous proposals for risk reduction and system viability are being studied. It is becoming clear that in Asia, a multi-country approach is needed to provide sufficient weight and strength to avert future crisis. Apart from asset pooling such as through currency swap arrangements and information sharing for early warning, strong political will and real co-operation are badly needed for Malaysia and its ASEAN partners to ride through the roughness of any future global upheaval.

6 Conclusions

Globalization will bring new opportunities of a growing global economy as well as challenges and threat to businesses and to the Malaysian economy, because the scope and intensity of competition will alter significantly based on easier market access. In the case of the electronics and auto industries in Malaysia, a world-wide response is to merge with or to acquire competitors, suppliers and even distributors depending on the strategic logic of each case. Some of these exercises that have already taken place have also affected affiliates located in Malaysia or in the ASEAN region. The anticipated border changes after 2003 with AFTA implementation may be affecting the auto industry in particular. With these strategic developments, firms are expected to have operational strategies that are different from those before widespread globalization. Creative innovations often based on new technologies of communication are expected to help reduce costs and keep efficient firms and affiliates in business. Co-operative strategies and ties will continue to take place between firms and among affiliates of the same corporate group. Besides, co-operation with competitors especially in R&D are also expected to increase significantly for cost advantages.

Malaysian firms should also seek opportunities for technological gains through strategic alliances with foreign investors with more advanced MNCs. With the new global economic order, the issue of relative equity share should become less important while that of real hands-on business operational management and control by Malaysians themselves – together with foreign partners – assumes greater importance. Opportunities from AFTA within ASEAN or elsewhere should be grasped. This can be achieved if Malaysia unites with ASEAN partners and like-minded nations to actively work towards common demands. As a first step, developing countries in Asia Pacific should develop a strongly-backed common agenda to address the unevenness of economic positions due to different levels of economic strength, development, market power, competitiveness and technology. Further concessions other than time extensions should be spelt out and sought when entering into any new round of international economic negotiation. Also, irrelevant issues other than those under negotiation should not be allowed to distract the attention of developing countries (e.g., human rights), while several basic concepts should be reviewed (e.g., reciprocity and level of economic development).

Again, the Asian economic crisis and progressive liberalization of financial markets have led to reforms in the financial sectors. Policy makers in Malaysia have been compelled to review policies that are relevant and to adopt policies and economic strategies that are needed to cope with the changes especially in the banking sub-sector. Further, the adjustments in government policies both from the host government as well as from government elsewhere will be relevant in the globalized environment, because policy shifts that arise from any part of the highly interconnected global economy will have bearings on businesses irrespective of the location of their operation. It is therefore important to keep alert of such changes and even to anticipate changes.

The CEPT scheme of AFTA that has been made known several years ago should be familiar to businesses by now. Many are already adjusting in anticipation. However, there are others, especially among the smaller businesses, that will not be ready. The disparity in productivity between the modern firms and traditional ones in Malaysia and the rest of ASEAN will become even bigger as we move past 2003. But the instabilities that will be brought by the changes may be reduced if firms keep themselves in the know and ensure that communication channels remain open with others that are relevant. Besides, suppliers and buyers, it is important that competitors within the trade should become dialogue partners as much as regulators from the public sector. Such openness will tell apart winners from losers as regionalism dovetails into the globalization process.

References

Malaysian Institute of Economic Research (1996) *Post–IMP Study: Interim Main, Report, Vol.II: Industry Studies: Transportation Equipment Industry Group*, MIER & DRI/ McGraw–Hill.

Malaysia (1998) *National Economic Recovery Plan*. Kuala Lumpur: Economic Planning Unit, Prime Minister's Department.

MIDA (1993) *Industry Brief: Electrical and Electronics Industries in Malaysia: Status, Prospects and Opportuniti*, Kuala Lumpur: MIDA

MIDA (1998*) The Automotive Industry in Malaysia.* Kuala Lumpur: MIDA

Ministry of International Trade and Industry (1995) *MITI Report 1994/95*, Kuala Lumpur: MITI.

Sieh Lee Mei Ling and Yew Siew Yong (1997) Malaysia: Electronics, autos and the trade–investment nexus, In Wendy Dobson and Chia Siow Yue (eds.), *Multinationals and East Asian Integration.* Ottawa and Singapore: IDRC and ISEAS, pp.131–152.

Sieh Lee Mei Ling (1998) Malaysia's Electronics Industry. In *The Effects of Liberalisation in Asia's Textiles, Clothing and Electronics Industries: Studies in APEC Liberalisation,* Canberra: Australian Department of Foreign Affairs and Trade.

Sieh Lee Mei Ling (2000) *Taking on the World: Globalization Strategies in Malaysia,* Kuala Lumpur: McGraw–Hill.

5 Globalization of Electronics Production Networks and the Emerging Roles and Strategies of Singapore Contract Manufacturers

Poh-Kam Wong
National University of Singapore

1 Introduction

Over the last two decades, non-Japan East Asia has emerged as a major production platform for the global electronics industry.Driven by global competition, electronics multinational corporations (MNCs) from advanced countries have increasingly extended their supplier bases and production networks to the various countries in East Asia. In 1998, the four Asian NIEs (Hong Kong, Taiwan, Korea and Singapore), the four ASEAN countries (Malaysia, Thailand, Philippines and Indonesia) and China together are estimated to have already accounted for over one-fifth of global electronics production (Elsevier, 1999), rising from less than 6% in 1985 and about 12.5% in 1990 (Table 5–1). It is also interesting to note that non-Japan East Asian electronics production had exceeded the total Japanese electronics production output for the first time in 1998, rising from less than one-third in 1985 and still less than half in 1990. Although this has happened partly to falling production within Japan itself – Japanese electronics production peaked in 1995 and declined thereafter – it is nonetheless remarkable that so much of electronics production has migrated to non-Japan East Asia within such a short period.

The growing importance of non-Japan East Asia is even more telling in the sub-sector of manufacturing of computer-related products. From about 8% in 1988, the estimated share of East Asia in computer equipment production had ballooned to 25% one decade later (Table 5–2). From slightly over one-quarter of Japan's computer equipment output in 1988, non-Japan East Asia's computer output approached one and a half times that of Japan a decade later.

While the expansion of manufacturing operations by global Original Equipment Manufacturers (OEMs) from the US, Japan and Europe accounted for the bulk of this rapid ascendancy of non-Japan East Asia as production platforms, the emergence of large indigenous OEM firms from the four Asian NIEs, particularly

Table 5–1. Electronics Production in Selected Asian Countries, 1985–1998

Country	1985	1986	1987	1988	1989	1990	1991	1992	1993	1994	1995	1996	1997	1998
	US$ million													
Japan	89,390	124,445	149,981	187,422	185,094	184,490	207,402	196,047	212,044	234,129	267,461	244,953	234,661	196,180
Total Asian NIEs	20,561	26,647	38,123	50,290	56,537	60,771	66,274	72,744	82,423	100,235	127,966	132,602	137,933	118,917
Singapore	4,458	5,315	7,543	10,653	12,518	14,992	16,709	20,245	23,556	31,599	39,783	43,597	43,554	37,850
Total ASEAN-4	4,120	5,224	6,800	8,853	11,579	14,714	18,284	23,193	29,243	38,750	49,334	55,507	58,063	54,490
China	na	na	7,588	10,436	11,801	12,039	13,663	15,954	17,797	23,456	28,290	33,370	na	49,268
Total NJEA [1]	24,681	31,871	52,511	69,579	79,917	87,524	98,221	111,891	129,463	162,441	205,590	221,479	195,996	222,675
World Total	481,708	518,961	559,095	644,624	658,038	699,098	738,791	748,186	778,570	877,863	1,039,293	1,059,496	1,051,191	1,085,613
	Percentage													
NJEA share of world production	5.1	6.1	9.4	10.8	12.1	12.5	13.3	15.0	16.6	18.5	19.8	20.9	18.6	20.5

Note: World figures for 1985 and 1986 are estimated using the CAGR for 1987–1990.

World figures for 1997 & 1998 and China figures for 1998 are forecasts at 1996 constant values and exchange rates.

[1] Non-Japan East Asia. Excludes China in 1985, 1986 and 1997

Source: Yearbook of World Electronics Data 1988–1998 & 2000, Elsevier

Table 5–2. Composition of Electronics Production in Selected Asian Countries, 1988 & 1998

	Japan	Singapore	NJEA [a]	World	Japan	Singapore	NJEA [a]	World
US$ million		1988				1998		
EDP	52031	4254	13696	167799	55966	22335	80608	324803
Office Equipment	5578	239	1701	17639	5103	342	3375	17313
Control and Instrument Electronics	6742	194	861	54347	7303	431	2240	83981
Medical and Industrial Electronics	5008	41	599	20700	5584	214	2066	37020
Radio communications (incl mobiles) & radar	8875	104	2549	79968	16868	958	10743	129587
Telecommunications	14727	245	4191	64237	16524	364	10324	107173
Consumer Electronics	35297	1789	19191	79454	16791	1914	30022	76685
Components	59164	3787	26791	160480	72040	11292	83296	311221
Total	189410	12641	75543	646612	196180	37850	222674	1087783
	Japan	Singapore	NJEA [a]	World	Japan	Singapore	NJEA [a]	World
Percentage of world share		1988				1998		
EDP	31.0	2.5	8.2	100.0	17.2	6.9	24.8	100.0
Office Equipment	31.6	1.4	9.6	100.0	29.5	2.0	19.5	100.0
Control and Instrument Electronics	12.4	0.4	1.6	100.0	8.7	0.5	2.7	100.0
Medical and Industrial Electronics	24.2	0.2	2.9	100.0	15.1	0.6	5.6	100.0
Radio communications (incl mobiles) &	11.1	0.1	3.2	100.0	13.0	0.7	8.3	100.0
Telecommunications	22.9	0.4	6.5	100.0	15.4	0.3	9.6	100.0
Consumer Electronics	44.4	2.3	24.2	100.0	21.9	2.5	39.1	100.0
Components	36.9	2.4	16.7	100.0	23.1	3.6	26.8	100.0
Total	29.3	2.0	11.7	100.0	18.0	3.5	20.5	100.0

Note: Radio communications (including mobiles) & radar was previously classified as communications & military electronics and then communications & radar

World and China 1998 figures are forecasts at 1996 constant values and exchange rates

[a] Non-Japan East Asia

Source: Yearbook of World Electronics Data 1988–1998 & 2000, Elsevier

the large Korean chaebols like Samsung and LG group and Taiwanese multinational firms like Acer and Tatung, has also been increasingly important over the last decade.

However, over the last several years, another major development appears to have emerged which is likely to herald important changes in the electronics production landscape of the world in general and East Asia in particular – the rise of global Contract Manufacturers (CM) that specialize in manufacturing electronics products solely for others, rather than under their own brands. While the subcontracting of manufacturing operations to others has been a practice by large OEMs for a long time, and East Asia indeed has been a major scene for such sub-contract manufacturing activities, the scale and scope of such manufacturing outsourcing has changed tremendously over the last ten years, resulting in dramatic transformation of the industrial structure for contract manufacturing. Whereas subcontract manufacturing tended to be undertaken by mostly small companies, often located in single countries, making either selected components or assemblying mainly matured, low-end products in the past, the last decade has witnessed the rapid ascendancy of large, global players with multiple manufacturing plants world wide. Moreover, these global contract manufacturers are taking on increasingly high-end, leading edge products, and handle the complete range of supply chain management services from procurement to delivery to end customers, with their OEM customers not having to "touch a single thing" in the process.

This development of global contract manufacturers (CMs) poses a significant challenge to both Japan and East Asia, not least because the global CM leaders in the world today are American, not Japanese or East Asian. The only exception is in the case of specialized semiconductor wafer fabrication ("pure foundries") where Taiwanese players like TSMC and UMC have become dominant. Moreover, while East Asia has been an important location for manufacturing plants by such global CMs,their operations are not confined to East Asia, but are spreading rapidly to many parts of the world, including back to the US itself.

In this paper, I examine the emergence of this global contract manufacturing phenomenon and its likely implications for Japan and East Asia by focusing on how one of the four East Asian NIEs – Singapore – has responded to the opportunities and threats posed by the rise of global contract manufacturing. The experience of Singapore is instructive, not least because Singapore has been one of the most important location in the world for advanced electronics manufacturing operations by both OEMs and CMs (Wong 2001a), particularly in computer-related equipment. In addition, Singapore has witnessed the growth of several indigenous CMs in recent years. While still behind the global leaders in terms of size and global reach, these firms have nonetheless grown rapidly and appeared to have competed well against the bigger players so far. By studying the co-evolution of both global CMs and indigenous CMs in Singapore, I therefore hope to draw lessons not only on how CMs would impact on East Asia as a platform for electronics production, but also on whether and how indigenous firms can compete in this industry.

This chapter is organized as follows. In Section 2, I briefly review the rise of global contract manufacturing industry as a phenomenon, its key drivers, and the leading players that dominate the industry today. Section 3 provides a brief overview of the changing role of Singapore as a CM hub, the emergence of key indigenous CM firms, their competitive performance, and in what ways their performance have been shaped by the strategies they have adopted. Section 4 concludes by drawing implications for East Asia and Japan from the experience of Singapore.

2 The Rise of the Global Contract Manufacturing Industry

The contract manufacturing (CM) industry, also known as the electronic manufacturing services (EMS) industry, provides manufacturing services to original equipment manufacturers (OEMs). Contract manufacturers take the detailed design specifications of a product from their customers and convert them to a finished product. The products involved can range from components to finished products.

The contract manufacturing industry had its beginnings over 25 years ago, when IBM asked SCI Systems, then a contractor for the US National Aeronautical and Space Administration, to produce computer parts on their behalf. The industry grew as other OEMs found that they could reduce costs by outsourcing their production needs to these manufacturing specialists (Lachica 1995).

CM can range enormously in terms of degree of sophistication. Based on discussion with industry participants, three useful dimensions of the degree of sophistication of CM can be identified. The first pertains to the scope of value chain activities or services that the CM can undertake. The lowest level is that of subcontract operations under ***consignment***, whereby the customers provide the CM with the direct materials; the CM perform the needed assembly operations and deliver the finished products back to the OEM customers. Some CMs handle only the subassembly of a key module rather than the entire end product itself. A higher level is that of ***turnkey*** operations, whereby the CM handles both the procurement of input materials as well as the assembly operations. The most sophisticated level is that of ***turnkey + ship/drop***, whereby the CM not only handles the inbound material sourcing and assembly operations, but also directly delivers the finished products to the end customers based on instruction by their OEM customers.

A second dimension of CM sophistication pertains to the level of process technological capabilities that it can undertake. For example, CMs may vary in terms of their printed circuit board assembly capabilities: some can do high speed surface mount on multi-layer circuit boards, while others can only handle through-hole operations. Some products require investments in chip-on-board (COB), flip-chip or Ball–Grid Array (BGA) processes, etc.

A third dimension of CM sophistication is the extent to which the CM can provide ***design*** services to the OEMs. CMs who are *Original Design Manufacturers* (ODM) are able to take product features/performance requirements from an OEM and churn out the design specifications themselves that meet those requirements, before proceeding to manufacture them based on their own designs. An even more sophisticated version of ODM is the so-called *Original Idea Manufacturing* (OIM), a CM that comes up with the original product idea in the first place and develops the detailed product design specification for it. It then offers the product idea for adoption by an OEM, who will put its brand label on it and to market it as if it the OEM's own product. The CM gains from the manufacturing contract from the OEM as well as possible design royalties, while the latter undertakes the cost and risk of marketing the products to end user markets.

Due to the diversity of CM players as measured in terms of the above dimensions, it is difficult to define the size and value added intensities of the CM industry with any degree of accuracy. Some firms manufacture their own products (i.e. they are OEMs themselves) as well as perform CM for others, e.g. Acer from Taiwan manufacture their own Acer-brand PCs as well as manufacture some Japanese – and American – brand PCs on a turnkey, ODM basis. Some CMs in turn outsource part of their operations to other subcontract manufacturers.

The above definitional problems notwithstanding, it is clear that CM as an industry has grown enormously over the last ten years. Moreover, this rapid growth is marked by the rapid rise of a number of independent, specialist CM that has reached the most advanced level on all three dimensions of sophistication identified above.

2.1 Rapid Growth of CM

Focusing primarily on independent players who are not OEMs themselves, the global contract manufacturing (CM) industry is estimated to have achieved remarkable growth in recent years, with output increasing from $59.3 billion in 1996 to a projected $178.0 billion in 2001 (Table 5–3). This represents a compound annual growth rate of 25%, more than three times higher than the 7% annual growth rate for global electronics production as a whole. The forecast compound annual growth rate of demand for CM for 1996 to 2001 for the US and Canada is particularly high, at 31%, while the markets in Western Europe and non-Japan Asia are also expected to undergo significant growth at 23% and 21% respectively. Japan, however, is expected to experience the lowest demand growth of 13% per annum.

The rapid growth in CM sales is largely attributed to increased outsourcing of supply chain activities from OEMs to contract manufacturers in PCBs and system subassemblies, particularly in the major electronics markets of North America, Asian and Europe. This is particularly true of the computers, peripherals and

Table 5–3. Worldwide contract manufacturing demand by region (US$ billion)

	*Asia**	*Japan*	*W. Europe*	*US & Canada*	*Rest of World*	*Total*
1996	6.4	13.0	10.5	27.2	2.2	59.3
2001 (projected)	16.5	24.0	29.8	104.2	3.5	178.0
CAGR	21%	13%	23%	31%	10%	25%

* Excluding Japan

Source: Roberts (1998)

telecommunications industries, and this trend is expected to continue for the next 10–15 years, until at least 60% of electronics manufacturing is outsourced (Electronic Business Asia 1999, Siew 1998). A similar rapid trend of increasing outsourcing to "pure foundries" has also been observed in the case of semiconductor manufacturing (Leachman, 2000).

2.2 Drivers for Increasing Outsourcing from OEMs to CMs

Factors both within the CM industry and within the OEMs themselves have created an environment where OEMs need to outsource a substantial proportion of their activities in order to save money and retain their market share (Roberts 1998).

First and foremost, OEMs are facing increasingly intense competitive pressure in the electronics industry. Electronics goods' life-cycles have shortened to less than two years whilst electronic product consumption has increased, especially in the personal computer, computer peripheral, disk drive, telecommunications and medical equipment markets. Time-to-market, time-to-volume and time-to-quality requirements have become more stringent and margins have shrunk (Wilson 1999, Siew 1998). Consequently, OEMs must now focus their energies on their core competencies such as R&D, product innovation, marketing and sales. Only by doing this will they be able to stay abreast of new technologies and develop and market new products in tandem with – or preferably ahead of – their competitors. Non-core activities are thus divested, including manufacturing, warehousing, logistics and financing (Roberts 1998, Electronic Business Asia 1999).

Large, independent CMs are the natural choice for taking over these outsourced activities. Unlike OEMs, large CMs have become experienced in quickly ramping up production, re-training staff and reconfiguring assembly lines and equipment, and so can manufacture with a lower resource cost. Furthermore, some of the leading CMs have expanded their services from printed circuit board assembly and subassembly to complete product assembly, logistics management, distribution, repair and warranty services. By using their services, OEMs can bring cheaper products to the markets in a shorter amount of time.

2.3 Growing Concentration of CM Industry

The CM Industry has become increasingly concentrated in recent years. As can be seen from Table 5–4, the four largest CMs in the world as of 1999 – Solectron, SCI Systems, Celestica and Jabil Circuit – had combined annual sales of US$22.4 billion, or over 30% of the $73 billion global EMS market in 1999 (Manufacturing Market Insider 2000). All four CMs have manufacturing plants located in US, Europe, Asia and Latin America. They have also developed regional centers for design, procurement and other value-added services.

Several economic factors have contributed to the growing concentration of CM services in the hands of such large, global players in recent years.

2.3.1 Economies of Scale in Purchasing

As CMs move from consignment manufacturing to turnkey production, they need to source for their own components. Since they purchase components in bulk, they can negotiate for discounts that individual OEMs or small CMs cannot. This

Table 5–4. Size & Performance of Leading Contract Manufacturers in the World, 1999

Company	*Solectron*	*SCI Systems*	*Celestica*	*Jabil Circuit*	*Total*
	US $ million				
Net revenue/sales [a]	8,391.4	6,710.8	5,297.2	2,000.3	22,399.7
	Percentage				
Share of 1999 global market	11.5	9.2	7.3	2.7	30.7
Gross margin	9.3	na	7.2	11.4	
ROS	3.5	2.1	1.3	4.6	
ROA	6.1	5.9	2.6	9.9	
CAGR of sales 1995–1999	42.0	25.9	62.5	37.5	
No. of manufacturing plants worldwide	44	34	27	15	
Other facilities [b]	13	na	6	6	
Number of employees	37,900	25,200	>23,000	18,000	
Year established	1977	1961	na	1966	

[a] Figure for Celestica is for revenue rather than net revenue

[b] Design, industry, warehousing, procurement offices, repair services, etc.

Source: Compiled from companies' 1999 annual reports, press release of Manufacturing Market Insider's Top 50 EMS companies

results in a significant cost saving, as components comprise 70%–85% of the product's cost (Siew 1998). Large CMs also have the bargaining power to shift part of the component costs to their suppliers, e.g. by forcing them to hold inventory.

2.3.2 Risk Diversification

CMs have many different customers, allowing them to maximize the use of factories which are costly to maintain[1]. It also reduces the impact of a decrease in demand from any individual customer. Relative to OEMs then, CMs have a lower risk of having to retrench staff or being left with excessive or outdated stock when demand falls.

2.3.3 Capital Requirements for Investing in the Latest Technologies

CMs keep themselves informed of new assembly and packaging technologies such as chip-on-board (COB), flip-chip (FC), micro-ball grid array (mBGA) and multichip modules (MCM). Incorporating these technologies allows them to produce goods cheaper and more efficiently than OEMs who are not manufacturing specialists, and so would generally not find it economical to keep informed of and invest in these technologies. In addition, the high capital costs of investing in the latest technologies for the most advanced products of their customers, while continuing to maintain a portfolio of process technologies required by key customers for their existing products, raise the economies of scale for efficient operations.

2.3.4 Fast Ramp up, Global Deployment Requirement of OEM Customers

As OEMs face increasingly short product life cycles, they increasingly prefer their CMs to be able to ramp up production fast, and to be able to handle simultaneous product launch world wide. Rather than having to deal with multiple manufacturers in different locations, the OEM customers therefore increasingly favour large CMs with large reserves of manufacturing capacity that are globally distributed.

[1] For example, SMT lines cost at least US$2 million each

2.4 Emerging Practices of Leading Global CMs

2.4.1 Widening of Range of Services

Large CMs now provide a wider range of services for their OEM customers. Traditionally, they conducted manufacturing services only, undertaking printed circuit board assembly on a consignment or turnkey basis. They have now expanded their services to incorporate the entire supply chain (Wilson 1999, Roberts 1998). This includes final product assembly (box-build), and order fulfilment and distribution, where the products are shipped to retailers and wholesalers. They also conduct warranty and testing services and do following up service and repair work on behalf of the OEMs.

CMs are also involved in the pre-manufacturing stage, in the design the product. Initially this was mainly in terms of the product's "manufacturability" since CMs are in a better position to advise on how to design a product in order to minimize its production cost and time. This is particularly true when the OEM is unfamiliar with manufacturing and manufacturing technology. However, leading CMs are now involved in ODM doing detailed product design and some have even become OIM.

2.4.2 Close Relationship with OEMs

The increasing involvement of CMs in a widening range of services is forcing CMs and OEMs to work together closely, a radical departure from the distant interactions they used to have. Tom Sansone, president of Jabil Circuit, notes that the two parties should ideally "behave as a single company – truly co-operative and integrated with no redundant resources or staffing on either side." This requires a great deal of trust on both sides. Sensitive information is shared as contract manufacturers are brought in to join OEM design sessions and their information systems are linked (Roberts 1998).

Since large OEMs generally have more than one CM, rival CMs sometimes also have to work together closely. As such they also need to be able to trust each other, sharing information they would not normally disclose to a competitor. One factor which facilitates this process is that OEMs rarely do anything to disrupt these relationshipsbetween the contract manufacturers.

2.4.3 Globalizing Scale of Operations

Manufacturing is now conducted closer to the end-markets, reducing shipping time and logistics costs. Thus Mexico is increasingly used as a manufacturing hub for the North American markets, and Eastern Europe for the European markets. China is expected to be the focal point of production for the Asian markets, although it is currently used mainly for low-cost, labour-intensive manufacturing.

However, even as manufacturing requirements become more globalized, OEMs are reducing the number of CMs they deal with. Consequently, a successful CM must have sufficient resources to sustain manufacturing operations in each region, particularly near the OEMs' major markets of North America, Asia and Europe.

Another benefit of having global manufacturing operations is that the CM can take advantage of the strengths of manufacturing in each region. For example, NatSteel Electronics has plants in Singapore, Malaysia, Indonesia, Thailand, China, San Jose, Mexico and Hungary. Low-cost areas such as China are used mainly when the products are mature, and so low-cost, high-volume manufacturing is required (Wilson 1999, Siew 1998). High-cost areas, such as Singapore are used for prototyping and higher value-added activities.

2.4.4 Investment in Supply Chain Management and Internet Technologies

To be able to cope with fast ramping up and ramping down, and to manage widely dispersed manufacturing plants and warehouses world wide, the leading global CMs need to invest heavily in supply chain management (SCM) and enterprise resource planning (ERP). Production, inventory, human resources, logistics, distribution, suppliers and distributors must all be monitored to optimize resource allocation. In addition, OEM customers are increasingly requesting instant access to information about their products' status (Siew 1998). Consequently, CMs are now having to invest in exploiting the internet to facilitate both internal operational coordination as well as information sharing with external parties.

2.4.5 Growth Strategies

CMs have been expanding through various means. One strategy is to merge with other CMs, or to acquire other companies. In some cases the CM buys their OEM customers' factories, as was the case when Flextronics International, Solectron Corp and SCI acquired Ericsson's factories in 1997, whilst NatSteel acquired some of Apple's manufacturing operations. Nokia and Philips have also sold their manufacturing facilities to CMs (Harbert 1998, Siew 1998). The advantage of buying plants from OEMs is the ready pool of customers' orders that comes with the plant. By contrast, other CMs such as Jabil Circuit prefer to build its own plants, reasoning that that it is easier to build a plant to its unique requirements than to convert one (Roberts 1998).

However, one problem CMs face in expansion is hiring suitable employees, particularly design engineers and program managers. Some companies such as Flextronics have even had to turn down orders from customers because of their shortage of engineers (Roberts 1998).

2.5 Implications for Newer, Smaller Entrants into the CM Industry

The growing concentration trends in the CM industry suggests that it is increasingly difficult for small and medium-sized contract manufacturers to survive[2]. Most large OEMs are reluctant to trust their business to small CMs without an established record. This is because of the diverse range of activities required, the resources needed to accomplish them and the enormous cost to the OEMs if the CM fails. Even if the CM does not fail, the cost of switching from one CM to another is very high, given the time-to-market pressures faced by the OEMs. This is especially true if the OEM's current CM is undertaking the entire range of product design, logistics and distribution activities on their behalf in addition to manufacturing.

New and small contract manufacturers are also likely to find it more difficult to obtain funds for expansion. This lack of working capital hinders them from establishing themselves more securely in the CM industry, for they will be unable to accomplish the rapid ramp up necessary as OEMs become more confident of them and increase their orders (Wilson 1999).

The clear implication is that newer entrants into the CM industry will have to either be prepared to grow aggressively, or to choose a specialization strategy by focusing on certain special product niches in the market where they can hope to differentiate through superior process capabilities.

Another strategy is for them to concentrate on working with new emerging OEMs which are still small in size but which may have the potential to grow into giants in the future. As the latter grows, the CM's hope is to keep its loyalty and to ride on its back. Indeed, one reason Solectron was able to grow to become the giant it is today is because of its early bet on Cisco as a customer. A variant of this strategy is to target those OEMs which were previously vertically integrated but are now seeking to outsource their manufacturing operations for the first time and may prefer newer CMs than those already working closely with their competitors.

Lastly, it is possible that some of the large CM incumbents may run the risk of growing too big and becoming excessively vertically integrated, thus ending up in the same situation as the OEMs (Wilson 1999). This may cause some of the large OEMs to re-consider the virtue of having some smaller CMs that are more flexible and provide better service.

3 The Changing Contract Manufacturing Role of Singapore

By adopting a strategy of attracting and leveraging foreign manufacturing MNCs, Singapore has benefited significantly from FDI by foreign firms in general and in

[2] Chester Lin, CEO of Natsteel Electronics, notes that it is difficult for a contract manufacturer to survive if it earns less than $1 billion (Wilson 1999).

the electronics industry in particular (Wong 2001a). Between 1985 and 1997, Singapore's production of electronics rose from less than US$4.5 billion to US$43.6 billion, or nearly a ten-fold increase in 12 years. Singapore's share of world production thus increased from 1.5% in 1985 to over 4% in 1997. Although Singapore's electronics output declined from 1997–98 as a result of cyclical downturn of the global electronics industry as well as some negative effects of the Asian financial crisis, it has since recovered strongly in 1999, and sustained through 2000.

While a major bulk of Singapore's electronics industry growth was driven by foreign MNCs' FDI accounted for around 85% of equity investment in electronics industry in the 1990s (Wong 2001a,b), an important consequence of this is the early emergence of Singapore as a recognized center for sophisticated manufacturing operations by global OEMs. To support such lead manufacturing plants, the Singapore government has developed among the best manufacturing infrastructures in the world – efficient sea-port and airport, excellent telecommunications and financial services, and a strong logistics and procurement services industry. The large number of world class manufacturing plants in Singapore has also created a sizable pool of trained manufacturing manpower from managers and senior process engineers to technicians and skilled operators. Moreover, a large base of supporting industries for the electronics industry in the form of various precision engineering firms such as metal stamping, electroplating, plastic injection molding, tools and fixtures making, etc. has also been spawned. This was particularly well-documented in the case of the magnetic hard disk drive (HDD) industry which has stimulated the development of an extensive range of supporting industries, both local and foreign, making Singaporethe largest HDD assembly hub in the world (Wong 1997,1999a).

It is in this context that Singapore was able to develop a fairly sizable contract manufacturing industry by the late 1980s, even before the rapid growth and concentration of the global CM industry was set in motion in the 1990s.

While there are no reliable data on contract manufacturing in Singapore, its overall size can be approximated by the printed circuit boards assembly (PCBA) industry group (classified as group 31195 under the Singapore Industrial Classification (SSIC) 1996) as covered by the Annual Report of Census of Production by the Economic Development Board of Singapore. As can be seen from Table 5–5, the PCBa industry output rose rapidly from less than S$780 million in 1986 to about S$3.3 billion in 1992. The industry output subsequently declined to less than S$3 billion for the next 3 years, but started to rise again and achieved almost S$4 billion in 1998. These figures probably underestimate the size of CM output, since some firms with some OEM products of their own may also provide CM services, and many firms classified as in the precision engineering industries probably engage in some amount of CM-related services as well.

Table 5–5. Size & Growth Trend of PCBA Industry (SSIC 31195) in Singapore, 1986–1998

Year	*Number of Establ't N.*	*Output S$mn*	*Number Employed L*	*Value Added* [a] *S$mn*	*Wages S$mn*	*Fixed Asset (K) S$mn*	*Total Sales S$mn*	*Export S$mn*	*Input S$mn*	*Other Expend S$mn*	*Estimated profit S$mn*	*Return on sales %*	*Return on assets %*
1986	10	777.77	2989	281.63	34.20	113.15	777.39	769.07	485.83	40.74	217.00	27.91	191.78
1987	19	905.26	3445	327.59	39.50	162.55	906.39	862.90	570.00	38.58	257.17	28.37	158.21
1988	45	2096.09	12300	755.37	147.05	225.63	2086.70	1658.29	1322.42	126.15	500.47	23.98	221.81
1989	54	2518.92	13544	807.71	175.42	319.66	2516.73	1888.95	1700.58	134.99	507.94	20.18	158.90
1990	62	2909.03	13508	912.66	212.17	374.17	2910.08	1879.63	1979.37	182.30	535.20	18.39	143.04
1991	66	2838.10	14064	734.03	231.79	387.24	2842.05	1887.86	1927.01	177.06	502.25	17.67	129.70
1992	67	3251.1	14052	728.27	249.29	379.88	3275.45	2271.05	2351.47	171.32	478.99	14.62	126.09
1993	62	2475.98	14077	515.97	256.63	337.13	2459.58	1398.81	1777.13	182.89	259.33	10.54	76.92
1994	59	2981.61	15088	573.79	294.58	362.58	2973.98	1690.56	2200.06	207.76	279.21	9.39	77.01
1995	68	2929.57	15637	505.52	325.98	405.66	2925.26	1230.57	2212.97	211.09	179.53	6.14	44.26
1996	67	3018.88	14137	532.79	322.46	381.96	3036.64	1486.87	2288.94	197.16	210.33	6.93	55.07
1997	65	3152.89	13382	532.04	318.63	377.82	3149.98	1355.08	2410.98	209.87	213.41	6.77	56.48
1998	62	3972.04	13030	600.21	343.85	378.02	3958.65	1668.62	3158.89	212.94	256.36	6.48	67.82
						Av. Growth % p.a.							
1986–98		14.6	13.1	6.5		10.6	14.5	6.7			1.4	-11.5	-8.3

Source: Report on the Census of Industrial Production (various years), Economic Development Board

Table 5-5. Size & Growth Trend of PCBA Industry (SSIC 31195) in Singapore, 1986-1998 (contd.)

Year	*Export/ Output %*	*Output/ Estab't S$mn*	*Labour/ Estab't*	*Val.Add/ Labour S$*	*Wages/ Labour S$*	*Val.Add/ Output %*	*Wages/ Val.Add %*	*Capital/ Labour S$K/L*	*Export/ Sales %*	*Growth of Output %*	*Growth of Val.Add %*
1986	98.88	77.78	299	94222	11443	36.2	12.1	37854	98.9	na	Base Yr
1987	95.32	47.65	181	95092	11467	36.2	12.1	47184	95.2	16.4	16.3
1988	79.11	46.58	273	61413	11955	36.0	19.5	18344	79.5	131.5	130.6
1989	74.99	46.65	251	59636	12952	32.1	21.7	23601	75.1	20.2	6.9
1990	64.61	46.92	218	67564	15707	31.4	23.2	27700	64.6	15.5	13.0
1991	66.52	43.00	213	52192	16481	25.9	31.6	27534	66.4	(2.4)	(19.6)
1992	69.86	48.52	210	51827	17740	22.4	34.2	27034	69.3	14.6	(0.8)
1993	56.50	39.94	227	36653	18230	20.8	49.7	23949	56.9	(23.8)	(29.2)
1994	56.70	50.54	256	38030	19524	19.2	51.3	24031	56.8	20.4	11.2
1995	42.01	43.08	230	32328	20847	17.3	64.5	25942	42.1	(1.7)	(11.9)
1996	49.25	45.06	211	37687	22809	17.6	60.5	27018	49.0	3.0	5.4
1997	42.98	48.51	206	39758	23810	16.9	59.9	28233	43.0	4.4	(0.1)
1998	42.01	64.07	210	46064	26389	15.1	57.3	29012	42.2	26.0	12.8

[a] Figures from 1986-1990 are for value added; thereafter figures are for net value added

Source: Report on the Census of Industrial Production (various years), Economic Development Board

The rapid rise of the CM industry from the mid-1980s to early 1990s was due to the emerging trend, even back then, of outsourcing of manufacturing activities, especially by computer and related OEMs. This can be regarding as the first phase of CM development in Singapore sparked by the arrival of early American CM pioneers like SCI as well as the birth of some local CM firms like Venture Manufacturing and Natsteel Electronics. These local CM firms were initially started by engineers and managers who have gained their experience from working in large OEM manufacturers in Singapore.

The subsequent decline in output of the CM industry in Singapore for the next several years was driven by rising labour cost and shortages, which forced many of these CMs to redistribute their more labor-intensive operations to lower cost locations in the region, particularly Malaysia. This can be regarded as the second, internationalization phase of Singapore's CM industry. During this period, all the leading foreign and local CMs in Singapore started operations outside of Singapore. While production in Singapore was scaled back in some cases, few if any completely shut down their operations in Singapore. Growing competition also resulted in rapidly eroding prices and declining margins in the CM industry in this period.

The third phase, starting in the late 1990s, is marked by a deepening and consolidation of the CM industry in Singapore. While internationalization continued, the key CM players in Singapore also invested in upgrading their Singapore operations to undertake advanced products assembly and to diversify into newer products such as telecommunication devices and information appliances. Some CM players also took over the factory operations of their customers (e.g. Omni Industries took over Apple's manufacturing plants). This, together with internaitonalization of production, resulted in declining share of export in total production output. Finally, mergers and acquisition began to occur in this period, the most dramatic case being the recent take-over of JIT (4th largest CM in Singapore at the time) and Li Xin (a plastics mold maker) by Flextronics in the second half of 2000. With these acquisitions (and other acquisitions overseas as well), Flextronics has now emerged as the third largest CM in the world.

Data compiled from reported revenues of the individual leading CM firms in Singapore lend further empirical support to the above analysis. As shown in Table 5–6, it suggests a higher rate of industry growth than the CIP data: From 1994 to 1998, the combined total sales of the 20 larger CM firms in Singapore (where data are available) rose up to S$8.74 billion. Since these firm level figures pertain to the total sales of these companies and hence include outputs from both their local as well as overseas plants, they suggest that overseas expansion of these CM firms in the 1990s has been faster than within Singapore. At the same time, they also suggest that the larger CM firms probably grew faster than the CM industry as a whole

4 Strategies and Performance of Singapore CMs

Despite the dominance of the global CM industry by large American firms, several Singapore-based CMs have been able to enter the industry over the years and established strong footholds. As can be seen from Table 5–6, there were more than a dozen Singapore CMs with annual sales exceeding S$100 million in 1998, with the five largest being Natsteel Electronics (S$2.48 billion), Flextronics (S$2.15 billion), Venture Manufacturing (S$731 million), JIT (S$580 million) and Omni Industries (S$415 million). The largest foreign CM operation in Singapore was SCI with sales of S$609 million. Although only Natsteel and Flextronics would rank among the top 10 CM in the world, the other three – Venture, JIT and Omni Ind would rank among the top 40 CMs in the world.

The importance of CMs in Singapore's local electronics industry can be appreciated if we examine the composition of the ten largest local electronics firms in Singapore in terms of sales: As many as eight of them are CMs, the exception being Creative Technologies (rank no. 3) and Chartered Semiconductor Manufacturing (CSM) (rank no. 5). Actually, CSM should be regarded as a CM as well, being the second largest "pure foundry" wafer fab in the world after Taiwan's TSMC. Similarly, among the next 10 largest local electronics firms, as many as eight can be regarded as having a substantial CM component.

The growth and profitability performance of the top Singaporean CM firms are found to compare well with the performance of the top four American CMs in recent years (Table 5–6). On average, the top 5 CM firms in Singapore grew at an average of 49% p.a. to 88% over the last 6 years, vs. about 26% to over 60% p.a. for the leading US CMs (see Table 5–4. earlier). In terms of profitability, the top 5 Singapore CMs achieved a 6-year average of ROS and ROA of about 3.6% and 6% respectively, vs. about 3% and 6% respectively for the US firms.

The relative success of these large Singapore-based CMs appears to have been due to a combination of factors. First was the favourable demand factor: Stimulated no doubt by the strong presence of OEMs in Singapore itself seeking to outsource part of their manufacturing operations to CMs, these indigenous Singaporean CMs were among the first in Asia to enter the CM industry to exploit this market opportunity.

Another factor was probably the lower barriers to entry that these firms encountered. They were able to enjoy certain level of trust with their first customers despite being relatively new; as mentioned before, most of these CMs were founded by managers and engineers who have worked for electronics OEMs in Singapore, and their first customers were typically their former employers. Indeed, in a number of cases, the employer actively encouraged and supported the formation of the CM by their ex-employees as part of the company's manufacturing outsourcing strategy. The presence of Singaporeans in the top management of some of these foreign MNC buyers probably facilitated the development of the initial OEM–CM relationships.

Table 5–6. Growth Trend of Leading Singapore Contract Manufacturers

Company	Major Ownership	Sales 1998 S$000	Sales Growth Rate 1992–1998 (%)	Average ROS 1992–98 (%)	Average. ROA 1992–98 (%)	Employment	Date Of Incorp.
NatSteel Electronics Ltd	Singapore	2458727	87.8	-0.7	1.6	8700	23/3/1981
Flextronics Singapore Pte Ltd	Singapore	1787592 [a]	1.2	7.1	8.2	na	21/11/1979
Venture Mfg (S) Ltd	Singapore	730650	48.7	7.4	12.7	2300	4/8/1984
Omni Industries	Singapore	415398	60.5	0.9	2.6	300	8/7/1995
JIT Holdings Ltd	Singapore	396452	76.7	2.0	5.1	na	na
SCI Mfg (S) Pte Ltd	USA	608685	4.3	3.0	8.6	1500	11/11/1983
GES (S) Pte Ltd	Singapore	404506	9.9	3.8	9.7	320	31/1/1981
Omni Electronics (S) Pte Ltd	Hong Kong	273342	45.9	1.8	4.5	750	25/2/1987
Wearnes Technology Pte Ltd	Singapore	231810	4.7	-2.5	-1.3	na	na
Foster Electric (S) Pte Ltd	Japan	150933	7.4	1.5	3.5	150	28/8/1972
Uraco Holdings Ltd	Singapore	136408	18.2	9.0	10.7	2500	9/11/1994
Eltech Electronics Ltd	Singapore	128001	4.4	-0.5	0.1	800	9/1/1989
PCI Ltd	Singapore	91702	-9.4	-1.6	-2.8	1940	8/12/1988
Brilliant Manufacturing Ltd	Singapore	71699	31.5	13.3	14.5	300	25/10/1984
Seksun Precision Engineering Ltd	Singapore	70335	21.6	8.4	8.4	280	12/1/1981
Speedy–Tech Electronics (S) Pte Ltd	Singapore	70355	16.2	5.7	7.6	62	24/9/1985
Tri–M Technologies (S) Ltd	Singapore	50467	-17.3	-1.0	0.2	807	2/2/1981
CAM International Holdings Limited	Singapore	50264	8.9	3.2	4.4	50	6/1/1994
Singatronics	Singapore	49472	-9.1	1.1	0.5	na	na
Kinergy Pte Ltd		27044	na	na	Na	na	4/1/1988
Total		8203842	21.8	3.2	5.9		

Note: [a]Figure for Flextronics International Ltd. Where full time series data is unavailable, statistics are calculated based on available data
Source: Singapore 1000 (various years), Stock Exchange of Singapore website, Companies' Prospectus and Annual Reports (various years), Asiaweek, 1992 to 1996

A third factor is the excellent logistics, communications and transportation infrastructure and the ready pool of manufacturing skills that were already in place in Singapore, making it possible for Singaporean CMs to reap home-base competitive advantages at least initially vs. CMs operating under less favourable home-base conditions. Other OEMs seeking CMs would also look to Singapore as a likely source, given the favourable reputation built up by Singapore as a manufacturing platform. Over time, as the Singapore-based CMs seek to globalize their operations, the home-base advantage probably lessens somewhat, but the excellent infrastructure probably still helps in facilitating global coordination. In particular, the availability of IT and internet manpower skills, coupled with the aggressive promotion of Singapore as a regional internet and e-commerce hub by the government, probably contributed to the Singapore-based CMs speed in developingtheir internet-enabled supply chain management and customer relationship management activities.

Last, but not least, the aggressive growth strategy pursued by the founders and key managers concerned was probably an important factor as well. The availability of capital through IPO on the stock market (coupled with a more favourable P/E ratio for manufacturing firms than say the Hong Kong stock market) has made it easier for the CMs to finance their ambitious growth. While some firms have chosen to diversify away from manufacturing to reduce risk, and still others have sought to enter into OEM products themselves, the more successful Singapore-based CMs understood the economics of the game, and steadfastly focused their resources on being the best manufacturing service providers to their customers. This "process specialist" strategy (Wong 1999b) appears to have paid off well. In addition, the CMs were also careful to adopt a diversified customer portfolio strategy, making sure that they do not become too dependent on any one customer or product segment. Venture Manufacturing, in particular, has been careful to focus on high profitability customer segments rather than just go for growth. Finally, all the major Singapore-based CMs have also invested aggressively in new process technologies to keep abreast of demands by customers.

5 Concluding Observations

In the 1960s, 1970s and 1980s, Japan became the discrete products manufacturing powerhouse of the world through innovations such as TQM, Just-in-Time Inventory Management, and Design for Manufacturability. Such strong manufacturing capability is widely recognized as having contributed significantly to the dominant global position of Japanese electronics companies in a wide range discrete products, especially consumer electronics. However, Japanese strength in manufacturing has developed in the form of a relatively closed, vertical hierarchical system whereby the large Japanese OEMs either produced everything themselves, or where outsourcing was done, it was primarily to a pyramid of Japanese suppliers and sub-contractors (the "Shitauke" system).

In the 1990s, it is American companies that have achieved relatively superior performance in a wide range of discrete product industries, especially information technology products. The resurgence of the US electronics industry in the 1990s has been widely attributed to its adoption of the manufacturing outsourcing strategy. On the one hand, to reduce their dependence on Japanese manufacturers who have become their competitors, US electronics companies actively sought out and promoted contract manufacturers from the Asian NIEs. On the other hand, leveragingthe strength of US in exploiting IT, new American CMs have also emerged that can undertake the entire value chain of manufacturing and supply chain management operations on a global scale, thus enabling the US OEM firms to concentrate on product innovation and marketing.

While it may still be too early to pronounce the superiority of the CM leveraging system of the US as was asserted by some scholars (see e.g. Sturgeon 1999), the striking differences in manufacturing strategy between US and Japanese electronics OEMs in the 1990s certainly warrant closer analysis. On the one hand, few Japanese OEM majors outsource manufacturers to independent CMs, and few independent Japanese CMs have emerged. On the other hand, US firms have outsourced extensively, and globally competitively CMs of American origins have emerged. It is thus intriguing to see if there is an inherent "home-base" advantage in the development of competitive CMs. Another interesting question is the extent to which the existence of independent, specialist CMs has supported a faster pace of product innovation by US firms and improved their

Table 5–7. Profitability of Major Electronics-related MNCs in Singapore, 1992/3–1997/8

	US-owned firms		Japanese-owned firms		European-owned firms	
	Return on Sales (%)	Return on Assets (%)	Return on Sales (%)	Return on Assets (%)	Return on Sales (%)	Return on Assets (%)
1992/93	7.5	13.6	1.7	4.0	1.3	3.0
1993/94	9.4	16.4	2.0	4.6	3.3	8.0
1994/95	9.8	15.8	2.3	5.9	3.9	8.7
1995/96	11.4	18.2	2.3	5.3	2.2	5.9
1996/97	11.3	17.2	-0.5	-1.1	3.7	10.6
1997/98	11.2	14.3	1.4	2.9	2.4	7.0

Note: Data pertain to only companies that are known to be involved in electronics manufacturing and exclude companies classified by the publisher as electronics but which only undertake sales and marketing or which are holding companies/headquarter operations where revenues pertain to sales in the region

Source: Estimated by author from Datapool, Singapore Industrial Companies 1000, 1994, 1996, 1999 and 2000 editions

time-to-market performance relative to the Japanese. While global data are not available, data I have compiled on the profitability performance of Japanese vs. US electronics firms operating in Singapore show a persistently large gap between Japanese and US electronics firms as measured by ROS and ROA (Table 5–7).

For non-Japan East Asia, the expected growing importance of the CM industry also holds a number of interesting implications. Firstly, East Asia can expect that an increasing proportion of manufacturing FDI decisions will not be made by the OEM majors themselves, but by the independent CMs. To the extent that home-grown CMs will have a higher tendency to root their more advanced activities in their home-base (headquarter, R&D, SCM and CRM system development and hosting, etc.), there is thus a national advantage to have strong indigenous CMs.

In view of the increasing globalization of CM operations, another implication is that East Asia countries will need to improve the competitive advantage of their supporting infrastructure and manpower skills to sustain their electronics manufacturing growth in the future. In particular, the entry of China into WTO, the growing importance of Mexico as a manufacturing platform for North America under NAFTA, and the growing integration of the former Eastern Europe into the European Union would put increasing competitive pressure on the less advanced East Asian nations like the ASEAN countries, while inducing the more advanced CMs from the East Asian NIEs to globalize faster.

Last, but not least, with the internet becoming increasingly important for enabling truly seamless, global SCM and CRM, CMs from East Asia need to invest aggressively in new internet and business-to-business (B2B) e-commerce technologies. The role of government in facilitating the development of such B2B e-commerce infrastructures may also become a more important factor in promoting the development of competitive CMs in the future.

References

Bettis, R. A., Bradley, S.P. & Hamel, G. (1992) "Outsourcing and Industrial Decline," *Academy of Management Executive,* 6(1): 7–22.

Dedrick, J. and K.L. Kraemer (1998) *Asia's Computer Challenge:Threat or Opportunity for the United States and the World?*New York:Oxford University Press

Dyer, J. H. (1997) "Effective Inter-firm Collaboration: How Firms Minimize Transaction Costs and Maximum Transaction Value," *Strategic Management Journal*, 18(7): 535–556.

Electronic Business Asia (1999) "Outlook 1999," *Electronic Business Asia (February)*: 24–34.

Elsevier (various years), *Yearbook of World Electronics Data,* London: Elsevier.

Frazier, G. L., Spekman, R.E. & O'Neal, C. R (1988) "Just-in-Time Exchange Relationships in Industrial Markets," *Journal of Marketing,* 52(4): 52–67.

Gibson, P. (2000) "Martinet with a Mission," *Electronic Business*, 1 August 2000.

Hamel, G., Doz, Y. L. & Prahalad, C. K. (1989) "Collaborate with Your Competitors and Win," *Harvard Business Review*, 67(1): 133–139.

Harbert, T. (1998) "A Wonderful World," *Electronic Business Asia (September)*: 20.

Jensen, O. (1996) "Competence Development by Small Firms in a Vertically-constrained Industry Structure," in R. Sanchez, A. Heene, & H. Thomas (Eds.), *Dynamics of Competence-based Competition: Theory and Practice in the New Strategic Management*, pp. 165–181, Oxford: Pergamon, Elservier Science Ltd.

Jorgensen, B. (2000) "Designing for Dollars," *Electronic Business*, 1 September 2000.

Lachica, E. (1995) "Contractors Reshape Electronics Business – Plants-for-Hire Thrive as Big Firms Farm out More and More Work," *The Asian Wall Street Journal*, 7 September 1995.

Leachman, R. (2000) "E-Commerce and the Changing Terms of Competition in the Semiconductor Industry," paper presented at the *Conference on E-Business Transformation: Sector Developments and Policy Implications*, Washington D.C., Sept. 26–27, 2000

Lee, J.R. & Chen, J.S. (forthcoming) "Dynamic Synergy Creation with Multiple Business Activities: toward a Competence-based Growth Model for Contract Manufacturers." In R. Sanchez & A. Heene (Eds.), *Research in Competence-based Research Advances in Applied Business Strategy series Volume C*, JAI Press, forthcoming.

Lei, D., & Slocum Jr., J. W. (1992) "Global Strategy, Competence-Building and Strategic Alliances," *California Management Review*, 35(1): 81–97.

Magretta, J. (1998) "The Power of Virtual Integration: an Interview with Dell Computer's Michael Dell," *Harvard Business Review*, 76(2): 73–84.

Manufacturing Market Insider (2000) "Top 50 Contract Manufacturers Exceed $46 billion," http://www.mfgmkt.com/top_50release.html

Markides, C., & Berg, N. (1988) "Manufacturing Offshore is Bad Business," *Harvard Business Review*, 66(4): 113–120.

Nishiguchi, T. (1994) *Strategic Industrial Sourcing: The Japanese Advantage*. New York: Oxford University Press.

Ohmae, K. (1989) "The Global Logic of Strategic Alliances," *Harvard Business Review*, 67(2): 143–155.

Peteraf, M. A. (1993) "The Cornerstones of Competitive Advantage: A Resource-Based View," *Strategic Management Journal*, 14(3): 179–191.

Porter, M. E. (1985) *Competitive Advantage: Creating and Sustaining Superior Performance*. New York: The Free Press.

Prahalad, C. K. & Hamel, G. (1990) "The Core Competence of the Corporation," *Harvard Business Review*, 68(3): 79–91.

Ring, P. S., & Van de Ven, A. H. (1992) "Structuring Cooperative Relationships Between Organizations," *Strategic Management Journal*, 13(7): 483–498.

Roberts, B. (1998) "Ties that Bind," *Electronic Business Asia (October)*: 38–44.

Sanchez, R. (1996) "Strategic Product Creation: Managing New Interactions of Technology, Markets, and Organizations," *European Management Journal*, 14(2): 121–138.

Sanchez, R., Heene, A. & Thomas, H. (1996) *Dynamics of Competence-based Competition: Theory and Practice in the New Strategic Management*, Oxford: Pergamon, Elservier Science Ltd.

Siew, T.K. (1998) *Electronic Manufacturing Services: Manufacturing the Future*, Emerging Markets Equity Research, Santander Investment.

Stalk, G. Jr., & T. M. Hout (1990) Competing Again Time: How Time-based Competition is Reshaping Global Markets. New York: The Free Press.

Stein, J. (1997) "On Building and Leveraging Competence Across Organizational Borders: A Socio-cognitive Framework," in A. Heene and R. Sanchez (Eds.), *Competence-based Strategic Management*, pp. 267–284. Chichester: John Wiley & Sons Ltd.

Straits Times (1998) "Contract Manufacturing," *The Straits Times*, 30 January 1998.

Sturgeon, T. (1999) *Turnkey Production Networks: Industry Organization, Economic Development, and the Globalization of Electronics Contract Manufacturing*, unpublished PhD dissertation, U.C. Berkeley

Teece, D. (1980) "Economics of Scope and the Scope of the Enterprise," *Journal of Economic Behavior and Organization*, 1(3): 223–47.

Teece, D. (1982) "Toward an Economic Theory of the Multiproduct Firm," *Journal of Economic Behavior and Organization*, 3(1): 39–63.

Ulrich, K. (1995) "The Role of Product Architecture in the Manufacturing Firm," *Research Policy*, 24: 419–440.

Utterback, J., & Abernathy, W.J. (1975) "A Dynamic Model of Process and Product Innovation," *Omega*, 3(6): 639–656.

Uzumeri, M. & Sanderson, S. (1995) "A Framework for Model and Product Family Competition," *Research Policy*, 24: 583–607.

Wernerfelt, B. (1984) "A Resource-Based View of the Firm," *Strategic Management Journal*, 5: 171–180.

Wilson, D.(1999) "Surfing the Contract Manufacturing Wave," *Electronic Business Asia (July)*: 33–40.

Wong, P.K. (1992) "Technological Development Through Subcontracting Linkages: Evidence from Singapore." *Scandinavian International Business Review*, 1(3): p.28–40, 1992.

Wong, P.K.(1997) "Creation of a Regional Hub for Flexible Production: The Case of Hard Disk Drive Industry in Singapore," *Industry and Innovation* , Vol.4, No.2. (Dec., 1997)

Wong, P.K. (1999a) "The Dynamics of HDD Industry Development in Singapore," Information Storage Industry Centre, Univ. Calif., San Diego, Research Report 99–03, July, 1999

Wong, P.K. (1999b) "National Innovation System for Rapid Technological Catch-up: An Analytical Framework and a Comparative Analysis of Korea, Taiwan and Singapore," paper presented at the DRUID Conference on National Innovation Systems, June, Denmark

Wong, P.K. (2001a, forthcoming) "Globalization of American, European and Japanese Production Networks and The Growth of Singapore's Electronics Industry," *International Journal of Technology Management*

Wong, P.K.(2001b, forthcoming) "Leveraging Multinational Corporations, Fostering Technopreneurship: The Changing Role of S&T Policy in Singapore," *International Journal of Technology Management*

Zajac, E. J., and C. P. Olsen (1993) "From Transaction Cost to Transactional Value Analysis: Implications for the Study of Inter-organizational Strategies," *Journal of Management Studies*, 30(1): 131–145.

Zizzo, T.(2000) "Euro-Growth," *Electronic Business*, 1 September 2000.

Celestica website and annual report

Flextronics website

Jabil Circuit website and annual report

JIT Holdings website

NatSteel Electronics website and annual report

Omni Industries website
SCI Systems website, annual report and 10K report
Solectron website and annual report
Venture Manufacturing website

6 Expansion Options among Hong Kong Electronics Firms: A Study of Effective Marketing Channel Strategies

T. S. Chan
Lingnan University

1 Introduction

Hong Kong is an important trading center located on the southern coast of China. It is the world's eighth largest trading nation measured in terms of value of merchandise trade in 1999 (Hong Kong Annual Report, 1999). In addition to its reliance on trade, Hong Kong's prosperity also depends heavily on the tourism and the provision of business and financial services. Hong Kong is the best example of a free enterprise economy. The Hong Kong government provides a sound regulatory structure for conducting business but with very little intervention, the tax rates are very low, and yet the infrastructure is very well developed.

The smallness of the domestic market brought about the intense pursuit of export opportunities amongst Hong Kong manufacturers, and all major manufacturing industries in Hong Kong are all export-oriented. With its geographical advantage of being the crossroad between the East and the West, Hong Kong has one of the busiest container ports in the world. Hong Kong is also one of the world's leading international financial centers, sharing the honor with cities like New York, London, and Tokyo. With its unique characteristics, Hong Kong is well suited for studying international expansion and marketing issues. The dynamics of Hong Kong's economy are attributed largely to adaptive entrepreneurs who are alert to opportunities and respond rapidly to change (Yu 1999). Over the past three decades, many of the Hong Kong manufacturing firms has expanded their business through effective international marketing structures and strategies as well as direct investment in production to maintain competitive advantages over their overseas competitors.

The electronics industry in Hong Kong is the focus of this study. Hong Kong's electronics industry is the largest merchandise export earner, which accounted for 31% of Hong Kong's total exports in 1998. In 1997, Hong Kong was the largest world exporter of calculators, radios and telephone sets. The industry also shares the biggest position of total foreign investment in Hong Kong, amounting to HK$20 billion in 1997. Well known for its adaptability to fast changing trends and consumer requirements, the electronics industry in Hong Kong produces sophisticated products such as consumer electronics from radios to televisions to communication electronics in modems, PABX and cellular phones, computer hardware and printing equipment, multi-layer circuit boards, liquid crystal displays, and semi-conductor devices (Hong Kong Annual Report, 1999).

The pressure of protectionism and the growing competition from other newly industrialized and developing economies have encouraged and motivated the efforts of Hong Kong electronics manufacturers to adapt new structure and formulate new strategies. Manufacturers must understand the changing environmental forces and use business strategies in production and marketing that correspond to the prevailing or anticipated changes. For examples, how could you build new channel arrangement while continuing to take advantage of existing channel structure? With the rising cost of manufacturing in Hong Kong, how could Hong Kong electronics manufacturers defend market coverage and share position relative to low cost producers from neighboring less developed countries (LDCs)?

This chapter explores the trends of structural modifications during international expansion among Hong Kong manufacturers. What roles do channel strategy and structure play in Hong Kong manufacturers' pursuit for international growth and expansion? How to plan and implement for international production? The objectives of this study are (1) to discuss the longitudinal changes in channel structure among Hong Kong manufacturers; and (2) to evaluate the expansion in international production and trace linkages of production decisions with marketing decisions. Specifically, this paper aims to understand the changing trends among Hong Kong electronics manufacturers in integrating forwardly from indirect exporting to direct exporting, and from setting sales subsidiaries to the establishment of wholesale/retail outlets in overseas markets. With the establishment of offshore production facilities by many Hong Kong firms, this study further explores their objectives and goals for setting up such production facilities. The pathways in becoming multinationals are also being investigated along the realm of the strategy and structure focus. Based on the analyses of empirical findings, a framework for strategy and structure in international expansion is proposed and a section on managerial and research implications is also provided.

2 The Research Literature

Recent contributions to the literature on the expansion of international activity of firms have distinguished between the initial act of FDI and sequential investment. Kogut (1987) related the international strategy of Multinational Enterprises (MNEs) to their learning experiences in coordinating domestic and foreign production. Along similar lines, Barlett and Ghoshal (1988, 1990) asserted that the complexities and varieties of different environments, which MNEs operated in, afforded these firms the opportunities to develop competencies and learning experience not open to domestic firms. More and more studies have targeted for explaining the growth of MNEs' activity rather than the reasons for the initial investment. So far there have been few quantitative research projects on this subject, only a small volume of case study materials emerged from field studies by Kogut (1985, 1987), Prahalad and Doz (1987), and Barlett and Ghoshal (1989).

The dominant approach in examining exporting and internationalization is based on empirical study (Bilkey 1978; and Kamath et al. 1987). Many of the articles reviewed by Bilkey and Kamath et al. (1987) utilized inductive techniques to answer the questions of why firms export, where to export, and what the motivations and obstacles are for successful exporting. Johanson and Wiedersheim-Paul (1975) investigated operating strategy for exporting and identified four stages: (1) no regular export activities; (2) export via agents; (3) establish overseas sales subsidiary; and (4) production in a foreign market. Bilkey and Tesar (1977) used stages in characterizing profiles of exporting firms. They identified six profiles according to export stages: (1) firm not interested in exporting; (2) firm responds only to external request for exports; (2) firm explores exporting; (4) firm experiments exporting; (5) firm becomes active exporter; and (6) firm becomes committed exporter. These studies identified the trends through investigating past development of firms, however, they did not probe into contextual factors which influenced the developments.

As this study involves tracking the modifications of channel structure, a review of literature in this area is in order. The few pieces of literature that discuss distribution channels in the international context have been directed toward the large MNEs from developed countries (Keegan 1972; Gilmour and Rimmer 1976; Ahmed, 1977; Picard 1982; Buckley and Pearce 1984; Kim and Kim 1993; and Murray et al. 1995). The area of distribution channels strategy used by other types of firms in their international marketing activities is almost completely overlooked. Consequently, there is limited prior experience to draw from in this area.

Cavusgil and Zou (1994) suggested that the "fit" between a firm's strategy and its context have a positive effect on export performance. Madsen (1994), on the other hand, provided a contingency view to successful export performance by linking export strategy and channel structure. Several recent studies have also examined how firms adapt to changes through focusing on product (Fraser and Hite 1990), marketing (Doyle et al. 1988) and manufacturing (Blois, 1986). Karunaratna and Johnson (1999) suggested that alignment of the exporter's and foreign channel intermediaries' goals could achieve positive operating climate and attain satisfactory trading relationships. Weber (2000) indicated the need to build closer relationships with channel members as an alternative way to improve distributor performance.

Many of the larger and more successful Hong Kong firms have expanded their international markets, established overseas marketing subsidiaries, and invested in offshore production facilities. As a firm increases its geographical scope and produces in more countries, the organizational structure needs to be reviewed or changed in view of its appropriateness. Various authors have expressed their views. Ghoshal and Nohria (1989) proposed that the organizational structure of an MNE should be suited to the resources available, the stage of development, and the external environment. They preferred an integrative structure for managing subsidiaries that operate in complex environments with abundant supply of local resources. Doz and Prahalad (1991) argued for an organizational structure to be based on multi-dimensionality and heterogeneity of MNE activity, with emphasis being given to managers of subsidiaries as basic units of decision making. On the contrary, Hedlund and Kogut (1992) suggested to emphasize the heterarchical attributes of MNE whose resources and competence are globally dispersed, where efficient horizontal communication at the functional and project levels is increasingly important.

This study represents an attempt to integrate the structural modifications among larger and more successful Hong Kong electronics firms, from expanding international channels to establishing overseas sales and marketing subsidiaries, and onto international production. These changes and developments will be incorporated into a framework which exploratively reflects the changing environmental forces facing the firms, and their strategic reactions which shape and determine the type and structure of international activity, at particular moments in time.

3 Change Channel Structures Among Hong Kong Firms

The electronics industry in Hong Kong has been flexible and adaptable in coping with the frequent changes in demand while at the same time maintaining external competitiveness. The manufacturing firms examined in this research are firms with Hong Kong ownership, thus excluding the channel implications between parent and subsidiary of non-Hong Kong multinational firms which might have very different motives for exporting and international production.

Using a series of longitudinal studies, Chan (1984, 1991, and 1997) focused on studying the structural changes in the export distribution channels, with the aim of exploring trends in distribution strategy. Data used for comparison represented three different time collection periods spreading over 13 years. Period I covers the period between 1976 and 1981 when Hong Kong's manufacturing sector went through a period of adjustment in view of the protectionistic sentiments in most developed countries, which marked the expansion of production to developed market countries. Period II (1982–1987) represents the aftermath of the oil crises which brought the world economy into a major downturn. The strategic changes in export channel structures would reflect the firms' attempts to survive the economic recession and remain competitive. Period III reflects the 1988–1994 period when the larger and more successful firms committed resources to combat this threat by investing in low cost production sites. The differentiation of time periods was used to reflect how these manufacturers managed or coped with the changes and made modifications that helped to maintain their competitive positions in the world marketplace.

After examining the adaptation of export channel structures at various points in time, Chan (1998) concluded with several observations. The use of multiple channels is very common among Hong Kong electronics manufacturing firms. Instead of relying on one particular type of intermediaries in the export distribution channel, Hong Kong firms are utilizing the services provided by a combination of Hong Kong based and/or foreign-based channel agencies or institutions. The trend of moving toward direct exporting continues. Hong Kong manufacturing firms are performing an increasing proportion of their export channel functions themselves through forward vertical integration in the export distribution channels. Hong Kong manufacturers are active in marketing their products internationally, from providing subcontracting manufacturing of international branded products for Hong Kong based foreign resident buyers to dealing directly with foreign based retail merchants in marketing Hong Kong made products. This represents a logical development. Once a firm established its own internalized export department, it would be in a better position to deal directly with channel agents and/or merchants located in the foreign markets which ensure continuity of channel relationships and continuous presence.

The linkages established between Hong Kong firms and their business customers reflect the drive to foster closer relationships with overseas partners/associates to enhance the magnitudes of direct cooperation. This is consistent with the study by Leonidou and Anna (1998) which revealed that the more a firm is involved in exporting, the more likely its relationships with overseas customers are to be characterized by greater resources and personal commitment, higher level of cooperation, and stronger feelings of satisfaction with both financial and behavioral performance. Hong Kong manufacturing firms normally will sell their finished products to whoever and whenever it is profitable, however, the opportunities for scale economies and the rapid changes in customer preferences among electronics products have led to more inter-firm linkages between Hong Kong manufacturers and overseas purchasing firms. On the other hand, many Hong Kong firms may welcome additional diversification in their distributing channel strategies, moving away from being the major supplying firms to large MNEs from the developed world.

The Hong Kong electronics manufacturing firms integrate vertically to get closer to their clients in foreign markets so that customer needs can be better served, as reliance on middlemen will automatically lead to loss of some control over their export marketing activities. Companies integrate to gain better control of their marketing destinies. Controls are designed to reduce uncertainty and increase profitability. As a result, quite a few Hong Kong electronics manufacturers committed direct investment in foreign marketing establishments.

These investment activities, such as setting up their own labels and selling through company owned sales subsidiaries and wholesale/retail distribution establishments in major market countries, came about as executives become more comfortable with the thought of owning and operating business in environments different from Hong Kong. Although not necessary in this sequence, dealing more often with foreign-based agents/merchants would encourage further integration in the setting up of foreign sales offices.

Such development of vertical forward integration in the export distribution channel is bringing Hong Kong manufacturers much closer to their customers in overseas markets. With more experience in overseas markets, manufacturers began to expand their involvement leading to the establishment of company-owned wholesale/retail outlets in overseas markets.

4 Survey of Offshore Production Facilities

Just as important as the need for control over exporting, Hong Kong electronics manufacturers also want control and efficiency in their production, and the result is horizontal integration and development toward becoming multinationals. This is the setting up of offshore production facilities. With the fast pace of changing technology, control of product development and production is very important for the timing of marketing activities. Therefore, several Hong Kong electronics firms invested in manufacturing facilities in DCs to be closer to the customers as well as attempting to overcome potential/actual trade barriers. On the other hand, taking into consideration the assembling of tiny parts in computers and other electronic products which constitutes a significant portion of overall production cost, several Hong Kong manufacturers established production facilities in lower cost LDCs to remain cost-competitive in their production.

A survey was conducted during November 1999 with the main focus on issues relating to the expansion in overseas production facilities among Hong Kong manufacturers. With the increasing number of Hong Kong manufacturing firms establishing overseas production, an important part of the questionnaire focused on the objectives and goals for setting up overseas production. A 5-point Likert scale was used to measure the relevance of various objectives and goals in the firms' decision to establish overseas production. An advance letter seeking cooperation was mailed prior to the sending the questionnaires to 300 larger and more successful electronics manufacturing firms in Hong Kong. Appointments were made by telephone for collection of completed questionnaires and personal interviews, if possible. Interviews were conducted mainly with managing directors or CEOs of the firms. Of the 62 respondent firms, 53 firms (85 percent) reported involvement in offshore production facilities and exhibited a wide range of gross export sales from slightly over US$10 million to over US$200 million. These firms also varied in terms of the size of workforce, with a range of 100 to 2500 workers. The years of export experience among these firms ranged from 12 to 36 years. This brief profile certainly reflected the successful performance of these firms in marketing to the global marketplace.

What are the objectives and goals of setting foreign manufacturing? Analysis of variance tests were performed on the objectives and goals of three different categories of firms. The three categories were based upon their expansion of manufacturing in different countries: Group A represented those firms which established production facilities in China only; Group B categorized those firms with production facilities in China and other LDCs, including Indonesia, Macao, Malaysia, Mauritius, Philippines, Thailand, and Sri Lanka ; and Group C firms included those with facilities in China, LDCs, and DCs such as Canada, United Kingdom, and the USA. This method of categorization provides three groupings with different degrees of involvement in overseas production; from one extreme end with Group A firms invested in China only to the other end of Group C firms investing in China, LDCs and DCs.

Table 6–1 provides the mean scores and rankings for the overall objectives and specific goals for setting up offshore production facilities. The objectives and goals were measured using a 5-point Likert scale with 5 being "extremely relevant" and 1 being "not relevant at all." Therefore, the higher the mean score, the more relevant the objective or goal. On the other hand, the lower the ranking, the more important the objective or goal. The statistical test of analysis of variance (ANOVA) was used, as it has the distinct advantage of being applicable when there are more than two means being compared.

Regarding the overall objectives for setting up offshore production facilities, "country experience" was reported as first in importance by Group C firms (with mean score at 3.69 and second for Group A firms (at 3.57), where Group B firms rated it in fourth place (at 2.64). As for the objective of "growth," both Group A and C firms rated it in fourth place (with mean score of 3.23 and 2.89 respectively) and Group B firms rated it in first place (at 3.73). The ANOVA test results indicated significant differences for these two objectives ($p<0.05$). Apart from these two objectives, all the others were fairly similar.

As for the specific goals of overseas production, Group A and Group B firms placed significantly greater importance on "lower labor costs" ($p<0.01$) and "lower land costs" ($p<0.01$) than Group C firms. As for the goal to "utilize disciplined workforce" it was significantly different between groups ($p<0.05$), with Group A firms rating it as more relevance than Group B firms, and Group B firms placing more relevance to it than Group C firms. In addition, the goals to "overcome trade barriers," "acquire technology," and "reduce transportation" were significantly different between groups ($p<0.01$), with Group C firms consistently placing more importance over firms in the other groups. Many of Hong Kong electronics manufacturers have relocated the labor-intensive processes to the Chinese mainland and/or other LDCs to maintain cost competitiveness. Yet there are a number of companies instill maintaining high value-added and/or capital-intensive production (especially for parts and components) in Hong Kong and/or those DCs.

Table 6–1. Objectives and Goals for Setting up Offshore Production Facilities

Objectives and Goal	Group A[a] Mean	Group A[a] Rank	Group B[b] Mean	Group B[b] Rank	Group C[c] Mean	Group C[c] Rank
	(N=22)		(N=16)		(N=15)	
OVERALL OBJECTIVES						
Profitability	3.76	1	3.46	2	3.32	3
Country Experience	3.57	2	2.64	4	3.69	1 *
Integration of Operations	3.41	3	3.22	3	3.48	2
Growth	3.23	4	3.73	1	2.89	4 *
Risk Diversification	2.87	5	2.56	5	2.53	5
SPECIFIC GOALS						
Lower Labor Costs	4.66	1	4.42	1	2.47	9**
Lower Land Costs	4.50	2	4.30	2	2.53	8**
Establish Connections	4.23	3	3.93	4	3.49	5
Combat Competition	4.12	4	4.32	3	4.37	2
Meet Customer Needs	3.85	5	3.21	5	3.22	6
Utilize Disciplined Workforce	3.43	6	2.98	7	2.28	10*
Obtain Local Sourcing	3.25	7	3.16	6	2.93	7
Overcome Trade Barriers	2.98	8	2.74	8	4.43	1**
Acquire Technology	2.57	9	2.59	9	3.71	4**
Reduce Transportation	2.36	10	2.44	10	4.10	3**

[a] Offshore production facilities established in China only.
[b] Offshore production facilities established in China and LDCs.
[c] Offshore production facilities established in China, LDCs, and DCs.

* $P<0.05$ (Analysis of Variance [ANOVA]).
** $p<0.01$ (ANOVA).

The experience of marketing to the US, Canada, and UK, as leading markets for Hong Kong products, has led Hong Kong manufacturers to build confidence in establishing production facilities there. Many of these firms had prior investment experience in setting up sales subsidiaries and other distribution arrangements. With its proximity to China, Hong Kong firms have had many years of trading and doing business with counterparts in China, such experience accentuated the close understanding between business partners. The return of sovereignty from British rule to that of a Special Administrative Region of China on July 1, 1997 further enhances the trade and investment linkages between Hong Kong and China.

Labor constitutes a significant proportion of costs in assembling electronics products. The cheaper the labor, the lower the costs and possibly higher profits. Those manufacturing firms that have established production facilities in China and/or LDCs would value the lower labor and lower land costs of these countries. For Group C firms which invested in DCs (in addition to China and LDCs), labor costs are certainly much higher and would not be a factor that influences the investment decision. In addition, the land costs could vary substantially depends on the specific locations within particular DCs which are being considered.

Diversities among different countries would mean different power bases for labor movements. In most cases, workers in Chinese mainland and LDCs are more likely to be subjected to straighter disciplinary control, whereas workers in DCs (such as US, Canada and UK) are often sheltered from straighter disciplinary control due to the strong union movements in those countries. Hong Kong manufacturers are fully aware of this background, and goals of their offshore production facilities decisions are often influenced by the labor factor.

Many Hong Kong manufacturers established production facilities in DCs in search of protection from trade barriers, as their products would be considered as "Made in USA" when a substantial portion of manufacturing was done in the US. By setting up production subsidiaries in market countries, products of a manufacturer would certainly be treated as domestic outputs rather than imports; these products would not be subjected to quotas and/or tariffs and might at times be the beneficiary of tariff walls put up to discourage foreign goods. From a technological standpoint, production technology (representing application of know-how leading to modification of equipment, improving plant layout, upgrading quality control and inspection procedures) is the common technological capability being transferred when Hong Kong firms established production facilities in LDCs. The most common reason for adaptation of imported production processes by Hong Kong firms was to take advantage of lower labor cost in these host countries. On the other hand, many Hong Kong firms established manufacturing subsidiaries in DCs to acquire new technology. The intention was to set up production in North American or Western Europe to gain insights into local innovatory capacity. When a Hong Kong firm plans for investment in production facilities in these regions, there are often powerful locational reasons toward locating foreign innovatory activities. For example, apart from being closer to their customers, three of the electronics manufacturing firms which participated in this study had set up production subsidiaries in the Silicon Valley in California to be closer to other inventors and suppliers of new technology. By locating closer to their suppliers and customers, opportunities would exist for reduction in transportation costs and improved efficiency in supply chain management. Johanson and Vahlne (1977) provided evidence to illustrate the internationalization process of Swedish multinationals, which started off initially through exporting to a country, then they set up sales subsidiaries; finally, they build production subsidiaries. Hong Kong firms have been on very similar paths, however, this study indicated that Hong Kong firms gained competitive strengths by focusing their strategies on operations that improve their advantages incrementally. Such behavior on the part of Hong Kong firms fits well with the strategic option theory (Bowman and Hurry, 1993; and Hurry, 1993).

5 A Conceptual Framework For Strategic Expansion

Based on the above findings, a framework for international expansion of Hong Kong manufacturing firms is presented (Figure 6–1). The development of this framework is intended to foster further research and facilitates greater managerial understanding and appreciation of the pathways to become multinational firms among Hong Kong manufacturers. Hong Kong manufacturing firms initially produce products out of their production facilities in Hong Kong and look for export opportunities in international markets. Typically, these manufacturers utilize multiple channels to reach foreign customers. With resident buyers who represent international companies in Hong Kong looking for original equipment manufacturing and/or subcontracting works, Hong Kong manufacturers could be engaging in indirect exporting. Another common mode of indirect exporting is to use the service of Hong Kong-based agent/merchant; instead of performing most of the export functions, these Hong Kong manufacturers are delegating to export channel intermediaries.

As export volume increases, more and more Hong Kong manufacturers would be establishing their own export capabilities in the form of direct exporting through company-owned export department. With more contacts and linkages with foreign-based agents/merchants, the more aggressive manufacturers would be in positions to set up overseas sales subsidiaries and/or wholesale/retail facilities in overseas markets, assuming that availability of resources is not a problem. This progression represents marketing investment and expansion along the international channels. The development of original design capabilities is also important to ensure the design is timely and of a good quality for the appropriate export markets. This is in line with what Barlett and Ghoshal (1988, 1990) have asserted that firms operating in a variety of environments are exposed to multiple stimuli that enable them to develop competencies and learning opportunities.

On the production side, production in Hong Kong might give way to lower cost production sites in LDCs such as China, Thailand etc. Cost reduction is one important factor to consider for such FDI, however, the level of productivity of workers from LDCs would be carefully compared. Moreover, the ability of Hong Kong headquarters to effectively manage these manufacturing facilities is an important factor deciding which of the countries to invest in. As a result, there seems to be greater interest in setting up production facilities in China as compared to other LDCs, primarily due to the similar cultural background among Chinese people in Hong Kong and China. Those manufacturers without marketing establishments in international markets would see production outputs from such

Figure 6–1. A Framework of International Expansion among Hong Kong Electronics Manufacturing Firms

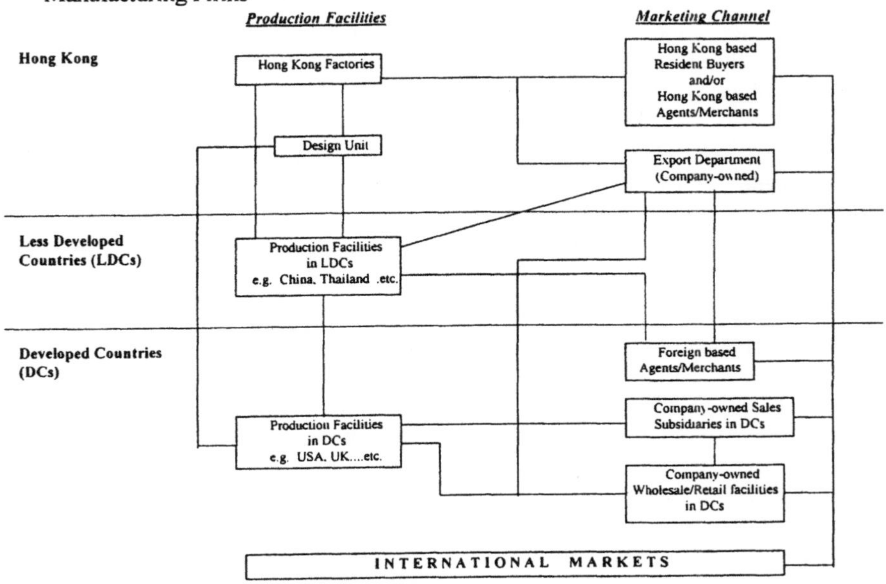

offshore production facilities be coordinated through the company's export department in Hong Kong. Products from offshore production facilities could be shipped through Hong Kong or directly to international markets, while the administrative workload and documentation are handled by the Hong Kong head office. Kogut (1989) related the international strategy of MNFs to their learning experiences in coordinating domestic and foreign production. The path of international production also reflects the interaction between the specific endowments of countries over time, as well as at a given moment in time.

With expanded involvement in DCs, Hong Kong manufacturers could be looking for integration of operations by establishing manufacturing subsidiaries in DCs. The case example of one electronics manufacturer would illustrate this point. This manufacturer expanded to the US with the establishment of two sales subsidiaries in 1978. Subsequently, the top management of the firm decided to set up a production subsidiary in Chicago with separate market research and wholesale distribution divisions in 1983. The Hong Kong factory (established in 1959) manufactures top of the line products and houses the design and technical support units, whereas the complete line of electronics products is manufactured in production subsidiaries in China (four facilities established between 1985 and 1992) and Thailand (one subsidiary established in 1994). The US production subsidiary produces mainly the high-valued top performers for the US market and provides repair and warranty maintenance services.

In addition to market proximity and protectionism considerations, the setting up of the US production subsidiary provides tremendous logistics support and market intelligence for important corporate decisions in the Hong Kong headquarters. Due to the substantial level of investment, the experience of operating in the US and the availability of human and financial resources are crucial for this FDI in the US.

This case example partially supports the general proposition put forth by Vernon (1966, 1974) that as a firm becomes more international it will first replace exports of low value items by foreign production, followed later by foreign production of high value activities. Prior to expanding production into low cost producing countries for the low-end products, the firm in this case established manufacturing facility in a DC for market presence and proximity to customers. The main explanation being that Hong Kong was a relatively low cost production center during the early 1980s. While the literature shows that large multinationals are continuing to account for the bulk of foreign production, it is worth observing the increasing internationalization of its production of MNEs from developing countries due to their technological development and the lowering of transportation and communication costs.

Within this framework, export channel structures of Hong Kong manufacturers could affect overall performance of firms through alternative channels and other administrative arrangements as well as FDI. The clear implication of this discussion is that different structures may be required for different kinds of multinational business activity and for different MNFs with different levels of competence and resource endowments. In addition, national and cultural differences are likely to influence the structure of MNEs. This conceptual framework could assist in future empirical operationalization in the fields of export and international expansion research.

6 Managerial and Research Implications

Faced with an ever-increasing intensification of international competition, marketing managers must formulate plans to improve the effectiveness of strategy for international business activities. It is important that managers recognize the potentials of channel integration as one of the strategic options. Deciding when and how to integrate vertically into overseas marketing channels is an important strategic consideration. Firms that learn more about the international marketplace through closer business cooperation with foreign-based agents/merchants or direct expansion overseas are better able to gain and sustain competitive advantages.

Horizontal integration of manufacturing facilities seems to be an appropriate mode when the intent is to meet customers' expectation of lower price and remain competitive amongst low cost producers, while at the same time not compromising product quality. The synergism inherent in vertical and/or horizontal integration of distribution channels enables these Hong Kong firms to be better able to adapt to dynamic environment changes. One must realize that such strategic changes do not come easy. The formulation of marketing channel strategy must be an essential part of senior management responsibilities. Besides, the modification of strategies must be proactive and spontaneous. Too many managers procrastinate and become too reactive to the surrounding environment. For firms from other developing countries seeking success in export markets, it is important to identify and select appropriate channel intermediaries. These firms must expend great efforts to identify the relevant distribution networks and their members, and strategic attempts should be made to cultivate relationships in order to move along the path of direct exporting.

In the formulation of FDI strategy, management teams are exposed to more diverse and complex environmental contexts in the host country (Huszagh et al. 1992, Miller 1993). The decision to establish an overseas sales subsidiary or manufacturing facility implies the need for increased efforts in management training and recruitment. The importance of human resources in terms of tangible and intangible skills must be available to affect successful channel integration and international expansion strategies. For example, tangible skills such as logistics methods to make available the required supplies (import or local) for production facilities in China and to move finished products from China to Hong Kong and then to the overseas markets must be in place. On the other hand, intangible relationship skills such as establishing trust with foreign channel members and conflict resolution skills with an understanding of inter-cultural differences are also essential. Long-term mechanisms or processes to acquire and apply this tangible and intangible knowledge must be developed. Indeed, as Adler and Ghadar (1990) have suggested, each stage in the internationalizing process of firms necessitates adjustments to the way in which MNEs recruit, utilize, train and remunerate their personnel.

The interdependence of strategy, structure, and staffing is very important in international expansion for MNEs from developing countries like Hong Kong. Existing structural and staff constraints often bear impact on strategic decisions. It is thus important to achieve good matching among those variables that facilitates strategic implementation (Deresky 1994).

It is recommended that managers from developing countries and emerging markets should evaluate various scenarios carefully before embarking on any major commitment of human and/or financial resources for international expansion. The key is to walk before running. Such evaluative processes could prevent negative consequences such as wasted time and unrecoverable sunk costs that often result from mistakes or failures. Once top management determined that excellent possibilities for export or FDI expansion exist, firms must commit adequate resources to the exporting or investment ventures. The riskiest venture occurs when the firm is not totally committed.

Decisions in these areas represent strategic-related variables that must be fully attended to. These decisions are the concerns of strategic management, as what Dunning (1993) referred to as ways in which managers plan and act to achieve their objectives. According to Dunning, strategic management embraces not only decisions as to how resources are acquired, created, utilized, and the way in which markets are identified and serviced, but on how transactions relating to these decisions are organized.

From a research standpoint, because of the paucity of research on the topic of MNEs from the developing world, a more refined theoretical approach to understand the nature of FDI by such multinationals is warranted. For researchers interested in studying the diversity among such MNEs, the proposed framework of international expansion offers opportunities for insight toward a more complete theory of growth and development of MNEs from the developing world. An interesting extension of this article would be to identify and examine additional relationships based on the proposed framework.

Strategic actions by the Hong Kong manufacturers indicate an interesting area for research into the issues of conflict and power in the expansion decisions, and in broader sense, research into the dynamic analysis of marketing entry timing and decision making in global industries. Oftentimes, firms from different industries might have different modes/forms of international expansion; therefore, it may be necessary to study international expansion trends and behavior on an industry-by-industry basis to account for any industry bias. In addition, how MNEs from different developing countries or emerging markets differ in their strategies for international expansion will be another area for future research.

Future studies should attempt to explore the actual mechanisms through which other MNEs from developing countries manage to achieve international expansion, and the performance implications of different growth and expansion strategies. Besides, comparative research (i.e. comparing Hong Kong firms with Singaporean or Taiwanese firms) in the area should be undertaken to further understanding these phenomena.

7 Conclusion

The Hong Kong electronics manufacturing firms under investigation have undergone major changes and development. The vertical integration of export distribution channels as an expansion strategy is evidenced by the findings of this study. The various forms of channel structural adaptations reduce the uncertainty and allow firms to gain a better understanding and predictive ability about their foreign market conditions.

The establishments of offshore production facilities by Hong Kong electronics manufacturers firms suggest a high degree of sensitivity of these firms to the marketing environment as well as their effective utilization of strategic options in the export channels. These manufacturing firms integrate horizontally to gain better control over their product mixes as well as marketing destinies. Such strategic actions by the Hong Kong firms indicate an interesting area for research into the issues of international expansion of multinational firms from newly industrialized countries.

The proposed framework discussed differs from previous ones in exporting literature by explicitly acknowledging the connection between export channel structure and production facilities as an international expansion strategy. Entrepreneurial firms from the developing world are expected to achieve successful performance through forward channel integration and international production activities which match the firms' strengths with the environmental forces. Testing propositions relating to this development should shed light on management practices and public policy programs.

References

Adler, N. And Ghadar, F. (1990) International Strategy from the Perspective of People and Culture, in *Research in Global Strategic Management* (Rugman A., ed.), Greenwich, CN: JAI Press.

Ahmed, A. Ahmed, (1977) Channel Control in International Marketing, *European Journal of Marketing*, Vol. II, Fall, 327-335.

Bartlett, C.A. and Ghoshal S. (1988) Managing Innovations in the Transnational Corporations, in *Research on Multinational Management* (Bartlett C. A., Doz Y. and Hedlund G., eds.). London: Addison–Wesley.

Bartlett, C. A. and Ghoshal S. (1989) *Managing Across Borders – The Transnational Solution*, Boston: Harvard Business School Press.

Bartlett C. A., Doz Y. and Hedlund G., eds. (1990) *Managing the Global Firm*, London and New York: Routledge.

Bilkey, W. J. (1978) An Attempted Integration of the Literature on the Export Behavior of Firms, *Journal of International Business Studies*, Vol. 9, pp. 33–46.

Bilkey, W. and Tesar, G. (1977) The Export Behavior of Small-sized Wisconsin Firms, *Journal of International Business Studies*, Spring/Summer, pp. 93–98.

Blois, K. (1986) Marketing Strategies and the New Manufacturing Technologies, *International Journal of Operations and Production Management*, Vol. 6, No. 1, pp. 34–41.

Buckley, P. and Casson. M. (1976) *The Future of Multinational Enterprise*, London: MacMillan.

Buckley, P. and Pearce, R. (1984) Exports in the Strategy of Multinational Enterprises, *Journal of Business Research*, 12, pp. 209–225.

Calof, J.L. (1993) The Impact of Size of Internationalization, *Journal of Small Business Management*, October, pp. 50–56.

Cavusgil, S. (1984) Organizational Characteristics Associated with Export Activity, *Journal of Management Studies*, 21, pp. 3-22.

Cavusgil, S. and Zou, S. (1994) Marketing Strategy–Performance Relationship: an Investigation of the Empirical Link in Export Market Ventures, *Journal of Marketing*, Vol. 58, No. 1, pp. 1–21.

Chan, T. S. (1984) *Distribution Channel Strategy for Export Marketing: The Case of Hong Kong Firms*, Research for Business Decision Series, Ann Arbor, Michigan: UMI Research Press.

Chan, T. S. (1991) Export Expansion Process for Electronics: A Study of Channel Integration Strategy, *Journal of Global Marketing*, Vol. 4(4), pp. 55–68.

Chan, T. S. (1997) The Use of Channel Integration as a Strategic Option: A Study of Hong Kong Clothing Manufacturers," *Asia Pacific Journal of Marketing and Logistics*, UK, Vol. 9, No. 1, pp. 36–59.

Doyle, P., Saunders, J. and Wright L. (1988) A Comparative Study of British, US and Japanese Marketing Strategies in the British Market, *International Journal of Research in Marketing*, Vol. 5, Vol 3, pp. 171–84.

Doz Y. and Prahalad C. K. (1991) Managing MNCs: A Search for a New Paradigm, *Strategic Management Journal*, 12, pp. 145–64.

Dunning, J. (1993) *Global Business: The Challenge of the 1990s*, London and New York: Routledge.

Fraser, C. and Hite, R. (1990) Participation in the International Marketplace by US Manufacturing Firms, *International Marketing Review*, Vol. 7, No. 5, pp. 63–71.

Ghoshal S. and Barlett C. A. (1990) The Multinational Corporations as an Interorganizational Network, *Academy of Management Review*, 15(4), pp. 603–25.

Ghoshal S. and Nohria N. (1989) Internal Differentiation Within Multinational Corporations, *Strategic Management Journal*, 10(4), pp. 323–38.

Gilmour, P. and Rimmer, P. (1976) Business Logistics in the Pacific Basin, *Columbia Journal of World Business*, Spring, pp. 63–72.

Hedlund, G. and Kogut B. (1992) Managing the MNCs: The End of the Missionary Era, in *TNCs and Organizational Issues* (Hedlund G., Ed.), UN Library on Transnational Corporations, London and New York: Routledge.

Hong Kong Annual Report (1999) Government Printer, Hong Kong.

Huszagh, S., Huszagh, F. and Hanks, G. (1992) Macroeconomic Conditions and International Marketing Management, *International Marketing Review*, Vol. 9, No. 1, pp.6–18.

Johanson, J. and Vahlne, J. (1990) The Mechanism of Internationalization, *International Marketing Review*, Vol. 7, No. 4, pp. 11–24.

Johanson, J. and Vahlne, J. (1977) The Internationalization Process of the Firm: A Model of Knowledge Development and Increasing Foreign Market Commitment, *Journal of International Business Studies*, Vol. 8, pp. 23–32.

Johanson, J. and Wiedersheim–Paul, F. (1975) The Internationalization of the Firm: Four Swedish Case Studies, *Journal of Management Studies*, Vol. 12, pp. 305–22.

Kamath, S., Rosson, P., Patton, D., and Brooks, M. (1987) Research on success in Exporting: Past, Present, Future, in Rosson, P. and Reid, S. (Eds.), *Managing Export Entry and Expansion*, Praeger, New York, NY.

Karunaratna, A. and Johnson, L. (1997) Initiating and Maintaining Export Channel Intermediary Relationships, *Journal of International Marketing*, Vol. 5, No. 2, pp. 11–32.

Kaynak, E. and Kothari, V. (1984) Export Behavior and Small and Medium Sized Manufacturers: Some Policy Guidelines for International Marketers, *International Management Review*, Vol. II, pp. 61–69.

Keegan, W. (1972) A Conceptual Framework for Multinational Marketing, *Columbia Journal of World Business*, Vol. VII, November, pp. 66–76.

Kim, S. and Kim, S. (1993) Motives for Japanese Direct Investment in the US, *Multinational Business Review*, Vol. 1, No. 1, pp. 66–72.

Kogut B. (1985) Designing Global Strategies: Profiting from Operational Flexibility, *Sloan Management Review*, 26, Fall, pp. 27–38.

Kogut B.(1987) A Note on Global Strategies, *Strategic Management Journal*, 10, pp. 383–89.

Leonidou, L. C. and Kaleka, A. (1998) Behavioral Aspects of International buyer–seller relationships: their Association with Export Involvement, *International Marketing Review*, Vol. 15, No. 5, pp.373–397.

Madsen, T. (1994) A Contingency Approach to Export Performance Research, in *Advances in International Marketing* (Axinn, C. ,eds.), Vol. 6, JAI Press, Greenwich, CT, pp. 25–42.

Mendenhall, M., and Oddou, G. (1986) Acculturation Profiles of Expatriate Managers: Implications for Cross-Cultural Training Program, *Columbia Journal of World Business*, No.4, pp. 73–79.

Miller, K. (1993) Industry and Country Effects on Managers' Perceptions of Environmental Uncertainties, *Journal of International Business Studies*, Vol. 24, No. 4, pp. 693–714.

Murray, J., Wildt, A., and Kotabe, M. (1995) Global Sourcing of US Subsidiaries of Foreign Multinationals, *Management International Review*, Vol. 35, No. 4, pp. 307–324.

Picard, J. (1982) The Management of Physical Distribution in Multinational Corporations, *Columbia Journal of World Business*, Winter, pp. 67–73.

Prahalad C. K. and Doz Y. (1987) *The Multinational Mission*, London and New York: The Free Press.

Weber, J. (2000) Partnering with Distributors to Stimulate Sales, *Journal of Business and Industrial Marketing*, Vol. 15, No.2/3, pp.154–162.

Yeoh, P. (1995) Contingency Relationships Between Entrepreneurship, Export Channel Structure and Environment: A Proposed Conceptual Model of Export, *European Journal of Marketing*, V. 29, No. 8, pp. 95–115.

Yu, T. (1998) Adaptive Entrepreneurship and the Economic Development of Hong Kong, *World Development*, Vol. 26, No. 5, pp. 897–911.

7 Issues on the Restructuring of the Korean Automobile Industry

Ki-Chan Kim
The Catholic University of Korea

1 Developments and Crisis of the Korean Automobile Companies

Unlike automobile industries in other developing countries, the Korean automobile industry obtained good results without being subordinate to multinational automobile companies. The industry has followed independent strategies, and daringly entered into advanced countries' markets. In 1997 the Korean automobile industry, which virtually started in 1962, was the 4th largest car-producing country in the world (2,818,000 cars) and the 6th largest car exporting country (1,317,000 cars).

After the Korean Financial Crisis of 1997, the Korean automobile industry underwent considerable restructuring. Many Korean carmakers (Ssangyong, Kia, Samsung, Daewoo) went bankrupt or were under legal management. In 1997, the long-established Kia Motors Corporation went into bankruptcy. Hyundai Motor Corporation took over Kia in 1998. After taking over Kia Motors Corporation, Hyundai merged Asia Motors and Kia Motor Sales into Kia Motors Corporation; and merged Hyundai Precision's Automotive Division into Hyundai Motor Company. Daewoo took ownership of Ssangyong in 1998. In April of 2000, Renault, based in France, took ownership of Samsung Automobile factory. Daewoo was put on the market again after Ford Motor Co. removed its bid for Daewoo.

As of September 2000, Hyundai and Kia fell under the same ownership. This means that the previous 9 Korean car makers (Hyundai, Kia, Daewoo, Asia, Hyundai Precision, Daewoo Heavy Industry, Ssangyong, Samsung Motor, Samsung Commercial Vehicle) have now merged into 4 companies (Hyundai/Kia, Daewoo, Renault–Samsung, Samsung Commercial Vehicle) (Figure 7–1).

Domestic car production in 1999 was 2.55 million, an increase of 30.5% from the previous year. Domestic demand for cars was 1.1 million (an increase of 41% from the previous year). Car exports were at 1.45 million (an increase of 6.4% from the previous year). The Utilization rate was 61.9% (an improvement of

Figure. 7–1. The Restructuring of the Korean Automobile Industry

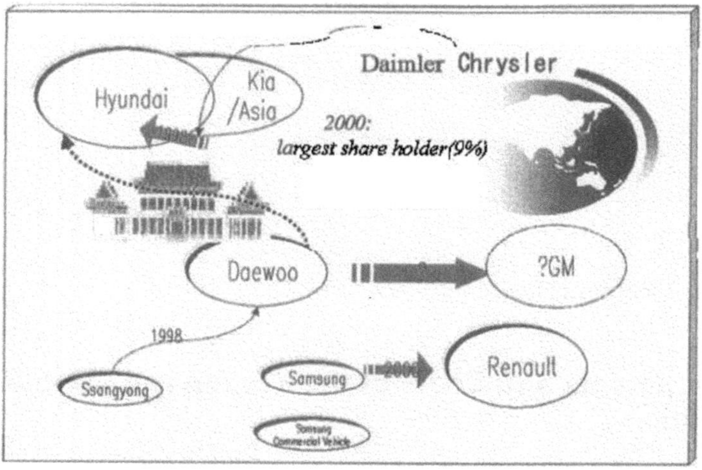

14.5% from the previous year). In 2000, domestic car production is expected to reach 3,160,000 units. Domestic producing capability is 4 million cars (2.65 million for Hyundai/Kia and 1.41million for Daewoo). The producing capability of Korean Automakers abroad is 750,000 cars for Hyundai/Kia, 820,000 cars for Daewoo, The total producing capability of Hyundai/Kia is 3.4 million cars, and for Daewoo 2.23 million cars. The following Figure 7–2 presents Korean automobile industry trends including production capacity, production, domestic sales and export from 1962 to 2000.

1.1 Hyundai & Kia

Hyundai took over Kia in 1998. In such mergers, problems have the potential of rising up, however in this instance it was not the case. In 1999, the first year of the merger, both companies combined realized an all time record of about 0.6 billion dollars in surplus. After the integration of Hyundai and Kia, Tier 1 suppliers have been decreased. As a consequence of this downsizing, modularization will advance rapidly and become more cost-efficient. Daimler Chrysler invested 430.9 billion won to take part in the capital increase of Hyundai Motors. The board of directors of Daimler decided to buy 9% shares of Hyundai Motors and to share capital on a reciprocal basis in 2000. As a result, Daimler became the largest shareholder (9%) of Hyundai Motors and will send one director to Hyundai Motors to be part of the company management.

Figure 7–2. Korean automobile industry trends

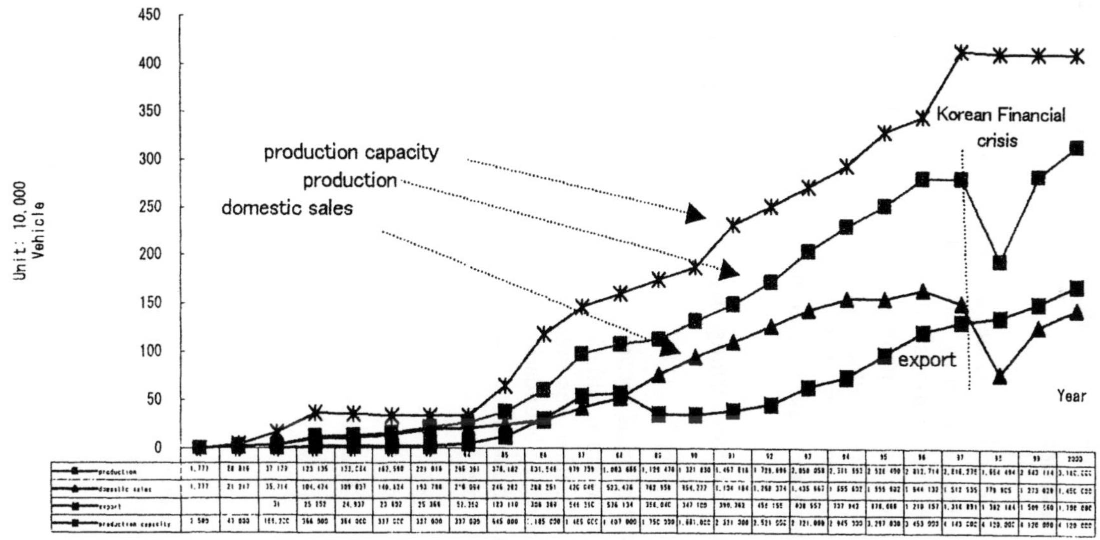

2 Issues concerning Korean automobile industry restructuring

The framework for issues development is shown in Figure 7–3 and Figure 7–4. The issues concerning the restructuring of the automobile industry can be classified into 4 parts as follows.

1. Those concerning the characteristics of the automobile industry itself
2. Those concerning the mega-merger era characteristics (time dimension)
3. Those concerning the geographical characteristics (space dimension)
4. Qualitative issues regarding internal competitiveness during restructuring

2.1 Issues concerning the characteristics of the automobile industry itself

The wall of crisis between countries. Why did the Korean Financial crisis of 1997 result in so much suffering of only Korean people and businesses when the trend of globalization was meant to have eliminated borders between countries? The international boundaries between companies are disappearing based on opportunity factors. However, there exists a great wall between countries based on crisis factors.

Figure 7–3. The framework for issues development

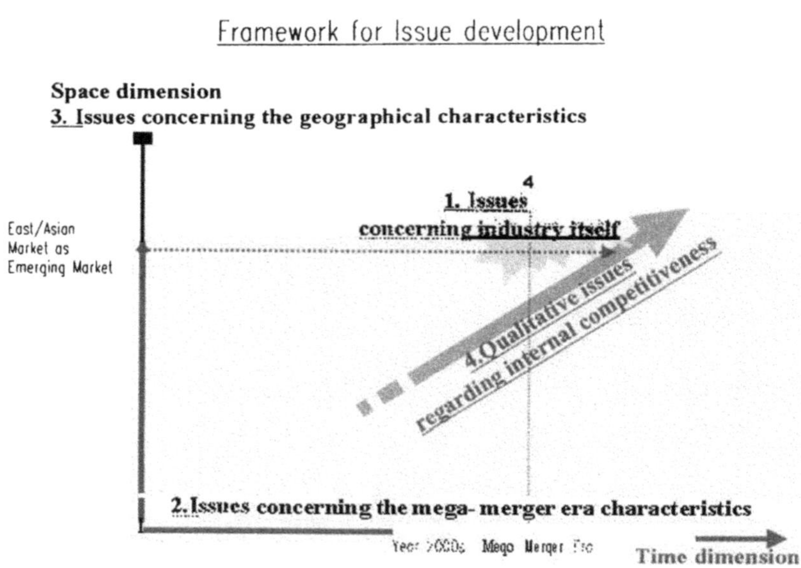

Figure 7–4. Two contradictory Mechanism for restructuring: Policy factor vs. Market factor

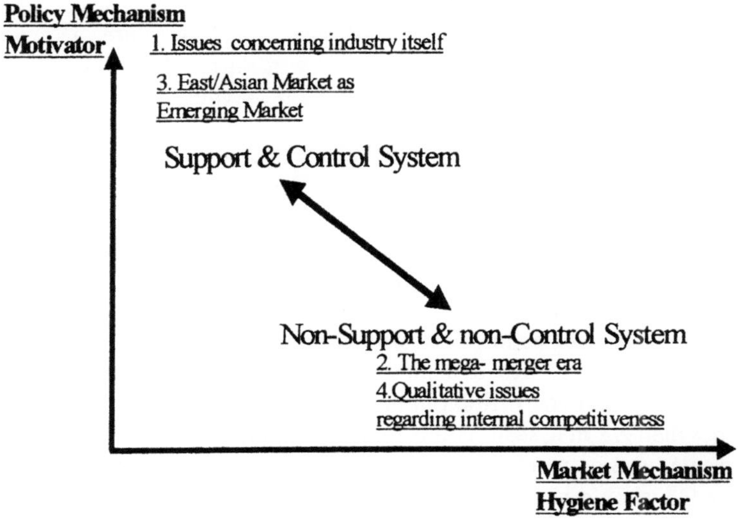

The weight of the automobile industry in Korea: the number of workers employed in vehicle and part related businesses are 223,924 (8.30 % of the manufacturing industry, 23.14% of the mechanical engineering industry). The total monetary amount of production is about 40 billion dollars (10.16% of the manufacturing industry, 32.05% of the mechanical engineering industry). Automobile exports amount to about 10 billion dollars.

Strategic importance of automobile industry. The competitiveness of the automobile is dependent upon the competitiveness of the overall industry comprising of product technology and the production technology accumulated from areas such as the country's basic materials, machine processing, petrochemical, and electronics industries. Therefore, Peter Drucker refers to the automobile industry as the industry of industries (IOI).

So, the automobile industry is a strategic asset to any nation. Government leaders, academics and business leaders all seem to worry constantly over the fate of the automobile industry.

2.2 Issues concerning the mega-merger era characteristics (time dimension)

At the beginning of 1980s, the Boston Consulting Group stated that in 1990s only the world's top 10 automotive makers will survive in the future. The scenario proposed was that after the latter part of 1990s and especially in the 2000s, such viewpoints would be reinforced well into the 21st century. Only 5 or 6 major automakers with a yearly production of over 4 million cars would survive. Pricewaterhouse Coopers identifies the global six, and the candidates as follows.

Global six: GM, Ford, Toyota, Volkswagen, Daimler–Chrysler, and Renault–Nissan.

Candidate: Honda, Mitsubishi, Peugeot, BMW, Fiat, and Hyundai.

Unexpected mega-mergers or alliances, as exemplified by the merger of Chrysler with Daimler–Benz, Ford–Volvo, Renault–Nissan, are taking place.

There were many debates in Korea with regards to the scenario of auto mega-mergers. Some people tended to believe that a Mega-merger was the tool for gaining scale for global competition in the next era. It's "myth of scale (Fujimoto, 1999)." They believe that scale is the source of competitiveness. In view of the myth of scale, some people believe that even Hyundai, the largest Korean Automobile Co, should be a member of a major company through such a M & A or alliance.

2.2.1 Lessons from Japan

The Japanese Ministry of International Trade and Industry (MITI) believed that the first requirement of an internationally competitive auto industry was high production scale. It proposed a series of plans to merge Japan's twelve embryonic car companies into a Japanese Big Two or Three to battle Detroit's Big Three.

What if these plans had succeeded?

The Japanese industry might have grown rapidly at first, but it would have posed no long-term threat to the established firms elsewhere in the world using the same techniques (Womack, Jones, and Roos 1990).

2.2.2 Two contradictory perspectives in the worldwide revolutionary transformation at the automotive industry

The automotive industry is undergoing a revolutionary transformation. There are two contradictory perspectives that offer an outlook as to how this transformation will take place (Fujimoto 1999).

2.2.2.1 Oligopoly perspective

The first perspective is that, through mega M&As, an industry wide reconfiguration will replace the current structure into an oligopolistic one. According to this theory, it is envisioned that approximately 5 companies who are

Figure 7–5. Automobile Production Share of Big 8 Companies

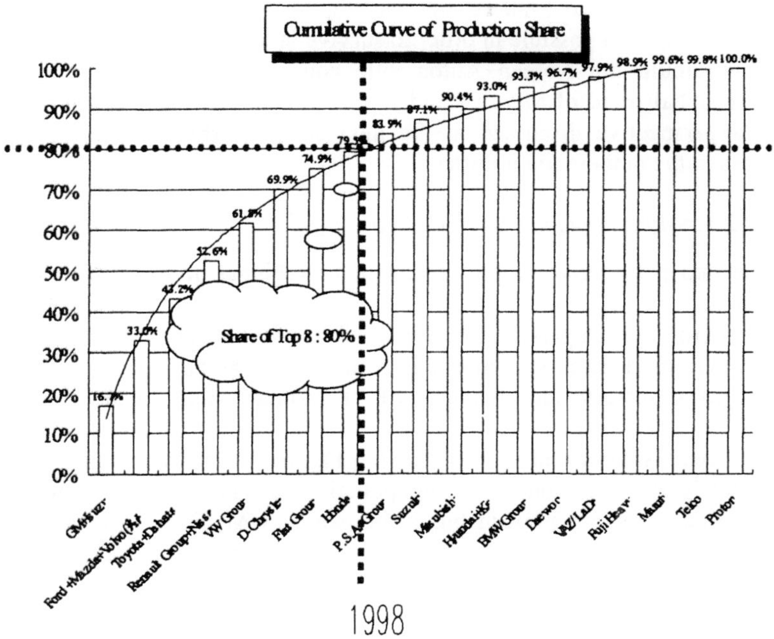

capable of producing over 4 million vehicles per annum will be able to survive. Consequently, other small to medium sized manufacturers will inevitably be merged into the major carmakers. The proponents of this theory argue that only a handful, roughly 20% of the car manufacturers supply approximately 80% of the global market.

The 80; 20 law in automobile industry of the world

As you can see from Figure 7–5, the Big 8 companies account for roughly 80% of the global market share. Equipped with advanced technological know-how and ample capital reserves, these corporations will lead the movement toward international integration and basically capture, if not monopolize, advance technology such as next generation environmental technology.

In 1998 among worlds total car production of 51.65 million cars, the big five companies (GM, Ford–Mazda, VW, Toyota, D–Chrysler) possessed 58% market share, the big 10 companies (those mentioned above and Fiat, Nissan, Honda, Renault, Peugeot–Citroen) possessed 81% of production market share[1].

[1] G.M Group: G.M–Fiat–Isuzu–Saab (Suzuki) , Ford Group: Ford–Volvo–Mazda–Land Rover, D–C Group: DaimlerChrysler–Mitsubishi, Renault/Nisssan Group: Renault–Nissan–Samsung.

On this point of view, only top 6 or 8 companies will survive in the global market." Minor Auto Makers, not the big 6 in the world, have to search for partners as soon as possible in order to survive in this new era of mergers."

How should the Korean Automobile companies respond or cope with the current global trend of Mergers and Acquisitions? My argument is based on the second perspective discussed in the next section, which concerns, the drastic changes in the automobile industry.

2.2.2.2 Regional division perspective

The second perspective is that there will be regional division of production via networks.

According to such perspective, corporations with independent management will exist where markets exist. Under this structure, the global market will be divided into regional sectors, and alliances will be formed where division of production occurs.

This trend is witnessed in the following Figure 7–6. If we look at the figure, we see a steady disintegration of the oligopolistic structure. Since the 1950s the global market share of the American big 3 companies, GM, Ford, Chrysler, have been decling. From the 1950s to 1996, the global market share of the American big 3

Figure 7–6. Global market share of the American big 3, GM, Ford, Chrysler: Steady disintegration of the oligopolistic structure

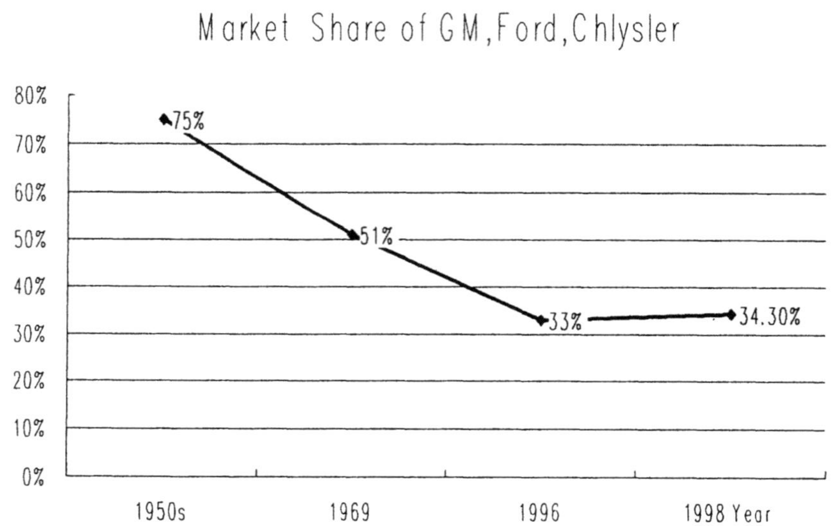

companies decreased from 75% to 33% by 43%. That is, despite the recent emergence of M&As, from a historical standpoint, we can see the overall dismantling of the oligopolistic structure.

On the other hand, car makers which produced over 1 million cars increased to 14 makers and car makers having the market share of over 1% are well over 17 companies.

As the following Figure 7–7 indicates, the global market share of the global big 3 corporations has declined quite rapidly from 75% in the 1950s (GM, Ford, Chrysler), 51% in 1969 (GM, Ford, Chrysler), 36% in 1996 (GM, Ford, Toyota) and 40% in 1998. Such advanced countries as USA, Germany, France, England, Italy and Japan have monopolized the worlds automobile industry. Along with each country's economic development, the automobile market has changed and the appearance of newly industrializing countries such as Korea has lowered their market share. In 1930s, these six countries possessed 99% of the market share. In 1980s it was 81% and in 1990s it has become 72%.

Boyer and Freyssenet (2000) state that the "big is beautiful" belief is a potentially dangerous one. The volume and diversity strategy is probably the most promising. There are many trials, but few successes exist. Therefore we can expect that the oligopolistic structure in the automobile industry steadily keep disintegrating shown in Figure 7–8.

Figure 7–7. Steady disintegration of the oligopolistic structure at the global big 3

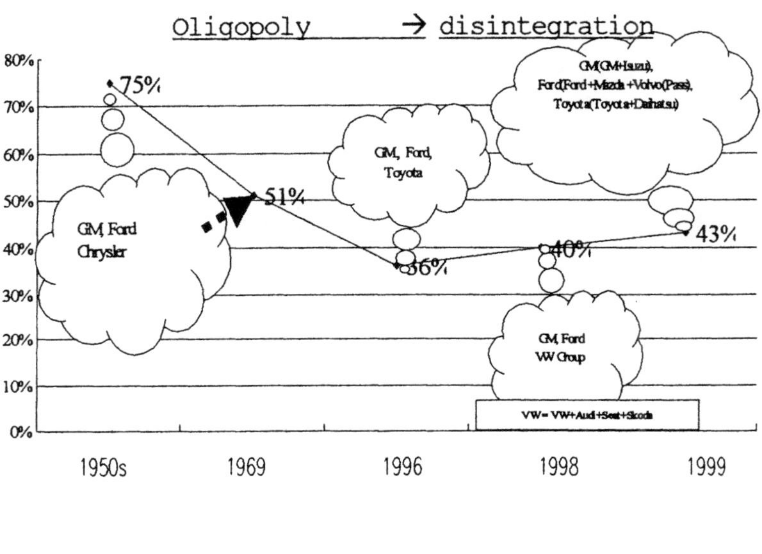

Figure 7–8. Expected Disintegration of the Oligopolistic Structure

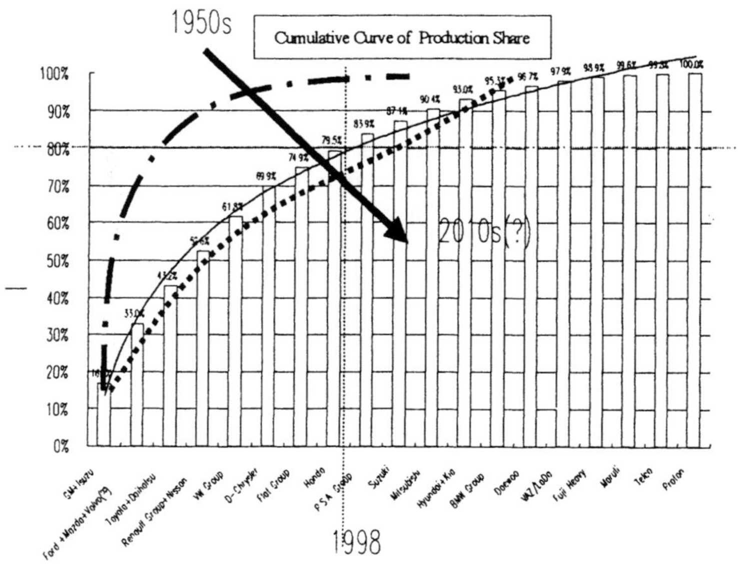

Figure 7–9. Auto Industry: The dilemma of the V Curve

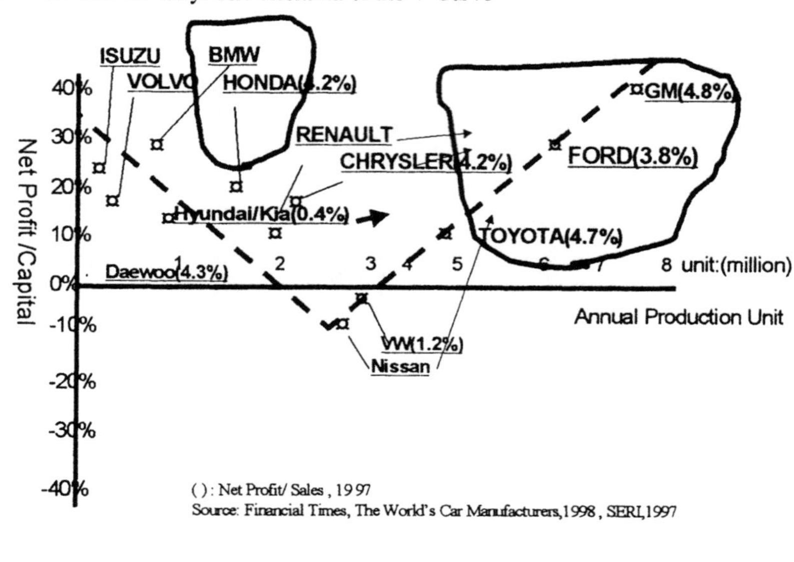

( ): Net Profit/ Sales , 1997

Source: Financial Times, The World's Car Manufacturers,1998 , SERI,1997

Figure 7–9 shows that each needs to select the mass production strategy or the focus strategy. That means "a compromising strategy is risky."For example, in the last 20 years BMW made as much profit as General Motors.

Let us discuss the evolvement cycle of the automobile industry. An evolvement cycle is the rate of evolution in industry. The evolvement cycle speed of each industry depends upon its product evolvement and process evolvement cycle. Since the era of the Ford Model T, the basic product architecture of the automobile has been rather integral, closed and stable. And within the basic industrial framework, this industry has been improving its industrial performance and technological advancement (Fujimoto 1999). Automobile companies typically refresh their car and truck models every 4 to 8 years. In this process domain, they expect that a billion dollars invested in an engine or assembly plant will remain vibrant for 20 years or more (Fine 1998).

Carmakers have to accumulate their capability evolutionally for the industrial marathon. The achievement of practical capability takes as long as the automobile evolvement cycle. They cannot get a practical result until at least one evolvement cycle. It is dynamic capability building competition. In this point of view "Scale can be regarded as a result of the firm's competitive capability, but it should not be regarded as its ultimate goal" (Fujimoto 1999). This contention based on dynamic capability building should be persuasive to Korea.

2.3 Issues concerning the geographical characteristics (space dimension)

2.3.1 East Asian Market as emerging market

In 2007, the East Asian car market forecasts that the Asia/Pacific will surpass each of the European and the American markets. In 2010, it is forecasted that the Chinese market will have motorization in full scale, the Asia Pacific area will be the center of the world market. Especially with China's joining the WTO, the opportunity for entering the Chinese market has become greater. The Korean automobile industry, which is close in proximity to the Chinese Market, has very good opportunities in variety of ways. 80–100% of the high automobile tariff will be reduced to 25 % by 2006 and the sea route from Korea might be the faster and cheaper trade route than the inland route inside China. The possibility of this is even higher since China has more rich people living close to the seaside. Also, in the case of the automobile parts industry, since China has lower localization rates, with respect to reliability, low price, production technology and management technology, Korean parts suppliers have the capability to develop into supply bases for China.

Particularly when it becomes possible to use North Korean low-cost work force, the competitiveness of the labor –intensive parts industry will be much

Figure 7–10. The geographical characteristics: proximity to the China market

higher. I think US based companies cannot make a car as cheaply as Korean car makers due to higher expenses. The automobile industry's competitiveness is related to various production and development factors. To be competitive in a late developing car market or any advanced countries' low-price market, an advanced country automotive manufacturer must be able to produce at low cost. Korean carmaker is one of best networking partners for producing automobiles at low cost (Figure 7–10).

2.3.2 If you can't beat them, buy them

The Koreans rushed into a near vacuum in America. The American makers build small cars now, but none are cheaper than $12,000, and they have no plans to take their brands further down the pricing scale, where profits, at least for a U.S.-manufactured vehicle, are hard to come by (Forbes Sep 18, 2000).

"We're not going to pour billions of dollars into a tiny segment in the U.S. that doesn't make money," says James P. Holden, chief executive of Daimler Chrysler Corp., the American branch of Daimler Chrysler.

Are successful efforts of Korean automakers in the U.S. market for small cars an invasion that General Motors, Ford and Daimler Chrysler should worry about? Definitely. So the Big Three have decided that if you can't beat them, buy them. Even with the reduced tariff, cars that are imported into the Korean Market cost twice as much as the same sized Korean cars. In the Korean market, Hyundai leads the world in delivering the most price competitive car when comparing quality and performance. Even if an advanced-country automaker localized the design on cars based on their own car model in Korea, they would still not be price competitive when comparing quality and performance. A very good example of this is the competition between Le Man, which was a GM model, and Excel in the late 1980s in Korea.

2.4 Qualitative issues for inner competitiveness in restructuring

2.4.1 Automobile Aftermarket as a new business opportunity

The automobile industry has reached its maturity stage as the most typical mass production industry. The life cycle of the automobile product is divided into "before maket" (the supply market of auto parts), the new car market itself, and the Aftermarket. In the life cycle of the automobile, the profit that can be obtained at the selling point is merely 10% and the remaining 90% comes from the car related service activities (after-market) after the car has been sold. Financial services, insurance services, repair services, and so on accompany the after-market. Accordingly, it is inevitable that the profit structure of a carmaker with no interest in the aftermarket will be weakened. One of reasons why Korean carmakers' profitability is becoming weak is that they have been focusing only on the 10% automobile selling profits.

There are 11,160,000 cars in the Korean aftermarket, in comparison with 1,500,000 in the new car market. In the US, the after automobile service market is 13.7 times (based on average vehicle life of 13.7 years (Field 2000)) of what the yearly new car demand of 15 million is. (The average life span of a car: US, Japan: 12 years, Benz: 20 years.)

2.4.2 New Concept Car

2.4.2.1 The Environmentally Friendly Safety Automobile

The development of environmental technology and ecologically safe production systems: Powertrain innovation, Hybrid & Fuel Cell techniques driven by fuel price, green car. It is expected that major carmakers, if successful in environmental technology development, will lobby for indirect restrictions that could result in the withdrawal of the automobile latecomers. In the case of the Korean carmaker, this New Concept Car challenge should be resolved through the technology network.

2.4.2.2 Mobile Office Car

As the digitalization of the world economy spreads and as the competition structure based on the completed product will be shifted to one based on parts and materials, the newly innovated parts and materials will be the source of creating new technology and new product.

Electronic technology and Internet driven e-business: The deepening of the integral design of electronics in automobile parts, intellectualization, telematics, and the mobile office.

2.4.2.3 Customization and electronic proximity

No longer are companies focusing on producing standardized products or services for homogeneous markets. Customization is the process in which the needs of the final customers are confirmed and fulfilled. As the feedback loop is reinforced, the niche markets become smaller: They begin reaching down closer to the "individual." "Greater and greater variety" blends into "more and more customization."

For example, 3DayCar Project (Graves 2000): To develop an organizational and process framework within which a customer's need for a vehicle can be fulfilled in three days, from order placement through manufacture and delivery. They have to shift their concept from 'stock–push', 'shop–floor Myopia' to 'build to order and customization'.

For such a speedy customization, managers realize that they could not achieve improved company performance solely, or even primarily, by concentrating on the factory. Rather, they must focus on customization and electronic proximity based on concurrently designing the customer-oriented product and the manufacturing process, that is, designing the product for the customer and manufacturability through electronic Supply Chain (e-SC) (Figure 7–11).

3 Future Scenario of Korea Auto Industry

3.1 Optimistic Scenario: Competitiveness and Growth Potential of Korea Auto Industry

3.1.1 Asian Market as emerging market

The East Asian Market is expected to increase in demand in the future. In the near future the East Asian Market, including Japan, Korea and China, will surpass each of the European and the American markets. In 2010, when it is forecasted that the Chinese market will be motorized, the East Asian Market will be one of the largest automobile markets. The Korean automobile industry, which is close to the Chinese Market, will have good opportunities (Figure 7–10).

The East Asian Market is expected to increase in demand in the future. In the near future the East Asian Market, including Japan, Korea and China, will surpass each of the European and the American markets. In 2010, when it is forecasted that the Chinese market will be motorized, the East Asian Market will be one of the largest automobile markets. The Korean automobile industry, which is close to the Chinese Market, will have good opportunities (Figure 7–12).

3.1.2 Cost competitiveness of Korean automobile industry

Furthermore, *the cars competing in Asia will not be high-tech cars for a while*. In this market the focus is to mass-produce cars at a low cost (production technology) and to accumulate know-how by circling fast around the experience (test) loop (process technology). From this point of view, Korean Automobiles will get relative advantages in capturing the East Asian Market based on a cheap cost structure.

When investigating the business feasibility, Daewoo carmakers are supposed to be making profits even with only 200,000 to 300,000 cars in production per year per platform. This was not properly accomplished however. In the case of mid sized cars, the minimum size for making profits is much smaller, in fact it is below 150000 cars. The reason for this is that Korea has world class price competitiveness with regards to development cost and parts cost.

The Korean auto industry offsets the demerits of smaller volume by this cost capability that enables production at lower cost. The economy of scale difference between 200,000 and 500,000 car production per year is approximately 5 to 10%. This demonstrates that the cost capability in the Korean auto industry can be attributed to more than the economy of scale. Comparing the similar case between Major automakers and Korea automakers, the automobile development cost of Major-makers was 4 times that of Korea's automakers.

3.1.2.1 Promotion cost of constructing new a factory and developing new cars in parallel.

It is known that 4 billion dollars was spent in the development of the GM compact car, Saturn. This is the result of promoting in parallel the construction of a new factory and the development of new cars. The expense used in the parallel promotion of the construction of Daewoo, Kun San Factory and Nubira, was about 1 billion dollars.

Figure 7–11. Customization and electronic proximity through electronic Supply Chain (e-SC)

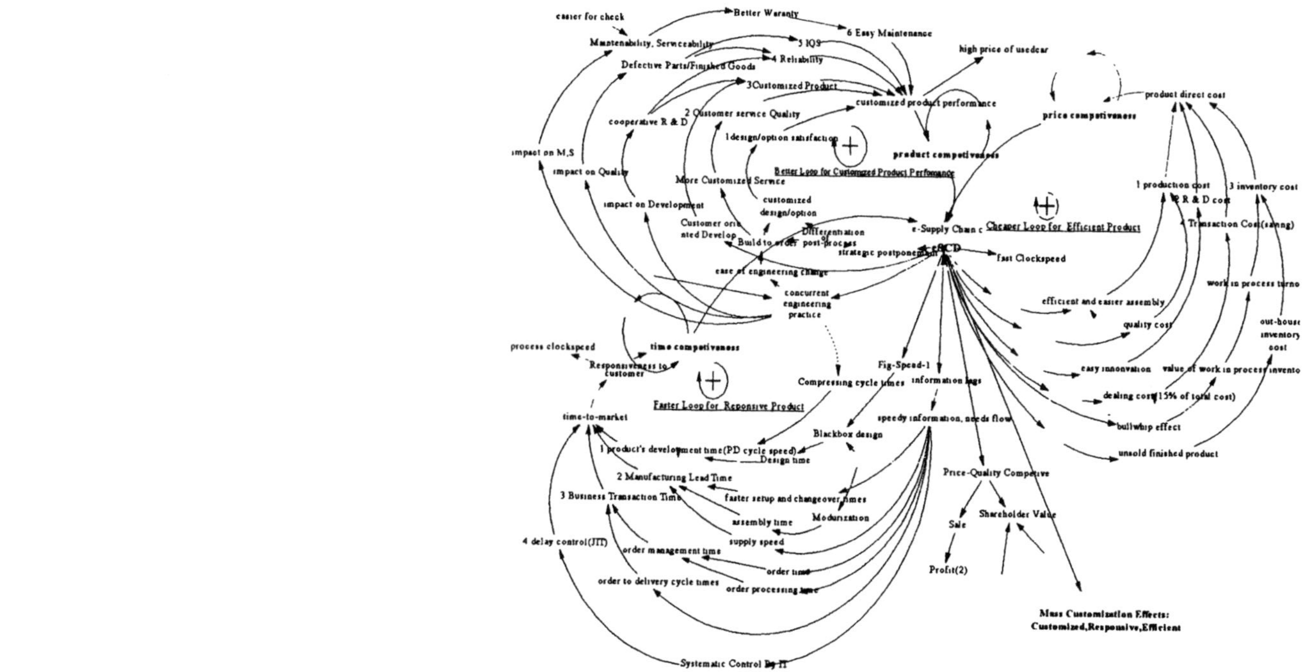

Source: Fine & Kim (2000)

Figure 7–12. Korean Car Maker Positioning

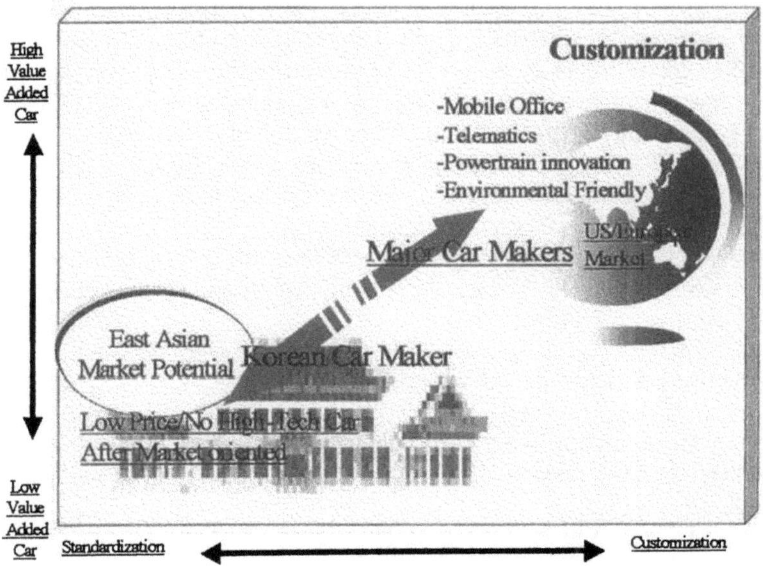

3.1.2.2 The comparison of the development cost of new cars

The development of the Chrysler Neon, which was the case of the entire change of P/F without building the new factory, has been known to cost 1.4 billion dollars. The similar case of Lezo and Magnus developments required 140–180 million dollars.

Even though Renault or GM(?) has taken ownership of some Korean Car Makers, these companies will still think of Korea as one of the production and development bases for managing the emerging East Asian Market. Korea is known for its strength in production technology. The product development technology area is relatively weak for most automakers.

However, because cost competition is fierce, the automobile R & D center must be located in close proximity to the automobile production base. To the extent that, in order to strengthen cost competitiveness, the development base should also accompany the automobile production base. Thailand, Indonesia, and China might be good as OEM bases but they still not possess enough competencies as production and development bases.

3.1.2.3 Cost competitiveness in Auto Parts Industry

Since about 60% of the entire production cost of a car is due to parts expenses, the reduction in parts related cost will determine cost competitiveness. The price of Korean auto parts materials, mainly consisting of steel, petrochemical, and electronics contribute more than 70% to the total materials for the auto, and are still comparatively low. Further more, by increasing of the rate of outsourced parts, systemizing parts, and improving modularity within each enterprise, automakers are trying to realize the cost saving effect. Recently, there has been rapid advancement of this kind of trend through platform integration and parts sharing.

Many Korean parts suppliers obtained QS9000, the quality certification of the US' 3 major automakers. There are not many countries that can produce reliable auto products at such a low price as Korea can.

3.1.3 Korean Autos Carve Niche in U.S. Market

Following the formula pioneered by Japanese automakers 30 years ago, Korean automakers got on Americans' shopping lists by selling dirtcheap compact cars in the U.S.

The three Korean companies selling cars in the U.S.–Hyundai, Kia and Daewoo – have seen their sales nearly double in a year, to 329,600 in 1999, according to Ward's AutoInfoBank. That's only 2% of the entire U.S. car market, but up from 1.1% the year before – a giant gain in an industry in which even the biggest players scrap for every tenth of a point of business. And, more pointedly, the Korean share of the U.S. small-car segment zoomed from 6.5% in 1998 to 14.9% so far this year, biting into U.S., European and Japanese business (Forbes Sep 18, 2000)

This year, Korean automobiles are selling better in the U.S. market this year. As of 92,000, Overall sales of Hyundai during the first seven months of the year jumped by 65% on an annual comparison this year. Kia Motor Co. and Daewoo Motor Co. has also enjoyed a visible rise in car sales in the U.S. market by 11.8% and 175% on an annual comparison each.

3.1.3.1 Hyundai plans $1bn US plant investment

Hyundai Motor, Korea's largest carmaker, is planning to invest more than $1billion to set up its first manufacturing plant in the US. The car company, which exports about 450,000 cars a year to North America, is drawing up proposals for a US plant capable of assembling 300,000 vehicles a year(October 2 2000, Financial Times).

3.2 Pessimistic scenario concerning Korean automobile industry

3.2.1 The characteristics of input capital for restructuring: Is GM a white knight or a black knight?

What is the significance of billions dollars proposed by major carmaker in acquiring Daewoo? Is it the value of entering the Korean domestic market or is it the future worth of the geographical network that will become critical in the East Asian emerging market?

Global major automakers' (such as GM, that can take over Korean Companies monopoly over R&D is the core capability. In this light, Daewoo's R&D might be reduced or actually closed down diminishing it to just becoming an OEM base. Daewoo may become OEM base by platform integration strategy. Historically, there have been bad experiences resulting from the collaboration between Daewoo and GM.

The strategy of the Korean automobile industry is to focus on the domestic market: major global automakers also wish to be aggressive in selling at a low price in the Korean market.

Last July, Daewoo's Bupyoung factory was stopped for 8 hours because Delphi cancelled its supply of auto parts temporarily. Delphi holds a 50% stake of Daewoo Precision Industries. A Daewoo Motor official explained his company had been experiencing a fund shortage and had requested the parts supplier to freeze the prices. Delphi responded by stopping their supply to Daewoo without any prior notice, leaving Daewoo at risk of an auto production shutdown. In the context of past experiences and traditional practices, this event embarrassed Daewoo a great deal.

Following Korea's 1997 financial crisis, major global auto parts makers continued to expand their operations in Korea. Foreign automakers took over more than 50% equity in about 30 domestic auto parts companies. Delphi Automotive Systems, an auto parts subsidiary of General Motors, took over a suspension plants from Daewoo (in 1998), Sungwoo (in 1999) and Korea Lucas Diesel(70% stake, 2000), These takeovers make it Delphi of the largest auto manufacturers in Korea in terms of sales. The U.S. auto parts maker, Gibbs, also took over the Munmak Plant of Mondo Machinery (1999). Mondo was the largest local auto parts maker until it sold off all of its four major plants in the country. Visteon, a subsidiary of Ford, took over Deukyang Industry (1999), local firm producing car-interior fittings, and is reportedly considering taking over a local firm producing car seats.

These domestic auto parts manufacturers produce core auto parts, including suspension and steering systems. Conflicts between Korean auto manufacturers, such as Hyundai, Kia and Daewoo, and these auto parts suppliers have arisen in recent months, particularly since the takeovers allowed the foreign firms to control the supply and price of auto parts in Korea.

Figure 7–13. The Korean automobile strength from the view of quality–cost competitiveness

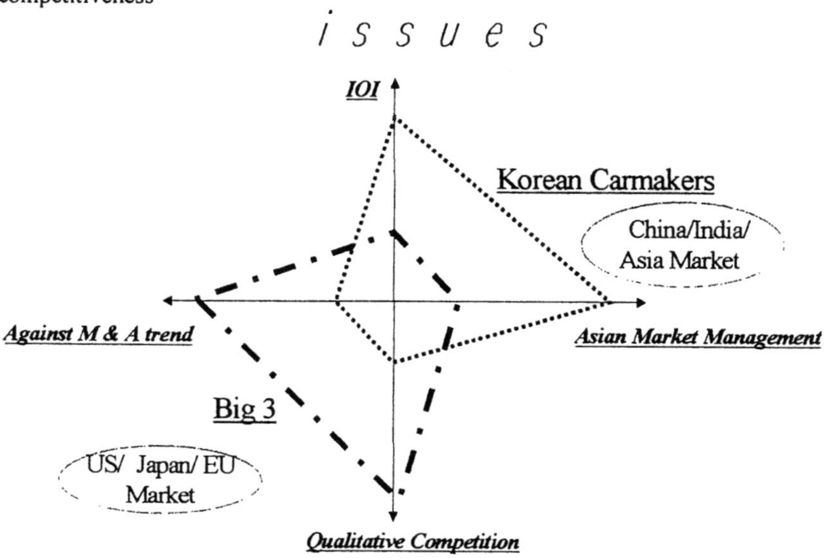

3.2.2 Only about 5 or 6 major makers Survival Scenario.

The automobile industry will be in fierce competition in the future due to the oversupply of 20 million cars. There is speculation that only about 5 or 6 major makers with a yearly production of over 4 million cars will be left alive.

The question becomes whether even Hyundai, the largest Korean Automobile Co, should be a member of major auto company through M & A or alliances?

Survival scenario of a few companies that developed the next generation automobile technology.

How would Korean carmakers as the new technology latecomer cope with such indirect environmental-related restrictions in the future market? Major carmakers, if successful in environmental technology development, will strongly drive for indirect restriction or the withdrawal of automobile latecomers from now on. This strategy is sometimes received as a serious plot in discriminating and excluding cars made by late entrants.

Can Korean carmakers resolve this New Concept Car challenge through their technology network?

Will electronics replace sheet steel as the most integral subsystem in the automobile, driving shifts in the relative strategic and financial importance of various members in the supply chain? (Fine 1998)

Figure 7–14. Cheaper strategy for east Asian market with low-cost car and compact car market in US

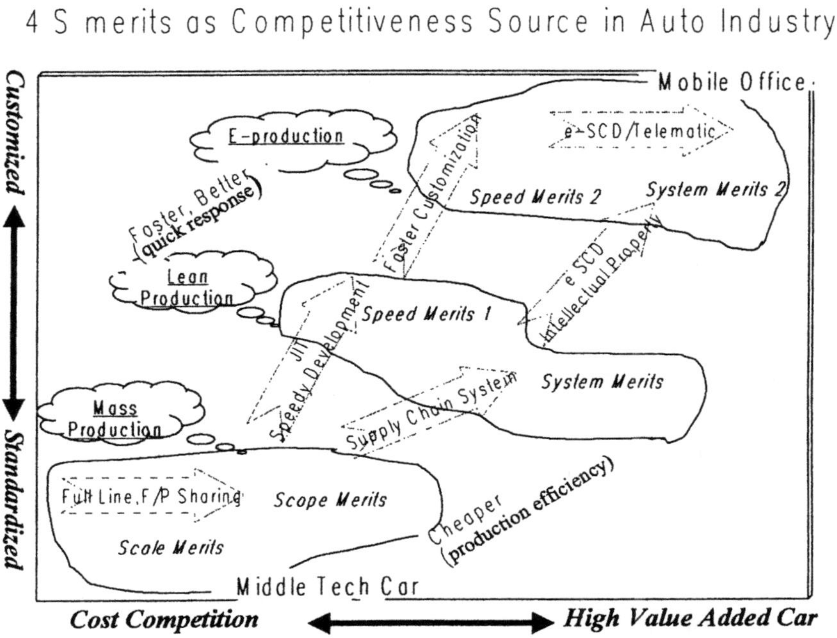

Hyundai has applied for the spin off of an automotive subgroup, including Hyundai Motor. The eight Hyundai automobile industry-related firms to be spun off have a total annual sales of W25.45 trillion, with assets of W28.59 trillion, and rank 5th in the country in terms of asset value as a group.

4 Discussion: Positioning Strategy in the world

The automobile industry is a strategic asset to any nation. Government leaders, academics and business leaders all seem to worry constantly over the fate of the automobile industry. In terms of the four main issues for the Korean automobile industry restructure, I want to address the following questions.

How should Korea carmakers compete with major car makers in the future? "Which position would suit Korean car companies best?" How should Daewoo Motor Co be dealt with?Figure 7–13 shows the strengths of Korea carmakers and the Big 3 (or even Big 5 or Big 6) carmakers in the world based on the 4 issues that I explained in Figure 7–3. The "IOI (Industry of Industry)" factor in Figure 7–3 is related to the issues concerning the characteristics of the automobile industry itself. "Against the M & A trend" factor in Figure 7–3 is related to the issues concerning the mega-merger era characteristics. "Asian market management" factor in Figure 7–3 is related to the issues concerning the geographical characteristics. "Quality competition" factor is regarding internal qualitative competitiveness during restructuring.

It is my contention that we must evaluate the Korean automobile strength from the view point of quality–cost competitiveness. Because I think the market they should target is the east Asian market with low-cost car and compact car markets in the US shown in Figure 7–13.

Then, which position would suit the Korea carmakers best among middle tech and low price strategy, mobile office and customization strategy and follower strategy? The Four S's shown in Figure 7–14 are the economy that the company should pursue for his competitiveness.

The four S's of economy are merits of scale, scope, speed and system. According to the characteristics of firm changes, the relative weight of the four S's will be different. Among the 4 S merits, cheaper strategy through scale and scope merits is more useful than faster or better strategy through speed and system merits for the time being. Because Korea carmakers have to target the east Asian market with low-cost car and compact car market in US shown in Figure 7–13.

Finally, I would also like to mention briefly the Daewoo situation. Daewoo has two options based on the pessimistic or optimistic scenario.

Based on the pessimistic scenario, Daewoo should be sold to anyone who want to buy, even though they want to pay for low price. Or, based on the optimistic scenario, Daewoo should be kept for the Korean economy. Daewoo may just as well be the public enterprise for the time being. The Korean Industry Bank can invest in Daewoo. At that time it may be committed by Hyundai as its manager.

References

Boyer, Robert and Michel Freyssenet (2000) "Megamergers and the Variety of Industrial Models," *IMVP sponsors Meeting*, Sep 28, 2000, MIT.

Clark, K.B. and T. Fujimoto (1991) *Product Development Performance*. Harvard Business School Press, Boston, MA.

Feitzinger, Edward and Hau L.Lee (1997) "Mass Customization at Hewlett–Packard: The Power of Postponement," *Harvard Business Review*.

Field,Frank (2000) "Green Cars," *IMVP sponsors Meeting*, Sep 29,2000, MIT.

Fine, C. H.(1998) *Clcokspeed-Winning Industry Control In the Age of Temporary Advantage*, Perseus Books.

Fine, Charles H. & Ki-Chan Kim (2000) "Customization effect of e SCD: Beyond 4 S merits."

Fujimoto, Takahiro (1999) "Global Alliances, Mergers, and Their implications for the Korean Auto Industry," *Seminar in Korean Industrial Oraganization Association.*

Graves, Andrew (2000) "The road to the 3daycar," *IMVP sponsors Meeting*, Sep 28,2000, MIT

Hyun, Young Suk (2000) "Case Analysis on the Oversea Car Maker Restructuring and Their Implication for the Korean Auto Industry," June 2000

Kim, Ki-Chan (1999) "The Future of Korean Automobile Industry," Yonsei University Economic Institute, 1999.10

MacDuffie, John Paul (2000) "Build-to-Order Process," *IMVP sponsors Meeting*, Sep 28,2000, MIT

Pine, B. J., Jr. (1993) *Mass Customization: The New Frontier in Business Competition*, Harvard Business School Press.

Pricewaterhouse Coopers (2000) *The Second Automotive Century*, 2000.

Williamson, O.E. (1985) *The Economic Institutions of Capitalism*, New York: Free Press.

Womack, James P. Daniel T. Jones, and Daniel Roos(1990), *The Machine that Changed the World*, HarperPerennial.

Yong-Wook Jun (1999) "Survival Strategy of Korean Car Makers in Mega Competition Era," Yonsei University, Economic Institute, 1999.10.

Finacial Times

Forbes, September 18, 2000

http://www.autonews.com

http://www.forbes.com

http://www.kama.or.kr/

8 Leveraging Capabilities: Models of Foreign Production in the Taiwanese Automotive Industry*

Teresa M. Lynch
Massachusetts Institute of Technology

1 Introduction

"Going global" by establishing or expanding foreign production capabilities has long played an important strategic role for firms in the automotive industry. Faced with high costs, falling profits, and loss of domestic market share in the 1970s and 1980s, American automotive firms turned to existing foreign affiliates for parts and finished vehicles, and bolstered production capabilities in lower-cost countries like Mexico and Canada. In the 1980s, the rising yen and growing trade frictions led Japanese firms to establish production sites in North America and Europe in order to protect market share in these regions. When crisis hit German automotive industry in the 1990s, extensive foreign investment allowed assemblers to spread design and development costs over much larger volumes, and spurred the globalization and domestic restructuring of German suppliers (Pries 1999). For automotive firms in each of these countries, expansion of global capabilities helped solve critical problems, and in the German and American cases, was an important component of a larger restructuring effort.

Today, challenged by a small and slow-growing domestic market, tariff reductions with likely accession into WTO, and a tight domestic supply of production and technical workers, firms in the Taiwanese auto industry face similar pressures to restructure domestic activities. Given the important strategic role of foreign investment in the restructuring experiences of automotive sectors in other countries, as well as the flurry of recent offshore investment across a range of Taiwan's manufacturing sectors, it is worth considering the relationship

* I would like to thank conference participants and colleagues at MIT's Industrial Performance Center for helpful discussions about the ideas presented in this paper. Special thanks to Momoko Kawakami, who provided detailed comments on an earlier version of this paper.

between foreign investment and domestic restructuring of Taiwanese automotive firms.

In this chapter, I examine foreign production patterns of Taiwanese automotive firms and find evidence of a dual pattern with regard to the relationship between foreign investment and domestic restructuring. One type of investment, which is evident among assemblers, as well as some suppliers, is aimed at maintaining or increasing overall production volumes given adverse conditions in the domestic market and expected reductions in tariff levels. For these firms, offshore investment represents an attempt to transfer skills and capabilities that have been developed within the (protected) domestic environment to new and in some ways, more hospitable market settings. Although many of the investing firms are concurrently reconfiguring domestic operations to lower costs, domestic adjustment and foreign investments do not constitute an integrated strategy, but appear to be distinct parts of a dual strategy in which domestic adjustments serve to maintain domestic market share, and foreign investments act to secure overall firm output levels in the event that domestic sales or margins collapse. In short, these offshore investments are aimed at market diversification, thus reducing firms' vulnerability to changes in the Taiwanese market.

These market-diversifying investments differ from typical market-seeking investments in the automobile industry. Unlike market-seeking investments, where market access *per se* is the primary goal, market-diversification strategies appear aimed as much at securing new regulatory environments as at gaining access to new customers. In addition, market-diversifying investments provide different benefits than typical market-seeking investments, which generate cost advantages by spreading design and development costs over higher volumes. Because Taiwanese assemblers and suppliers tend to produce vehicles and parts designed by their foreign partners, higher production volumes will not necessarily generate cost savings. Instead, these investments provide an opportunity to take advantage of foreign market structures that provide some protection for local producers.

A second type of foreign investment is also evident among Taiwanese automotive firms. These investments are not driven by specific changes in the domestic environment, such as likely WTO accession, but reflect on-going attempts to restructure domestic activities as Taiwan's comparative advantage within the region changes. As conditions in domestic product and labor markets change, these investments enable firms to move low value-added or labor-intensive products to foreign sites, creating opportunities for domestic plants to shift to new product lines without abandoning existing customers or markets. In some cases, these investments are accompanied by the transfer of some lower-end engineering and design tasks to foreign sites, thus reducing costs and freeing domestic staff to focus on higher-end engineering and design tasks. In contrast to market-diversifying investments, which largely reproduce domestic operations, these upgrading investments often yield a complex division of labor between offshore and domestic sites.

These two distinct patterns have interesting implications for examining patterns of globalization and "hollowing out" of employment and capabilities in industrial economies. For firms that have pursued only market-diversifying strategies, the dichotomous nature of foreign production and domestic restructuring means that the level and types of future activities at domestic plants is likely to be largely independent of the success or failure of globalization efforts. However, because of the overlap in product lines at home and host sites, it could appear that firms have in effect transferred production from domestic to foreign plants. As a result, if domestic plants were to be less competitive after WTO accession, subsequent declines in domestic production and employment might appear to have been caused by the transfer of production to from domestic to foreign sites. In fact, though, because of the independent strategic role of these investments, foreign activities and domestic economic outcomes will be largely independent (but coincident) phenomena.

For firms that have integrated foreign investment and domestic restructuring strategies, though, levels and types of domestic activities are strongly linked to the role foreign sites in absorbing price-sensitive product lines and providing access to lower-cost engineering and technical workers. In these cases, because foreign and domestic plants manufacture different products, it could appear that success or failure at domestic plants is independent of foreign activities. In fact, though, these investments allow firms to continue to exploit their experience and expertise in product areas in which Taiwan has lost its comparative advantage, and create space for domestic plants to move into new product areas. In these cases, what appear to be distinct or even independent foreign activities can, in fact, have real implications for the level and characteristics of output and employment at domestic plants.

These findings call into question the reliability of macro or aggregate approaches for understanding the causes and consequences of foreign investment. As these patterns illustrate, even when home country, host country, and sector are identical, multiple investment strategies, each with different implications for domestic economies can exist. In the case of Taiwanese automotive firms, this duality is due in part to the unusual attributes of the primary host country, China, which has attracted vast amounts of foreign investment because of its promising market, but also because of its abundance of qualified, low-cost production and technical labor. As such, it might not be easy to generalize from this case. That said, the findings still suggest that understanding the linkages between foreign and domestic production requires disentangling the multiple pressures that underlie foreign investment decisions, and identifying the specific roles that foreign investments play in firms' market and production strategies.

2 Domestic Problems

Measured by some key indicators, Taiwan's auto industry seems reasonably healthy. In contrast to the rapid decline in output and employment in other traditional sectors, like textiles and garments, the automotive sector has actually grown over the past decade. Between 1989 and 1999, output increased from $4.7 to $9.1 billion US and employment from 66,000 to almost 76,000 (Directorate-General of Budget 2000; MOEA various years). Even relative to other auto-producing countries, the assembly and supply sectors continue to make significant contributions to national output and employment, accounting for 1.3% of total employment in 1998, compared to, for example, 1.0% in the U.S. in the same year (Directorate-General of Budget 2000; US Department of Labor 2000).

Despite its relatively strong recent showing, the Taiwanese automotive industry faces a number of challenges, some the result of the large number of producers, others the result of a small and slow-growing domestic market. Despite the small internal market, there are currently ten assemblers in Taiwan, five of which account for virtually all of the island's vehicle production. Each of the top assemblers is owned in part by large foreign assemblers: Mitsubishi owns 21percent of China Motors Corporation, Nissan owns 25 percent of Yulon, Toyota and Hino own 49 percent of Kuozui, Honda owns 13.5 percent of San Yang, and Ford owns 70 percent of Ford Lio Ho (TTVMA 2000).

Although the commercial and personal vehicle market in Taiwan grew rapidly between the early 1980s and mid-1990s, when sales rose from about 100,000 to almost 600,000 units annually, it has actually shrunk in the last few years and future market growth is expected to be modest (Noble 1996; TTVMA 2000). These problems are compounded by the large number of assemblers, which contributes to low capacity utilization rates and kept any single firm from producing 100,000 vehicles in recent years.

Industry observers expect the number of assemblers to decline to four or five in the next few years. The surviving domestic producers, however, could face greater competition from imports. In the latter half of the 1990s, despite vehicle tariffs of 30 percent, imported vehicles accounted for between about 15 and 25 percent of domestic sales (TTVMA 2000). And although industry observers disagree about the likely degree of import penetration when tariffs fall from 30 to 17.5 percent with (expected) WTO accession, there appears to be a consensus that the import ratio will rise significantly from its current level of 15 percent (see, e.g., Taipei Times 1999; EIU 1998). The full effect of WTO accession, though, will not be immediate, as tariffs reductions and rising import quotas will be phased in as part of a negotiated transition period (Barnes 1999).

The supply sector is also likely to be strongly affected if tariff or local content rates are reduced or eliminated as part of WTO accession. Despite a core of strong firms, there are significant gaps in domestic supplier capabilities, a situation that has contributed to low average domestic content of vehicles. Current regulations require domestic assemblers to achieve 50 percent local content and some models, like China Motors' Varica, which uses a Taiwanese-produced engine, and the Freeca, with a local content rate near 90 percent, rely almost wholly on locally-produced parts (Noble 1996; FT Asia Intelligence Wire 1997). Still, the overall local content ratio of domestically produced vehicles is only between 50 and 60 percent, with most of the remaining parts coming from Japan.[1] In 1999, Taiwan imported US $1.25 billion in components from Japan, the equivalent of about one-third of total Taiwanese consumption of parts that year (TTVMA 2000; Veloso, et al. 1998).[2] Many of these imports were drivetrain parts, reflecting continued Taiwanese dependence on foreign partners for most engines and some other critical parts and components (TTVMA 2000; Jiji Press Ltd. 1997; EIU 1995).

Despite these challenges and constraints, the past decade has witnessed the emergence of new capabilities and strategies at some of Taiwan's leading automotive firms. Two of the largest assemblers have established some independent research and design capabilities, and both appear to be taking on more important roles in the Asian strategies of their Japanese partners. One has emerged as an important source of complete knock-down (CKD) kits for its partner's assembly sites in ASEAN; the other hopes to design six new passenger, van, and heavy-duty models in the next few years, and recently helped remodel a vehicle for production and sale on the mainland (Taipei Times 2000; AFX News Limited 2000). Both companies are also committed to aggressive foreign investment strategies and, as will be discussed, have begun to secure new production sites outside of Taiwan.

3 Domestic Solutions?

Like many firms around the world, Taiwanese automotive firms are facing imminent challenges associated with liberalized markets, greater competition, and regional and global overcapacity. Often times, these types of pressures will spur firms to reduce costs in order to compete in existing product areas, or to move into new product areas and markets. However, the standard prescriptions that accompany these strategies, for example, improving price-quality ratios of goods or increasing sales in regional or international markets, could be difficult for

[1] Veloso, et al. (1998) report that average local content is 50%; TTVMA (2000) suggests local content is about 60%. Trade data confirm that actual local content is somewhere between these estimates. See footnote 2.

[2] In 1998, Taiwanese components firms produced about $4B US, of which about $2.1 B was exported. Assuming that parts and components produced domestically but not exported are for OEM sales, as are the $2B in imported parts and components, then total domestic OEM consumption is about $3.9 billion. Of this, $1.9B, or about half, is produced locally. (Trade data from TTVMA 2000.) Actual vehicle assembly will add additional local content. In addition, some assemblers might make parts in–house that are consumed domestically but not counted in estimates of domestic parts production.

Taiwanese firms to implement given current domestic labor market conditions and the larger political economy of auto production in Asia.

Some managers report that price pressures have been intense for the past few years and one noted that assemblers already require his firm to meet expected post-WTO prices.[3] However, the domestic production environment might not be amenable to further cost reductions. Like other firms in so-called traditional industries in Taiwan, many components manufacturers have difficulty finding and retaining domestic workers at current wage levels and must bring in foreign workers to fill low-skilled positions, a practice that also saves on labor costs. There are legal limits, though, on the number of foreign workers firms can use, as well as on-going domestic debate regarding the desirability of using these workers. Given these conditions, Taiwanese automotive firms are likely to find it difficult to reduce labor costs and could even face further upward pressure on domestic wages.

Another option, increasing sales in regional and international markets, is likely to be difficult to achieve and at best, would provide only a partial solution. Despite policies specifically aimed at increasing exports to Japan (Noble 1996), Taiwan's major export market in Asia, absolute levels remain low. Some Taiwanese suppliers report that the on-going recession in Japan has led to more outsourcing and dual sourcing, as well as greater willingness of Japanese firms to utilize technological capabilities in lower-cost countries such as Taiwan. These changes, though, have not (yet) translated into a greater presence in Japanese supply chains. While exports to Japan now account for about 6 percent of Taiwanese components exports, compared to only 2 to 3 percent in the mid-1980s, Taiwan's share of total Japanese parts imports actually dropped slightly during the 1990s and Taiwan's imports from Japan remain about ten times higher than their exports (Tomisawa 1987; TTVMA 2000).[4,5]

Taiwan's parts suppliers currently do not have a strong foothold in regional markets outside of Japan, in part because of only modest integration of sourcing channels across east Asia. Despite earlier hopes that Taiwan would emerge as a regional center for parts production, only three of Taiwan's fifteen largest export markets are in Asia. Exports to two of these countries, Philippines and Indonesia, are concentrated in high-end OEM parts for "Asian" cars like Mitsubishi's Freeca, but combined exports to these countries totaled less than $100M US in 1999 (FT Asia Intelligence Wire 1997; TTVMA 2000). Given the changing political economy of automotive production in east Asia, especially the on-going shift in

[3] This particular managed commented that, "For us, WTO happened three years ago" (interview 2000).

[4] JETRO (1999) data indicate that in 1998, Taiwanese parts imports from Japan were about 7 times greater than exports; TTVMA (2000) data indicate that imports were 12.5 times greater than exports in 1998 and 9 times greater in 1999.

[5] The proportion of Japanese parts imports originating in Taiwan dropped from 8.2% to 7.6% between 1993 and 1998 (JETRO, various years).

investment and production to promising markets in lower-wage countries, room for increased production and exports from Taiwan might be limited.

Buoyed by expectations that Asia (outside of Japan) would be the site of the highest growth in vehicle production in the medium-term, automakers invested heavily in ASEAN, where vehicle assembly doubled in the first half of the 1990s, and China, which has attracted investments from most of the world's major assemblers (Sturgeon and Florida 1999; Sako 1996). This trend gained momentum in the latter half of the 1990s when Japanese automotive firms invested heavily in the region; between 1995 and 1999, 21 percent of all contracted Japanese investment in the transportation sector was destined for China or ASEAN, compared to just 11 percent in the 1989–1994 period. (See Table 8–1) Despite the crisis-induced drop in automotive demand in ASEAN, Japanese firms, which hold a 80 to 90 percent market share, remain committed to a long-term presence in these markets; where possible, some firms have attempted to bolster depressed production levels by exporting from these sites (Legewie 2000a; Mori 1999). This has contributed to rising vehicle exports from more developed production locations, like Thailand.

The surge in investment and production in ASEAN and especially China could present a number of problems for Taiwanese automotive firms. These investments likely signal that earlier hopes that Taiwan might serve as an export platform for the China market are unlikely to materialize,[6] and open the possibility that Taiwan could become a target for future vehicle exports from China, a situation that could arise if vehicle demands falls on the mainland and assemblers there are committed

Table 8–1. Japanese Foreign Investment in Transportation Sector, 1989–1999

	1989–99	1989–94	1995–99
Average Annual Investment, 100M Yen	2,749	2,164	3,452
Destination			
Europe	25.9%	28.6%	23.8%
North America	35.3%	40.0%	31.8%
Other	16.7%	15.5%	18.2%
Asia	21.2%	15.0%	25.9%
Low-wage east Asia	16.9%	11.3%	21.1%

Notes: 1) Figures represent contracted investment;
2) "Low-wage east Asia" includes ASEAN and China

Source: Calculated by author from outward investment data compiled by Ministry of Finance, Japan (2000).

[6] See, e.g., Noble 1996.

to running plants at high capacity.[7] Because export patterns from the mainland are likely to be driven by the overall Asian strategies of international assemblers that have invested there, it is difficult to predict if assemblers will look to export from the mainland and whether Taiwan would present a likely market for these vehicles. Given rising overcapacity in Asia and the world, though, existing production and trade patterns are likely to come under pressure in the near future.

The dominance of Japanese firms in Taiwan's auto sector – and indeed, throughout Asia – has had the effect of limiting Taiwanese suppliers' exposure to European and American assemblers and has contributed to Taiwan's limited presence in OEM supply chains outside of Asia. Although half of all parts and components produced in Taiwan are sold in foreign markets, most are for the aftermarket, with approximately 30 percent of all exports going to the US aftermarket alone (Veloso et al. 1998). These exports tend to be concentrated in generic parts and components, rather than higher-quality replacement parts for specific models or OEM sales. In fact, only a few Taiwanese firms have broken into even lower tiers of the supply chains of European and American assemblers.

Some observers suggest that Taiwanese firms have difficulty breaking into international supply chains because required volumes strain or exceed the capacities of all but the largest firms. Others add that an increase in firm size is unlikely because Taiwanese customs and culture place a high value on firm ownership, thus inhibiting merger and acquisition activity and encouraging successful entrepreneurs to start new businesses rather than grow existing ones (see, e.g., Biggart and Guillen 1999). Regardless of whether firm characteristics can be explained by cultural factors, it is certainly true that firm size has an influence on strategy and performance. As the data in Table 8–2 show, there is a strong relationship between firm size and sales in foreign markets; OEM suppliers with high levels of exports tend to be significantly larger than those with lower export ratios.[8,9] Some of this relationship, of course, is definitional: high levels of exports will drive up sales and output figures. Still, firms in this group seem to be

---

[7] A shift to an export strategy seems likely given regulations against laying off workers because of economic conditions.

[8] It is likely that some, if not most, of the exports of OEM suppliers in Taiwan are in aftermarket products.

[9] Firms in the data set were chosen on the basis of having received QS–9000 certification. Original data are based on surveys by China External Trade Development Council (CETRA), Taipei, Taiwan. Minor modifications were made by the author based on data available in individual companies' websites and/or annual reports. For one firm, a large 1st–tier supplier, QS–9000 certification could not be confirmed. Some of the 79 firms originally in the data set were excluded because their primary business was deemed to be in a sector other than automotive components, usually electronics or motorcycle parts production, and estimates of their automotive–related production or employment were not available. Many of the remaining firms in the data set also sell in sectors other than automotives but either data on the proportion of auto–related business were available or the proportion of non–automotive was judged to be fairly small.

Table 8–2. Trade Patterns of Taiwanese Components Firms, 1998

Group	Average Output ($US M)	Exports as % of Output	Major Export Destinations	Destination of Exports (%) Asia	Japan	Other	N.America/Europe	US
LOW–exp	$21 M	3%	Southeast Asia, US, Japan, Chin	69%	11%	58%	31%	22%
MED–exp	$25 M	16%	US, Japan, Australia, China	53%	22%	31%	47%	24%
HIGH–exp	$46 M	50%	US, Europe (UK, Italy), Japan	27%	15%	12%	73%	44%
Aftermarket	$25 M	93%	US	6%	3%	4%	94%	72%

Notes:

Data sources: See footnote 9. In the data set from which these statistics were drawn, there are 28 LOW–exp firms, 22 MED–exp firms, and 14 HIGH–exp firms. (See Table 8–4)

Definitions: LOW–exp: firms with Taiwanese OEM business and export ratios less than 10%
MED–exp: firms with Taiwanese OEM business and export ratios between 10% and 33%
HIGH–exp: firms with Taiwanese OEM business and export ratios greater than 33%
Aftermarket: no OEM sales

Other: It is likely that some, if not most, of the exports of OEM suppliers in Taiwan are in aftermarket products.
Asia does not equal sum of Japan and Other because of rounding.

qualitatively different than those with lower export ratios: they represent some of the few Taiwanese firms that have broken into foreign OEM supply chains and as will be discussed, seem more likely to utilize foreign production sites as part of larger restructuring efforts. Thus, it appears that the dominance of small firms in Taiwan's automotive sector does, in fact, have real implications for export and foreign production strategies.

4 Foreign Solutions?

Given the structural impediments to wholesale domestic upgrading, foreign investment seems like a natural solution to the problems facing Taiwanese automotive firms. By establishing foreign plants, Taiwanese firms might alleviate demand side problems created by the small and saturated domestic market, low volumes, and falling tariffs; and supply side problems associated with rising wages, high land costs, and tight domestic supply of production and technical workers. Moreover, in cases where Taiwanese firms were to invest on the mainland, they would gain access to a market that is currently four times larger than Taiwan's and is expected to undergo rapid growth in future years (see, e.g., Shimokawa 2000).

Among Taiwanese assemblers, only two have invested or are likely to invest in foreign production capabilities. One reason for this, naturally, is the power of foreign partners to shape trade and investment patterns of Taiwanese assemblers: reliance on foreign partners for basic model designs, as well as key drivetrain components, forces them to negotiate export and investment initiatives with their partners (Noble 1996). As Noble notes, "Control over engines [gives] Japanese mother firms effective veto power over any Taiwan export or investment plans" (1996, p.20). Still, as evidenced by recent offshore investments by Taiwanese assemblers and what appears to be growing roles in their Japanese partners' strategies, control over design *per se* might not be the critical factor in dictating the ability of firms to shape the levels and types of foreign activities.

Taiwanese assemblers will face greater competition from imports when tariffs fall with likely WTO accession. Although domestic output levels could be reduced, those assemblers with offshore investments could compensate with higher production volumes elsewhere in east Asia, where investments have been concentrated. One leading assembler began investing outside Taiwan in the mid-1990s, when it purchased five percent of an assembly operation in southern China (Nobles 1996). In late 1999, the same assembler purchased a share of its partner's operations in the Philippines and soon after, assumed management control (Moises 2000); and in late 2000, it purchased a 25 percent share of another Chinese assembly operation, where it will oversee production of 20,000 vehicles. This last investment followed on a May, 2000 agreement by its stockholders to earmark 20 percent of the company's value for investment in China (Agence France Presse 2000).

A second assembler has followed a similarly aggressive offshore investment strategy. In the mid-1990s, the company signed a 50/50 JV agreement with a provincial government in southern China to establish assembly operations and proceeded to build a plant with potential capacity of 150,000 vehicles per year, on a site that can be expanded to accommodate production of 300,000 vehicles. In 1996, the company began small-scale production; output levels have increased steadily and are expected to reach 25,000 in 2000 and 60,000 in 2001 (China Economic Review 1996; AFX News Limited 2000).

Aggressive offshore investment strategies of these Taiwanese assemblers appear to contribute to two objectives. By investing in other sites in east Asia, the firms greatly increase their production capacities and perhaps more important, gain direct access to promising markets that will remain protected for at least a few more years. If Taiwan joins WTO, import taxes on vehicles will decline from their current 30 percent to 17.5 percent by 2007, by which time import quotas will also be phased out (Barnes 1999). Although mainland tariff reductions would be more rapid under WTO, dropping incrementally from the current 80–100 percent to 25 percent in 2006 (Zachary 2000), the absolute levels of protection will remain higher on the mainland for at least the next five or ten years. Similarly, the ASEAN Free Trade Agreement (AFTA), which is scheduled to go into effect in 2002, caps tariffs at 5 percent, but only for intra-regional trade. And as some observers suggest, even after 2002, "there is a strong possibility that non-tariff barriers will grow in importance and continue to hinder the free flow of goods and thus a deeper integration of the automobile industry" (Legewie 2000a, p. 241).

With investments outside Taiwan, then, these assemblers can potentially offset any losses in the domestic market share and help ensure their survival – or even growth – regardless of domestic demand and the extent of post-WTO import penetration in Taiwan. These investments provide access to more hospitable market structures, diversify the markets and production sites of the investing firms, and reduce vulnerability to changes in the domestic market. In addition, by taking lead roles as investors and managers at foreign sites, these Taiwanese assemblers can potentially increase their power or even independence vis-à-vis their foreign partners.

At the same time, these investments seem unlikely to mitigate domestic problems or strengthen domestic capabilities, and could eventually displace some production at home plants. Some observers have noted that if production costs prove lower at new offshore site, vehicles could be exported back to Taiwan (Taipei Times 1999), an outcome that could cannibalize production from plants in Taiwan. Similarly, although offshore investments could help assemblers increase total production volumes, unless Taiwanese-designed vehicles or engines are produced at new sites, Taiwanese brands might not be strengthened or independent technological capabilities greatly enhanced. As such, offshore investments might not significantly improve the long-term viability of Taiwan as a production site. Instead, these investments offer individual assemblers the opportunity to diversify the markets in which vehicles are produced and sold, and to assume larger roles in their partners' regional strategies.

Interestingly, a similar market-diversification strategy appears to drive investment strategies of some Taiwanese suppliers, including some that have followed Taiwanese assemblers to new production sites. For these suppliers, offshore investments tend to reproduce domestic operations: foreign plants often make the same products as home plants, and output from these plants is often sold to other Taiwanese firms or is exported back to the home plant. For some of these supplier investments on the mainland, geographic isolation from major auto-producing regions like Shanghai and the (currently) closed nature of mainland supply networks mean that opportunities to develop new customers are likely to be limited. Thus, these investments do little to expand the customer bases of firms and have not (yet) generated a strong division of labor between mainland and home operations. (For examples, see firms 1 through 5 in Table 8–3)

As currently configured, these foreign plants seem unlikely to contribute to domestic cost-cutting or upgrading efforts. Despite labor costs on the mainland that are one-tenth to one-third of those in Taiwan, low volumes, high duties, and in some cases, low productivity, mean that overall production costs can be higher than in Taiwan. While some costs will decline as volumes increase and workers gain experience, other costly practices, such as importing basic raw materials, are likely to be required across the mainland for some time. Because these plants are dedicated to producing the same or similar parts as the home plants, they currently offer few opportunities to create divisions of labor between home and host sites or otherwise contribute to upgrading of product lines in Taiwan.

These investments, though, provide a type of insurance: by providing direct access to some of the world's most promising markets, they represent an opportunity for firms to maintain or even increase overall production levels regardless of future conditions in the domestic market. Perhaps not coincidentally, new production sites on the mainland, as well as in ASEAN, resemble the current (i.e., pre-WTO) environment in Taiwan, where production volumes are relatively low and tariffs offer some protection against imports. More important, perhaps, is the strong likelihood that these new production sites are likely to remain somewhat protected, at least in the medium-term. Even with accession into WTO, China's vehicle tariffs, for example, will drop only to 25 percent by 2006 (Zachary 2000), which is just below current tariff rates (30 percent) in Taiwan.

A second type of foreign investment is also evident among Taiwanese automotive firms. These investments do not appear to have been motivated by expected changes in the domestic trade and regulatory environments, but are part of a nearly constant upgrading of domestic operations. These investments often contribute to domestic restructuring by providing lower-cost sites from which to export and manufacture labor-intensive products, and in some cases, perform engineering and design tasks that are costly to perform in Taiwan or for which domestic engineers and technicians are difficult to find. These plants also provide lower-cost export bases to third countries, such as Japan, thus extending the life or

Table 8–3. Characteristics of Mainland Plants of Taiwanese Auto Supply Firms

Plant	Type of Firm	Number of Employees	Mainland Customers	Exports	Division of labor between Taiwan and China
1	JV (all Taiwanese partners)	<100	Taiwanese assemblers and suppliers	Some back to parent firm in Taiwan	None; same products made at both sites
2	Wholly-owned	<100	Taiwanese assemblers (80%)	20% to parent firm	Makes some older products no longer made in Taiwan; hope to increase exports to 50%
3	Wholly-owned	<100	Taiwanese assemblers (90%)	None	None, but firm sources technologically-demanding parts from Taiwan
4	Wholly-owned	<100	Taiwanese assemblers; hope to sell to Japanese assemblers in the future	None; hope to export to Taiwan and Japan in future	Firm hopes to shift lower-technology products to mainland
5	Wholly-owned	<100	Taiwanese assemblers	None	None; same products made at both sites
6	Taiwanese managed; owned by Japanese parent	100-<250	European, American, and Japanese JV assemblers	Some to Taiwan	Some low value-added products moved to mainland and exported back to Taiwan
7	JV (Japanese partner)	250+	European and American JV assemblers	80% to Japan, US, Europe	Make same products, mainland plants are now export base; in future, Taiwan to focus on design, high-tech products
8	JV (Chinese partner)	250+	Foreign assemblers, Japanese parent of Taiwanese firm	Design work "exported" to Taiwanese parent	Slowly shifting design and engineering tasks to mainland to take advantage of availability and cost of engineers
9	JV(Taiwanese, Japanese partners)	250+	Foreign (e.g., American) suppliers on mainland	80+%, most to Japan	Part of strategy to shift production of lower-skilled products to mainland
10	Wholly-owned	100-<250	Aftermarket	Export (% n.a.)	Mainland plant makes low-end components. Initial designs and pilot projects in Taiwan. Ship parts from mainland and Taiwan to a third production site in North America.

increasing the profitability of existing product lines. (For examples, see firms 6 through 10 in Table 8–3)

With these investments, Taiwanese firms are able to exploit what many see as their natural advantages on the mainland, including their ability to communicate with Chinese workers, firms, and local officials, and their experience in establishing and running plants with low break – even points. At the same time, these investments can provide an opportunity for Taiwanese firms to gain exposure to major international assemblers with JV projects on the mainland. Although only a few wholly-owned Taiwanese firms are part of the supplier network of SAIC – the largest Chinese automotive firm and the JV partner of VW and GM – some Taiwanese firms have used joint ventures with foreign partners as an entrée into this and other supply networks on the mainland. And by teaming with foreign partners, these firms often secure additional export channels – for example, partners' home plants – that allow them to produce at high volumes without relying on exports back to Taiwan.

Despite the stark differences in the characteristics of these two types of investments, they share some interesting similarities. Both types of investments are motivated by changing conditions in the domestic environment. In the case of market-diversifying investments, the salient factors are related to product market conditions, including domestic demand and likely changes in tariff and other regulatory structures; in the case of upgrading investments, changes in factor prices, especially rising land and labor costs, are more important. Interestingly, the organization of supply relations at new sites is also similar. Foreign plants of both investment types report reliance on other Taiwanese firms as suppliers. In some cases, this reliance is in the form of imports from Taiwan; in other cases, firms source directly from mainland plants of other Taiwanese firms. For some Taiwanese automotive firms, then, offshore investments reproduce and reinforce supply arrangements developed in the domestic arena.

5 Emerging Patterns, Open Questions

The existence of (at least) two distinct patterns of foreign investment in the Taiwanese automotive sector illustrates the potential of globalization to shape domestic firms and economies in complex, and even contradictory, ways. The first pattern, which involves the reproduction of capabilities and production of existing product lines at new sites, provides an opportunity for firms to reduce their dependence on an increasingly competitive domestic market and diversify markets in which they sell and produce. These investments could help ensure the survival or even growth of firms in the post-WTO period and thus avert a situation in which firm capabilities and human capital developed over decades are made obsolete by changing product markets and regulatory conditions.

The second pattern of investment, which is characterized by transfer of existing product lines and functional tasks to new sites, provides opportunities for firm growth, development of new customers, and upgrading of product lines at domestic plants. As such, these investments directly shape the types and levels of production and non-production activities and employment at domestic plants. By providing lower-cost sites from which to export to third countries, as well as exposure to European, American, and Japanese firms, these investments help firms broaden their customer bases. Interestingly, then, both types of investments act to reduce dependence on the small and competitive domestic market, but in fundamentally different ways.

Not surprisingly, some firms utilize both types of investments in their globalization strategies. Data from a sample of Taiwanese automotive firms show that of the roughly one-third of firms with some type of foreign investment, about 40 percent have invested in multiple sites. In addition, almost half of firms with plants in Fujian Province, where Taiwanese foreign assembly is concentrated, have also invested in other sites, usually on the mainland or in ASEAN. (Although some of these other investments could be in non-automotive sectors, like motorcycle parts, they suggest, in any case, a diversified approach to foreign production.) However, firms with a diversified foreign investment strategy seem to represent only a small portion of all Taiwanese suppliers: of the 64 firms represented in the sample, only 23 have foreign plants and of these, only 10 have two or more plants outside of Taiwan (See Table 8–4). Thus, while it is clear that foreign production plays a key role in the competitive strategies of some Taiwanese automotive firms, the future of a large number of suppliers is likely to depend on their ability to adapt to changes in the domestic environment.

Across the Taiwanese automotive sector, future activities could be shaped as much by developments in the larger east Asian automotive complex as by the domestic and foreign production strategies of individual firms. One key factor, of course, will be the evolution of sourcing patterns of Japanese firms and in particular, the extent to which east Asian countries, including Taiwan, are further integrated into sourcing networks. Shimokawa (2000) suggests that the regional division of labor within east Asia is likely to deepen as the region continues to emerge from the financial crisis. A second critical issue involves the extent to which Taiwanese plants will be utilized to complement or support their Japanese partners' plants in ASEAN by, for example, increasing their supply of parts and CKDs to these sites.

The most important influence on the future direction of the Taiwanese auto industry, though, is likely to be the development of the auto industry on the mainland, and the challenges and opportunities this will create. One crucial question is whether and how China's automobile capabilities will be integrated into the existing east Asian production network. One possibility is that Japanese assemblers will continue to pursue regional complementarity schemes in east Asia, and American and European assemblers will use mainland plants only to serve the China market. In this case, mainland production capacity would be used to serve only the local market and production capabilities currently being developed in China would be only marginally integrated into existing regional

Table 8–4. Foreign Investment Patterns of Taiwanese Components Firms, 1998

Group	Average Output ($US)	Firms in Sample	Percentage of firms with Investments	Total # of Plants	Location of Plants: Fujian Province	Location of Plants: Other China	Location of Plants: Total China
LOW–exp	$21 M	28	25%	14	43%	36%	79%
MED–exp	$25 M	22	45%	12	66%	17%	83%
HIGH–exp	$46 M	14	43%	12	25%	50%	75%
Total		64	36%	38	45%	34%	79%

Notes:

Data sources: See footnote 9.

Definitions:
LOW–exp: firms with Taiwanese OEM business and export ratios less than 10%
MED–exp: firms with Taiwanese OEM business and export ratios between 10% and 33%
HIGH–exp: firms with Taiwanese OEM business and export ratios greater than 33%

arrangements. Under these conditions, events on the mainland would have only limited effect on trade and production levels in other countries in east Asia.

A radically different approach, though, is suggested by the integration of Spain and Mexico into the regional production systems of American assemblers. Development of production capabilities and capacities in these countries came at the expense of existing automotive plants in the regions (see, e.g., Lynch 1998). In order to support high and steady levels of production at new plants in Spain and Mexico, these sites began to export vehicles and as a result, displaced production at existing plants in the regions. If the major assemblers were to integrate Chinese production sites into existing regional arrangements, the potential for a significant re-shuffling of market and production arrangements across east Asia could be high.

References

Baum, Julian. (1999) "Ready and Waiting," *Far Eastern Economic Review*, April 22nd.

Biggart, Nicole Woolsey and Mauro F. Guillen. (1999) "Developing Difference: Social Organization and the Rise of the Auto Industries of South Korea, Taiwan, Spain, and Argentina," *American Sociological Review*, Vol. 64, p4p.722–747, October.

Directorate-General of Budget. (2000) *Monthly Bulletin of Earnings & Productivity Statistics*, No. 317, Accounting and Statistics, Executive Yuan, March.

Economist Intelligence Unit. (1995) "Taiwan: Regional Components Centre for South–East Asia?" *Motor Business International*; 4th quarter.

Economist Intelligence Unit. (1998) "Taiwan and the Main ASEAN Markets: Outlook Reassessed," *Motor Business International*; 4th quarter.

Japanese External Trade Organization (JETRO) Various years, *White Paper on International Trade*, Tokyo.

Landers, Peter. (1999) "Long, Hard Road," *Far Eastern Economic Review*, April 8th.

Legewie, Jochen. (2000a) "Driving Regional Integration: Japanese Firms and the Development of the ASEAN Automotive Industry," *In Facing Asia: Japan's Role in the Political and Economic Dynamism of Regional Cooperation* (Verena Blechinger and Jochen Legewie, editors), Munich: Iudicium.

Legewie, Jochen. (2000b) "Cars Get No Vroom From Afta," *Far Eastern Economic Review*, May 4th.

Lynch, Teresa M. (1998) Leaving Home: Three Decades of Internationalization by American Automotive Firms, MIT IPC Working Paper #98–007, Cambridge MA, October.

Ministry of Finance, Japan. (2000) Outward Direct Investment, County and Region, Data available from Ministry of Finance Japan website.

Ministry of Economic Affairs (MOEA). Various year,. *Industrial Production Statistics Monthly*.

Moises, Evangeline L. (2000) "Enterprisers: Getting the Pulse of the Customer," *Business World* (on-line), September 14th.

Mori, Minako. (1999) "New Trends in ASEAN Strategies of Japanese-affiliated Automobile Parts Manufacturers," *RIM: Pacific Business and Industries*, Vol. 1, No. 43, pp. 12–27.

Noble, Gregory W. (1996) Trojan Horse or Boomerang: Two-Tiered Investment in the Asian Auto Complex, Berkeley Roundtable of the International Economy, Working Paper #90, November, Berkeley, California.

Pries, Ludger. (1999) "Restrukturierung and Globalisierung der deutschen Automobilhersteller—Sogeffeckte fuer die Zulieferer," *Industrielle Beziehungen*, Vol. 6, No. 2, pp. 125–150.

Sako, Mari. (1996) Restructuring and Global Strategy of the Japanese Automobile Industry and its Perspective, Working Paper MITJP 96–15, Cambridge, MA: MIT Japan Program.

Shimokawa, Koichi. (2000) Reorganization of the Global Automobile Industry and Structural Change of the Automobile Component Industry, Presented at 8th Annual Gerpisa Conference, "The World That Changed the Machine: The Future of the Auto Industry for the 21st Century," Paris: June 8th–10th.

Sturgeon, Timothy. and Florida, Richard. (1999) *The World that Changed the Machine*, Final Report to the Alfred P. Sloan Foundation, Cambridge, MA: International Motor Vehicle Program, May.

Taiwan Transportation Vehicle Manufacturers' Association (TTVMA). (2000) *Annual Report of Taiwan's Automotive Industry, 1999*, Taiwan.

Tomahawk, Konini. (1987) Development and Future Outlook for an International Division of Labor in the Automobile Industries of Asian NICS, A briefing paper for First Policy Forum, International Motor Vehicle Program, May 5th.

Veloso, Francisco., Romero, Jorge Soto, and Amsden, Alice H. (1998) *A Comparative Assessment of the Development of the Auto Parts Industry in Taiwan and Mexico: Policy Implications for Thailan,.* Cambridge, MA: Massachusetts Institute of Technology, March.

Zachary, Kathleen. "WTO–No! China Braces for Big Shake-Out," *Ward's Auto World*, November.

Accounts from various on-line news sources.

9 The Changes in the Automobile Industry in Thailand

Thamavit Terdudomtham
Thammasat University

Kreingkrai Techakanont
Thammasat University

Peera Charoenporn
Thammasat University

1 Introduction

In Thailand, the automobile industry has been developed since the early of 1960s. Then, it has expanded rapidly since the latter half of the 1980s. The domestic sales of new vehicles increased from 101,624 units in 1987, to 589,126 units in 1996. Consequently, the domestic production reached its peak at 547,312 vehicles in 1996. However, due to the 1997 economic crisis, the domestic sale drastically decreased to 363,156 vehicles in 1997, and 144,065 vehicles in 1998. As a result, the domestic production decreased to 156,130 vehicles in 1998. Although the domestic production increased to 327,101 vehicles in 1999, the automobile industry still has a huge excess capacity.

Recently, the automobile industry in Thailand has drastically changed. For example, it has been more export oriented after the 1997 economic crisis. The competition in the domestic market has intensified due to the entry of the US Big Three. In addition, local auto part industry also has been in structural changes. These changes resulted jointly from several factors. The major factors include the economic crisis, trade liberalization, and the changes of global automobile industry.

This chapter studies the changes of Automobile Industry in Thailand. Three factors are hypothesized as the reasons of the changes; economic crisis, trade liberalization, and the changes in the global automobile industry. Trade liberalization includes the abandon of local content requirement following the commitment to WTO, and ASEAN agreements. After domestic demand decreased sharply due to the economic crisis, the automobile assemblers temporarily stopped or reduced their production. They also adjusted by being more export oriented and reducing production cost by using more local parts.

With the consolidation and mergers in global automobile industry and direct investment from GM and Ford in Thailand, the dominant role of Japanese assemblers in Thailand has been challenged. GM and Ford also brought the competitive bidding system for outsourcing to Thailand. In addition, every assembler has employed global outsourcing strategy more extensively after the abandon of local content requirement. However, auto assemblers and global suppliers plan to increase localization in order to minimize cost.

For auto part makers in Thailand, they can be divided into four groups: global Tier 1 suppliers, local Tier 1 suppliers, Tier 2 suppliers, Tier 3 and lower suppliers. Along with the investment of the US big three in Thailand, several Tier 1 global suppliers from the US and Europe have set their own subsidiary companies in Thailand or purchased the majority share of Thai companies. After the crisis, some local Tier 1 suppliers were taken over by Japanese or Western firms, or shifted to other business. In addition, some of them were downgraded to be Tier 2 suppliers. This is because of their financial problems and their lacking of product design capability.

Under the competitive bidding system with the world standard of management and product, local auto part makers are forced to integrate into global supply networks, improve management, productivity, and so on in order to survive in this business. For local SME with family business style, they have some difficulties with this system. However, for auto part makers who can join the networks of global suppliers, they have a good opportunity to expand.

This chapter aims to offer some evidences of the impacts from the recent economic crisis, trade liberalization, and the changes in global automobile industry. The adjustment and structural changes of assemblers and auto part makers are discussed. The paper divided into 6 parts: (1) historical background; (2) the economic crisis (impacts and response); (3) trade liberalization; (4) global changes and impacts on automobile in Thailand; (5) major changes of automobile industry in Thailand; and (6) concluding remarks.

2 Historical Background[1]

A brief historical background of automobile industry is discussed here in order to understand its current situation.

---

[1] See discussions in Thamavit (1997)

2.1 Emerging of automobile industry in Thailand (1961)

In 1960, a number of investors received licenses and incentives for investing in automotive assembly. Anglo–Thai Motor, the first automobile assembly factory in Thailand, began to operate in 1961. In this early period, the import duty on CBU passenger cars, pickups, and trucks were 60, 40, and 20 percent respectively, while the tariffs on CKD passenger cars, pickups, and trucks were 30, 20, and 10 percent respectively. Providing incentives for investment under the 1960 Industrial Act and protecting with high tariff on CBU cars were two major policies establishing automobile industry in Thailand.

2.2 Beginning of Local Content Requirements (1971)

In 1971, the Automobile Industry Development Committee (AIDC) set the local content requirement (LCR) at 25 percent for the assembly industry. However, the LCR became effective three years later, on December 31, 1973. This is the beginning of auto parts industry in Thailand. In 1970s, the production of peripheral auto parts, small-pressed body parts, and auto parts based on casting process increased significantly.

2.3 Import Ban on Small CBU Cars and Rising Tariffs (1978)

In 1978, the government increased tariffs on CBU passenger cars to 150 percent and CKD passenger cars to 80 percent, and imposed an import ban on small CBU passenger cars (with engine size 2300 c.c. and smaller) due to an increasing trade deficit.

2.4 New Local Content Requirements (1987)

The AIDC, assemblers and the auto part makers agreed to set the LCR at 54 percent for passenger cars, 45 percent for heavy and light trucks, 61 percent for petrol pickups, and 72 percent for diesel pickups in 1987. These LCR ratios were imposed during the period of 1987–1999.

Along with the high domestic economic growth, the demand for automobile increased rapidly during the period of 1988 and 1990. However, the domestic production failed to meet the demand. As a result, the prices of automobile were very high.

2.5 Partially Liberalization (1991)

To decrease domestic prices of cars, the government lifted the ban on the imports of CBU in April 1991, and decreased the tariffs and business taxes on import cars in July 1991. The tariff for large CBU cars (over 2300 cc) decreased from 300 percent to 100 percent, for small CBU cars from 180 percent to 60 percent, and for CKD cars from 112 percent to 20 percent. As a result, the share of imported CBU cars in the domestic market increased.

2.6 Export Promotion (1995)

In 1995, the Ministry of Industry announced "The Automobile Industry Export Promotion Project" for the period of 1996–2000. Meanwhile, the Board of Investment grants incentives to automobile assemblers who produce cars for export. However, until the 1996 crisis, the export of automobile was small. After the crisis, the export of automobile has increased significantly.

On the other hand, domestic market of automobile industry still is protected by high tariff rates. Currently, the import duty on CBU passenger cars and pickup passenger cars is 80 percent. While the import duty on OEM passenger cars is 33 percent.

3 The Economic Crisis: Impacts and Response

Thailand had a remarkable economic growth during the period of 1987–1995. However, in July 1997, the country had to float its currency due to the loss in foreign reserves, the chronic current account deficit, and the huge external debt. The baht was sharply depreciated from 25.8 baht per a US dollar in July 2, 1997, to 56.5 baht per a US dollar in January 1998.

Due to the loss in foreign reserves, the Thai government had to ask for emergency financial assistance from the International Monetary Fund (IMF) in August 1997. Under the IMF recommendations, the Thai government tried to keep the surplus of government budget, and the stability of exchange rate. To stabilize the exchange rate, the Bank of Thailand kept domestic interest rate at very high. The inter-bank rate was over 20 percent in 1997 and early 1998. To keep the budget surplus, the government increased value added tax, excise tax and import tariff. The tight fiscal and monetary policies decreased the domestic aggregate demand sharply.

Under this crisis period, the domestic demand for automobile decreased drastically. The domestic sale of new vehicles decreased from 589,126 units in 1996, to 363,156 units in 1997, and 144,065 units in 1998. The main reasons for the drop of demand are summarized as follows.

- The growth of GDP decreased from 8.8 percent in 1995, to 5.5 percent in 1996, and became negative growth in 1997. As a result, income of consumers decreased significantly after the crisis. Moreover, the number of unemployed increased.

- The Bank of Thailand ordered to close 56 insolvent finance companies in 1997. It caused credit shortage of car hire purchasing.
- On August 16, 1997, the government increased "value added" tax from 7 percent to 10 percent. On October 14, 1997, the government increased import tariff on CBU cars to 80 percent. Surcharge (10 percent) was also imposed on the import (Bank of Thailand 1998, 1999).

Following the drop of domestic sale, the domestic production decreased from 559,428 units in 1996, to 360,303 units in 1997, and 158,130 units in 1998. Assemblers adjusted by temporarily stopping production, reducing production, and cutting the number of workers or working hours as shown in Table 9–1.

Furthermore, the automobile assemblers have increased the export after the crisis. Unico (1999) reports that after the crisis, Japanese assemblers still keep their plans to have production bases in Thailand. Thus, they began to increase

Table 9–1. The Adjustment of Auto Assemblers in Thailand

Assemblers	Adjustment
Toyota Motor Thailand	Production Stoppage in Nov.–Dec.1997; production Reduction since January 1998; increased exports in 1998.
Isuzu Motor Thailand	Production Stoppage in November 1997.
Siam V.M.C. Yarn Yon	Production Stoppage in August 1997; laid off workers.
Honda Cars Man. (Thailand)	Reduced production; laid off workers.
Siam Motors and Nissan	Reduced production and working hours.
Siam Nissan Automobile	Production stoppage in August 1997.
Bangchan General Assembly	Production Stoppage in August 1997; laid off workers
Thai Rung	Laid off workers.
MMC Sittipol	Reduced production and working hours; increased export.
Thai Hino Industry	Production Stoppage in Sept.–Dec. 1997; reduced wages and working hours; increased export.
Thonburi Automotive Ass.	Reduced production and working hours.
Y.M.C. Assembly	Reduced production and working hours; laid off workers.
Thai Swedish Assembly	Production stoppage in August 1997; lowered wages.
Mazda Motor	Production stoppage in August 1997. Transfer production line to Auto Alliance (Ford–Mazda).
Auto Alliance Thailand (Ford–Mazda)	Began to operate in July 1998. To respond to the crisis, it increased export ratio, and reduced output from the plan.
General Motor	Reduced investment by cutting capacity from 100,000 unit per year to 40,000 unit per year.

Source: Nipon (2000), Bank of Thailand (1999), and Minako Mori (2000)

export after the crisis. For example, Honda began to export small passenger cars (Honda City) to Singapore and Brunei in July 1997.

It is noteworthy that due to the sharp depreciation of Baht, assemblers tend to increase local content and outsourcing in order to minimize cost.

4 Trade Liberalization

Thailand has recently liberalized trade on automobile. First, with the commitment to WTO, It eliminated the local content requirement on automobile industry in 2000. Second, under ASEAN Free Trade Area Agreement, Thailand will reduce import tariff on automobile. In addition, Thailand also joins The ASEAN Industrial Cooperation (AICO) scheme. The trade liberalization has shaped automobile industry in Thailand.

4.1 The Abandon of Local content requirement

Historically, the government began to impose the local content requirement in 1971. In the beginning, the local content requirement was imposed at 25 percent. Then, in 1987, it was increased to 54 percent for passenger cars, 61 percent for petrol pickup and 72 percent for diesel pickups. In addition, pickup assemblers were required to use only locally produced engines. For diesel engine production with BOI privileges, the minimum local content was 20 percent in 1989, and increased to 70 percent in June 1996. It also included five compulsory parts; cylinder heads, cylinder blocks, camshafts, crankshafts, and connecting rods (Thamavit 1997).

The local content requirements had encouraged significantly investment in local auto parts industry. The number of firms in the auto parts industry had increased significantly during the period of 1974–1996. The BOI (1999) reports that the number of firms in the auto parts and component parts industry currently is 700, of which 200 is in the OEM market, and the rest is in the REM market.

Based on her survey, Maruhashi (1995) concludes that the local content requirement increased localization of auto parts in Thailand. However, it did not encourage the subcontracting system directly. For some auto parts, the automobile assemblers prefer in-house production to subcontracting.

Unico (1999) reports that assemblers utilized 70–80 percent of local content in one-ton pickup trucks for domestic market in 1999. But for exporting one-ton pickup trucks, the local content ratios were 36–75 percent. For passenger cars, assemblers generally utilized 54 percent of local content. However, for the ASEAN model (Soluna), Toyota utilized 73–74 percent of local content (The Nation, September 24, 1999).

The Thai government has abandoned the local content requirement for automobile industry since January 1, 2000. The elimination of LCR is expected to have following effects.

1. For automobile assemblers, according to a report of The Nation (October 1, 1999), General Motors, Ford, Volkswagen, Toyota, Nissan and Renault, and Daimler Chrysler have developed a global part-sourcing strategy. Toyota's executive managing purchasing said that its operation in Thailand would implement a global part-sourcing strategy in the year of 2000. As a result, for models with low domestic production quantity such as Toyota Camry, Toyota may not use local parts due to lacking of economy of scale.

2. For auto part makers, Sayan (1998) made a survey of the impacts of the elimination on members of Auto Parts Producers Association, and members of Auto Parts Industrial Group. In his survey, 69 percent (34 firms out of 49) are Thai-owned firms. The survey results are summarized as follows.

- For all samples, 73 percent expected that they would receive negative impacts after the elimination of LCR. The negative impacts are the decrease in sale volume and the decrease in price. For the adjustment after the elimination, 37 percent of them give the first priority on product development and waste reduction.
- For small auto part firms with annual sale below 50 million baht in 1997, half of them expected that the prospect of auto part industry would be not quite good in 2000. For the adjustment after the elimination of LCR, some planned to set joint venture with foreign investors.
- For large auto part firms with annual sale exceed 500 million baht in 1997, they expected that the annual sale would increase in 2000. The Thai-owned firms in this group are also looking for joint venture with foreign investors.
- The majority of Thai-owned firms is SME. Among 34 Thai-owned firms, 62 percent of Thai-owned firms expected that their annual sale would decrease after the elimination of LCR. Most of them faced financial problem and decreasing price of their products in 1998

4.2 The Liberalization under ASEAN

Indonesia, Malaysia, the Philippines, Singapore and Thailand established the Association of Southeast Asian Nation (ASEAN) in 1967. Then, Brunei Darussalam joined in 1984, Vietnam in 1995, Laos and Myanmar in 1997, and Cambodia in 1999. As a result, the ASEAN has 10 member countries with a population of about 500 million.

4.2.1 Tariff Reduction

In terms of intra-ASEAN trade, five original member countries signed ASEAN Preferential Trading Arrangement (PTA) in 1976 and implemented it in 1977.

However, the PTA did not have significant impacts on the intra-ASEAN trade because it included only a small part of the intra-ASEAN trade, and the margin of preference was small.

At the fourth ASEAN summit in 1992, the ASEAN leaders unanimously agreed to establish ASEAN Free Trade Area (AFTA) by implementing the Agreement of the Common Effective Preferential Tariff (CEPT). According to the CEPT Agreement, the tariff rate on the imports from intra-ASEAN region will be reduced to 0–5% in 2008.

During the period of 1993–1999, the implementation of the CEPT Agreement has been accelerated its time frame. At the 26th ASEAN Economic Ministries (1994), the ministers agreed to move the deadline of the CEPT from 2008 to 2003. Then, at the sixth ASEAN summit in Hanoi (1998), the ASEAN leaders accepted to speed up the realization of AFTA to the year 2002. In addition, at the 13th AFTA Council meeting (1999), ASEAN ministers agreed to eliminate import duties on all products by 2015 for the six original members and by year 2018 for the new members of ASEAN.

However, the ASEAN has a temporary setback. While the time frame of implementation of the CEPT Agreement has been accelerated, Malaysia recently asked for a delay on tariff reduction on the import of automobile. According to the CEPT agreement, Malaysia has to reduce tariff on CBU cars from over 65% to 20% in 2000. Finally, Malaysia was allowed to delay tariff reduction on automotive products for five years.

Despite an unexpected set-back of AFTA accelerated process toward free trade as a result of a delay tariff reduction of some items by some ASEAN members, the ASEAN free trade area will be eventually moved forward by ASEAN countries for their long-term benefits. The reasons are as follows.

First, the ASEAN trade agreements have provided some real benefits to ASEAN countries. For example, Thailand's export to five original ASEAN countries increased from 14.8% of the total export during 1983–1985, to 19.1% in 1995. However, as a result of the Asian economic crisis, Thailand's export to ASEAN countries significantly decreased from 21.65% of the total export during 1996–1997, to 18.4% during 1998–1999. In addition, the potential market integration of ASEAN has been an important factor of an increase in foreign direct investment in Thailand, especially in the automobile industry.

Second, ASEAN countries have a significant progress in completing AFTA objectives. The six original ASEAN countries agree to include 98.4% of tariff lines into the inclusion list of CEPT scheme. Only 1.6% of tariff lines of these six countries is included in Temporary Exclusive List, Sensitive List, and General Exception List. In addition, ASEAN countries also have ASEAN Industrial Cooperation scheme (AICO), ASEAN Industrial Joint Venture, and ASEAN Investment Area (AIA).

Third, multinational firms investing in ASEAN countries strongly support the market integration of ASEAN. On the other hand, foreign investment is expected to rise markedly if the full integration of ASEAN market is materialized.

4.2.2 The ASEAN Industrial Cooperation (AICO)

The ASEAN signed the ASEAN Industrial Co-operation scheme (AICO), the parts exchange program, in April 1996. AICO provides following privileges: (1) 0–5 percent import duty rates immediately, (2) local content accreditation, and (3) no restriction on the export of the AICO products for the participating countries.

As of June 1999, ASEAN had received 46 AICO applicants, of which 33 came from Thailand. Thailand's projects comprised 28 automotive projects, two electrical appliance projects, one agricultural engine project, and two food processing projects. Among 33 Thailand's projects, 15 approved projected are two from Toyota, three from Honda, three from Denso, two from Volvo, and one each from Kayama, Thai Steel Cable, Matsushita, Yanmar and Sony (The Nation June 18, 1999).

Under this scheme, the intra-ASEAN trade of auto parts has expanded. Assemblers can utilize supporting industry in the whole region of ASEAN.

5 Global Changes: Impacts on Automobile Industry in Thailand

The automobile industry in Thailand is only a tiny part of global automobile industry. While global automobile industry produced light vehicles over 51 million units in 1998, Thailand's domestic production of passenger and commercial cars was 144,065 units in 1998. In addition, most of the assemblers in Thailand are multinational firms and joint ventures. As a result, the automobile industry in Thailand is determined by the global automobile industry. Recently, the global automobile industry has following major changes.

5.1 Strategic Alliances and Consolidation

Since global automobile industry has an over capacity and fierce competition, major assemblers have actively formed strategic alliances or mergers. The examples are the merger of Daimler–Benz and Chrysler Corporation, Isuzu Motor and Suzuki acquired by GM, the Renault and Nissan alliance, and Mazda acquired by Ford.

In Thailand, Auto Alliance Thailand (Ford and Mazda) has increased the domestic market share of Ford significantly.

5.2 Changes in U.S. Big Three relationship with Suppliers

Gereffi (1999) pointed out that in the 1990s, U.S. Big Three redefined their relationship with suppliers in three aspects. First, the responsibility for products design and inventory program has been shifted to suppliers. Second, auto parts that are sourced from suppliers have changed from individual parts to entire subassemblies. The outsourcing of complete system and modules can reduce significantly the cost of auto assemblers. Third, the Big Three reduced the number of their direct suppliers and offering them longer contracts.

Under this system, most of local auto part makers (Thai owned firms) in Thailand can not be a real Tier 1 supplier because they don't have a capability of product design.

5.3 Technological Changes

The introduction of new technology into the industry has important impacts on the global automobile industry. The internet auction site of assemblers, the innovation in microelectronics and materials are examples of new technology. The new technology provides more flexible and well-coordinated system of production for the industry.

6 Major Changes of Automobile Industry in Thailand

Recently, the automobile industry in Thailand has drastically changed due to the recent economic crisis, trade liberalization, and the changes of global automobile industry. Its major changes are summarized as follows.

6.1 Auto Assemblers

To respond to the economic crisis, the auto assemblers reduced the production and became more export oriented. With trade liberalization and global changes, auto assemblers have utilized global part-sourcing strategy. Lastly, with the investment of the US big three and global mergers, the dominance of Japanese cars in Thailand has been challenged.

6.1.1 The Reduction of Production

Facing the fall in domestic demand, assemblers generally adjusted by temporary stoppage of production, reducing production, reducing the number of workers and working hours (Table 9–1). As a result, the domestic production of automobile decreased by 35.59 percent in 1997, by 56.11 percent in 1998 (Table 9–2). Due to the economic crisis, the domestic sale of new vehicles sharply decreased by 38.36 percent in 1997, and 60.33 percent in 1998 (Table 9–3).

For a new comer, General Motor delayed the opening of its production line, and reduced its capacity from 100,000 unit per year to 40,000 unit per year. It commenced its production in May 8, 2000, about two year later than its initial plan.

However, Thai economy began to recover in 1999. The domestic sale of automobile has increased since 1999 (Table 9–3). Thus, the domestic production also began to increase in 1999 (Table 9–2).

Table 9–2. Domestic Production of Automobile in Thailand

(Number of vehicles)

Year	Passenger Car	Commercial Car	Total	Growth rate (%)
1961	310	215	525	N.A.
1962	908	276	1,184	125.52
1963	1,817	1,628	3,445	190.96
1964	3,978	3,289	7,267	110.94
1965	4,408	5,687	10,095	38.92
1966	4,898	5,749	10,647	5.47
1967	6,211	6,607	12,818	20.39
1968	7,209	6,779	13,988	9.13
1969	6,110	6,030	12,140	(13.21)
1970	6,604	4,063	10,667	(12.13)
1971	9,017	5,997	15,014	40.75
1972	11,630	7,755	19,385	29.11
1973	17,935	9,499	27,434	41.52
1974	17,572	14,891	32,463	18.33
1975	15,524	15,467	30,991	(4.53)
1976	15,333	25,729	41,062	32.50
1977	18,564	47,310	65,874	60.43
1978	21,869	45,200	67,069	1.81
1979	21,602	45,137	66,739	(0.49)
1980	23,441	50,544	73,985	10.86
1981	26,650	60,509	87,159	17.81
1982	24,629	52,655	77,284	(11.33)
1983	33,945	75,314	109,259	41.37
1984	36,127	74,910	111,037	1.63
1985	24,861	58,244	83,105	(25.16)
1986	21,046	53,116	74,162	(10.76)
1987	29,333	68,815	98,148	32.34
1988	54,459	99,724	154,183	57.09
1989	58,761	154,787	213,548	38.50
1990	73,766	231,077	304,843	42.75
1991	76,938	206,177	283,115	(7.13)
1992	104,565	223,393	327,958	15.84
1993	144,449	275,582	420,031	28.07
1994	109,830	325,231	435,061	3.58
1995	127,640	398,040	525,680	20.83
1996	138,579	420,849	559,428	6.42
1997	112,041	248,262	360,303	(35.59)
1998	32,008	126,122	158,130	(56.11)
1999	72,716	254,385	327,101	106.86

Source: The Thai Automotive Industry Association, and Federation of Thai Industries.

Table 9–3. Domestic Sale of automobile in Thailand

(Number of vehicles)

Year	Passenger Car	Commercial Car	Total	Growth rate (%)
1961	3,542	3,318	6,860	N.A.
1962	4,658	3,680	8,338	21.55
1963	9,096	6,303	15,399	84.68
1964	11,178	9,891	21,069	36.82
1965	10,974	13,724	24,698	17.22
1966	14,984	15,835	30,819	24.78
1967	23,316	26,115	49,431	60.39
1968	27,898	36,188	64,086	29.65
1969	24,376	41,069	65,445	2.12
1970	21,828	27,438	49,266	(24.72)
1971	18,008	26,595	44,603	(9.46)
1972	18,027	26,156	44,183	(0.94)
1973	30,175	39,843	70,018	58.47
1974	29,211	44,644	73,855	5.48
1975	23,388	54,729	78,117	5.77
1976	20,699	57,642	78,341	0.29
1977	25,480	75,843	101,323	29.34
1978	23,233	66,034	89,267	(11.90)
1979	22,043	66,816	88,859	(0.46)
1980	26,840	62,361	89,201	0.38
1981	27,672	62,372	90,044	0.95
1982	27,356	63,830	91,186	1.27
1983	32,779	85,732	118,511	29.97
1984	31,500	82,049	113,549	(4.19)
1985	22,097	63,125	85,222	(24.95)
1986	22,481	55,973	78,454	(7.94)
1987	27,116	74,508	101,624	29.53
1988	38,768	107,712	146,480	44.14
1989	47,705	160,538	208,243	42.16
1990	65,864	238,198	304,062	46.01
1991	66,779	201,781	268,560	(11.68)
1992	121,441	241,546	362,987	35.16
1993	174,169	282,299	456,468	25.75
1994	155,670	330,008	485,678	6.40
1995	163,371	408,209	571,580	17.69
1996	172,730	416,396	589,126	3.07
1997	132,060	231,096	363,156	(38.36)
1998	46,300	97,765	144,065	(60.33)
1999	66,858	151,472	218,330	51.55

Source: The Thai Automotive Industry Association, and Federation of Thai Industries.

6.1.2 More Export Oriented

In Thailand, there is a huge excess capacity of automobile assembly after the crisis. In 1998, the capacity was utilized only about 17 percent (Table 9–2, and Table 9–5). The excess capacity is due to a sharp fall in domestic demand, and over investment in the boom period to serve the expected growing demand.

With the excess capacity and the fall in domestic demand, assemblers have been more export oriented. In overall, the export of vehicles increased sharply from 16,419 cars in 1996, to 42,218 cars in 1997, 66,772 cars in 1998, and

Table 9-4. Automobile Import and Export 1972–1999

(Number of vehicles)

Year	Import				Export			
	Passenger car	Commercial car	Total	Growth Rate (%)	Passenger car	Commercial car	Total	Growth Rate (%)
1972	7,248	17,348	24,596	NA	8	11	19	NA
1973	12,780	29,558	42,338	72.13	0	0	0	(100)
1974	11,639	30,929	42,568	0.54	3	0	3	NA
1975	7,864	38,892	46,756	9.84	3	6	9	200
1976	5,366	31,913	37,279	(20.27)	6	0	6	(33)
1977	7,002	33,706	40,708	9.20	2	4	6	0
1978	2,487	24,989	27,476	(32.50)	2	1	3	(50)
1979	1,166	17,987	19,153	(30.29)	10	74	84	2,700
1980	685	7,861	8,546	(55.38)	7	35	42	(50)
1981	400	6,331	6,731	(21.24)	2	24	26	(38)
1982	683	4,088	4,771	(29.12)	4	24	28	8
1983	767	7,588	8,355	75.12	1	3	4	(86)
1984	1,922	7,597	9,519	13.93	2	17	19	375
1985	1,292	4,871	6,163	(35.26)	12	8	20	5
1986	474	2,510	2,984	(51.58)	20	26	46	130
1987	4,334	4,727	9,061	203.65	488	40	528	1,048
1988	6,735	3,974	10,709	18.19	14,121	314	14,435	2,634
1989	7,263	1,795	9,058	(15.42)	9,032	631	9,663	(33)
1990	10,153	3,289	13,442	48.40	5,826	442	6,268	(35)
1991	12,857	11,292	24,149	79.65	15,688	144	15,832	153
1992	22,583	19,326	41,909	73.54	2,384	1,586	3,970	(75)
1993	44,279	12,115	56,394	34.56	3,781	8,532	12,313	210
1994	36,657	4,838	41,495	(26.42)	14,294	7,086	21,380	74
1995	41,931	6,934	48,865	17.76	1,623	7,182	8,805	(59)
1996	25,185	8,039	33,322	(32.01)	926	15,493	16,419	86
1997	10,808	5,781	16,589	(50.07)	564	41,654	42,218	157
1998	1,023	1,526	2,549	(84.63)	6,773	59,999	66,772	58
1999	NA	NA	7,100	178.54	NA	NA	125,702	88

Source: The Customs Department of Thailand

125,702 cars in 1999 (Table 9–4).

Among assemblers, Mitsubishi Motors Corporation in Thailand is the largest exporter of CBU cars. It exports pickup trucks to Europe, and passenger cars to New Zealand. It planned to export about 60,000–80,000 units in 1999 (Bank of Thailand, 1999). Toyota Motor Corporation began to export Thai–made pickup trucks to Australia and New Zealand in October 1998. Toyota planned to export 20,000 units annually (Minako Mori 2000). Honda began to export small passenger cars (Honda City) to Singapore and Brunei in July 1997, and to export Honda Accord to Australia and New Zealand in 1998. Honda planned to export about 7,000–8,000 units in 1999.

New comers, Auto Alliance Thailand (AAT) and GM, have been more export oriented. AAT (Ford and Mazda) began to produce in May 1998, and export in December 1998. In 1999, AAT became the second largest exporter of CBU cars with over 30,000 units. GM began to produce in May 2000, and planned to export 80 percent of its 40,000 annual production in this year.

Table 9–5. Capacity of Automotive Production in Thailand (1999)

(Number of vehicles)

No.	Assemblers	Passenger cars	Pickups	Trucks and Buses	Total
1	Toyota Motor Thailand	100,000	100,000	-	200,000
2	MMC. Sittiphol	42,000	118,000	14,400	174,400
3	Isuzu Motor Thailand	-	110,000	20,000	130,000
4	Siam Nissan Automobile	-	78,000	3,900	81,900
5	Honda Cars Manufacturing Thailand	50,000	-	-	50,000
6	Siam Konlakan and Nissan	31,200	-	-	31,200
7	Bangchan General Assembly	20,000	-	-	20,000
8	Thonburi Assembly	13,500	-	1,400	14,900
9	Y.M.C. Assembly	12,000	-	-	12,000
10	Thai Rung Union Car	9,600	-		9,600
11	Hino Motor Thailand	-	-	9,600	9,600
12	Thai Swedish Assembly	6,000	-	-	6,000
13	Siam VMC Automobile	-	6,000	-	6,000
14	Motor and Lee cheng	-	-	200	200
15	Auto Alliance Thailand	-	201,000	-	201,000
	Total	284,300	613,000	49,500	946,800
16	General Motor Thailand	40,000	-	-	40,000
	Total	324,300	613,000	49,500	986,800

Note: General Motor Thailand has operated its assembly line since 2000.

Source: Ministry of Industry.

6.1.3 Dominance of Japanese Cars in Thailand

Most of vehicles in the domestic market are Japanese made. Japanese assemblers, such as Toyota, Honda, Isuzu, and Mitsubishi have their share in the domestic market over 80 percent for many years. Toyota captured the largest share of passenger car market, about 36.3 percent in 1999. For commercial cars, Isuzu had the highest share in domestic market, about 37.5 percent in 1999. In overall, Toyota had the highest share at 36.1 percent in 1999.

Generally, the domestic market share of European and US assemblers is small. However, the domestic market share of Ford, the US assembler, increased from 0.9 percent in 1995, to 3.9 percent in 1999 (Table 9–6). Ford Operation Thailand expected that the share of Ford in pickup truck market would increase to 8 percent in 2000 (Thansettakit newspaper 14–17 May 2000). Moreover, some Japanese assemblers were taken over by the US and European firms. For example, Isuzu was taken over by GM. Nissan was taken over by Renault. Thus, in Thailand, Japanese assemblers have been challenged by the US and European assemblers, including their alliances.

Table 9–6. Automobile Market Share in Thailand

(Unit: Percent)

Brand Name	1995			1999		
	Passenger cars	Comm. cars.	Total	Passenger cars	Comm. cars.	Total
Toyota	29.0	29.1	29.1	36.3	35.9	36.1
Isuzu	0.0	27.5	19.7	0.7	37.5	25.0
Nissan	8.4	18.2	15.4	12.8	7.8	9.5
Mitsubishi	11.1	13.1	12.5	6.1	10.1	8.7
Honda	16.9	0.0	4.8	30.4	0.0	10.3
Benze	8.0	0.3	2.5	1.6	0.0	0.5
GM	3.1	0.0	0.9	0.2	0.1	0.1
BMW	3.0	0.0	0.8	2.8	0.0	0.9
Volvo	3.3	0.1	1.0	1.4	0.0	0.5
Ford	2.6	0.3	0.9	0.0	6.0	3.9
Hyundai	4.5	0.0	1.3	2.4	0.0	0.8
Daewoo	2.0	0.0	0.6	1.0	0.0	0.3
Others	8.2	11.5	10.6	4.4	2.6	3.3
Total	100.0	100.0	100.0	100.0	100.0	100.0

Sources: Pacific Business and Industries (1996), and Toyota Motor Thailand.

6.1.4 Changes in Part Supplier Relationships

Historically, in terms of part supplier relationship, there are differences between the US system and Japanese system as follows.

- The US assemblers utilized either internal procurement or short-term contracting. On the other hand, Japanese firms have employed a long-term relationship with a limited number of independent suppliers that seem to mix element of market and hierarchy. The long-term relationship substitutes for ownership in protecting specific assets used in American style.
- In the US system, design-intensive products were often procured internally (Monteverde and Teece 1982). For part outsourcing, products were designed typically by the US assemblers. On the contrary, Japanese auto-firm normally relies on their supplier to do actual design of the product (Holmatrom and Robert 1998).
- Traditional American style relies on market bidding, short-term contract, and strictly inspection. On the contrary, Japanese assemblers rely on trust, long-term relationship.

Following the trade liberalization, there is the new trend of combining the advantages of both systems in the automobile industry.

In Thailand, there are three major changes in the relationship between auto assemblers and part suppliers as follows.

- Automobile assemblers have utilized a global outsourcing strategy, especially after the abandon of local content requirement. GM and Auto Alliance Thailand (Ford and Mazda) are leaders in this strategy.
- The use of "Modularization" has appeared in Thailand. Auto Alliances Thailand (Ford and Mazda) tries to use more local parts, reduces in-house facilities and orders auto part makers to send auto parts in form of module.
- The US automobile assemblers, especially GM and AAT, have utilized a competitive bidding system for part outsourcing. On the other hand, Japanese assemblers have employed Japanese subcontracting in Thailand for several decades. However, it is expected that Japanese assemblers such as Toyota in Thailand will move gradually toward competitive bidding system.

In 1999, Isuzu which was taken over by GM, employed the global outsourcing strategy for a new model of pickup (so-called I 190) by the competitive bidding system. The bidding was held in Japan. This model will be produced in Thailand in 2002. Many global suppliers participated and won the bidding. Only a few Thai firms were allowed to bid directly and received the order of a few simple parts. Many Thai firms will have to down grade from Tier 1 to Tier 2 suppliers for Isuzu. This is a major turning point of the relationship between auto assemblers and local part suppliers.

6.1.5 Building Part Supply Base of the US Big Three

Along with their direct investment in Thailand, Ford and GM set up their part suppliers in Thailand and other ASEAN countries. They invited their Tier 1 global suppliers to invest in this region in order to build up their part supply system. In addition, part suppliers prefer to locate near assemblers' plants in order to minimize their transportation cost and to delivery on time. Thus, global suppliers, such as Visteon, Delphi, and Dana Corporation invested in Thailand. These global suppliers also have to build up their networks including Tier 2 and Tier 3 suppliers in this region.

6.1.6 Increasing Localization

Auto assemblers tend to increase localization in order to minimize cost of inventory, transportation, and fluctuation of exchange rate. For example, Toyota aims to increase localization to 100 percent. It is noteworthy that the production of exported cars, for some models or some assemblers, has less localization than the production for domestic market. For example, Isuzu (Thailand) produces a model for Australia market by using imported parts about 80 percent.

In addition, global auto part suppliers such as Delphi also aim to maximize local content.

6.2 Auto Part Makers

The recent economic crisis, trade liberalization, and the changes in global automobile industry have substantial impacts on the auto part industry in Thailand. In Thailand, auto part makers may divided into four groups: (a) Tier 1 global suppliers who are subsidiaries of transnational companies or joint ventures, and work closely with assemblers to develop products and supply directly to assemblers; (b) Tier 1 local suppliers; (c) Tier 2 suppliers; and (d) Tier 3 suppliers. The changes in the auto part industry in Thailand are discussed as follows.

Along with the investment of the US big three in Thailand, several Tier 1 global suppliers from the US and Europe have set their own subsidiary companies in Thailand or purchased the majority share of Thai companies. They regard the operation in Thailand as a part of their global network. These global suppliers have formed their networks including Tier 2 and Tier 3 suppliers in Thailand. For example, Delphi has formed its network with about 20 suppliers in Thailand. In Delphi network, all of suppliers are joint ventures, and none is pure Thai own company.

The economic crisis had two major effects on local auto part makers. First, due to the decrease in domestic sale and production of cars, the demand for auto parts decreased sharply. Second, their foreign debts in terms of Baht increased drastically after the depreciation of Baht. At the same time, there was liquidity crunch in the Thai economy. As a results, it is very difficult for local part makers to survive without outside financial aid. Most global suppliers, especially Japanese firms increased their capital in local joint ventures after the crisis. However, the majority of Thai partners could not increase capital in joint ventures. Thus, the foreign investors have increased their ownership and control in joint ventures.

According to Unico (1999), among 117 Tier 1 suppliers for Toyota, 40 suppliers are local suppliers. After the crisis, many of local suppliers have withdrawn from the auto parts industry. For example, the Siam Cement Group sold its equity in Thai Engineering Product Co., Ltd. (machining and aluminum casting), Nowaloha Industry Co., Ltd. (iron casting), and Siam AT Industry Co. Ltd. (machining), to Aisin Takaoka (Toyota Group) in 1999. In addition, the Siam Cement Group announced that the auto parts business was not its core business anymore.

On November 4, 1999, the Sammit Motor Group, a major local producer of auto parts, announced that it was switching from a purely auto parts producer to the agricultural machinery business, and planned to have 50 per cent of its total revenues from new business within the next five years. The Group president explained that it was unable to become an international player because its costs were higher than those of competitors (The Nation November 5, 1999).

On the other hand, Thai Summit group and Thai Rung have diversified by producing auto parts, and parts for other industries, such as electrical appliances and agricultural machinery.

Most of local auto part makers have to down grade themselves from Tier 1 suppliers to Tier 2 suppliers, or from Tier 2 suppliers to Tier 3 suppliers. It is expected that there is no real Tier 1 local suppliers. There are three major reasons. First, local firms have limited capabilities. Specifically, they lack of design capabilities. While automobile assemblers have shifted the responsibility of design to suppliers. Second, the US and European global suppliers came in Thailand with the US big three. These global suppliers are much superior than local firms in terms of technology, management, and financial aspects. Third, many local Tier 1 suppliers have taken over by global suppliers or foreign firms after the recent economic crisis as discussions in above.

Under the globalization in automobile industry, part supplier relationship in Thailand moves toward competitive bidding system with the world standard of management and product. To survive in the global competition local part makers must get the standard of QS9000. Many local part makers have improved their production and received the certificate of QS9000. For joint ventures, it is easy to improve their capabilities in order to qualify for the standard of QS9000. However, with family business style, local suppliers who are SME have difficulties to improve their capabilities in terms of quality control, engineering, and management. Moreover, under the competitive bidding system with the world standard of management and product, all assemblers demand the reduction of the price of auto parts periodically. Thus, local auto part makers are forced to reduce their cost of production or improve their productivity.

After the recent crisis and a fall in domestic demand, auto part makers also try to increase their direct export the same as automobile assemblers. Auto parts can be exported either (1) indirect export (in the export of CBU cars), or (2) direct export such as OEM parts and REM parts. In terms of direct export of auto parts, the majority is the export of global suppliers, such as Thai Arrow Product Co. Ltd. (export of wiring set) and Denso. Nipon (2000) reported that a Thai–Japanese joint venture that used to supply seat belts for domestic market only, has exported to its parent company in Japan, and began to export to Mexico. It is expected that the export of after-sales parts or REM parts also increase.

In addition, after the economic crisis, under the Thai Auto Part manufacturer Association (TAPMA), about 20 local auto part makers have formed "Auto part Exporter Club." This club aims to promote and cooperate among themselves for auto part exporting. However, this club is a new and weak club.

Finally, under the new environment, some of local auto part makers who can not improve themselves have to go out from the business. However, some of them can adjust themselves and join the network of global suppliers. The new environment provides threat and opportunities for local auto part makers.

7 Conclusion

In Thailand, the automobile industry has been developed since the early of 1960s. In the beginning period, the Thai government employed two major policies for this industry: granting incentives for private investment and protecting with high tariff on CBU cars. Then, the government promoted local auto parts industry by imposing local content requirement on the auto assembly. In the boom period of Thai economy (1987–1996), the automobile industry expanded rapidly. However, this industry shrank drastically after the 1997 economic crisis. Recently, it has recovered since 1999.

After the economic crisis, the automobile industry, both assembly and part making, has drastically changed. These changes resulted from three major factors: the recent economic crisis, trade liberalization, and the changes in global automobile industry. Trade liberalization includes the abandon of local content requirement following the commitment to WTO, and ASEAN agreements. The global changes in automobile industry include global consolidation and mergers, the change in assemblers' relationship with part suppliers, and technological changes.

The major changes in automobile industry in Thailand can be summarized as follows:

1. After the economic crisis, automobile assemblers and auto part makers decreased the production and have been more export oriented. With the excess capacity and the fall in domestic demand, the export of CBU cars of auto assemblers in Thailand and auto parts has increased significantly after the 1997 crisis. Under the plans of parent companies, auto assemblers in

Thailand have exported CBU cars to Singapore, Brunei, Australia, New Zealand, and some European countries. Following the recovery of domestic market and increasing export, the domestic production of automobile has a positive growth rate in 1999–2000.

2. With the consolidation and mergers in global automobile industry and direct investment from GM and Ford in Thailand, the dominant role of Japanese assemblers in Thailand has been challenged. GM and Ford also invited their part suppliers to invest and build up their networks in Thailand. Moreover, they also brought the competitive bidding system for outsourcing to Thailand.
3. With the abandon of local content requirement, the automobile assemblers have employed global outsourcing strategy more extensively. However, auto assemblers tend to increase localization in order to minimize cost of inventory, transportation, and fluctuation of exchange rate. For example, Toyota aims to increase localization. In addition, global auto part suppliers such as Delphi also aims to maximize local content. It is noteworthy that the production of exported cars, for some models, has less localization than the production for domestic market.
4. For auto part makers in Thailand, they can be divided into four groups: global Tier 1 suppliers, local Tier 1 suppliers, Tier 2 suppliers, Tier 3 and lower suppliers. The major changes of these suppliers are as follows:

- Along with the investment of the US big three in Thailand, several Tier 1 global suppliers from the US and Europe have set their own subsidiary companies in Thailand or purchased the majority share of Thai companies.
- After the crisis, some local Tier 1 suppliers were taken over by Japanese or Western firms, or shifted to other business. In addition, some of them were downgraded to be Tier 2 suppliers. This is because of their financial problems and their lacking of product design capability.
- Under the competitive bidding system with the world standard of management and product, local auto part makers are forced to integrate into global supply networks, improve management, productivity, and so on in order to survive in this business. For local SME with family business style, especially Tier 3 and lower suppliers, they have some difficulties with this system. However, for auto part makers who can join the networks of global suppliers, they have a good opportunity to expand.

References

Bank of Thailand (1998) "Automotive Industry in Crisis," *Monthly Bulletin.* Vol.38, No.2, February. (In Thai)

Bank of Thailan (1999) "Automotive Industry in Crisis and Trend," *Monthly Bulletin.* Vol.39, No. 7, July (In Thai)

Board of Investment (BOI) (1999) The Executive Report: *Thailand's Automotive Parts Industry..*

Gereffi, Gary. (1999) *A Commodity Chains Framework for Analyzing Global Industries*. Duke University, August 12.

Holmatrom, Bengt and John Robert. (1998) "The Boundaries of the Firm Revisited," *Journal of Economic Perspective*. Fall, pp. 73–94.

Krailerk, Ampika. (1998) *Managing Productivity Improvement in the Auto-parts Manufacturing Industry for the Future*. Thailand Productivity Institute.

Maruhashi, Hiroko. (1995) "Japanese Subcontracting System in Thailand: A case Study of The Thai Automobile Industry," M.A Thesis, Faculty of Economics, Thammasat University.

Mori, Minako. (2000) *New Trends in ASEAN Strategies of Japanese-affiliated Automobile Parts Manufacturers – The Role of Exporting and Priorities for the Future*. Center for Pacific Business Studies.

Monteverde, K. and Teece, D.J. (1982) "Supplier Switching Costs and Vertical Integration in the Automobile Industry," *Bell Journal of Economics*, 13: 206–213

Nobeoka, Kentaro. (1996) "Alternative Component Sourcing Strategies within the Manufacturer–Supplier Network: Benefits of Quasi-Market Strategy in the Japanese Automobile Industry," *Kobe Economic & Business Review*, 41, 69–99

Poapongsakorn, Nipon. (2000) *The Thailand Automotive Industry*.

Poapongsakorn, Nipon. and Fuller, Belinda. (1998) "The Role of Foreign Direct Investment and Production Networks in the Development of the Thai Auto and Electronics Industries." *JETRO–IDE Joint Symposium*.

Chanwipapwong, Sayan. (1998) "Development Strategy for The Industry Affected by WTO Agreement: A case study of TRIMs: Local Content Requirement." Thesis, Witthayalai Pongkan Ratcha-anachak (Kingdom Defense College), (In Thai)

Terdudomtham, Thamavit. (1997) "The Automobile Industry in Thailand." A paper prepared for the project Analysis and Review of Competitiveness in Selected Industries in ASEAN, submitted to ASEAN secretariat, Bangkok: Thailand Development Research Institute, 1997.

The Nation, a newspaper in Thailand, various issues.

UNICO International Corporation (1995) *The Study on Industrial Sector Development: Supporting Industries in the Kingdom of Thailand*. Japan International Cooperation Agency (JICA) and Thailand, Ministry of Industry.

UNICO International Corporation (1999) *The Follow-up Study on Supporting Industries Development in the Kingdom of Thailand*, Japan International Cooperation Agency (JICA) and Thailand, Ministry of Industry, September.

Appendix: List of Interviews

Srisuddee, Anuporn. General Manager, Product Development Department, Isuzu Motors Co., (Thailand) Ltd.

Phaoenchoke, Kaewkow. Assistant General Manager, Thai Rung Union Car Public Company Limited.

Wuttiprasittipol, Lertsak. General Manager, Purchasing Administration Department, Isuzu Motors Co., (Thailand) Ltd.

Siripoke, Nontasak. Division Manager, Purchasing Division, Honda Cars Manufacturing (Thailand) Co., Ltd.

Jungroongruangkit, Pattana. President, Thai Summit Group companies.

Chung, Russell Kirk. Asia–Pacific Director, Delphi Global Purchasing, Delphi Automotive Systems.

Chaiwongwutikul, Tawatchai. Assistant Manager, Purchasing Department, Toyota Motor Thailand Co., Ltd.

Rerkchavee, Warin. General Manager, Summit Steering Wheel Co., Ltd.

Kitaphanich, Yongkiat. Vice President, Somboon Malleable Iron Industrial Co., Ltd. (Somboon Group Companies)

10 Reevaluation of the International Division of Labor in Japan's Automobile Industry in Asia

Koichi Shimokawa
Tokaigakuen University

1 Introduction

At present there are signs of financial stabilization and recovery across the whole Asian region, even though the financial crisis had a tremendous impact on the automobile market and production in Asia. In 1999, Japanese, European and American automobile manufacturers put an end to production reductions in ASEAN countries and have started to increase production. Therefore, it is expected that the automobile industry in Asia will revive, sooner or later, in the 21st century. It is also expected that, after two years of economic crisis and production reductions, an innovative system for the international division of labor will be established when concerned parties reexamine the existing system with its limitations. This system had been established to complement the real international division of labor, with focus on technology transfer and production and supply systems for the domestic markets of each Asian country.

Most of the automobile manufacturers reduced their production during the economic crisis. However, it is believed that while promoting exports, due to the depreciation of local currencies, these manufacturers were preparing to increase the domestic production rate of auto parts because of the high cost of imported parts and further promotion of intra- and interregional divisions of labor. Obviously, the economic crisis brought on the turning point. As a part of my attempt to look at the future of the automobile industry in Asia, which has reached a turning point, I would like to analyze the presence of Japanese automobile manufacturers in Asia, especially in terms of direct investment, trends in the international division of labor, and the impact on technology transfer and the auto parts industry that these may have.

Before the Asian monetary crisis occurred, the strategy of Japanese automobile manufacturers for the Asian markets was to expand the international division of labor especially in ASEAN countries while establishing a foothold in the Chinese market, which offered the largest growth potential for the 21st century. The international division of labor linking ASEAN countries, Taiwan and South Korea was only regionally oriented, its aim being to develop a regional division of labor and contribute to the domestic production in each country in expectation of the development of markets within the region. There was no assumption of a rapid price increase of imported parts due to the devaluation of local currencies or the export drive for completed cars. The underlying idea was to gradually develop international competitiveness through an expansion of the international division of labor of AICO (ASEAN Industry Cooperative Organization), in anticipation of the establishment of AFTA (ASEAN Free Trade Area), which was scheduled in 2003.

In the wake of the Asian economic crisis, Japanese automobile manufacturers are holding off expanding the international division of labor but taking aggressive action to enhance competitiveness in exports by increasing the domestic production rate. This approach is quite contrary to the electric and electronics industries, which have made progress with a complementary international division of labor. They are now further reinforcing the division of labor as part of a global strategy and upping exports to extraregional markets.

What the future has in store will depend on how concerned parties go about steering the international division of labor in automobile production in Asia as a production base with a potential for global development. On this point, I would like to study the future development of an international division of labor in Asia's automobile industry and try to reevaluate it in a comparison with what electric and electronics industries have done.

2 The Presence of Japanese Automobile Manufacturers in Asia and the History of Local Production

The presence of Japanese automobile manufacturers in Asia has become increasingly significant in various ways. The influence of Japanese automobile manufacturers is seen mostly in Taiwan and ASEAN countries, followed by South Korea. Mainland China and India have just started technological tie-ups and other projects on a trial basis (Table 10–1). Especially in China, which had adhered to a policy of accepting only a limited number of newcomers to protect the three big, three small and two tiny state enterprises, Japanese automobile manufacturers allowed Volkswagen to get ahead of them in large-scale manufacture with the Shanghai project. Japan went ahead only with truck production and related technological tie-ups but did not have any major production base there. However, Daihatsu established a production base for compact cars in Tianjin as a joint venture with Tianjin Automotive Industrial Group Company. This production base provided a foothold for Toyota to open a small-sized car and engine factory. Honda started assembly operations for the ACCORD at the Guangzhou Automotive Industrial Group Company after the French automobile manufacturer Peugeot withdrew. In addition, motorcycle-related projects by Honda and Suzuki are starting to make progress in various locations in China. However, all of these

Table 10–1. Automobile Market in 13 Asian Countries

	94	95	96E	2000E
Southeast Asia Total	3,526	3,561	3,790	5,800
Korea	1,556	1,556	1,600	2,200
China	1,337	1,403	1,550	2,700
Hong Kong	57	60	60	60
Taiwan	576	542	580	740
ASEAN Total	1,202	1,459	1,561	2,165
Thailand	486	572	610	900
Malaysia	200	286	310	400
Indonesia	326	384	400	600
Philippines	103	28	145	240
ASEAN 4 Countries	1,116	1,370	1,465	2,040
Singapore	38	42	45	45
Vietnam	28	22	25	50
Myanmar	19	25	26	30
South Asia Total	539	739	920	1,500
India	470	629	800	1,300
Pakistan	69	110	120	200
13 Asian Countries Total	5,266	5,759	6,271	9,365

(units: thousand)

Source: TED Seminar, Mr. Mashu Kato, Trends and Prospects of ASEAN Automobile Market and Automobile/Parts Industries

Note: 1995 figures for China, Hong Kong, Vietnam, Myanmar, India and Pakistan are estimated.

projects are in the so-called sowing stages with another ten to twenty years to bear results.

India has the second largest population in the world after China. Suzuki established a major base in India – with an annual production of more than 0.2 million multi-model type cars modeled after the compact car ALTO as a joint venture with Maruti Udoyog Ltd. and is gaining the early profits expected of an early arrival in the market. However, European and American manufacturers have also entered the market and other Japanese manufacturers like Toyota and Honda have set up footholds to make their entry.

In South Korea, while three major automobile manufacturers – Hyundai, Kia and Daewoo – dominated the market, production under license, capital and technological tie-ups had long been carried out between Hyundei and Mitsubishi, Kia and Mazda, and Daewoo and General Motors. However, around 1988, at the time of the Seoul Olympic Games, these South Korean manufacturers made progress in establishing systems that would enable them to develop on their own. The relations with the Japanese manufacturers started to gradually weaken. In addition, since major Japanese manufacturers Toyota and Honda had not historically been involved, tie-ups at the assembly level were limited. As for auto parts manufacturers, however, quite a few technical tie-ups and joint ventures were formed especially in sophisticated electronics, press, cast and engine components and underbody parts. The South Korean automobile industry had been trying to enter the world market and import materials and parts that were significantly value-based from Japan. In fact, when the yen sharply appreciated between 1985 and 1987 after the G5 meeting, despite the high costs due to the strong yen, the volume of imports from Japan continued to increase, thus contributing to a huge trade deficit between South Korea and Japan. In addition, the South Korean government gave approval to the Samsung Group to enter the automobile industry, putting an end to the domination of the three major automobile manufacturers. This move fueled competition and the total production capacity reached 3.5 million cars per year, which constituted a surplus of more than one million cars annually.

It was in 1997 that the financial crisis hit. In the process of financial and economic reconstruction under strict supervision by IMF (International Monetary Fund), large financial groups and business exchanges underwent restructuring. Kia eventually went faced bankruptcy and was placed under legal control in 1997. Samsung Motors also went bankrupt, leaving just Hyundei Motor and Daewoo Motor to dominate the South Korean automobile industry. However, Daewoo Motor ran into trouble over the dissolution of the group and financial support, with GM winning exclusive negotiating rights. It turned out that there was a breakdown in the sales negotiation between Daewoo Motors, banking group and GM. In place of General Motors, with the existing alliance relationship with Daewoo Motor, is expected to come into play for the acquisition. Moreover, Renault of France, which was already in a technical tie-up with Nissan, bought out Samsung Motors and made Kia a subsidiary of Hyundei. Daimler–Crysler then approached Hyundei–kia to forge a global tie-up with the manufacturer. Thus the Korean automobile industry finds itself today right in the center of on-going worldwide restructuring. Eventually the wave of international restructuring that foreign companies are forcing with tie-ups are expected to reach beyond the vehicle assemblers to the parts manufacturers. As for Japanese automobile manufacturers, though South Korea virtually abolished import tariffs on automobiles and opened the way to total liberalization, their efforts to export and sell in Korea have not made much progress so yet.

Therefore, it is not an overstatement to say that ASEAN countries and Taiwan were the only countries in Asia where Japanese automobile manufacturers maintained a strong influence or presence in the region. Yet, 90% (or over 80%) of the cars domestically produced in Taiwan and ASEAN countries were developed by Japanese automobile manufacturers and manufactured through joint ventures.

In Taiwan, 0.44 million cars are produced annually by as many as 12 manufacturers where most of them have been developed by Japanese automobile manufacturers. This includes Mazdas produced by Taiwan Ford, the second largest automobile producer in Taiwan. The total investment in Taiwan Ford was

NT$ 555 million, 70% of which came from Canada Ford. Toyota, Nissan, Mitsubishi, Honda and Taiwan Ford manufactured 80% of the automobiles. In Taiwan, there are not as many large industrial groups like South Korea, thus many companies have formed joint ventures with Japanese manufacturers. However, there are many owner-operated companies, and this has prevented mergers as the government had hoped. Unlike South Korea, no manufacturer in Taiwan has been groomed for large-scale production of over several hundred thousand cars.

Compared to this, the ratio of direct investment by Japanese automobile manufacturers is low. In fact, Toyota Motor, which joined only in 1986 after a request by the Taiwanese government, invested only 22% of the total NT$ 2 billion (49%) in Kuozui Motors, 25.2% coming from Hino Motors Ltd. and 1.8% by Mitsui and Co., Ltd. Among the remaining companies, Nissan Motor Co. invested 25% of the NT$ 1.6 billion of Yuron Motors, Mitsubishi Motors Corp. and Mitsubishi Corp. invested 15.95% and 5.47%, respectively, of the NT$ 667 million capitalization of China Motor, and US Honda invested 13.5% of the NT$ 4.868 billion of Sanyang Industries" capitalization.

Seeking to join the WTO, Taiwan has reduced tariffs on European and US cars to 30%. As a result, imported passenger cars account for over 30% of the passenger car market. The ninety primary suppliers and part of about 200 small and medium parts manufacturers in Taiwan offer excellent technology and quality. Both the public and private sectors in Taiwan have been making efforts to nurture these suppliers and parts manufacturers so as to incorporate them into the network of global parts suppliers.

In particular, the parts manufacturers of the Toyota and Nissan groups have entered the market in the form of joint ventures with active involvement in technology transfer. If this move is successful, it is possible Taiwan will be an auto parts supply center for the world in some fields, especially electronic parts, just like Acer is for personal computers. With its location and given a positive development of exchange with the Chinese mainland, Taiwan could develop various automobile-related projects. However, the problem is that it is uncertain how relations between China and Taiwan will develop after the return of Hong Kong to China. Instead, the division of labor in ASEAN countries, where Japanese automobile manufacturers have a strong influence, are more likely to be practical.

The ASEAN region, where Thailand, Malaysia, Indonesia and the Philippines once produced 1.4 million cars annually, has been attracting the most attention of all Asian countries with its tremendous potential for demand. As was mentioned at the beginning, the Asian currency crisis in the ASEAN region of Thailand, Indonesia, and South Korea caused a decline in automobile demand in 1997. Although this decline in demand seemed to continue for two to three years, there was a recovery in demand as these countries made operational adjustments and carried out restructuring.

Japanese automobile manufacturers have historically had a tremendous presence in the ASEAN region, noting that 90% of all cars domestically produced in this region are produced with the cooperation of Japanese manufacturers in domestic production and technology transfers.

Among Japanese automobile manufacturers, Toyota and Mitsubishi started SKD (semi-knockdown) operations as early as the late 1960s continuing into the early 1970s, in response to requests by local governments for cooperation in domestic production. Today, Toyota and Mitsubishi have the strongest influence in the ASEAN region followed by Honda, which started with motorcycle production, and Nissan, which is now trying to catch up. As far as the automobile industry is concerned, direct investments from Japan were relatively low in ASEAN countries. This is because ASEAN countries, especially Malaysia and Thailand, followed a policy of indirect investment from overseas, rather than direct foreign investment from Japan, and introduced a policy of indigenization of components, thereby giving preference to domestic resources. This was especially in the field of automobile industry.

From the early stage of import of completed cars and carrying out repair work, assembly production was carried out in the form of SKD (semi-knocked-down), KD (knocked-down) and CKD (complete-knocked-down) production. At the same time, the domestic market received protection. However, although the protection of the domestic market promoted technology transfer and domestic production to a certain extent, production volume was restricted and cost penalties were inevitable due to high tariffs placed on imported parts in order to promote domestic production. The result was that costs were twice resulted with costs twice as high as Japanese-made products and quality lower in comparison to international standards. In order to ease this situation, ASEAN Complementation (an agreement for reciprocal complementation in automobile production) was concluded among the five countries, the founding members of ASEAN, in 1969. Yet, it ended up only as a desk plan since it was difficult to decide on the autoparts to be produced by the member due to conflict of interests in auto parts trading amongst the countries. At the background of the failure to supplement the ASEAN Complementation. There were the differences in automobile industry policy of the separate ASEAN countries, which emerged in the 1980's. However, the major problem lay in the difference in policy decisions among ASEAN countries: whether to deregulate foreign currency introduction in order to aggressively invite foreign investment and introduce yet sophisticated technology needed for full-set automobile production, or to actively prepare for free trade areas in Asia, such as AFTA (ASEAN Free Trade Area); or to place emphasis on protection of domestic industries. However, through experiencing these trials and tribulations and complications, ASEAN countries began to achieve progress in the local production of automobiles and technology transfers, with consequent expansion of domestic markets. The financial crisis hit Asia at this time.

3 The Development of an International Division of Labor in Asia, Especially in ASEAN Countries, and Technology Transfer

As stated earlier, within the Asian region, direct investment and operation of Japanese automobile and auto parts manufacturers have historically had the strongest presence in Taiwan and ASEAN countries. South Korea and China had their own policies for domestic production and strictly limited the inflow of foreign capital, especially direct investment by Japanese assemblers. In contrast, ASEAN accepted investment by these Japanese assemblers and auto parts manufacturers in the form of joint ventures with local companies under the name of technology transfer, even though they were also pursuing a policy of domestic production. Furthermore, they were seeking an international division of labor on a regional basis. Of all the ASEAN countries, the Japanese manufacturers made the maximum investment in Thailand. In 1998, the production capacity of Thailand reached over 1 million cars, including European and US cars; Japanese manufacturers accounted for 80% of it. The future development of a regional complementary division of labor in components and parts production among the four major ASEAN countries should not be overlooked when it comes to the automobile industry in the ASEAN region. As mentioned before, the ASEAN Complementation was being worked out among ASEAN countries, from the late 1960's, led by the four major ASEAN countries, as a plan to promote a division of labor in auto parts production and reciprocal complementation. The idea was that, if production were divided among countries rather than producing all parts in a single country, for example, producing engines in country A, transmissions in country B and pressed parts in country C, the cost would be reduced considerably because of the merits of scale.

The complementation plan began with this concept but ended up as a desk plan since each country had their own domestic production plan and there was a conflict of interests over the allocation of parts to be produced. It was difficult to solve because some countries had surpluses and others deficits in the auto parts trade. Thus it resulted in a failure of the complementation plan. The underlying cause of this failure was the low standards of industrialization of ASEAN countries and the different degrees of industrialization within them.

In the late 1980's, the industrialization of the four major ASEAN countries grew and the domestic automobile production plan started to get on track. The, BBC (Brand of Brand Complementation) was started at that time. In the BBC scheme, a specific automobile manufacturer offers reciprocal complementation for parts of a specific brand car, and import tariffs on those parts are reduced considerably. Some manufacturers, such as Toyota, Mitsubishi and Nissan, started to use this system. Among ASEAN countries, the concept of a complementary division of labor was expanded to parts and materials. AICO (ASEAN Industry Cooperative Organization) was established as a comprehensive and full-scale agreement on reciprocal complementation in an anticipated response to the sharp reductions of import tariffs to be implemented under AFTA (ASEAN Free Trade Area), which was scheduled for 2003 (Table 10–2).

What is worth noting about AICO is that it will help promote a division of labor and cooperation among parts manufacturers, while helping to form a network not only within the region but also beyond.

When AICO was put into effect in November 1996, nineteen companies, mainly Japanese, applied. But, no companies have actually operated under AICO before 1999. Thailand gave approval to a total of nine companies to apply for AICO, including Japanese automobile manufacturers (Toyota and Honda), auto parts manufacturers (e.g.: Denso Corp.) and home electrical appliance manufacturers (e.g.: Matsushita Electric Industrial Co.), as well as Volvo and Goodyear. However, Malaysia and Indonesia refrained from granting approval to any company because of concern about the impact on domestic industries. Later, in 1988, Matsushita and Volvo were given the go-ahead to apply for AICO.

As for BBC, though the ASEAN Secretariat gave approval for projects, AICO certification required approval of the Ministry of Industry of each country, which is why its implementation was delayed.

According to Japanese automobile manufacturers who have applied for AICO certification, each country demanded a foreign currency balance (import-export balance between two countries) from each manufacturer when it applied for AICO certification. (P.27 op. cit. by Research Division of Japan Finance Corporation for Small Business).

There is no doubt that the basic concept of AICO will greatly contribute to the development of a regional international division of labor in the ASEAN region if it functions at full scale. However, there are differences in expectations and the degree of domestic automobile production among the ASEAN countries, as well as the fact that the problem of balancing trade in auto parts still remains to be solved before a division of labor can be strengthened. Furthermore, the currency crisis in 1997 discouraged each country from liberalizing trade in key industries, such as the automobile industry. However, if ASEAN countries hold off on trade liberalization for a long time, the ASEAN market will become less attractive because of non-tariff barriers, which could curb direct investments in ASEAN. In such case, ASEAN would be unable to compete with China and India in attracting more direct investment. Therefore, though AICO is presently not functional, if the ASEAN economy recovers by the time AFTA (ASEAN Free Trade Area) and CEPT (Common Effective Preferential Tariff) agreements are established, a full-scale international division of labor will be introduced and a production and supply network for auto parts will be established linking Japan, Taiwan and other countries.

In this way, regional reciprocal complementation by leading Japanese automobile manufacturers is underway though the system has been applicable to a limited number of auto parts.

Table 10–2. Comparison of BBC and AICO Plan

	BBC	AICO
Contents	(1)Expansion of Mass-Production Effect (2)Remove obstacles to private business by reducing high tariffs set to protect the domestic parts industry and reducing vehicle production cost. This enables support for the distribution of the specific parts of the specific model of the specific brand in the local countries.	Promote infrastructure in interest of WTO trade deregulation through trade/investment expansion in order to enhance the mutual profits and competitiveness in each country and promote economic development in the ASEAN region. CEPT adoption was prolonged to 2003, thus the AICO Plan was temporarily adopted in 1996 in order to make adjustments for each ASEAN country by 2003. Also, the ASEAN automobile industry is expected to improve in the long-run in terms of income and technical standards. But, the need of each country to reduce cost by promoting the localization and mutual complementation among countries was one of the factors for the early adoption.
Background	Originated by the AIC approved by the 14th ASEAN Foreign Ministers' Conference in 1981. In 1982, Mitsubishi Automobile Industries proposed to "(1) reduce the import parts tariff to half, (2) recognize imported parts as domestic parts and include in the calculation of the domestic production ratio, when each country mutually accommodates parts with high cost priority." In 1987, at the 3rd Summit, an agreement was reached to promote the BBC Plan by the Manila Declaration, and in 1988, it was approved and signed at the ASEAN Cabinet Economic Ministers Council.	
Items Included	Automobile Parts	Finished Products / Mid-process Products / Raw Material
Applicable Term	From October 1988 until the start of AICO	Until the start of CEPT (2003)
Applicants	Domestic Automobile Manufacturers (Brand Owners)	Manufacturers in each country
Authorizing Party	ASEAN Office	Industrial ministry in each country.

Terms and Conditions	—Limited to automobile parts. — BBC products meet PTA (ASEAN special privileged decision) regulations on the place of origin. a. Single ASEAN content exceeds 50% b. Cumulative ASEAN content exceeds 60% — Manufactured according the International Quality Assurance Standards — Competitively priced for the general marketplace.	— Established in "each ASEAN member country" and operating business. — Minimum 30% of country's share — Material-sharing or corporate cooperation. —Corporations conducting business established by multiple participating countries, which cooperate to manufacture AICO products. —Domestic manufacturing ratio of designated parts exceeds 40%. — Approved as AICO products when raw material is imported if CIF amount is less than 60% of the export FOB amount.
Benefits	—Domestic manufacturing approval —50% exemption of CDK tariff.	—To be included in the domestic manufacturing ratio. — 0–5% performance tariff is applied (available only for the participating companies who handle AICO approved parts).
Issues	—Advantages and disadvantages become evident for governments in each country due to their own domestic automobile, manufacturing programs. —Each country advocates the production of more value-added parts (engines and transmissions), which leads to conflicts. —BBC has a special program for large automobile manufacturers, thus the early shift to CEPT is necessary. Also, more opinions call for a program to promote small to mid-size local industries. —After submitting the application to the ASEAN office, opinions of each industrial ministry of each country must be asked. This is a complicated process because approval must be granted by all ASEAN participating countries.	—Each country's does not progress at the same pace. —Approval by the government (of importing and exporting countries) is done simultaneously and the importing and exporting countries need to negotiate. Both benefits and losses will be evident and conflicts may affect the supporting industries such as a delay in permits is expected for automobile related industries. —Because of trade imbalances, it is possible that the CKD package that categorizes parts by manufacturers under the control of each country's automobile companies, may not be approved. In this case, the manufacturer must apply for AICO approval.

Source: Small to mid-size Finance Corporation Investigation Dept., Previous document, p.26, A Re–created document from the ASEAN office documents.

Figure 10–1. Outline of Toyota's Components Complementation Plan 1990

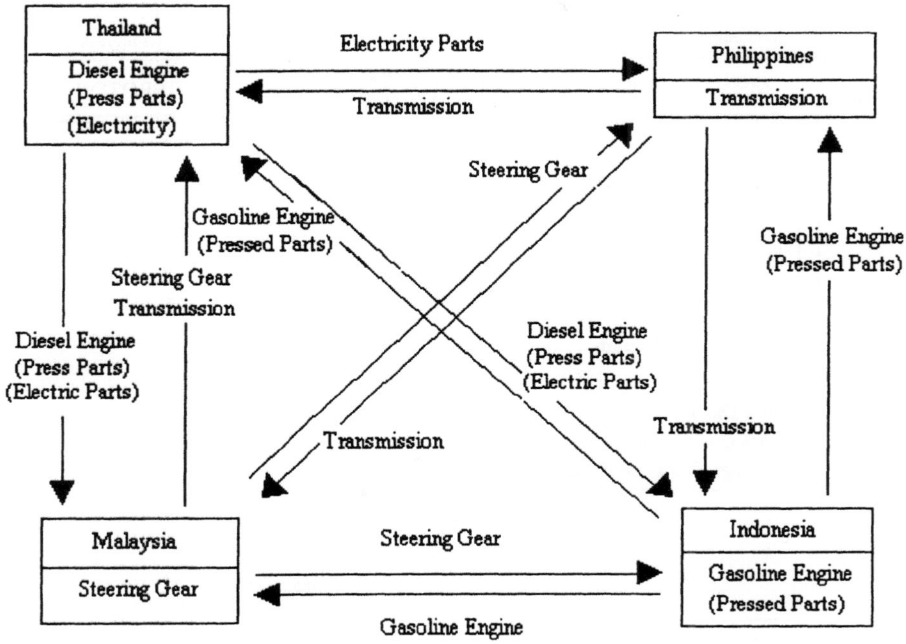

Source: Toyota Motors, Automobile Market in Asia and Oceania, 1990.

An outline of the regional reciprocal complementation of Toyota and Mitsubishi by BBC is shown in Figures 10–1 and 10–2. These figures show how an international division of labor made progress.

The currency crisis occurred when operations were starting to shift from BBC to AICO. It is believed that Japanese manufacturers will improve domestic production rate, strengthen the international division of labor and start exporting outside the region due to the high cost of imported auto parts from Japan.

Another notable point about the automotive scene in the ASEAN region is that the major Japanese automobile manufacturers are trying to establish a full-scale production system for Asian cars through a division of labor, especially in Thailand. Cars produced in this region were largely commercial vehicles due to road and traffic conditions in ASEAN countries. For example, Toyota developed an original commercial vehicle model "Kijang" which was mainly produced in Indonesia. However, it should be noted that the prospect of market expansion for passenger cars began to attract attention and led to the production of Asian passenger car models in Thailand, such as the SOLUNA by Toyota and the CITY by Honda.

Figure 10–2. Outline of Mitsubishi Component Complementation in ASEAN

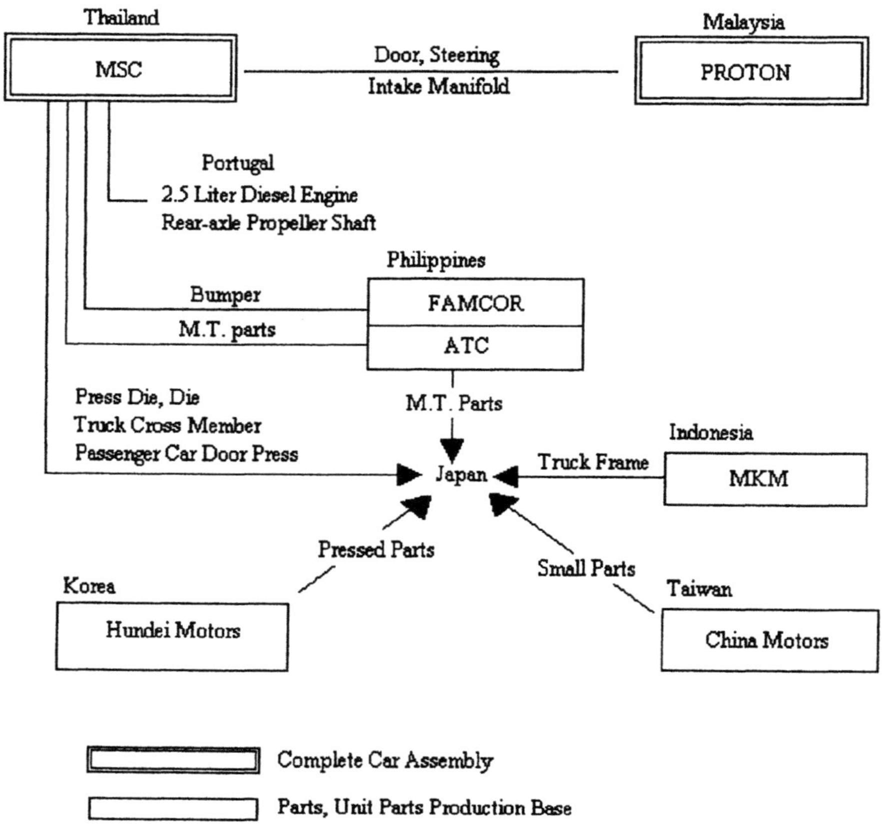

Source: Mitsubishi Research Institute, Automobile Industry Report 1, 1994.

As mentioned above, an international division of labor in the automobile industry centered on ASEAN countries has begun and is operated mainly in the form of a division of manufacturing processes for a limited number of parts and components. This is because the international production rate for auto parts is low in this region and a large number of parts, materials and intermediate resources have to be brought from Japan.

However, the BBC requires 50% of ASEAN-made parts and it is imperative to improve local content and the regional division of labor due to the high cost of imported parts from. In the period up to 1996, the year before the economic crisis, Thailand and Malaysia saw an increase in domestic production rate for each major auto part, while imports from Japan declined considerably. It is inferred that local production of parts and components increased during this period. On the contrary, the Philippines and Indonesia saw an increase in imports except for certain parts. In Thailand, local production of power trains and engine supplements progressed, reflecting the effect of local production regulations. On the other hand, imports of bodies and accessories increased, which was probably because the demand shifted to various passenger cars on the development of the domestic market.

However, other than car bodies and accessories, the progress of domestic production was outstanding in general. In particular, Malaysia, thanks to her domestic production policy for national cars, became less dependent on imports in all areas. The Philippines became less dependent on imports of underbody parts, transmission and steering parts, while imports of power trains, engine supplements, bodies and accessories increased. This trend implies that demand for high value-added passenger cars expanded along with the political stability in the country, while domestic production was not making progress in the various areas of parts production. Indonesia did not see much change on the whole, but it is noted that local production of engine supplements and power trains was lagging, while domestic production of underside parts made progress (p.39 op. cit. by Research Division of Japan Finance Corporation for Small Business). In conclusion, when it comes to a local complementary division of labor, there are considerable differences in the degree and content of domestic production among countries. This is because each country has a different domestic production policy and their respective automobile markets are in various stages of development. Therefore, in order to develop a regional complementary division of labor for the automobile industry in the ASEAN region, political adjustments are needed for such issues as protectionist tariffs aimed at promoting domestic production and trade imbalances. But more importantly, production across the whole region should be intensified at all levels of manufacture, from finished cars to parts. In this sense, the recent economic crisis may have helped intensify production.

4 Asian Economic Crisis and Countermeasures Taken by Japanese Automobile Manufacturers

The Asian economic crisis was triggered by the Thai Baht crash of July 1997 and subsequently involved mainly ASEAN countries. This economic crisis forced Japanese automobile manufacturers who had been pursuing an international strategy in Asia centering on a regional complementary division of labor mainly in ASEAN countries to reexamine their strategy and take emergency action to change direction, even if only temporarily. The total annual sales volume of automobiles in the four major ASEAN countries was close to 1.5 million in 1996 and declined to 1.3 million in 1997. After August 1997, the sales volume declined drastically in contrast to the period up to July. Compared with the same month in the previous year, the volume declined by 60 to 80% – a drastic fall. This implies the factory operation rate declined to a level of about 30 or 40%, while sales volume is believed to have declined by more than half after 1998.

Faced with a drastic situation, Japanese automobile manufacturers took short-term and long-term measures (Shown in Table 10–3). The short-term measures included a reduction in production, temporary suspension of operations, freeze on investment plans, and postponement of the introduction of new models, reduction in workforce and price increases. Most notably, they raised advance payment and purchase prices, and had meetings to discuss joint support measures in order to prevent local parts manufacturers who were financially disadvantaged from going bankrupt. This shows that the Japanese automobile manufacturers realized the importance towards a post-crisis strategy of providing support to local parts manufacturers, whom they had been helping for a long time develop through cooperation in domestic production and technology transfers. As for the reduction in workforce, they tried to keep skilled workers who played a central role at the work place, and carried out training for them in Japan. The long-term measures included the promotion of intraregional procurement and expansion of exports of both finished cars and auto parts outside the region. In addition to these

Table 10–3. Trends of Japanese Automobile Manufacturers after the Currency Crisis

Reduction in Production	–Place of origin/Temporarily-terminated operation. –Terminated outsourcing production. –Froze investment plans. –Postponed the introduction of new models.
Reduction in Workforce	–Reduced temporary workers/full-time workers.
Measures for Sales	–Increased sales price due to a raise in imported raw materials. –Upped sales promotion. –Special implementation of Auto Loans.
Local Parts Manufacturer's Support	–Advance payments –Increased parts purchasing price –Council to discuss support measures by cooperative efforts among Japanese finished automobile manufacturers.

(Temporary Measures)

Changes in Purchasing / Clients	–Promotion of local/regional supply purchasing. –Expansion of exports (finished car/parts)
Financial Support for Local Corporations	–Increased investment and investment ratio by Japanese companies.
Concentration of Plants	–Concentrated on domestic manufacturing centers by closing the old plants.
Technology / Quality System Plants	–Implement employee training in Japan. –Obtain ISO etc.

(Long-term Measures, Reorganization of the Production System)

Source: Previous documents, Paper by Ms. Minako Mori.

fundamental strategic measures, investment was made in local companies and intensive production bases were set up.

As stated, these measures including the temporary emergency measures, were adopted by Japanese automobile manufacturers faced with the Asian economic crisis on the assumption that the ASEAN market would eventually grow in the mid to long-run, and that the regional trade liberalization would progress. Figures 10–1,10–2 illustrates the prospects of regional reciprocal complementation and a structure of a division of labor up to the establishment of AFTA in 2003. The left section "Post-Currency Crisis" shows the situation up to date after the crisis, and suggests that approaches should be considered from two aspects to counter stagnant market growth: when trade liberalization makes progress and when trade liberalization gets stranded. It also suggests that these post-crisis approaches are to be considered in anticipation of the growth of the ASEAN market in the post-AFTA era, and the progress of trade liberalization. A competitive edge in exports should be gained not only through the progress of reciprocal complementation in auto parts production thanks to a mass-production effect but also a specialized division of labor according to each country.

5 Perspectives of the Southeast Asian Automobile Industry in Recovery

At the end of last year, I had an opportunity to visit Malaysia and Thailand to investigate automobile plants and automobile market trends. My opinion based on my overall impression, is that they have somehow overcome the nightmare economic crises, which occurred three years ago. Meanwhile, they are getting indications, which show that they are overcoming various troubles and steadily raising the operation ratio to prepare for this recovery, while reinforcing exports to take advantage of the currency depreciation.

The major problem however is that in the last 3 years while they were involved in tackling the economic crises, globalization in the world automobile industry proceeded rapidly. Globalization and liberalization influenced the strategies of Japanese automobile manufacturers and parts manufacturers whose principles were the cooperation for domestic production and the construction of a division of labor in the ASEAN region. Here, I would like to describe prospects for the development of the Southeast Asian automobile industry, which is now facing this kind of critical turning point.

First of all, concerning market trends in both countries, Malaysia reached its peak of 404,789 units in 1997, when the economic crises occurred, and dropped to 60% i.e. 163,851 units in 1998. The forecast for 1999 was to level off around 160,000; however, the rise in demand occurring in the latter half of the year, ensured a production volume of 280,000 to 290,000 units.

Figure 10–3 shows approximately three-quarters of the peak level; therefore, Malaysia's recovery pace was much quicker than expected. This was achieved because of the introduction of a fixed exchange rate system, which was introduced at the time of economic crises as an emergency remedy, and accelerated the recovery of the economy. The government also implemented the installment interest rate cut in order to boost domestic automobile demand and recovery.

Compared with this, Thailand, which reached a peak of 589,000 units in 1996, dropped to 363,000 during the crises in 1997. Moreover, in 1998, it dropped even more, down to 144,000 – a mere quarter of that at its peak. In November 1999, it reached 181,000, which means in December it would reach 200,000 at best (Figure 10–4).

In the case of Thailand, it recovered to one third of its peak, showing a slower pace of recovery compared with that of Malaysia. This is because Thailand proceeded with dissolution of bad debt including automobile loans while depreciating the Thai baht; the extent of its government intervention was lesser which kept the demands low. In Thailand, the fairly rapid recovery is expected to take place in the next two years.

It is needless to say that the economic crises in 1997 brought unprecedented difficulties on automobile manufacturers in both countries. Drastic reductions in production and plant integration, as well as the elimination of jobs, were the problems that had to be tackled. Besides the response at the plant level, support was provided in various ways: to boost automobile loans to help dealers; and

Figure 10–3. Shift of Malaysian Automobile Market

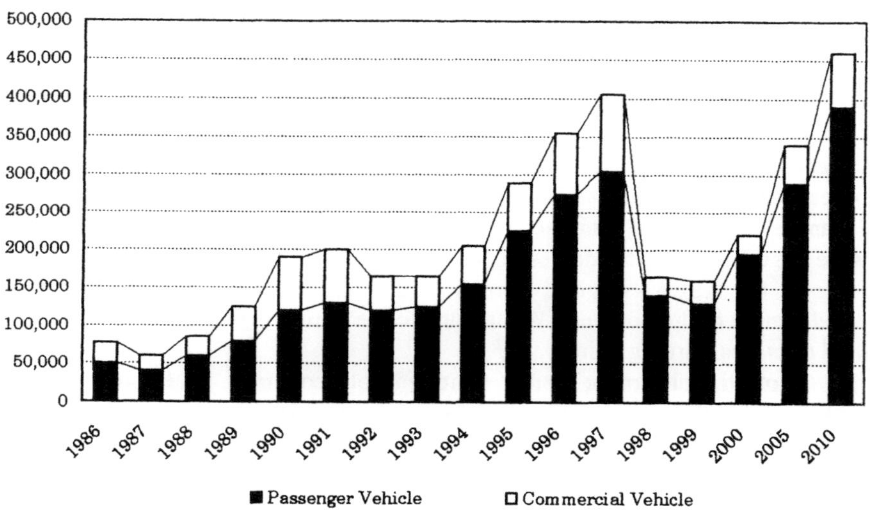

Figure 10–4. Thailand's Overall Market

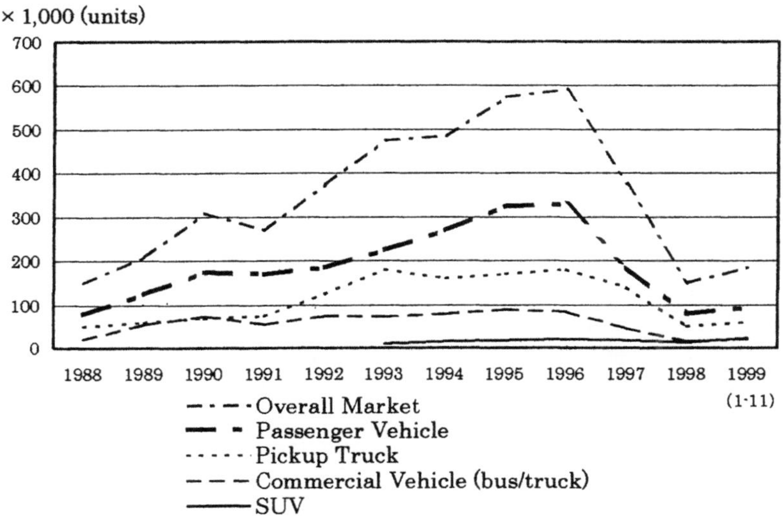

advanced payments or the raising of unit prices of parts for local parts manufacturers who were facing the danger of bankruptcy. Especially, in Thailand, Japanese automobile manufacturers extended their joint cooperation to support local suppliers.

The methodology of labor adjustment during drastic production cuts varies by country and company. In Malaysia's case, the government has strict regulations to maintain employment; the number of layoffs is relatively small. In the case of their national car manufacturer, "Proton," the employment has been maintained by changing the work shift from two shifts to one, and sending excessive labor to the army for training, or to vendors, or used for grass-cutting or painting work which were outsourced to other companies. In this way, employment has been maintained but the company also tried to survive by drastic wage cuts of 50% to 70%.

Malaysia in general, has a tendency towards labor shortage at the second national car manufacturer, "Produre" (aligned with Daihatsu). They dispatched their key workers to Daihatsu in Japan for training of various techniques, instead of implementing layoffs. Thai manufacturers commonly adopt this approach.

Malaysia Toyota, whose unit production is around 10,000 to 20,000 and doesn't have many employees, has unitized cooperative parts to increase jobs directly related with exports, and strive to achieve ISO 14000 certification with the cooperation from employees. This is how they avoided layoffs.

In Thailand, demands slumped more seriously than in Malaysia. Considerable job elimination was implemented. In order to survive, Thai Denso, which had 1,100 employees, eliminated 30% of the jobs through voluntary retirement, and dissolved contracts with outsourced workers. In the midst of the economic crises, even those employees who stayed had only 3 or 5 working days in a month, therefore, many employees reluctantly complied with voluntary retirement programs, and no designated and enforced retirement occurred.

Thai Toyota faced similar situation, and could somehow survive by introducing voluntary retirement and the elimination of outsourced workers. However, in order to prepare for the economic recovery, they also provided off-the-job-training in Japan, or dispatched workers to support production in Vietnam. They also concentrated on educational training and to be certified by ISO 9000 and 14000 as Thai Denso did, in order to assure key human resources and labor for future recovery. Therefore, the labor turnover rate, which was once high, lowered after the economic crises and the labor retention rate and employees' confidence in the company is said to be growing. However, the weak point is the serious shortage and high mobility of engineers and managers.

In this way, even in the midst of the crises these companies came up with countermeasures, with due consideration to their next movement. Among these countermeasures, the target of their concentration was the reinforcement of exports to take advantage of depreciated currencies, as well as the reinforcement of an international division of labor for finished cars and components in the ASEAN region. In addition, the appreciated yen raised the price of imported parts, thereby making it necessary for them to use domestically produced parts to raise the local procurement ratio, even if this is undesirable.

Actually, in Thailand, the export of finished cars was doubled from 50,880 units in 1998 to 101,865 in 1999, and the export of engines increases from 109,578 units to 290,202 units. Finished cars are mainly exported to Australia and the Middle East, while components are exported in the ASEAN region and its neighboring countries. Therefore, in the case of Thailand, one third of the annual production of 300,000 units is exported.

In the case of Malaysia, which is predominated by domestically manufactured cars, the export of finished cars has benefits such as tax exemption and parts import. Although emphasis is on export of finished cars, Malaysia has yet to reach the level of Thailand in exports. Rather, non-national car manufacturers characterize Thailand and suppliers like Denso and Ikeda, which utilize the AICO (ASEAN Industrial Cooperation) scheme, and reinforce a mutual completing supply of components.

Concerning the mutually complementing division of labor it was slowed temporarily due to the economic crises, but eventually recovered. Especially, Indonesia, which was reluctant to complete a division of labor in the ASEAN region, has been compromising recently, and the mutual complete division of labor including Thailand, Malaysia, and Indonesia, as well as the Philippines has been showing signs of development.

Then, what would be the issues for the Southeast Asian automobile industry situated under those circumstances? First of all, these might be defined by their methodology to take advantage of lessons they have learned through difficult experiences during the economic crises and their preparation for the future era of liberalization involving AFTA as well as the globalization proceeding in the automobile industry.

Especially, during the economic crises, they made efforts to foster and retain skilled workers without implementing forceful layoffs even though an incredible production cut was required. This has contributed to the improvement in the retention ratio of local workers as well as the quality of labor. It allows for a plant operation that doesn't depend on low labor cost but is concerned more with different labor practices in the different countries. What is required additionally is to foster engineers, and the selection of foreign employees – both of which are crucial for human resource development.

In association with their experiences to support local suppliers during the economic crises, it would be an urgent task to foster the secondary and tertiary suppliers. In Southeast Asia, many secondary and tertiary suppliers have problems with quality assurance and delivery control. The primary suppliers, many of which are Japanese companies, have had a great deal of bitter experiences. Automobile manufactures and Japanese suppliers should cooperate to foster the secondary and tertiary local suppliers, and this is indeed an extremely urgent issue.

The automobile industry in Southeast Asia utilizes the lessons learned from their experience during the economic crises, and is making efforts to reinforce a regional division of labor in order to reinforce their exports and implemented diversified strategies concerning their positions as manufactures.

However, even in this region, the waves of globalization have been surging, accompanied by the deadline of liberalization of capital and transactions by the AFTA (ASEAN Free Trade Agreement) in association with the WTO. The deadline is set for 2003. Concerning this liberalization, attitudes vary for countries. For example, Thailand affirmatively welcomes the entry of Japanese companies and foreign companies as well, and Malaysia wants to foster their national car manufacturers to make them serve as export bases like those in the electric and electronics industries.

Malaysia is expected to postpone the liberalization by AFTA in order to protect the national car manufacturers but will nonetheless fail to stop the surge of internationalization and will thus have to move towards liberalization. The dilemma that Malaysia may suffer if they postpone the liberalization is that Thailand will have consecutive entry of American and European companies and may grow to be the export base for Southeast Asia.

Moreover, in this era of globalization, GM, the Ford–Mazda alliance, Delfy, Bisteon, and Bosch have started to establish their operations based on large-scale global strategies. This trend is drawing considerable attention from the Japanese manufacturers and suppliers, who are finally starting to ride the wave to recovery after sacrifices in the domestic production and severe economic crises.

6 The Development of the International Division of Labor of Japanese Electric Appliance and Electronics Industry in Asia

In terms of an international division of labor, Japanese electric appliance manufacturers are far ahead of automobile manufacturers who have mainly shared production in the ASEAN region. An international division of labor has been rapidly expanding not only in the production of color televisions, electric refrigerators and electric washing machines but also VTRs and air conditioners. And, since the second appreciation of the yen in the 1990's, production in China and ASEAN countries has shot up. For example, as shown in Table 10–4, the total number of production bases for video tape recorders in Asia exceeds the total number in Europe and the United States combined. The nature of the international division of labor of the electric appliance industry is not limited to regional complementation but is expanded to a global scale. Beginning in the 1990's, production bases for video tape recorders were shifted from Europe to Asia, mainly to Malaysia (Table 10–4). The international division of labor in the production of video tape recorders and air conditioners is conducted not only in the form of a regional complementary division of labor according to manufacturing process, but also in a form of horizontal division according to item and model.

In terms of an international division of labor in Asia, Japanese electric appliance and electronics manufacturers are far ahead of Japanese automobile manufacturers. There are three factors; (1) rapid expansion of the local market, (2) speedy establishment of production bases for parts, and (3) easily transferred manufacturing lines with advanced technology. I'd like to comment on how such

Table10–4. Number of Overseas Production Centers of VTRs by Region

Year	Total	Asia Other	Singapore	Malaysia	Thailand	Indonesia	Philippines	China	Europe Total	USA	Other
1988	36	5	0	0	0	0	1	0	21	5	6
1990	40	12	0	7	0	0	0	0	19	2	7
1993	48	22	2	9	0	2	0	2	17	2	7
1996	42	22	2	7	0	2	0	3	11	3	6

Source: EIAJ, Overseas Corporations List, Annual research takes place in May.
Report by Japan Finance Corporation for Small Businesses No.97–3, Establishment of the New Divisional Production System for Home Electronic Appliances among ASEAN and Japan, p.61.

an advanced international division of labor was achieved, as well as on the regional complementary division of labor and what role was played by the establishment of the system for the international division of labor at the time of economic crisis, including its future development.

The production volume of electric and electronics appliances in Japan peaked at 7.88 trillion yen, in 1991 and then declined yearly to 5.37 trillion yen, a decline of 33%. In contrast, imports of electronic appliances and electric appliances for home use amounted to ¥330 billion and ¥140 billion, respectively, in 1995. (Report by Japan Finance Corporation for Small Business No.97–3, "Establishment of a new system of the division of labor between Japan and ASEAN countries in the electric appliance industry" p.1) This 33% decrease in production within a span of only four years implies progress in the shift of production to Europe, the United States and Asia. The increase in imports was largely from Asia due to advantages in logistics. Table 10–5 describes operations of Japanese electric appliance and electronics manufacturers in Asia by period and country. According to Table 10–5, the period of import substitution in the 1960s was relatively short and the period of transition to export-oriented production came relatively early. This table also shows that export-oriented production became dominant after 1985 due to the first appreciation of the yen and again after 1992 with the second, and developed to full scale in all countries for every item.

Most noticeable is production transfer to Singapore and Thailand during the period of transition to export-oriented production. The number of production items and manufacturers in Singapore and Malaysia increased after the yen's first appreciation, while an increase was seen in Indonesia, the Philippines and Chine after the yen's second appreciation. Export-oriented production was rapidly promoted as the shift of production to overseas accelerated following the above-mentioned stages. Therefore, although there are considerable differences between products in the overseas production percentages of major electric appliances, those percentages sharply rose as a whole.

Given the fact that electric appliance markets in Europe and the United States had reached maturity and labor costs were no longer competitive, the development of operations in Asia, as shown in Table 10–5, represents the rapid rise in production ratios in Asia and contributed greatly to these figures. The production of electric washing machines and electric refrigerators, – everyday-use products that are closely connected with cultures and customs in each region – did increase but only little. Both the rate with which production was moved overseas and the rate of increase were high in color televisions, microwave ovens, stereos and video tape recorders. This indicates that the shift to overseas production – mainly of audio-visual electric appliances – was fast particularly in Asia and that production of these product lines was global, further developing the network of an international division of labor.

The shift to overseas production of the Japanese electric appliances and electronics industry progressed and some product lines, such as audio-visual appliances, started an international division of labor on a global scale. This trend

Table 10–5. Expansion Time, Country and Business of Japanese Electronics Production Centers

	Import Substitution Period	Export-oriented Production Period	Full-Development Period for Exports		Total (Number of Main Locations)
	1960–69	1970–84	1985–92	1993–97	
Korea		Home Appliances (3), VTRs(1)			7
Taiwan	Home Appliances(6) Color TVs(1)(5) Air-Conditioners (1)(5) Picture Tubes(5)	VTRs (3)	Compressors (4)		17
Hong Kong		Home Appliances (1)			5
Singapore	Home Appliances (1) Washing Machines(1)	Television(5)(7) Home Appliances(4)(5) Compressors (6) Color TVs (1) Picture Tubes (5)	Air-Conditioners (1) Color TVs (1)(3)(4) Compressors (1) VTRs(4)	Picture Tubes (3) Color TVs (1)(5)	29
Malaysia	Home Appliances (6)	Air-Conditioners (6) TVs (5) Color TV (2)	Home Appliances (2) Washing Machines (2) Refrigerators (2) Color TVs 3)(6) Compressors (5)(6) VTRs (2)(3)(5)(7) TVs (5) Air-Conditioner (5)(6) Picture Tubes (6)(7)		31

Thailand	Home Appliances (1)(4)(6)(7) Refrigerators (7) TVs (7) Washing Machines(7)	Home Appliances (5)(6) Refrigerators (5) TVs (5) Air-Conditioners (5)	Picture Tubes (4)(7) Color TVs (3) Compressors (7) Home Appliances (2) VTRs(5) Home Appliances(2)(4) Air-Conditioner (2)(4)(6)(7)	Compressors (1)(5) Refrigerators (1)(5) Washing Machines(4)(5)	35
Indonesia		Home Appliances (1)(6)	VTRs(1)(6) Home Appliances(7) Color TVs (2)	Compressors (1) Refrigerators(1)(2) Color TVs (1)(2)(3)(4)(5) Home Appliances (5)	25
Philippines	Home Appliances(6)	Color TV(2) Washing Machines(2)		Refrigerators(5) Compressor(5) Color TVs(6) Washing Machines(1)	12
China		Color TVs(1)(5) Air-Conditioners (1)	Picture Tubes (5)(6) Home Appliances(6) Washing Machines(6)	Refrigerators(1)(2) Home Appliances (1)(2)(6)(7) Compressors (1)(4)(5)(6)(7) Air-Conditioners (1)(5)(6)(7) VTRs(6) Washing Machines(1)(2)(5) Picture Tubes(3) Color TVs(2)(3)(4)	54
Total (Number of Main	16	42	84	73	215

Note: Numbers in ( ) indicate corporations by number as follows (1) Sanyo, (2) Sharp, (3) Sony, (4) Toshiba, (5) Hitachi, (6) Matsushita, (7) Mitsubishi.

Source: Weekly, Toyo Economics, List of Corporations with Overseas Expansion in 1996, Created based on Toyo Economic Shinpo.

was noticeable especially in Asia. It is attributed to the fact that a relatively small amount of investment in factories in Asia was sufficient for these product lines and, in some cases, technology transfer was carried out easily by bringing in the latest automated lines. In addition, the structures of these products were not as complicated as automobiles. These products have just one-tenth the parts of an automobile, which consists of as many as twenty thousand parts. It is relatively easy to standardize parts for these products which helps reduce the overall number of parts and subsequently accelerates the expansion of an international division of labor. Furthermore, there are not as many bulky parts or components in these products and logistics made for a cleaner transition into an international division of labor.

In this respect, there were differences in the conditions facing automobile manufacturers and electric and electronics manufacturers. For automobile manufacturers, export-oriented production was still in the distant future as they had just started a regional international division of labor in shifting from BBC to AICO.

So, what impact did the Asian economic crisis have on the electric and electronics industry, which had strengthened both regional and international division of labor and had become export-oriented? There is no detailed data concerning this aspect, but media reports at that time show that high-priced goods, such as houses and automobiles were the most affected by the economic crisis. Of course, home electric appliances – so-called "white products" – were largely for domestic markets rather than export, so considerable production reductions seems to have been carried out. On the other hand, export-oriented products, such as audio-visual related products, including their parts and components, actually saw improvements in their export competitiveness due to currency devaluations and the fact that production was carried out almost at full capacity. This was, of course, achieved on the assumption of a high ratio of local procurement that would make production less dependent on costly imports from Japan, particularly so with audio-visual related products, which already had the latest automated production lines from the early stages. Though this figure was but one-tenth of that of automobiles, they were successful by placing more emphasis on exports to developed countries in Europe and the United States despite the stagnant domestic economy. It is reported that Minebea and Sanden (air-conditioners) plants in Thailand operated at full capacity even though they were not audio-visual related, in contrast to the partial closures of automobile factories.

As stated, electric appliance and electronics manufacturers incurred relatively less damage from the economic crisis compared to automobile manufacturers and recovered much more quickly. This is because electric appliance and electronics manufacturers started transferring export-oriented production overseas and preparing a system that would enable an international division of labor, as well as a regional division of labor, quite early.

7 The Outlook and Reevaluation of the International Division of Labor of Japanese Automobile Manufacturers in Asia after the Economic Crisi: Relationship to Global Restructuring and Future Outlook

Having experienced first-hand the Asian economic crisis, electric appliance and electronics manufacturers undertook well an international division of labor, whereas the automobile industry stood in quite a different position. However, this difference is also attributed to their structural differences as industries that are pursuing their own strategic aims in Asia – a high growth potential market. While the market for durable consumer goods in Asia started with electric appliances and shifted to electronic information equipment, the automobile industry also expanded the market at the same time. But, the great difference in unit price and the difference in the degree of transportation and industrial infrastructure available caused a gap in market scale.

To put it plainly, the market for electric appliances and electronics was in the growth period, while the market for automobiles were just about to grow. Therefore, the degree of damage inflicted on these two industries by the economic crisis was quite different. Since the electric appliance and electronics industry had a certain degree of market scale and some products were strongly export-oriented, the industry incurred relatively little damage. On the other hand, the automobile industry was investing in factories with a view of expanding production to full scale when it was hit head on by the economic crisis. In addition, if observed over a longer period, the electric appliance and electronics industry switched from import substitution in the early stages to export-oriented production relatively quickly. This, and the expansion of the market for electric appliances and electronics products in Asia helped them considerably. As for their moving into Asian countries, the electric appliances and the electronics industry of set makers, that is to say assemblers and their parts manufacturers, was relatively coordinated. On the other hand, since the structure of the automobile is sophisticated and complicated, the transfer of electronic, precision-manufactured and sophisticated parts and materials, such as metal molds and rough casting materials, tended to lag behind.

The advancement of assemblers into the region and the domestic production of parts did not go smoothly or in a balanced way. Furthermore, since the transfer of production was carried out relatively smoothly, the electric appliance and electronics industry was able to shift to hi-tech fields such as high-definition televisions and information appliances, in order to alleviate the hollowing-out effect on Japan's domestic industry that grew as companies moved overseas. This helped separate production through a kind of horizontal division of labor. A horizontal division of labor could be achieved in the automobile industry in the future, but it would be difficult, under the present conditions, to switch to a horizontal structure to the extent that the electric appliance and electronics industry did.

It is undeniable that the economic crisis hampered the development of a regional complementary international division of labor of Japanese automobile manufacturers in the ASEAN region. The crisis happened just when the industry was about to see a growing demand for automobiles in the region and the emergence of a full-fledged market for public consumption, like the one for the electric appliance and electronics manufacturers, toward the year 2000. In addition, an international division of labor on a global scale and involving China was not developed in the automobile industry since, in the midst of the economic crisis, temporary closures and production reductions were implemented at many factories of Japanese manufacturers in Thailand, Indonesia and Malaysia. These countries were to become the core of a regional international division of labor in the ASEAN region, but the development of an international division of labor now had to be postponed.

Nevertheless, signs of recovery continue to show in automobile production in Asia, especially in the ASEAN region, along with an overall recovery from the economic crisis. During the two years of recession, though still insufficient, gradual progress can be seen in financial system reform, increased transparency of business conducted by industrial groups, the elimination of special enterprises and the liberalization in foreign capital investment. This region still has great potential demand for automobiles just as it had for electric appliances. Besides, the latest economic crisis made Japanese automobile manufacturers realize that it was risky to rely on an automobile market of only one country. As a result, it will be a strategic tendency to establish an international division of labor.

The conflict of interests between countries over trade in auto parts, which are to be allocated among the countries in the region, was the biggest impediment to the development of an international division of labor for the production of components with ASEAN countries at the core. However, since it is inevitable in this global era to uphold AFTA and CEPT schedules toward the year 2003, the problem should be solved eventually. At the moment, Thailand is playing a central role and the issue is now centering on an adjustment of interests with Malaysia, which gives priority to its national interests and national manufacturers, and the most populous ASEAN country, Indonesia. However, for new development in the 21st century, they will be forced to give up minor differences in order to accomplish a common goal. Another impediment to the development of an international division of labor was that technology transfers of auto parts did not reach the local lower-end suppliers. Though, during the recession, support measures were taken for local suppliers, smaller suppliers with no competitive margins were forced out of business through restructuring. Therefore, from now on, production recovery will be pursued while improving competitiveness in cost and quality. The currency crisis brought prospects of a future advantage because of a substantial competitive edge in exports and a rise in costs of imported parts and materials. In this respect, it is imperative to shore up parts suppliers on the lower end. In addition, the economic crisis brought a kind of strategic turning point, switching local production from domestic-oriented to export-oriented. Of course, the currency conditions favorable to exports do not directly bring cost, quality and technology in line with international standards. In order to enhance competitiveness in exports, it is essential to enhance operator skills. In this respect, Honda and Suzuki sent several hundred local operators from their factories in Thailand to their Japanese factories for six months of training in order to enhance their skills while they cut back on factory operations in Thailand. From the mid-to long-term perspective, this policy aims to enhance competitiveness in exports and prepare for an international division of labor. Recovering from the Asian economic crisis, preparations are underway, for the present, to reinforce a regional international division of labor with the ASEAN region as a core and eventually establish an international division of labor of global scale.

In any case, as private businesses reduce production, integrate factories and restructure to cure the ills brought on by Asia's economic crisis, the impact of global restructuring in the automobile industry is having an impact on the future of the Asian automobile industry and its hoped-for international division of labor. The big changes in Asia are that all of Korea's automobile manufacturers, are now in some sort of tie-up or group run by western automobile manufacturers and that the wave of restructuring has hit Asia's largest automobile producing country, Japan, and brought all manufacturers except for the Toyota Group and Honda into a tie-up with GM, Ford or Daimler–Crysler. These global manufacturers from the west have focused their strategy on the soon-to-be largest automobile market in the world i.e. Asia and targeted South Korean and Japanese manufacturers to achieve these goals. It obviously is too risky to challenge the Asian markets alone because of the geographical and cultural gaps that separate them. In particular, Korea is for them a wise production base for the future markets in North and Northeast China and coastal areas of Russia, whereas teaming up with Japanese manufacturers who have been present in ASEAN for a long time offers also excellent merits.

Injecting this global restructuring into Asia will conceivably change the division of labor in all Southeast Asia. The transition to AICO, a WTO-like arrangement, will lead ASEAN to take liberalization measures, which will accelerate the investment of western manufacturers in Thailand and other countries, the increase in production by Japanese automobile manufactures and the reduction in parts production. In fact, Toyota announced that they would procure all parts locally by the year 2003 to avoid exchange rate risks. In Thailand, already local production is progressing with materials and intermediate parts such plastic and molded parts, which at one point were the weak points in the production chain. If secondary and tertiary parts manufacturers and the necessary engineers can be developed, 100% local parts procurement would no longer be just a dream. European and American parts manufacturers are making inroads into the region in hoards. Eyes will be watching to see if they will concentrate in Thailand, create a new division of labor across ASEAN or develop their division of labor across all of Asia and not just ASEAN, as well as what environmental technology strategy they will bring with them.

References

Chusho Kigyo Kinyu Koko (Small to mid-size Finance Corporation) Research Dept., (1998) *Automobile Industry Trends in ASEAN and Effects to Our Domestic Small to Mid-size Parts Manufacturers*, Chusho Koko Report, No.98–1, April.

Ditto, (1997) *Establishment of a new system of the division of labor between Japan and ASEAN countries in the electric appliance industry*, No.97–3, June.

Ditto, (1999) *Japanese small to mid-size companies going through the economic crisis in Asia*, Report by Japan Finance Corporation for Small Businesses No.99–2, July.

Kitamura, Kayoko. (1997) *Advancement of industrial structure in East Asia and Japanese industry*, Asia Economic Research.

Itagaki, Hiroshi. (1997) *Japanese economic production systems and East Asia:* Hybrid factories in Taiwan, Korea and China, Minelva Books.

Sogo Kyoiku Kikaku (1997) (Total Education Planning), *Asia Automobile Market Data Book.*

Abo, Tetsuo. Itagaki, Hiroshi. Ueyama, Kunio. and Kawamura, Tetsuji. (1991) *Japanese Production System in USA*: "Usage" and "Application" for Localization," Toyo Economic Shinpo Press.

Hayashi, Tadayoshi. (1989) Development and international divisions of labor for the automobile industry in East Asia, *Economic Management Theories*, Volume 8, issue 1, 2, March, Yachiyo Gakuin University.

Ishiro, Katsuji. (1991) Current situation of parts supply in Taiwan, Kayoko Kitamura version, *Current situation of parts supply in NIES equipment industries*, Asia Economic Research.

Inoue, Ryuichiro. Urata, Shujiro. and Kohama, Hirohisa. (1990) *Industrial policies of East Asia*: For the new development strategies, Japan Trade Promotion Bureau.

Kawakami, Momoko. (1995) Capital and technological introduction from Japanese corporations in the Taiwan automobile industry, *Asia Economy*, Volume 36, issue 11, Asia Economic research.

Kumon, Hiroshi. (1992) Japanese automobile factories in Taiwan, *Social labor research*, Volume 39, issue 2,3, Social Science Dept. of Hosei University.

Kwo Peigyo, (1994) Labor policies in Taiwan and establishment of 'self-labor movement': labor movements in the 80s, *Economic Theories*, issue 8, Kyoto University.

Shimokawa, Koichi. (1990) Taiwan automobile industry in the transition phase, *Economist*, July 24, issue.

Ditto, (1996) Summary of visit to the Toyota Astro, *Nikkan Automobile Newspaper*, August 6.

Ditto, (1996) Summary of visit to the Astro/Daihatsu, *Nikkan Automobile Newspaper*, August 24.

Ditto, Development of direct investment and international divisions of labor of Japanese automobile industry in the Asia region, *Keiei Shirin*, Volume 35, issue 3.

Shoichiro, Sei. (1989) Production system and technological standards of the Taiwan automobile parts industry, *Annual Report of the Economic Research, Kanto Gakuin University*.

11 The Tire Industry: A Comparative Study About the Strategy of Internationalization of French and Japanese Multinationals

Françoise Guelle
Université Jean Moulin-Lyon 3

1 The Tire Industry

1.1 Top Three Makers

Strong postwar popularity of the automobile supported the redevelopment of the tire industry, which increased its capital investment, expanded the product lines and continued to growth through the 1970s. The technological innovation of the radial tire allowed French tiremaker Michelin to improve the major qualities of its tires and to expand abroad. In the early 1970s, competition among radial tire makers became severe in the US as well as in Europe, instead, insulated in Japan, Japanese carmakers bought Japanese tires knowing they inferior to European ones. That support provided them with the resources and the time to improve and progress, both in terms of market and technology to internationally competitive levels.

Next came a sluggish economic era, and demand for automobiles, and, by association, for tires has matured. Sales volume has been stagnant in the long term, the life of cars has become longer. As regards the age of automobiles, in light of this mature demand, auto sales will mainly come from replacement demand and therefore are not likely to grow substantially in the future.

Tire production by leading manufacturing countries is connected with the automobile core markets (Japan, US, Europe), even if tires are classified in the statistics as a rubber product rather than a car component. The United States are the world's largest tire-producing nation with 264 million units, Japan is the second largest tire producer with 160 million units : they together account for 39.7% of tire

Table 11–1. Tire Production by Leading Manufacturing Countries and World Tire Production by Geographic Area (1997)

Countries	%	Geographic Area	%
USA	24.7	North America	27.8
Japan	15.0	Asia/Oceania	28.4
Korea	5.4		
France	6.2	Europe	23.9
Germany	5.1		
United Kingdom	3.0		

Source: Japan Automobile Tire Manufacturers Association

production worldwide (Table 11–1). The other major countries are France, South Korea, Germany and the United Kingdom[1].

Tire production is a capital intensive industry, and scale merits through intensive production are necessary to increase cost competitiveness. In response to the globalization of the car companies, tire makers must secure orders through overseas operations, and so international reorganization has been encouraged in the last two decades. Worldwide reorganization began in the 1980s, the level of oligopoly rose mainly from 1984 to 1989 due to the advancement of Japanese makers into Europe and US and to the advancement of European makers into US. Looking at the world top three companies in the tire industry, it is clear that mega-firms are ranked highest (Table 11–2).

After the Asian economic crisis, US and European companies have been positively expanding their activities into Asia. The tire oligopoly is entered in a new phase of concentration and progressed particularly since 1999 as the top 3 makers were actively involved in alliances or acquisitions. Faced with their combined share of nearly 60%, lower-ranked groups will probably have to regroup for strength.

Bridgestone, Asia's Number One and Michelin, Europe's Number One are ranked just after Goodyear, World's Number One. Their principal business is the development, production, distribution and sales of tires and related products and services. They manufacture and market, in most regions of the world, a road line of rubber tires for automobiles, trucks, buses, tractors, farm implements, aircraft, industrial equipment and various other applications, in each case for sale to original equipment manufacturers and in the replacement markets. They made giant strides in the implementation of the growth and cost strategies through increased productivity, continuous restructuring and strategic acquisitions. Market share gains are undoubtedly the main objectives, but in a very competitive, mature industry, fast growth can be achieved only through successful acquisitions, joint ventures and strategic alliances. Their vision is to be ranked as the best tire

[1] Japan AutomobileTire Manufacturers Association, *Tire Industry of Japan*, 1999.

Table 11–2. Tires World Share by Makers

(%)

1986		1996		1999	
Top 3 makers	*46.2*	*Top 3 makers*	*53.5*	*Top 3 makers*	*59.6*
Goodyear	19.3	Michelin	18.6	Goodyear	22.6
Michelin	17.9	Bridgestone	18.3	Bridgestone	18.5
Bridgestone	9.0	Goodyear	16.6	Michelin	18.5
Continental	8.0	Continental	6.6	Continental	6.3
Firestone	6.6	Sumitomo	5.7	Pirelli	4.3
Uniroyal Goodrich	6.1	Pirelli	4.5		
Pirelli	6.0				
Sumitomo	5.6				
Yokohama	3.5				
Toyo	1.8				

company in the world and gain, or regain, a position as the undisputed leader in the industry.

1.2 Top Three Maker's Visions

- Bridgestone, A Word from the President Yoichiro Kaizaki[2]: *"Lead; Or be Led; Bridgestone already is a tire-industry leader. Our goal, however, is to be more than "a" leader. We are determined to be "the" leader."*
- Goodyear, A Word from the President Samir G. Gibara[3]: "Leadership in our markets and industry is our goal for the 21st century. We intend to make Goodyear No.1 or No.2 in every market we serve and to be the low-cost producer among the three major global tire and rubber companies.
  My vision by the end of the year 2000 has Goodyear ranked by all measures as the best tire and rubber company in the world."
- Michelin, A Word from Edouard Michelin[4]: *"Michelin is more determined than ever to sharpen its competitive edge on the European continent and to progress in the Americas and in Asia. (...) In Asia, we have won new positions in several large developing markets and we are determined to become number 2 in this zone ... before 2005 !"*

2 The strategy of Bridgestone

Bridgestone, A Word from the President Yoichiro Kaizaki:

[2] Bridgestone Annual Report, May 2000.

[3] Goodyear1996 Annual Report.

[4] Speech given to the CGEM shareholders meeting, 26 May 2000.

"Lead Or be Led Bridgestone already is a tire-industry leader. Our goal, however, is to be more than "a" leader. We are determined to be "the" leader."

2.1 Bridgestone's US Deal

Bridgestone has long dominated Japan's tire industry with a 40 to 50 per cent share on the domestic market. But 20 years ago, Bridgestone tires were regarded with contempt by western customers. The first thing many western car buyers did when they bought a Japanese car was to insist that the Bridgestone be replaced with Michelins, Pirellis or some other quality make of radial tire.

In the 1980s the Japan's tire producers were pushing aggressively into mergers with or acquisitions of Western companies. This interest reflected new corporate strategies to cope with the yen appreciation and win a business of Japanese automakers stepping up production at their US plants. Japanese tire makers had no choice but to follow. As a result, the world's tire market was being greatly concentrated. "*Of the world's tire makers, only three will be able to survive in the foreseeable future*" suggested Bridgestone president Akira Yeiri in 1988[5].

Clearly the yen appreciation was having a great effect on the makers. The exports were no longer profitable. Another major factor was the Japanese automobile industry's advancement into North America and Europe. However two giants, Goodyear in the US and Michelin in Europe stand in the Japanese maker's way. There was no rapid alternative other than M&As to expand the overseas operations.

Specifically, Japan's Bridgestone Corp. has been forced to move production to the US. It commanded nearly half of the Japanese replacement tire market and supplied carmakers in Japan with 35% of new car tires. But when Japanese carmakers began building plants in the US and Europe in the 80's, it was slow to follow its customers abroad. While other Japanese companies like Sumitomo Rubber with the acquisition of Dunlop were developing overseas production plants and marketing channels, Bridgestone stayed mostly at home.

2.2 Firestone's Purchase

When Bridgestone bought a truck tire plant from Firestone Tire & Rubber Co. in 1983, it inherited big trouble. Productivity at the money-losing plant was dismal, and labor relations were even worse. After 6 years, however, productivity at the plant has been soared. It set up another plant a few years later. But so far it has captured less than 2 per cent of the US replacement tire market.

Firestone, with its strong market share in Detroit and production facilities in South America, Europe, and the US provided a quick remedy. *"Looking at it from*

[5] *Nikkei*, February 18 and 21, 1988.

a worldwide strategic point of view, we felt this was a necessity," President Akira Yeiri explained in 1988, when the Japanese tiremaker bought the rest of Firestone. Since Bridgestone paid $2.6 billion after a counteroffer from Italy's Pirelli helped by France's Michelin (Pirelli wanted production facilities in the US and Michelin hoped to get the distribution network), it is still the most expensive acquisition of a foreign manufacturer by a Japanese company. Rising its bid surprisingly high, Bridgestone showed its urgent need for US production and blue-chip American name's acquisition. In 1989, it committed an additional investment of $350 million to double its US capacity for radial truck tires.

But Firestone was especially hard to digest, even if Bridgestone emerged as a new power. Bridgestone's purchase of Firestone gave the company a foothold in Europe which it otherwise would not have had. From a strategic standpoint, this acquisition enabled Bridgestone to become a truly global company with tire manufacturing operations in over 20 countries on six continents. Moreover, the acquisition gave Bridgestone an immediate foothold in Europe where the company took ownership of six tire manufacturing plants (one of which was subsequently closed) and a tire technical center in Italy. Clearly Bridgestone couldn't have entered the European market so quickly had it attempted to do so through "greenfield" facilities, because the European tiremakers Michelin and Pirelli are tough competitors. The takeover of Firestone was an inevitable choice to become a global auto tire maker.

Firestone did probably not have survived without Bridgestone support. 1989 to 1992 was a difficult period, especially 1990 and 1991 when daily losses exceeded $1 million. Bridgestone spent $1.5 billion on facility modernization. Shortly after the takeover, Firestone productivity levels were around 50 to 60 percent of Bridgestone in Japan. Obviously improvements were made at Bridgestone/Firestone in order to push the productivity levels to be around 70 percent of Bridgestone's. Under Japanese management, the company has focused on manufacturing efficiency and product quality, emphasizing long-term market share gains. Despite General Motor's decision to drop Firestone as a North American supplier, there was ample possibility of supplying Japanese carmakers in the US. At that time, Nissan and Honda already have plant in the US and Toyota was due to open a plant, with Mazda and Mitsubishi Motors following in 1989.

Despite problems it faces, Bridgestone/Firestone has been profitable ever since. From 1993, the first year in the black, accumulated profits have grown to $544 million in 1997 for Bridgestone/Firestone, which passed Bridgestone Japan in 1997 in sales. Bridgestone/Firestone produced 53 million at those facilities in 1997, more than double 1991 levels. The multibrand strategy – centered on the Bridgestone, Firestone, and Dayton brands – has produced sales growth.

The decision to construct a new $435 million passenger radial and light truck plant in Aiken, South Carolina, was taken because of a capacity shortage in the United States and Canada, Bridgestone/Firestone had to import nearly 5 million tires from Japan. The plant produces around 25,000 radial tires per day which translates into 8 to 9 million units per year since 1999. One of the corporate goals is to reduce imports from Japan, eliminate them if possible, and produce 100 percent of the North American requirements locally. Bridgestone/Firestone currently makes car and truck tires at 8 North American plants including seven in the US and one in Canada.

Before the alliance between Goodyear and Sumitomo/Dunlop in 1999, Bridgestone as a group holded an estimated 18 to 19 percent share of the global tire market and was running neck and neck with Michelin for the industry's top spot, while in total rubber products, including tires, the company has been the world leader for nearly a decade.

2.3 Firestone's Recall

Bridgestone/Firestone, Inc., is recalling some 6.5 million tires since August 2000. The company's massive recall – the second-largest in US history – will cost Bridgestone between $400–$500 million in fiscal 2000. To meet the increased demand , Firestone is doubling production in its plants and maximizing the volume of its imports, but the customer may replace its recalled tires with a competitor's brand. The tires being recalled were linked to an unusually high number of accidents, mainly involving Ford Motor Co's Explorer sports-utility vehicles equipped with Firestone tires. Sales account for 17% of overall Bridgestone/Firestone sales, a little over 7% of group sales, while truck tires and other divisions have not been affected. There as been no impact on sales in markets other than North America, and the company's financial base is likely to remain strong despite the huge recall's effects. The Firestone brand, which Bridgestone has worked hard to restore over many years, has been severely hurt. There have also been reports that Ford is dissatisfied, so it seems possible there will be some impact on the two companies' future relationship. This problem will provide rival companies like Michelin and Goodyear a chance to regain competitiveness and gain new market shares. If Bridgestone is forced to scuttle the Firestone brand, the Japanese maker would lose its coveted status as a major player in the global tire market.

Depending on the results of the investigation of the US National Highway Traffic Safety Administration (NHTSA), this issue will have a major impact in the following areas[6]:

1. business development in the North American market, which, including exports, accounts for some 40% of consolidated sales
2. the company's relations with automakers other than Ford
3. the chance of restoring the Firestone brand
4. the reputation of the Firestone brand
5. the possibility of compensation claims regarding responsibility for manufacturing.

[6] Tire recall punctures Bridgestone rating, *Nikkei Weekly*, October 2, 2000.

2.4 Bridgestone in ASIA

Bridgestone operates 46 tire plants on 6 continents and develops tires globally through technical centers in Japan, the USA and Europe. The strength of Bridgestone is in Japan. Before the acquisition of Firestone, Bridgestone was only manufacturing tires in Asia (Table 11–3).

Japan is the second largest car-owning country in the world, next only to the United States. Automobile production in Japan has been falling since the economic bubble burst. It is 70% of that in fiscal 1990 (13.59 million vehicles) and failing to reach the 10 million for the first time in 1998 in 20 years since 1978. Domestic sales have been falling due to recession and exports are declining after peaking in fiscal 1985 due to the expansion of production capacity overseas on four core regions: Japan, the US, Europe and Asia. This trend affected all the Japanese tiremakers.

Bridgestone, number One in Asia, is very strong in Japan. Flexible, high-productivity factories keep the global production network functioning smoothly. The 9 Japanese plants can adjust product specifications and production volumes quickly and provide exports to help their counterparts around the world cope with fluctuations in demand. They also are the main sources of high-performance tires, aircraft tires and tires for trucks and buses.

In Japan, Bridgestone is accelerating expansion of its chain of franchised tire retailers since 98, boosting the number of MR Tireman outlets and Tirekan retailers. The move is in preparation for the full-scale entry into the Japanese market by major western tiremakers (Table 11–4).

In Southeast Asia, the tire manufacturing has a long history. Bridgestone's globalization began in 1965 in Southeast Asia, where the company has produced tires in Malaysia, the company's first overseas production since World War II. The Asian manufacturing network has grown steadily and now comprises tire plants throughout Southeast Asia and also in Taiwan, India and China. The strategy of Bridgestone is to grow by building a presence in emerging markets (Table 11–5).

Table 11–3. Bridgestone Tire Plants Worldwide

Geographic Area	1987	2000	Change
North America	1	10	+9
South America	0	7	+7
Europe	0	6	+6
Africa / Middle East	0	4	+4
Asia (included Japan)	12	16	+4
Oceania	1	2	+1
Total	14	45	+31

Table 11–4. Bridgestone's Japan Tire Plants:

1.Kurume Plant
2.Tokyo Plant
3.Nasu Plant
4.Hikone Plant
5.Shimonoseki Plant
6.Tosu Plant
7.Tochigi Plant
8.Amagi Plant
9.Hofu Plant

Table 11–5. Bridgestone Asia Tire Plants

1.Rangsit Plant Thai Bridgestone Co., Ltd.	1969
2.Nong Khae Plant Thai Bridgestone Co., Ltd.	1995
3.Bekasi Plant P.T. Bridgestone Tire Indonesia	1973
4.Karawang Plant P.T. Bridgestone Tire Indonesia	1999
5.Hsin–Chu Plant Bridgestone Taiwan Co., Ltd.	1982
6.Kheda Plant Bridgestone ACC India Ltd.	1998
7.China Shenyang	1999
8.China Tianjin	2000

In the1980's Japanese tire manufacturers intensify move to overseas productions, setting up plants in the US, Europe, but also joining hands with local producers in Taiwan and South Korea in order to cash in on those countries' lower production costs and expanding automobile industries. In 1987 Bridgestone has raised its holding in its Taiwan subsidiary, Bridgestone Taiwan, to 80% in order to bolster the production set-up[7].

Bridgestone is accelerating its foreign investments in Asia since 1998, specialy towards China, India and Indonesia.

In Southeast Asia, Bridgestone began mass production at its second Indonesian tire plant in 1999. That plant along with one of the two factories in Thailand, is becoming a strategic production center for serving markets worldwide. The Thai and Indonesian operations serve local demand and also export large volumes of tires. 1998 was the first year of operation for the production and sales joint-venture in India.

In China, Bridgestone moved carefully, expanding its presence in the tire market by consolidating the Chinese distribution organization. In 1999, Bridgestone acquired its first tire factory in Shenyang, which makes truck and bus tires, and in early 2000 its second Chinese tire plant, which the South Korean Kumko set up in 1996 in Tianjin, that makes passengers car tires. Bridgestone

[7]Tire manufacturers intensify move to overseas production, *The Japan Economic Journal*, March 28, 1987

decided to purchase the factory, as the Chinese government has restricted additional tire plant construction to check excessive inflow of foreign companies into its tire market. The move makes Bridgestone the second Japanese tire maker to start operations in China, following Toyo, which has been producing tires with a local group since 1995. Both Michelin and Goodyear have plants in China.

Bridgestone is under increasing pressure to meet targets of 20% global market share, it is the first significant acquisition since Goodyear and Sumitomo agreed a global alliance earlier to become the world's largest tire company.

3 The Strategy of Goodyear

Goodyear, A Word from the President Samir G. Gibara:

"Leadership in our markets and industry is our goal for the 21st century. We intend to make Goodyear N°1 or N°2 in every market we serve and to be the low-cost producer among the three major global tire and rubber companies. *My vision by the end of the year 2000 has Goodyear ranked by all measures as the best tire and rubber company in the world.*"

An agreement since 1996 allowed Goodyear to produce tires for two Sumitomo Rubber Industries Ltd. subsidiaries in the United States in exchange for production of Goodyear tires in Japan. For the first time in 1996, Goodyear supplied tires to the Japanese market from its Indonesia and Taiwan facilities. Previous Japanese imports were supplied from the United States and Europe.

In 1998, Goodyear unveiled an ambitious five-year plan to almost double its size and establish clear leadership of the global tire industry. At that time, Michelin was the current number one. The alliance between Goodyear and Sumitomo Rubber makes Goodyear a stronger competitor. Under this business alliance, Sumitomo Rubber transferred its Dunlop tire business in the U.S. and Europe to Goodyear in september 1999. Sumitomo Rubber will start producing automobile tires at a new plant in Indonesia from 2002, supplying Japanese automakers in Southeast Asia. It will also export to Japan. The capacity is 10000 tires a day. The existing plant, which went to operation en 1997 will also boost the capacity to 6000 auto radial tires per day from 4500.

In the Philippines, Goodyear acquired the tire assets of Sime Darby to double capacity of an existing plant, which is the country's leading tire producer. This new plant gave Goodyear a cost-competitive base for production in Asia and is used for export in the AFTA trading markets. It significantly strengthen the position in the region, opening new markets in the rest of Asia.

The start-up acquisitions in China are moving forward with the Dalian Tire Plant, Liaoning Province, undergoing expansion, producing Goodyear brand tires for the China market. The Qingdao Engineered Products plant now supplying automotive hose to the region.

India, with a population of more than 900 million, and an expanding OE market, has considerable potential for growth. South Asia Tires, the tire joint venture with Ceat in India was operating at capacity in 1997. It supplies a full line of modern radial passenger and truck tires to meet the burgeoning Indian market.

4 The Strategy of Michelin

Michelin, A Word from Edouard Michelin:

"Michelin is more determined than ever to sharpen its competitive edge on the European continent and to progress in the Americas and in Asia. (...) In Asia, we have won new positions in several large developing markets and we are determined to become number 2 in this zone ... before 2005 ! "

Michelin was founded in 1889. The company's turnover in 1999 was 13,7 billion Euros. Michelin employs 127 000 persons world-wide. It is headquartered in Clermont–Ferrand in France. Main brands are Michelin, B F Goodrich, Uniroyal, Kléber, Riken, Wolber, Stomil, Laurent.

The global strategy for profitable and durable growth will lead to a more balanced repartition of the turnover over five years in the three major zones : Europe, the Americas, Asia, while at the same time consolidating its leading position in the entire (East and West) European market.

4.1 Michelin in Asia

In Asia, Michelin is determined to become number 2 in this zone ... before 2005 ! But, Michelin's Asian sales accounting for only 6.8 per cent of the group total in 1997. Given the spectacular growth of car output and the steadily increasing importance of the region in the world economy, it was natural that Michelin moved in :

- Japan : Joint-venture agreement with OKAMOTO (1988), the smallest Japanese tiremaker : Ohta factory, Gunma (Japan).
- Thailand : Signature of an agreement for a joint-venture between Michelin and Siam Cement : factories at Laem Chabang (1988), followed by NongKhae and Phra Pradaeng.
- Philippines : Continuation of Michelin's collaboration with Siam Cement resulting in the Manila factory.
- China : Joint-venture with Shen Yang Tyre Factory : Shen Yang factory (from 1996).
- India: joint-venture (from 2000).

Michelin is trying to break into distribution in Japan, which has been closely guarded by the Japanese competitors until recently. The economic crisis has led to cracks in this system, and it is up to take advantage of the opportunities that are now emerging. The penetration with Toyota, Nissan, Honda, and the reconfiguration of distribution's channels will open the replacement market more widely. This market is essential for Michelin, and it is profitable.

As regards possible changes in the structure of auto parts procurement induced by industrial reorganization including alliances of carmakers with foreign capital, Michelin will increase its presence as a global supplier in Japan. In 2000, Toyo which ranks second in the Japanese market with a 20% share, has teamed up with a subsidiary of Michelin, with a view to winning more business from Nissan Motor. The joint-venture will supply vibration-absorbing rubber components for use with new engines being developed jointly by Nissan and Renault, the Japanese automaker's top shareholder. Toyo will supply Nissan and Michelin will serve Renault[8].

The Chinese market, which is already one of the major markets in the world for trucks and buses, is developing rapidly in all categories. With this evolution in mind, Michelin opened a commercial office in Beijing as early as 1989. An agreement has been signed in 1995 between the town of Shen Yang and Michelin to create a joint venture in China. The new company, named Michelin Shen Yang Tire Company, will be 90 % owned by Michelin. The plant has a large production capacity for radial Michelin tires for passenger cars and light trucks. Production started end of 1996 and is mainly supplying the Chinese market. The agreement also includes exclusive technical assistance by Michelin for the production of bias tires undertaken by the Shen Yang parent company founded in 1973.

Michelin, which ranks after Goodyear and Bridgestone in global sales would eventually need to complement its international growth plan by making some kind of alliance or even acquisition in Asia. Medium-sized tiremakers would either merge or join the club of large companies. Takeovers are likely to accelerate reorganization of the world's tire market, which is mature, which makes it difficult for newcomers to expand their shares of the market.

5 Conclusion

As automakers expand production overseas, suppliers are being forced to supply their products to automobile plants all over the world. As a result, competition is intensifying in the whole tire industry as makers compete among auto makers. Competition will becomes more borderless, prices will converge worldwide.

Most of the recent strategic alliances in the tire industry are intended to achieve mutual complementarity through expanding horizontally in geographical areas.

[8] Nihon keizai shimbun, May 9, 2000.

The alliances allow a mix of multiple brands to be marketed. This aspect of complementation concerns marketing areas. Tire makers have gone global independently, but starting a business overseas from zero involved significant risks as well as time and costs. The fastest way to expand sales areas is through acquisitions. US market is key, but second-tier makers have difficulties faced to the strength of top three makers in the oligopoly. Japanese tiremakers have established strong business bases in Asia, but foreign makers did not have strong bases in Asia, either. For area complementation, they are looking to the ideal partner among Asian companies experiencing financial difficulties.

References

Asian Development Bank, Thant Myo, Min Tang, Kakazu Hiroshi (eds.) (1998) *Growth Triangles in Asia, A New Approach to Regional Economic Cooperation*, Second Edition, Hong Kong, Oxford University Press,.

Beechler, Schon L. and Bird, Allan. (eds.) (1999) *Japanese Multinationals Abroad, Individual and Organizational Learning*, New York, Oxford University Press.

Darmon, Olivier. (1997) *Le grand siècle de Bibendum*, Paris, Hoëbeke.

European Rubber Journal (November 1999) Global Tyre Report, , Crain Publications

Hout, Thomas. Porter, Michael. and Rudden, Eileen. (1994) " How Global Companies Win Out," in *The Harvard Business Review Book Series*: *Global Strategies, Insights from the World's Leading Thinkers*, pp. 29–46.

Japan Automobile Tire Manufacturers Association (JATMA) (1999) *Tire Industry of Japan*, Tokyo, 27p.

Kierzkowski, Hendryk. (ed.) (1984) *Monopolistic Competition and International Trade*, New York, Oxford University Press.

Krugman, Paul. "Import Protection as Export Promotion: International Competition in the Presence of Oligopoly and Economics of Scale," in Kierzkowski Hendryk (ed.), *Monopolistic Competition and International Trade*, New York, Oxford University Press, pp. 180–193.

Lottman, Herbert. (1998) *Michelin, 100 ans d'aventures*, Paris, Flammarion.

Low, Linda. and Toh, Mun Heng. (eds.) (1993) "*Regional Cooperation and Growth Triangles in ASEAN*," Singapore, Times Academic Press.

Michelin (2000) *Oser – To dare*, CD Rom, Clermont-Ferrand.

Moulin-Bourret, Annie. (1997) *Guerre et industrie, Clermont-Ferrand 1912–1922: la Victoire du pneu*, Clermont-Ferrand, Institut d'études du Massif Central, Tome I + Tome II.

Ohmae, Kenichi. (1994) "The Global Logic of Strategic Alliances," (1989) reprinted in *Global Strategies, Insights from the World's Leading Thinkers*, The Harvard Business Review Book Series, pp. 109–128.

Perlmutter, Howard V. and Heenan David A.(1994) "Cooperate to Compete Globally," (1986) reprinted in *Global Strategies, Insights from the World's Leading Thinkers,* The Harvard Business Review Book Series, pp. 129–141.

Porter, Michael E. (1985) *Competitive Advantage, Creating and Sustaining Superior Performance.* New York: The Free Press, 557 p.

Ramstetter, Eric. (1998) "Measuring the size of foreign multinationals in the Asia-Pacific," in Thompson Grahame (ed.), *Economic Dynamism in the Asia-Pacific,* New York, Routledge, pp. 185–212.

Westney Eleanor D. (1999) "Changing Perspectives on the Organization of Japanese Multinational Companies," in Beechler Schon L., Bird Allan (eds.), *Japanese Multinationals Abroad, Individual and Organizational Learning*, New York, Oxford University Press, , pp.11–29.

http://www.goodyear.com/us/corporate/
http://www.bridgestone–firestone.com/
http://www.bridgestone.co.jp/
http://www.michelin.fr
http://www.RubberNetwork.com/xmatrix/index.htm

12 Evolution of Global Product Development Strategy: A Case of "Asia Car"

Takahiro Fujimoto
The University of Tokyo

Yasuo Sugiyama
Kyoto University

1 Introduction

The purpose of this paper is to explore dynamic aspects of strategy formation in global product development. By describing and analyzing design and organizational choices of some Japanese automakers for products targeting the Southeast Asian markets, particularly in Indonesia, we aim to better understand how international manufacturing firms try to balance goals that often contradict: to adapt their products and activities to local requirements, and to enjoy scale or scope economies through standardized global operations and resources. We pay special attentions to the dynamic nature of a firm's capability-building or organizational learning, through which its product design strategies, organizational capabilities, and its environments *co-evolve* over time.

Practitioners and researchers in international management have long discussed how a multinational manufacturing firm balances the benefits and costs of global standardization and local adaptation. Product design and development for emerging markets (for example, Asian developing countries) has been an area where this trade-off problem was particularly difficult to solve. Globally standardized designs, exemplified by "World Car," often failed to attract local consumers (Sinclair 1983), whereas so called "low cost vehicles" (that is, simplified models specifically designed for such local requirements) seldom prevailed as dominant products in the emerging markets. Based on these past lessons, today's multinational auto firms tend to choose a more subtle and sophisticated approaches in making trade-off between local-specific designs and global-standard designs. One of such design strategies is to use old platforms that may have already been terminated in the home market but to develop new derivative models that are optimized to various local conditions. We may call this approach "Old Platform Derivative." We see some examples in Japanese models for Indonesia, which we will analyze in details later on.

Researches on the global-local trade-off in product development themselves are by no means new. In the field of international marketing, for example, the product design choice between global standardization and adaptation to the local needs has been one of the central issues (Levitt 1983; Douglas and Wind 1987). Also, the role of global integration and local responsiveness has been emphasized in the literature of international management (Prahalad and Doz 1987, Bartlett and Ghoshal 1989).

However, most of the existing analyses tended to treat this global-local issue as that of static optimization under given constraints. In other words, there has been an implicit assumption that managers of the multinational firms can make deliberate and optimal strategic choices, given their environmental and resource-capability conditions in both home countries and local markets at a certain point in time.

This assumption is not necessarily appropriate in the real setting, though. Considering the bounded rationality of managers, uncertainty of the local environmental conditions, and cumulative nature of firm's organizational capabilities and managerial resources, it would be more realistic to assume that the global firms find effective solutions to this through trial and errors, and that their product design strategies are formed in a more or less path-dependent way[1]. Also, such strategies may have been realized in a way that managers neither foresaw nor intended in advance – an "emergent strategy" (Mintzberg and Waters 1985). What the company needs for effective strategy formation in such unpredictable situations is a certain dynamic capability for not only intentional learning but also for opportunistic (ex-post) learning (Fujimoto 1999).

Besides, when the environments change unpredictably, what used to be an optimal design solution may turn out to be a sub-optimal one in the next period, and the company may not be able to adjust its strategies and resources instantly. Also, the strategic choices, once implemented, would affect the environments and capabilities: a dynamic process which results in a cumulative interactions, generating a gap away from the optimal choices. Thus, over-adaptation or miss-adaptation may be the rule rather than the exception at least in the short run. The importance of organizational capability in global strategy implementation has been emphasized in a number of past researches (Prahaladand Doz 1987, Bartlett and Ghoshal 1989), nevertheless, they were not well connected to the notion of dynamic interaction among strategy, capability and environment.

In this paper, taking into account the above possibilities of path dependence, emergent strategies, over-adaptation and so on, we apply a dynamic view of

[1] The concept of path-dependency tends to be applied to depict the situation that the later outcome depends on small events beneath the beginning of its history due to their positive feedback (Arthur 1989). In this case, it is unpredictable which outcome is "selected" in path-dependent manner. On the other hand, the concept of path-dependency here means that the capability accumulated by learning from past activities and decision-makings play a key role for present decision making, and it is not strongly related to the self-reinforcing.

strategy formation and capability-building to the case of international product development in Indonesian automobile industry. More specifically, we try to answer the following questions about the international product development strategies of Japanese automobile makers for Indonesian markets:

1. *Context:* What was the situation that the automobile firms were facing in Asia (Indonesia), including market size and needs, government regulations, manufacturing/design capabilities of local operations, supplier systems, etc.?
2. *Strategy Formation:* How did the firms choose a particular strategy in terms of product design choices? How did they choose locations of development organizations and product development processes for Asia (Indonesia)?
3. *Competitive Results:* How did the above strategic choices affect competitive performance of their products in Asia (Indonesia)?
4. *Co-evolution:* How did the strategic choices affect local market needs and local manufacturing capabilities, as well as their evolution?
5. *Over-Adaptation:* Did the companies suffer from the problem of over-adapting their product designs to the local environment? If so, how and why?

These issues will be discussed with the illustration of a case of product development strategy of Japanese automotive firms for Indonesian markets. We pay special attention to the case, partly because the dynamics process of path-dependent strategy formation and over-adaptation was particularly obvious in this country. In section 2, we elaborate our framework for analyzing dynamic aspects of international product development. In section 3, this framework will be applied to explain the strategy of the Japanese automotive makers' product development for country specific vehicle in Indonesia. Then we will sum up the discussion in section 4.

2 Global Strategy of Product Development: A Dynamic View

2.1 The Types of International Product Design Strategy and Their Competitive Effect

In this section, based on the research question mentioned in the beginning, the framework of analyzing international product development strategy will be presented in view of the newly emerging markets such as Southeast Asia.

In general, the strategic decision-making regarding international product development can be roughly divided into the following: 1) Strategies for product design itself and 2) Strategies regarding the configuration of product development organization. The brief explanation of each is given below.

Figure 12–1 represents a framework to comprehend the product design strategy in the global context. In this framework, we first classify the design strategy of product in terms of the width of its target market (Takeuchi and Porter 1986). Global design is the design which physical structure is basically the same as that for home or other countries' market. This strategy tends to be chosen when the demand condition of emergent market is relatively similar to that of other market. On the other hand, local design is the design which physical structure is somewhat different from that for home or other countries' market. This strategy tends be chosen when the market demand there is different and independent from that of other country. These choices reflect the similarity of market among countries.

Second, we also classify the strategy based on the linkage between new product development and the existing platform (or core component) of product. We include this classification because it reflects the applicability of new design, and the cost of development and manufacturing of the product. When product is developed on *newly developed platform*, the development cost is higher, but the range of allowance for adoption of new design might be wider. On the other hand, in the case of *applied old platform*, relatively smaller tolerance for application of new design is allowed in new product development. While the degree of freedom in design change is small, the cost necessary to produce a new model would be reduced.

With above classification, four typical types can be extracted which functional characteristics are summarized as below.

1. Global design product using newly developed platform

This is the typical example of global standardization (Levitt 1983). The major advantage of this strategy is development cost saving. Investment cost for production equipment can also be shared for imported parts, but this is not the case for locally produced parts, which require double tooling anyway. Another

Figure 12–1. Product Design Strategy for Local Market

	Global Design	Local Design
New Designed Platform	I	II
Applied Old Platform	III	IV

advantage is that the model can incorporate the state-of-the-art technologies, but this often means over-specifications and cost increase. Also, manufacturing quality is high due to the supply of products of which their function had already been proven.

2. Local design product using newly developed platform

In this type, either the platform developed only for the local market and the rapidly transferred platform from the current models is available. In the case of rapid transferred platform, the main advantage is a balance between design adaptation and scale economy. Although additional investment is needed for product development, cost saving is still significant here, particularly when the original project and the derivative projects are overlapped (Cusumano and Nobeoka 1998). Investment cost can also be saved for those parts produced centrally and imported for local assembly. These models can also incorporate the latest technologies, but this often means over-specification from the emerging markets' point of view. Investment cost saving may also be limited for those parts produced locally, since this usually means double tooling.

On the other hand, in the case of platform developed only for the local market, design adaptation to local markets and design simplification for local production base are emphasized for achieving the cost and quality competitiveness simultaneously. It does not pursue cost saving by development and investment cost saving, though.

3. Global design product using old platform

This strategy calls attention to Vernon's concept of product cycle. Vernon (1971) predicted that the market and production site would sift from developed country to developing country as the product gets matured and standardized. The main advantage of this strategy is cost saving both in product development and capital expenditure for production equipment. This is particularly the case when the old equipment can be transferred to the local production facilities. Another potential advantage is that the old product designs tend to be simpler and thus easier for the local producers/suppliers to handle. Besides, it is a proven technology, which is less risky from manufacturing quality's point of view. Its major disadvantage, however, is the very fact that the design is old. In the information age, consumers of the emerging markets also know what is sold outside their country. Simply old designs would not attract such customers even with extremely low prices.

4. Local design product using old platform (Old Platform Derivative)

This is also a strategy aiming at the balance between design adaptation and scale economy, there may be more significant cost reduction in this case. As for the carried-over parts and the platform, most of the tools and equipment may be transferred to the local facilities without much additional cost. Development cost can also be saved. The design is also less subject to the over-quality problem that the new platform may suffer from, but the overall design of such models may be still attractive to the local customers, which enhances the likelihood of being accepted as new models by the middle-class customers in emerging markets. This approach, however, may need a high level of product development capabilities, because using old platform often means more constraints for the engineers of the derivative products than the case of new platform. We call this strategy as "Old Platform Derivative" for the sake of convenience.

In static sense, it is recommended for global enterprises to select the most appropriate strategy taking into account the various conditions such as market characteristics, market size, and nationalization policies in each country.

2.2 Types of International Configuration in Product Development Organization

Also, the configuration of activity is one of the critical issues that global strategy is to address (Porter 1986), since it is related to the utilization of location advantage (Dunning 1981). For product development strategy, the choice of location (the deployment or allocation of resources) for product development organization is the focal issue[2]. Product development organization consists of various functional activities such as product planning, designing, prototyping, testing, process engineering, and so on (Clark and Fujimoto, 1991). Each activity has choices of location between the home country and the local country. As for Asian models, there is a strong tendency to concentrate in the home country, which will be discussed later. The decision about the configuration depends mainly on the stickiness of information (von Hippel 1994), and the scale effect for development activities (Ghoshal 1987).

In the case of models produced and sold locally, which part of the activities is to be transferred to the local site and which part is to be left in the home country will be decided according to the stickiness of the problem-solving information exchanged among the local market, local production facilities and the development organization of the home country. This in turn will decide the location distribution of international development organization.

Although product development is essentially a production of information assets as opposed to physical products (Clark and Fujimoto 1991), its performance may still be affected by certain scale factors in terms of the number of projects executed at each unit. For example, at least several projects may be needed for efficient use of such developmental tools as prototyping equipment, supercomputers for simulations, and testing facilities. When only one project is executed for local product development, it may have to use the central facilities in the home country for this reason.

---

[2] Needless to say, product design strategy and location strategy have reciprocal influence on each other. This line of argument, however, is omitted in this article.

2.3 The Path-dependent Selection of Strategy (Emergent Strategy)

Companies do not necessarily make the rational and ex-ante selection of a product development strategy described above. Rather, it seems more appropriate to think that the choice was attained emergently in the successive decision-making at each time.

If global product strategy is determined by the cumulative decision-making of the past and environmental constraints, the explanation found in the existing static global strategy theory, which is based on an implicit assumption that managers of the multinational firms can make deliberate and optimal strategic choices, is not sufficient. In order to explain the path-dependent decision-making in global strategy, the framework including dynamic capability building and the co-evolution of strategy, capability and environment are indispensable.

As the selection of strategy is restricted by the condition of accumulated capabilities, the strategy selection consequently becomes dependent on the path of the strategy selected in the past. For example, the above "Old Platform Derivative" strategy might possibly be achieved through two paths.

The first path comes from the classical transfer strategy in which the old model which is no longer produced in the home country is transferred without any change. This however overlooks the fact that the local needs also do progress and advance in their own pace. The old model gradually loses customers in the local market as they learn more about the products, often comparing the local models with the more advanced models sold in the home country. Faced with the sluggish sales of the old model, makers typically try to overcome this crisis by introducing a derivative and locally adapted model. As a result, a derivative model based on the old platform is developed, which is the ex-post, rationalized selection made possible by learning, rather than the strategic selection intended from the start.

The second path possibly resides with the case in which the local model, which had been planned as a derivative model from the current platform in the home country, consequently becomes a derivative model based on the old platform as a result of the model change in the home country. This happens because of the time lag between the model changes in the home country and the local market, attributed to the difference in production volume and the degree of competition. In cases where the local production was obliged by the nationalization regulation, the intervals of model changes tend to be prolonged in order to collect the local capital investment in production equipment. In the home country, on the other hand, model changes tend to be frequent to win the severe market competition, followed by the swift introduction of models in which new technology is applied. As a result, the local models are left behind as old platform based models. Thus, the local model based on the old platform happens to be a strategic choice as an unintended, consequence.

2.4 The Co-Evolution of Strategy, Capability and Environment, and the Possibility of Excessive Adaptation

Strategy is not only determined by environment and organizational capability, but also influential to the market environment and organizational capability in a long run. Influence is reciprocal, and strategy, environment and capability co-evolution. Figure 12–2 is a brief summary on how the choices of strategy are affected by past experiences and affect in the future.

Irrespective of whether it is intentional or not, enterprises are the entities which accumulate capability through the execution of strategy. The trajectory of resource accumulation and the evolutionary path of environment, both of which affect the decision-making, do not necessarily match, and there is also a possibility that the strategy appropriate at one time may become inappropriate as the environment and resources change (Leonard-Barton 1992).

Figure 12–2. Dynamic View of Strategy

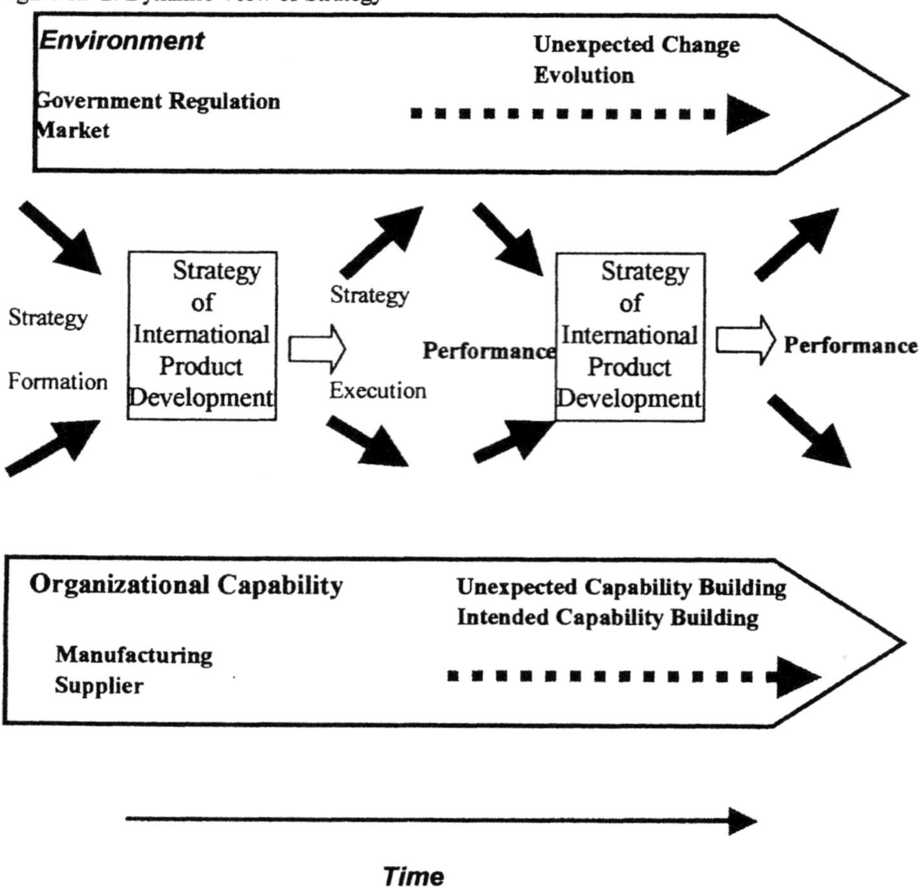

There is a possibility of miss-adaptation or excessive adaptation. For instance, although "Old Platform Derivative" does appear fit to the local conditions, somewhat resolving the dilemma of cost reduction and meeting local needs, it does not address the perspective that the customers and production capability in the local market also evolve. "Old Platform Derivative" may in fact fixate the local needs, and accelerate the fragmentation of demand and production system by nation. In other words, the introduction of this model might possibly hinder the movement towards the homogeneity of market needs and local production capability. It may be possible that flexible development system generates inflexible models. Concrete examples of such dynamic process are as follows:

1. *The Adaptation to the Local Production Capability.* Even globally standard designs sometime require modification in the local market due to lower local capability and differences in production volume. This modification enables the production of a model that fits the local production capability, while, on the other hand, this adaptation eliminates the pressure on the local production system to improve its capability.
2. *The Adaptation to the Local Market Condition.* Although the introduction of a locally adapted model through the locally adapted designing based on the local platform boosts local sales, this consequently isolates the local customer taste from the international market, which therefore adversely affects the competitiveness of the local products. In addition, as the possibility of the international market deployment of the products will be lowered, the production volume cannot increase without expanding markets in foreign countries, which in turn hinders the improvement of manufacturing capabilities.

In other words, "Old Platform Derivative" strategy is adopted in a pass-dependent manner, and price and non-price competitiveness will be enhanced in the local market. In this aspect, this strategy excels in balancing the pursuit of scale economies and the adaptation to the local needs in design. When looked at dynamically also from the perspective of the evolution of organizational capability and market needs, however, there is a problem that the local adaptation of products lessens the pressure for global homogeneity, including the improvement of capabilities and the advancement of market needs from a global point of view. This may be called the "over-adaptation" condition of product development strategy, which may weaken the resistant power against environmental change.

As a matter of fact, for the Japanese makers which had introduced the locally fit models in Southeast Asia, the paradox of "flexible organizational capability generates inflexible products" became manifest with the economic crisis in the region. The merits of local adaptation is naturally emphasized when the local market is growing, but when it is shrinking, the standardization of design which enables the export to other regions is a priority, and the over-adaptation to the local market becomes problematic. The Asian Crisis after 1997 has dramatically revealed this problem.

On the other hand, strategy and corporate environment are similarly related to each other with reciprocal influence. The co-evolution of the corporate products and the customer needs clearly indicate this relationship. Companies adopt a product strategy to adapt to the customer needs, and by using their products, customers learn about the products. As a result, the customers come to have new needs, demanding their products new adaptation. The products, which had been adaptive to the customer needs, become obsolete, and the companies cannot survive without introducing products that satisfy the new needs. Customer needs and products, having gone through such process of co-evolution, become oriented towards finer differentiation (Clark 1985). The adoption of a strategy for local adaptation lowers the pressure for the advancement of market needs from a global perspective, but rather develops the needs specific to the local market. This consequently isolate the needs from the global market, depriving the efficacy of the strategy which had once been effective, which may in turn deteriorate the global competitiveness.

Thus, from a dynamic perspective, companies engage in accumulative decision-making while repeating the failures of under-adaptation and over-adaptation, which is paralleled by the evolution of market needs and local production capability. Through the experiences of recurrent adaptation over time, learning organizations may accumulate certain dynamic capabilities in the long run, by which the firm can re-adjust the product strategies quickly to the environmental changes (Teece, Pisano and Shuen 1997). Such dynamic point of view would be crucial in looking at global strategy.

In the next section, we will focus on this particular design strategy from a dynamic point of view. That is, we will analyze not only how this strategy achieved the products' competitiveness in the local market at a certain point in time, but also how this strategy was chosen through a certain path-dependent sequence of decisions, as well as how such strategic choices affected the companies' capabilities and environments over time.

3 A Case Study: The Product Development Strategy of Asia Car

In this section, we apply the framework proposed in the last section to the case of automobile product development for ASEAN markets. Especially, we analyze the case of the development of Indonesia specific vehicle of Japanese automakers, because the case is one of the most appropriate examples to illustrate our argument. We discuss the product design strategy for adapting to its local environment, the formation of organizational capability to realize it, and the organizational inertia formed by that capability. First, we overview the specific condition and history related to especially Indonesian auto industry, as well as the Japanese automakers' product development strategies as a response to such conditions. Then we will discuss more about dynamic aspect of this issue thorough the case of the development processes of two Indonesian models and capability building of the firms will be described. Finally, we discuss the environmental change caused by recent economic crisis, and the appeared vulnerability because of the over-adaptation against it.

3.1 Context and Conditions: The Indonesian Auto Industry

First, we analyze the environmental condition for product development for the Indonesian market. We describe the situation that the automobile firms were facing in Indonesia, including government regulations, market size and needs, dominant strategy in the past and so on.

3.1.1 Government Regulation and Its Consequence

Since the late 1960s, many of the governments of Asian developing countries have adopted import-substitution policies for their automobile sectors through protection of local production operations from imports. The Indonesian government adopted the localization policy in 1969, prohibiting any import of complete auto products, obliging foreign automakers to employ locally capitalized makers for CKD assembling, and restraining the entrants of foreign assembly makers. This was followed by the adoption of the policy promoting the localization of commercial vehicles in 1976, which favored the custom for the CKD import of commercial vehicles, while concurrently encouraging the domestic parts procurement.

Such local-content policies, however, mean governmental protection of local assembly and parts manufacturing operations which do not have sufficient international competitiveness because of their limits in manufacturing capabilities, production scale, material availability, technologies, and so on. Compared with the Japanese domestic operations, which are known for their world-class competitiveness in both quality and productivity, the operations in ASEAN countries tended to lack competitiveness for exporting vehicles and components. Their low wage rate could not make up for their low productivity.

The above-mentioned disadvantage of local operations vis-a-vis the Japanese counterparts has been particularly serious in the case of parts manufacturing, which tends to be more capital-intensive and scale-sensitive than vehicle assembly. As a result, cost competitiveness of the locally produced vehicles tended to decrease as local content ratio increased. Manufacturing quality of local parts was also low in many cases. This often meant that the automakers had to modify parts designs in order to match them to the local manufacturing conditions.

The New Automotive Policy came into effect in 1994 in an aim to strengthen the competitiveness of domestic automakers, which liberalized the import of complete auto products and lowered the custom imposed on parts import. This effort nevertheless eventually marked a considerable setback as a result of the contraction of the domestic market. Although the governments of Asian developing countries, in recent years, have attempted to shift from import-substitution to export-promotion policies in some other sectors, such a transition was difficult in the automobile sector, in which the above-mentioned vicious cycle of increasing localization and decreasing competitiveness was quite common.

As an alternative measure, some of the developing countries, since the 1970s, have attempted to promote mutual exports and imports of components or vehicles inside a certain regional communities such as ASEAN, aiming at larger production scale for each local operation. Typical examples include so called BBC (brand-to-brand complementation scheme) in ASEAN auto-producing countries, which actually facilitated intra-firm trade of certain components among the Japanese automakers' component factories within this region. The impacts of such regional complementation policies on competitiveness of their products have been limited, though.

3.1.2 Market Conditions

In terms of the unit of sales, the Indonesian market has shown a great expansion from the outset of the 1990s (Figure 12–3), yet the demand took an acute down turn due to the economic crisis, and it decreased sharply from 387 thousands in 1997 to 58 thousands in 1998[3]. Moreover, the 1997 crisis resulted in a dramatic shrinkage of the combined ASEAN market to about 400,000 units, or less than one third of the peak volume. Prior to the Asian economic crisis, however, the automakers had been predicting a rapid market growth of in this region based on the robust market performance from late 1980s to the mid 1990s. In response to such market expectations, as well as continued government policies for local production, the Japanese automakers and parts suppliers had continued to invest on local assembly and parts production, as well as development of specific local models[4].

The low per-capita income naturally results in the relatively low diffusion rate of vehicles, which is below 3 per cent in Indonesia. Per capita GNP of Indonesia amounted only to US$980 in 1995, which was one twenty-seventh of the U.S.A., and one fourth of Brazil. Even in the 1990s, the average monthly salary for a

[3] "Asia Pulse," 16 March, 1999; 17 March, 1999

[4] Doner (1991) described the historical dominance of Japanese firms in Southeast Asia. As success factors, he pointed out its long-term orientation and flexibility both in strategy and production.

Figure 12–3. Automobile Sales in Indonesia

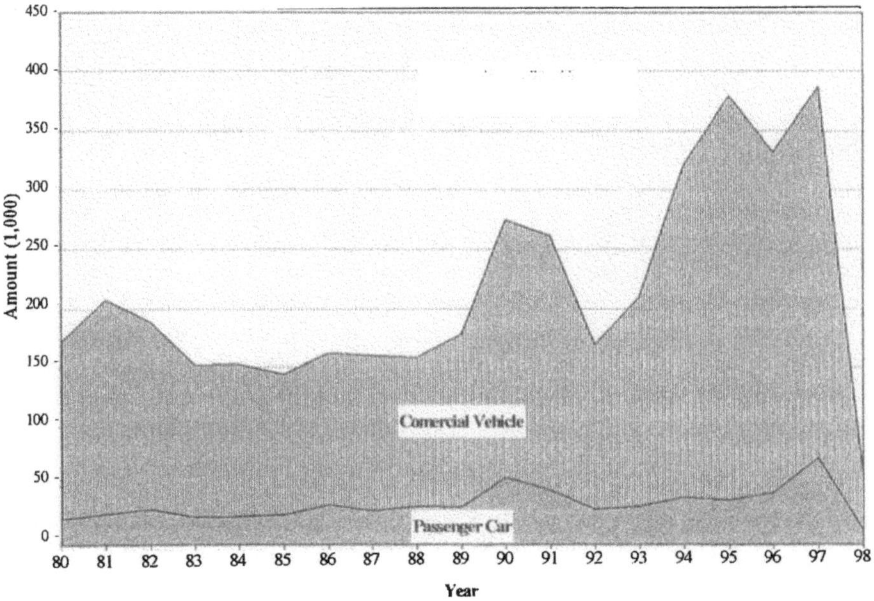

Source: LTCBR (1997) p5, Nikkan Jidosya Shinbunsya (1999) p229, and Asia Pulse 16 March, 1999; 17 March, 1999.

senior manager of a major company was approximately US$130[5]. In terms of price, therefore, low-priced cars have been in most demand excluding the small market for luxurious high-class passenger cars. In the areas outside of cities and suburbs, in particular, this road condition has enhanced the demand for specifications usually required for trucks, such as waterproof quality, especially for low-priced passenger cars. On the other hand, meeting the quality standard for the mass-produced vehicles in Japan has not been a necessity in product development for this particular market.

Despite the efforts of ASEAN countries to build an integrated regional market, patterns of automobile user needs have been rather diversified from country to country. As indicated in the Table 12–1, the difference in consumer choices of vehicle types across the ASEAN countries is remarkable. While nearly 80 per cent of total sales is derived from passenger car sales in Malaysia, it is less than 30 per cent in Thailand, and in Indonesia, it is only 10 per cent of total sales. Difference is also seen within the commercial vehicle category. Where pick-up trucks comprise a major segment in Thailand, van (or mini-bus) type vehicles are the

[5] According to the interview with the manager engaged in Indonesian operation.

Table 12–1. Diversified Auto Market in ASEAN 4

	Passenger Car		Comercil Vehicle	
Thailand	163,371	(28.6%)	408,209	(71.4%)
Indonesia	37,835	(10.0%)	340,861	(90.0%)
Malaysia	224,991	(78.7%)	60,801	(21.3%)
Philippines	71,195	(55.6%)	56,967	(44.4%)

Source: LTCBR (1997) p5

primary commercial vehicles sold in Indonesia. Such a diversified demand structure prevented the automakers from pursuing scale-economy through introduction of a single product design to all the ASEAN countries.

The consumer needs in Indonesia center on commercial vehicles as briefly mentioned above. Above all, they show a strong preference for van typecommercial vehicles, which is characteristic of the Indonesian market. There are several reasons for this slanted needs. First of all, there have been the tax favoring commercial vehicles as mentioned above, which has led to the substitution of the major portion of the demand for passenger cars with commercial vehicles. In Indonesia, the purchaser class of passenger cars has been limited to a small portion of high income bracket from the start, and that of commercial vehicles had mostly been small to medium-sized transportation companies. With the birth of middle income class, however, the purchaser class of low-priced passenger cars has generated. They tended to buy van type commercial vehicles because of the tax system which favored commercial vehicles. The consumers used to purchase commercial vehicles that came in the form of cab chassis only, and have the local servicing manufacture and attach the rear body by the primitive method of sheet metal processing. The technique they used was quite rough, with the low precision in matching rear body and cab chassis, applying putty where there were gaps.

The typical customer for the van type vehicles was the people who are capable of employing drivers and maids. It was required for these customers that their driver, maids as well as baby sitters if they had children besides the family members could get on the same car, which therefore created the demand for passenger cars which accommodated more than 7 people. Under these circumstances, the needs for the development of van type commercial vehicles as the products to substitute the passenger cars emerged.

3.1.3 The Dominant Product in the Past

The above-mentioned environmental conditions, including small market size, diversified user needs, relatively low income, and insufficient capabilities of local factories and suppliers, makes designs of the difficult and subtle. While several firms try to develop a country specific vehicle for Indonesia, Toyota could introduce it to the market most successfully. Toyota started their investment in Indonesia in 1971, which was the joint venture with Astra International, a local conglomerate. Almost four years had past after the government of Indonesia first approached to automakers

Kijang was and has been the most popular vehicle in Indonesia and defined as an Indonesian car, fully designed specially for Indonesia. In 1977, six years after the establishment of joint-venture between Toyota and Astra, the first Kijang was introduced in Indonesian market. Kijang was designed to adapt the local needs of Indonesian domestic market, for use to transport agricultural products and building material around the rural area. Kijang had no doors. Although that feature was beyond the imagination of the engineers in Toyota, they could adopt that design thanks to the input from local stuff. Kijang even had no rear body (upper) and the part covered by upper body was only around the front seats. The rear body was produced in the local servicing as above mentioned. The first Kijang and its successor kept the position of most popular car in Indonesian automobile market constantly. The second Kijang, the successor of the first Kijang, sifted their design a little to be more stylish, however they still remained the same in terms of their cost competitiveness. In 1989, a basic grade of Kijang was sold by only $5,700, which was less than one third of the price of their main passenger car, the Corolla[6].

3.2 Strategy Choice in Product Design

3.2.1 Country Specific Vehicle as a Concept of Product Design

Following the conditions mentioned above, the Japanese makers have introduced the products developed with the concept of the country specific vehicle for Indonesia. The concept signifies the model which was developed in order to adapt to the demands in the particular country and to sell free of tax by satisfying the localization standards fixed by the government for the parts of the commercial vehicles. The tasks involved in the product design of them were to develop the model that was fit for the local production environment, low cost, and that met the local needs, which fit the ideas advocated in the 1970s such as "appropriate technology" (Jequier 1976).

As an instance, Model X is the product that Firm A developed especially for the Indonesian market, which is produced in the local factory of joint-venture with the local capital[7]. As for the units of production of Model X, they are about six-seventh for MPV (Multi-Purpose Vehicle) types and about one-seventh for pick-

[6] The description here is based on "Fortune" January 2, 1989, p16, "Institutional Investor" November 1991, p105.

[7] The data on the development of Model X in this section was collected mainly by the interview with several managers of Firm A in June 1997.

up types. The present model is the third generation, with the last model change done in 1997.

Firm B's Model Y is also the product planned as the country specific vehicle for Indonesia[8]. They initiated its development in 1992 as "the car to change the scene in Indonesia," and started the production three years later, in 1995. Although they started to be produced in Malaysia, China and Vietnam after a while, it was planned as the country specific model for Indonesia at the time of initial development. There are three types of vehicles, including van type complete products, semi-complete products shipped to a local parts servicing, and pick-up types, each of which has been produced in about the same proportion.

3.2.2 Parts Sharing: The Application of Old Platform of Home Country

The product design strategy for these vehicles were the local design using old platform, that is "Old Platform Derivative" in our terminology. The equipment cost was cut down by applying the parts of old models in the home country to many of the primary parts in any model, and it was unusual to find cases in which sharing of the parts with the current models in Japan was observed. If the designs of the current models for Japan were applied unchanged, the quality of many of the parts would exceed the customer needs, which would cancel out the effects of development cost reduction in terms of materials and facilities.

In the development of Model X, its suspension and transmission were applied unchanged from the first generation, although its frame was remodeled. When the first generation of the model was introduced, the core components such as engine were imported from Japan, sharing their design with the home country model at that time. Since then, although production site was transferred from Japan to Indonesia, the facilities used for its production remained unchanged. For example, the production facility for engines is the one that had originally been transferred from Japan to Australia, which was further transferred to Indonesia. By transferring facilities, they minimized the investment.

Firm A try to utilize old facility as much as possible, even some design change are inevitable. The current engine of Model X is an expanded version of one that was used for first generation. 1,100cc overhead-valve-style engine of the popular passenger car in home country was used in first generation. Then it was expanded to 1,500cc, which was still insufficient and therefore was further stroke up to 1,800cc for the application to current Model X.

The engine room is about the only part that was developed with parts sharing with the current models in Japan. While they had initially planned to apply the headlamps of a home model to Model X, they cancelled the application due to problems in adjustment.

---

[8]The data on the development of Model Y in this section was collected mainly by the interview with Chief Engineer of Firm B in October 1997.

In the case of Model Y, the "Old Platform Derivative" was applied through the path from the classical transfer strategy. Firm B was formerly produced the model transferred without any change. Then, the Model Y was developed using the old platform of it. Therefore, despite the press release explaining that it was a wider version of a model in Japan, what this model is sharing its structure with is an old model of Indonesia, and in fact, the model sold in Japan and Model Y are totally different in their physical structures. By and large, they succeeded in halving the equipment cost and largely reducing the development cost by applying the platform of an old model.

3.2.3 The Fit between the Trajectory of Strategy and the Progress of Local Technology

Firms have to adapt their strategy to fit the local environment such as local production capability. As for Model X, the quality standard in the evaluation of design was substantially relaxed. Out of necessity to develop a low-cost product that fits the local environment, chief engineers have been more flexible in their judgments and occasionally given OK to designs that did not meet the Firm A standard. The local production capability, for example, may be sufficient to manufacture press parts, but may present trouble in matching the parts. The rigid application of the same standard for evaluation is therefore not practical in order to sustain the production. Table 12–2 contains a list of cases in which design was adapted to the local production capability.

As such, the level of quality even for Model X is considerably low, far from the level that could be exported to Japan. For the time being, the possible destination for exports remains limited to the South Pacific countries outside the

Table 12–2. Cases of Design Adaptation to the Local Production Capability

Instrumental Panel	Due to the low capacity of resin injection casts, steel was partly applied. Although the total injection required a 2,000-ton machine, local makers only possessed 1,300-ton ones. In 1997, the problem had already been resolved as one of Firm A supplier had 3,000-ton machines locally.
Seat Cover	The local products are used, of which technological level is low. Leather is weak, and fabric is prone to yield to pressure and to whiten. They do not meet the quality standards of Firm A proper. Although starch used is not of good quality and easily cracks, they conceded to use it as import costs more.
Steel Sheet	In Japan, stripped material (rolls) is used and its yield is high at 70%, but locally, it is low at 64,5% as sheet material is used. As they complement it by recycling, zinc plated steel sheet cannot be used. Therefore, the warranty for no rust and no holes are shortened to 3 years and 5 years, respectively, from 5 years and 10 years, respectively, applied in Japan.

Source: Field interviews

ASEAN region. Export to the Middle East is possible in terms of quality, which however is precluded due to temperature problem. While the temperature occasionally reaches 50 degrees centigrade in the Middle East, Model X is likely to have problems if it gets over 35 degrees centigrade. Moreover, there is practically no emission control or safety standard in Indonesia, and the measures taken for the safety purposes are on a totally different level from those in Japan. As the addition of emission control costs more than 100 US dollars, it is not adopted placing priority on cost. Although air conditioning is in place, the model is not at all equipped to function in the chilly climate, with no heater or defroster and the tire chains not applicable. Thus, the priority placed on the cost reduction as the country specific model for Indonesia largely limited the market for export as a consequence.

On the other hand, the local technology and production capability, which are the targets of their adaptation efforts, have been progressing, resulting in the corresponding, gradual upgrade of parts design. In Model X, several improvements have been made from the previous model, in line with the progress of the local capability. First of all, the major change took place in its styling. This was to meet the change in the demand in Indonesia, as well as to adapt to the advanced parts production technology of the local suppliers. For instance, the improvement in styling was possible because of the improved glass technology of the local supplier, or more concretely, of the use of three-dimensional curved surface glass. Glass is a part which has always been locally procured from the first generation of Model X. While it was initially one-dimensional, it gradually shift to two-dimensional and to three-dimensional curved surface that they finally came to be capable of handling.

Besides, it is also important that they came to be capable of applying highly advanced production technology, along with the expansion in production scale. Look at welding as an example. With the first model (monthly production of 500 to 1,000 units), double sheet welding were frequently used to flat body to minimize fixed cost. On the other hand, with the current model, more advanced techniques such as single sheet welding and closed section were applied, which resulted in lighter body and higher rigidity. This enabled the reduction in the number of parts as well as a 30 per cent cut in per unit cost by decreasing the weight by 30 kilograms.

3.2.4 The Effect of Product Development Capabilities on Product Design

In order to adapt to local conditions, product development capability to attain flexibility based on the agility in development speed and lower development cost may play a significant role to choose the strategy. According to Clark and Fujimoto (1991), the Japanese automakers during the 1980s tended to outperform the Western counterparts in lead times and productivity of product development. The high performance of the Japanese auto makers as above has been supported by a set of organizational capabilities for early and integrated problem-solving, including parts suppliers' ability to take part in component design (Asanuma 1989), high manufacturing capability that supports the development process (for example, prototyping and die-making), overlapping problem-solving between product and process engineering, strong project management (for example, heavy-weight project manager system), and so on.

Due to the lower development cost of Japanese firms and its organizational capability to implement "Old Platform Derivative" strategy, it becomes possible for them to develop the model specific for the country of small number of production. In fact, Japanese makers announced the development of Asia specific car in mid-90s taking advantage of these characteristics, and some models were actually introduced to Asian market. The characteristics of these models are that each model has a specific target country. While Honda City, Toyota Soluna mainly aimed at Thai market, Toyota Kijang and Daihatsu Espass were originally planed to target Indonesian market.

3.3 Strategy Choice in Configuration of Activities

3.3.1 The Choice of Configuration

As mentioned above, in case of product development for ASEAN market, Japanese firms tend to concentrate their product development organizations in the home country. Coupled with the small number of local suppliers with sufficient technology and prototyping capability in Indonesia, the actual situation is that local development is not feasible. Looking at the actual configuration of activities, in the case of Model X, everything up to design prototyping was done in Japan in principle, which was then transferred to the local site from the stage of trial production in facilities. Locally, it was the technology department that engaged in the development. Their central responsibility was the inspection of locally procured parts. The only exception was the deck of their pick-up truck which was designed locally.

There was a similar systematic division in which product development was done in Japan and process engineering was done locally in the case of Model Y, although the local staff in charge of the process engineering took some business trips to Japan for preparation. Out of two stages of design prototyping, the first one was done with the parts almost all from the Japanese suppliers, but the second one aimed at nearly 100 per cent local parts procurement. In practice, approximately 60 per cent of the total parts used was local in the second design prototyping. Among the Japanese suppliers who participated in the first prototyping, those who maintained the local affiliation (about 60 per cent of them) were asked to locally start the mass production of their parts under their own initiative. While both prototypes were all tested in Japan, everything was done locally from the trial production in facilities. They tried to make commitment in supplier selection from Japan, as the staff at the local production base will just repeat what the suppliers say after showing them the specifications of the parts required, reflecting their lack of capability to judge the suppliers capability.

As for the process engineering, press dies and outer sheet metal are procured in Japan, while interiors are procured locally. The press dies for exterior, which must be finished beautifully, need to be procured in Japan. In this case, any modification to the dies is done on a business trip base from Japan. They dispatch not only the die designers but also those in charge of processing. As for injection dies, larger ones (such as instrumental panels) are transferred from Japan or Taiwan, and smaller ones such as bumpers are procured locally.

3.3.2 The Effect of Product Development Capabilities on International Configuration

The centralization of development organization permits the active use of capabilities accumulated in the development department in the home country. In the case of Model Y, the development was carried out in the same organization as the domestic models without the establishment of a specialized project team. This organizational structure was adopted based on their prediction that having the overseas department as a separate organization would hamper the acquisition of cooperative assistance from each functional department related to development such as design and evaluation. It was reported that even in the development of Model Y without a special project team, there were some delays in the schedule in the areas of design and process engineering attributed to the tendency seen in each department to neglect the overseas operations and to be reluctant to cooperate. It is presumed that it would have been even more difficult to gain cooperation from the domestic side of operation, if the department was organizationally separate.

The effect of the accumulated capabilities in the process engineering department based on the past experiences in development is also noteworthy. As the Model Y was the first overseas specific model that they developed anew, the process engineering department for overseas operations at that time was not familiar with overlapping problem-solving. The role of this department had previously been limited to the overseas exploitation of the existing model produced in Japan, which only required replicating the established manufacturing process of the vehicle, of which the design had already been finalized. This time, however, they could not effectively handle the consecutive changes made in design in the process. Or conversely, the effect of having development in Japan must have been even higher, if the process engineering department had accumulated the capability in the overlapping style development pertaining to overseas production.

3.4 The Strategy Implementation and Its Effect on Environment and Capability

For the development of locally adapted products, the maintenance and further extension of the rapid and highly flexible development process that takes advantage of the high "integrated problem-solving capability" in Japan is indispensable. However, this strength in the home country, which was facilitated by the high capability of suppliers and die makers in Japan, adversely contributed to the development of local production capability in overseas.

3.4.1 Simplification of Development Process

If the product development cost was high, the development of the local specific vehicle will be a futile discussion. While the Japanese makers had maintained product development with relatively small cost, they further realized the low-cost development process for the development of specific models for overseas through its innovation.

In the development of Model Y, for instance, the dies and tools for prototyping were not manufactured in order to cut down development cost. Because the policy was not to use the prototype dies, the designing had been proceeded with the utmost deliberateness from the start in an attempt to concentrate design changes in the early stages of development. This type of managerial attempts are often called as "front-loading" of problem-solving in the product development (Thomke and Fujimto 1998). From the second design prototyping, the manufacturing of the prototype parts was carried out in mass production facilities. As a consequence, the second prototyping practically became trial production, and they succeeded in shortening the total lead time despite the lengthened time-period to reach the stage of the second prototyping. Although the lead time for Model Y was 3 months longer than that for other models in the domestic market, it is actually short considering the fact that it was for the first local specific vehicle.

With the success in the new development process that minimized the use of prototyping facilities, this process with less trial production has been transferred back to the development of vehicles for the domestic market. The chief engineer in the development of Model Y, has later been engaged in the development of the model for the domestic market.

3.4.2 Overcoming the Rigidity to Capability Transfer

In maintaining the organizational pattern which has supported the product development capability of the Japanese companies, the satisfaction of the localization policy for parts as well as the adoption of the design strategy which entails the development of the local specific parts have been the strong restraints. In particular, the fact that the automakers have been dependent on the capability of suppliers as indicated by their involvement in development has created some problems in developing parts specifically for the local market.

In cases in which there are joint-venture parts suppliers in the local market, this does not seem to present a major problem. In developing Model Y, they attempted to maximize technological transfer even in the cases of Black Box Parts in order to promote the localization of parts. Yet, when local suppliers highly invested by Japanese suppliers were available such as the suppliers of shock absorbers, springs, and tires, Firm B let the local production base to select a local Japanese supplier while providing them with the specification. Firm B has also asked their Japanese suppliers to send their engineers to the local site and make drawings physically at local site. They persuaded their suppliers to carry out the Black Box Parts operation with the transfer of engineers by mentioning the advantage of this contract, that were the easier follow-up after the initiation of production and the accelerated transfer of parts technology.

However, when there is no local joint venture but only technologically affiliated partners available in the local market, there is a need for the transformation of Black Box Parts to Detail Controlled Parts in localizing parts production. In the case of Model X, although Firm A holds a simplified drawing, all other information not present in the drawing as well as the detailed drawings required for production are retained by the parts suppliers, which did not therefore lead to the accumulation of know-how and knowledge sufficient for designing these particular parts on Firm A side. Taking outside mirrors as an example case, Firm A transferred the drawing which Firm A asked its supplier to draw, since there was no designer in Firm A who could draw them. In addition, there are cases when they ask their parts suppliers to give technological assistance to their local makers, which sometimes become problematic. For instance, a Black Box Parts supplier conducted technological assistance to a local supplier in the development of mufflers. The mere transfer of drawing, however, failed to transfer the latent know-how, which resulted in the low silencing effect of the final products.

In such cases of technological assistance, parts suppliers cannot recover the cost by parts sales after full-scale production is started, which diminishes their merits. Therefore, their incentive to engage in technological assistance becomes inevitably small, which has tended to result in the relatively low local capability compared to the cases in which parts are produced locally through overseas investment. Thus, in the cases of technological affiliation, the development of the parts which had originally been the Black Box Parts appeared to present numerous problems, often calling for confirmation and modification in the stage of trial production. In developing the local specific parts, their organizational patterns that entailed supplier's involvement in development rather presented obstacles under the condition of the localization policy for parts.

Even with the Detail Controlled Parts, there are cases in which the knowledge pertaining to design was accumulated in both parts and die suppliers, which occasionally led to problems in localizing production. When the Detail Controlled Parts was adopted, parts suppliers also occasionally made modifications in design, taking into account the manufacturability at the trial production stage in Japan. When localized, the know-how of the suppliers will no longer be available. Furthermore, when die suppliers are localized, problems are likely to arise in the manufacturing process eventually, as the local suppliers will only produce what is drawn in the given designs. This is also attributed to the history that die suppliers have solved their problems in manufacturing by themselves in Japan. In the case of Model Y, there have been many instances in which drawings and the products did not match in practice when they tried to apply the parts used in the old models in Japan. This necessitated some alteration in their facilities in order to match the tools and facilities to the drawings. Similarly, this was due to the fact that delicate modifications were made at the actual work site in the production of the previous model. While the suppliers and die makers' own accumulation of knowledge constituted the strength in the home country, which was facilitated by the established organizational pattern of integrated problem-solving, it adversely contributed to the local production in overseas.

3.5 The Asian Crisis and the Manifestation of "Over-Adaptation"

3.5.1 Asia Crisis and Problems of Asia Car

Despite some fluctuation, the automotive market in Indonesia had shown a constant growth, and the demand for automotive had started to penetrate into the middle class in addition to the limited high-income class. Model X and model Y have been provided to such middle class as the home-use cars (mini-vans) that fit the local specific needs at a relatively low cost. In this sense, these models can be evaluated as the product design strategy with a relatively good balance between the adaptation to the local demand pattern and the achievement of scope economy and scale economy through the international sharing of parts and platforms.

However, the acute fall of Rupiah in September 1997 following the outbreak of Asian currency crisis, coupled with the domestic political crisis that started from the riot in Jakarta in May 1998, drastically shrunk the automotive market, driving many of the local auto makers and parts makers into the discontinuation of operation. Many dealers' outlets were destroyed in the riot, and with the overseas Chinese population running out of the country for safety, the local business became in fact paralyzed. The demand from the middle class, which had been the driver engine of the automotive market, almost ceased to exist, resulting in a large drop in yearly demand to 60 thousand units (less than one sixth of the previous year). The political confusion has continued for 1999, and a sign of recovery in the automotive demand has not been observed except for the relatively stable demand from the upper class. It is showing a sharp contrast with the Thai market, although in the same ASEAN market, which has already been back on a growth curve since 1999.

Following the drastic contraction of the local market, the problems inherent in the model X and model Y, which are the low-cost cars based on the old platform, fit to the local needs in Indonesia, became manifested. The problems include, first of all, the limited possibility of improving price-competitiveness by currency depreciation, because of the models' low local content (below 50 per cent for model X) compared to Thai and Malaysian counterparts, magnifying the effect of currency fall on the cost-up of parts import.

The second problem is that the adaptation of design locally fit to the Indonesian market (or Southeast Asia) in the cases of model X and model Y has precluded the export to other regions (such as Europe, North America, Middle-East and Oceania) from a non-price competitive perspective. In short, these can be consequently regarded as the cases of "over-adaptation" to the local market (Fujimoto 1999). In the case of model X, for example, as the export of complete car products had been sluggish, despite the increased export of engines to Japan, the decrease in the domestic demand directly led to the drastic fall in the domestic production as a result. This is in contrast to the pick-up trucks produced in Thailand by Toyota, Mitsubishi Motors, Isuzu, Nissan and Mazda, and to the fact that the passenger car of Honda, "Accord," has been exported to the Australian market which has been showing a robust growth in recent years. These pick-up trucks or Accords turned out to be fortunate cases in which the models had a stronger character as the "global model" which can be highly evaluated in different region.

3.5.2 Manifestation of Over-adaptation

The "Old Platform Derivative" strategy, represented by X and Y, had been the most appropriate strategic selection in the Indonesian market prior to the Asian Crisis, which appears to have been reflected in the market performance. Moreover, in the development of such models, the Japanese auto companies seem to have adopted flexible development process, free from the development routine and design standards of the products for home market. Ironically, this flexibility in international product development, however, appears to have resulted in the generation of a model overly adapted to the local demands. It can be said that this dilemma of flexible development process generates inflexible (marketability) models became manifested by the Asian Crisis.

At present, some Japanese companies, including A, seem to be aiming at the development of a model with design and technology content that can be successful in other regions (such as Japan) as the next generation of Asian models. There is undoubtedly the consideration gained from the experience of the current model which placed excessive focus on the local demands.

3.5.3 Necessity of Dynamic View

It is nevertheless misdirected to dismiss the problem of over-adaptation manifest in the Asian Crisis as a simple miss-judgement of strategy. As long as "the limit of rationality" of present companies is presupposed, it is not realistic to consider that the present condition had been predictable prior to 1997 when the Asian markets were booming. It is not until they fell into the condition of "over-adaptation" as a result of the Asian Crisis that they start the designing and marketing attempts to achieve a deeper level of compatibility between global marketability and local adaptation. It is not reasonable to think that the "over-adaptation" situation had been predictable before the environmental change of Asian Crisis occurred.

As seen in the above, companies that face the uncertain environment with radical changes experience numerous situations of "under-adaptation" and "over-adaptation" in the short-term. In the longterm, they gradually become more capable of balancing the local adaptation and global efficiency by transforming the design strategy in a pass-dependent manner, and accumulating the dynamic capabilities through such transformation, having been learning from these experiences. At the same time, the customer needs in each country also become more sophisticated, which lead to the global convergence in some aspects, while retaining notable regional difference in other aspects. Thus, the essence of global product development in the automotive industry cannot be grasped correctly unless the dynamic strategic model is applied, which explains that the strategic selection, environment, and organizational capability *co-evolve* while influencing one another.

4 Conclusion

In this article, we have indicated the importance of the dynamic perspective in considering global strategy. By looking at the Indonesian case, in particular, the significance of a pass-dependent organizational capability in the adaptation to local environment as well as the vulnerability of the over-adaptation against environmental change have been clarified. The followings are the summary of discussion in this paper.

1. The ASEAN automobile markets are relatively small, diversified, and constrained by relatively low income levels of the customers. Their supplier base is also different from that of the home country.
2. Such conditions create a trade-off between local adaptation and international standardization that the product developers of the auto firms have to balance.
3. In product design strategies, one of the most commonly used one is a derivative product from an old platform. It requires sophisticated product

development organization and capabilities, but may achieve a good balance between the two forces.

4. In resource configuration strategy of the Japanese automakers in Asia, even compared with their North American and European operations, product development for Asian cars tends to be centralized in the technological centers in Japan. Certain problem solving capabilities are moved to the local facilities, where local information is "sticky," though.
5. Such choices of product design strategies may be formed through a series of path-dependent (or emergent) strategic choices, rather than a deliberate decision making based on foresights.
6. The strategic choices, once they are made, may then affect the patters of evolution of both market needs and organizational capabilities. While the derivative approach based on the old platform requires sophisticated product development capabilities, the strategic choice forms new capability suitable for its strategy through the execution of it.
7. Sometimes, the cumulative effects of strategic formation and market evolution, together with unexpected market changes such as the Asian economic crisis, may result in the problem of "over-adaptation." It is difficult for the firms to avoid this kind of problems.
8. Through the experiences of adaptation, over-adaptation and lack of adaptation over time, learning organizations may accumulate certain dynamic capabilities in the long run, by which the firm can re-adjust the product strategies quickly to the environmental changes.

These findings show the necessity of dynamic framework to grasp the global-local trade-off rather than static one. In dynamic perspective, firms select the product strategy cumulatively, with repeating the failures of under-adaptation and over-adaptation, which is paralleled by the evolution of market needs and local production capability. Such dynamic point of view might be crucial in looking at global strategy.

References

Arthur B. (1989) Competing technologies, increasing returns, and lock-in by historical events. *Economic Journal*, Vol.99, March: 116–131.

Asanuma B. (1989) Manufacturer-supplier relationships in Japan and the concept of relation-specific skill. *Journal of Japanese and International Economics*, 1–30.

Bartlett C. A. and Ghoshal S. (1989) *Managing Across Borders: The Transnational Solution*. Boston. MA: Harvard Business School Press.

Clark K. B. (1985) The interaction of design hierarchies and market concepts in technological evolution. *Research Policy*, 235–251.

Clark K. B. and Fujimoto T. (1991) *Product Development Performance: Strategy, Organization, and Performance in the World Auto Industry*. Boston, MA: Harvard Business School Press.

Cusumano M. and Nobeoka K. (1998) *Thinking beyond Lean.* New York, NY: The Free Press.

Doner R. F. (1991) *Driving A Bargain: Automobile Industrialization and Japanese Firms in Southeast Asia.* Berkley and Los Angels, CA: University of California Press.

Douglas S. P. and Wind Y. (1987) The myth of globalization. *Columbia Journal of World Business*. Vol. 22, Winter: 19–29.

Dunning J. H. (1981) *International production and the multinational enterprise.* London; Boston : Allen & Unwin.

Fujimoto T. (1999) *Evolution of Production System at Toyota.* New York, NY: Oxford University Press.

Ghoshal S. (1987) Global strategy: an organizing framework. *Strategic Management Journal,* Vol. 8: 425–440.

Jequier N. (ed.) (1976) *Appropriate Technology.* OECD.

Nikkan Jidosha Shinbunsha (1999) *Jidosha Sangyo Handobukku. (Auto industry handbook).* Tokyo, Japan: Nikkan Jidosha Shinbunsha.

LTCBR (1997) ASEAN jidousha sangyo: buhin sangyo no kyosoryoku to nikkei buhin meika no sinshutsu. (ASEAN automobile industry: the competitiveness of component industry and expansion of Japanese suppliers.) *Soken Tyosa,* May 1997 no.72

Leonard-Barton D. (1992) Core capabilities and core rigidity; a paradox in managing new product development. *Strategic Management Journal,* Vol. 13: 111–125.

Levitt T. (1983) The globalization of markets. *Harvard Business Review,* Vol. 61, May–June: 92–102.

Mintzberg H. and Waters J. A. (1985) Of strategies, deliberate and emergent. *Strategic Management Journal,* 246–275.

Porter M. E. (1986) *Competition in Global Industries.* Boston, MA: Harvard Business School Press.

Prahalad C. K. and Doz. Y. (1987) *The Multinational Mission.* New York, NY: The Free Press.

Sinclair S. (1983) *The World Car: The Future of the Automobile Industry.* New York, NY: Facts on File, Inc.

Takeuchi H. and Porter M. E. (1986) Three roles of international marketing. in Porter M. E. (ed.), *Competition in Global Industries.* Boston, MA: Harvard Business School Press.

Teece D. J., Pisano G. and Shuen A. (1997) Dynamic capabilities and strategic management. *Strategic Management Journal,* 509–533.

Thomke S. and Fujimoto T. (1998) The effect of "front-loading" problem-solving on product development performance. Harvard Business School Working Paper #98–10.

Vernon R. (1971) *Sovereignty at Bay: The Multinational Spread of U.S. Enterprise.* New York,NY: Basic Books.

von Hippel E. (1994) Sticky information and the locus of problem solving: implications for innovation. *Management Science,* 429–439.

13 Taiwanese Technology Transfer to China: The Automobile Industry as a Case Study

Cheng-Cherng Chen
National Taiwan University

1 The Current Situation in the Chinese Automobile Industry

1.1 The Proportion of Buses

In 1953, the first Chinese automobile plant was opened. From this time to the early 1980's, trucks were heavily manufactured and very few buses and passenger cars were manufactured. For example, as shown in Table 13–1, in 1983, 57.15% of vehicles produced were trucks, and the percentage of buses was only 2.6% while the percentage of passenger cars was a mere 2.5%. The reason is that military and infrastructure needs were emphasized in this period.

Since the late 1980's, the situation has been different. The manufacture of buses and passenger cars is encouraged, and truck manufacturing has declined relatively. As shown in Table 13–1, in 1998, the percentage of vehicles manufactured which were trucks declined to 29.7%, while the percentage of buses rose to 22.5%, and the percentage of passenger cars rose further to 31.2%. The reason is that China is freeing its economy, and the society is becoming richer, and demand for buses and passenger cars is gradually increasing.

1.2 The Passenger Cars

As shown in Table 13–1, vehicles are classified into 13 different kinds. Passenger car and buses are two categories which are increasingly being demanded. It is well known, that the technical level of engineering required for truck and passenger car is extremely different. You may have the ability to manufacture trucks, but this does not imply that you can manufacture passenger cars. In order to satisfy the increasing demand for passenger cars, China has to raise its engineering standards.

Table 13–1. Vehicle Classification and Volume

Unit: vehicle (%)

Classification	Volume					
	1983	1984	Λ	1996	1997	1998
Trucks	137,100 (57.15)	179,846 (56.8)		537,673 (36.5)	465,098 (29.4)	483,419 (29.7)
Buses	6,211 (2.6)	6,990 (2.02)		267,236 (18.1)	317,948 (20.1)	366,553 (22.5)
Passengers	6,046 (2.5)	6,010 (1.9)		391,099 (26.5)	487,695 (30.9)	507,861 (31.2)
M 13.Specially equipped 14.Chasis	62.263 (26.0)	85,348 (27)		167,651 (11.4)	178,644 (11.3)	195,653 (12.0)
Total	239,886 (100)	316,367 (100)		1,474,905 (100)	1,582,628 (100)	1,629,026 (100)

Source: China Automotive Technical Research Center: 1999 China Automotive Industry Yearbook, 1999 (Aug.), p. 5.

Here we note that the light commercial car which belongs to the category of buses is the object of our study in our paper. We shall explore it later (see 2.5).

As restricted by the Chinese Government, the number of passenger car makers is six, namely the so called "Three Bigs and Three Smalls." The details of these Three Bigs and Three Smalls are shown in Table 13–2. But aside from this. I will make two remarks.

1. As will be discussed later, the Chinese Automobile Industrial Policy emphasizes that in order to enjoy the merit of economies of scale and product quality, before 1995 no new licence was given to produce passenger cars. It stuck with the six companies. In October 1997, the Chinese Government permitted a new passenger car maker: Shanghai General Motors (SGM) which is a joint venture company formed by the Chinese Shanghai Automotive Industrial Co. (SAIC) and American General Motors (GM). Because of the importance of GM in the world automobile industry and the Chinese government's intention to balance the bargaining power of European (VW and Citroen) and American (Chrysler and GM) companies, the Chinese government gave permission to GM. The Three Bigs are now the Four Bigs.

2. Originally Guangzhou Peugeot Auto Co. was a joint venture of Guangzhou Auto and Peugeot. In May 1998, Japanese Honda Co. replaced Peugeot. Now here are two Japanese companies among "The Four Bigs and the Three Smalls."

Table 13–2. The Status Quo of Chinese Passenger Car Manufacturers

	Company	Partner (Share %)	Content	Model
The Four Bigs	FAW–VW Auto	VW(40)	1988 (May), Audi TC [1989 Audi and VW: M&A], 1991(Feb), VW JV	Audi 100, Golf, Jetta, Passat
	Shenlong	Citroen(30) Dongfeng(70)	1992 (May),JV	Citroen ZX Series (1.3–1.6)
	SVW	VW(50)	1984.10.10,JV 1985.09.01,Production start	Santana
	SGM	GM(50)	1997 (Oct.), JV 1999 (Apr.) production start	Buick/Regal 100,000 /year
The Three Smalls	Tianjien Auto	Daihatsu Toyota	1986 Charade Knock-down 1998 TJ 7131 U (Toyota Engine 8A–FE)	TJ Series (Charade)
	Guangzhou –Honda Auto	Honda(50)	1998 (May), JV 1999 Production Start	Accord 30,000/year
	Beijing Auto	Chrysler(31)	1993 (Dec.), AMC JV AMC and Chrysler: M&A	BJ 2021 (Cherokee)

*JV: Joint Venture, TC: Technical Cooperation
Source: 1999 China Automotive Industry Yearbook, 1999 (Aug.), and interview

2 A Profile of the Fujian Southeast Motor Co. (SEM)

2.1 The Joint Venture

Legally the Taiwanese investor is not allowed by the Taiwan government to invest a large amount of capital in China (Figure 13–1). Due to this reason, the Taiwanese investor used to have to invest in China through roundabout methods. The Taiwanese "China Motor Corporation (hereafter referred to as CMC)" is not allowed to invest in China[1]. It owns a 100% share of the "Hwa-Wai Co." located

[1]The Taiwanese "China Motor Corporation, Ltd." (hereafter CMC) was founded by Dr. T. L. Yen in June 1969. In October 1970 CMC signed a technical licencing agreement with Japanese Mitsubishi Motor Co., and in June 1986 CMC、 Mitsubishi Motor Co. and Mitsubishi Trading

in the U.K. Virgin Islands. "Hwa-Wei Co." and the Chinese "Fuzhou Motors Co." on Sept. 19, 1995 established a joint venture company. It is called the "Fujian Southeast Motor Co. (hereafter referred as SEM)."

The capital share of SEM held by Hwa-Wei Co. is 50%, and that of Fuzhou Motors Co. is also 50%.

Figure 13–1. Location of SEM Plant by Fuzhou (Chin-Kou) City

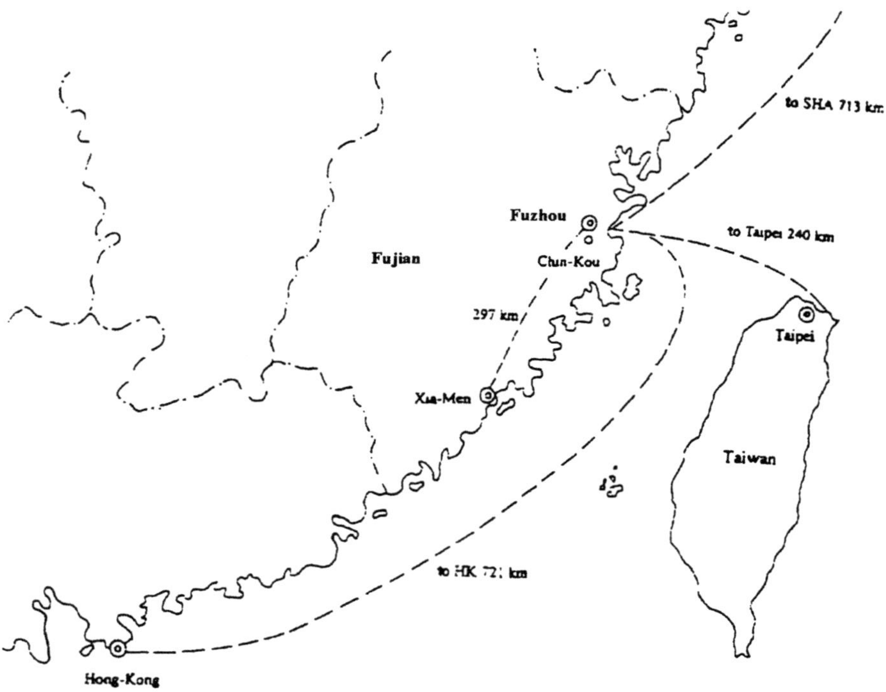

Co. became a joint venture company of which CMC owns 75%, Mitsubishi Motor Co. 19% and Mitsubishi Trading Co. 6%. Since 1981 Chairperson Mm. Vivian Wu Yen has directed the company and Mr. Kenneth K. T. Yen is the Executive Director of Board. CMC has a managerial phylosophy of "Harmony、Innovation and Excellence in life" and holds of the principle of "The Customer is King".CMC has manufactured a big variety of light commercial cars and sedans using Mitsubishi Motor Co.'s model and Mitsubishi models CMC has modified. Among these both Delica and Freeca models are the first manufactured in China. I am grateful to CMC members of Vice General Manager Wen–cheng Hwang, Manager Shih–ho Chang, Vice Manager L. C. Lin, Mr. Michael C. D. Cheng and Director H. Y. Chu for valuable conversations and providing unpublished material.

2.2 The Board of Directors

The Board of Directors of SEM consists of 12 directors. 6 directors are asigned by Fuzhou Motors Co., and the other 6 are asigned by Hwa-Wei. Chairman of the board of directors is appointed by Fuzhou Motors Co., and the vice-chairman is appointed by Hwa-Wei. Such a distribution of board members is a general pattern regulated by the Chinese Government's "Implementation of the Investment Protection Law for Taiwanese (Dec. 1997)."

2.3 The Chief Executive Officer

The general manager is appointed by Hwa-Wei. Vice general managers are to be 2 to 3 persons, and among them Fuzhou Motor Co. recommends 1to 2 persons and Haw-Wei recommends 1 person.

Aside from the managers of the engineering and financial departments which are appointed by Fuzhou Motor Co., the managers of the other six departments are appointed by Hwa-Wei.

2.4 Technical Cooperation

The Taiwanese "China Motor Corporation (CMC)" (Hwa-Wei) has many years experience in manufacturing small and medium-size trucks and passenger cars. Therefore, it is already in a position to transfer technology to SEM.

2.5 Products

As we stated before, the Chinese Automobile Industrial Policy was to grant no other licences to new passenger car makers before 1995. For this reason, SEM manufactures two light commercial cars, the Delica (DN 6470) for 11 persons and the Freeca for 8 persons. In fact, the Taiwanese CMC has manufactured the Delica and Freeca for many years. Therefore from the point of view of engineering experience, cost containment and market demand, the selection of these two models was wise. But the final ambition of SEM is to manufacture passenger cars.

3 Technology Transfer

3.1 Definition

A process of transferring a technology is from one place (firm) to another place (firm), is defined as a technology transfer.

A technology transfer consists of not only engineering, but also management. The scope of it depends on the technical agreement upon which both licenser and licensee agree. The technical agreement regulates all matters concerning the product and service to be licensed, such as the exclusivity of manufacturing and distribution rights, the area in which the product may be sold, technical documentation, personnel assistance, quality control, modifications and improvements, product liability, royalties, the use of trade marks, and trade secrecy.

3.2 General Background

I wish to explain generally why the Taiwanese automobile industrial technology can be transferred to Fujian province. The points are as follows:

1. Fujian is a poor area: Geographically 80% of Fujian province is covered by mountains and the rest is poor land for agriculture. Owing to the poverty people in this land have historically emigrated to South East Asia Taiwan and other areas. The people of Fujian were a great source of overseas Chinese.
2. Backwardness of industry: Due to its poverty the industries have not been developed in the last hundred years. Fujian has no well built infrastructure, modern electrical power plants and integrated mills etc..
3. The opening of this Special Economic Zone (SEZ) was delayed: Since 1980 China has launched many Economic Free Zones, such as Shenzhen, Shanghai, Guangzhou, etc., and the economy of these areas has been growing rapidly. Fujian province was opened as a SEZ in 1990. The delay in opening means less development of the province.
4. The close relationship: Taiwanese ancestor mainly came from Fujian province. Both Taiwanese and Fujianese have a common language (dialect) which is not spoken by people in other Chinese provinces. At the same time they have a common culture, custom and religion. In this sense Taiwanese and Fujianese feel that they are like a family and work together easily.
5. CMC is a qualified car-maker: CMC was founded in 1969. In 1970 CMC got a technology transfer from Mitsubishi Motor Co.. Since then CMC has manufactured a large variety of light commercial cars and sedans. CMC is qualified to transfer both engineering and management technology to SEM.
6. CMC has initiative: Since CMC has shown initiative both by a car maker SEM and the suppliers who are coming from Taiwan to SEM, SEM could

manufacture a car which satisfies the conditions of "Quality, Cost, Delivery and Speed."

3.3 Car Manufacturer

3.3.1 The Technical Agreement

The content of technology transfer depends on the technical agreement which defines the rights and the obligations of both licensor and licensee. As I am going to discuss technology transfer, I have to review first the technical agreement.

In Aug. 8, 1998 CMC (licensor) and SEM (licensee) signed a technical agreement. Here I emphasize four important articles as follows:

1. Definition
   - A. Licensed Products: SEM MOTOR VEHICLES mean all kinds of vehicles, identical in specifications with CMC MOTOR VEHICLES, including the light commercial car DELICA series manufactured with technical assistance rendered by CMC pursuant to this agreement.
   - B. Import Parts: Parts and components SEM imports from CMC for the manufacture of SEM MOTOR VEHICLES.
   - C. Locally Manufactured parts: parts, components and accessories of SEM MOTOR VEHICLES which are manufactured by SEM or purchased from local parts suppliers for SEM.
   - D. Replacement Parts: Parts, components and accessories of SEM MOTOR VEHICLES which SEM imports from CMC for the purpose of repairing SEM MOTOR VEHICLES.

   Concerning to the above mentioned definitions, I make the following remarks:
   - A. Concerning "Licensed Products." So called "SEM MOTOR VEHICLES mean all kinds of vehicles" is restricted to the "DELICA series" light commercial car. If SEM wants to build another different model of cars or trucks, it is necessary to sign another agreement.
   - B. Concerning "Import Parts." So called "parts and components SEM imports from CMC" means import parts (and components) from non-CMC firms are not "Import Parts." This concept directly concerns the amount of running royalty.
   - C. Concerning "Replacement Parts": "Parts which SEM imports from CMC for repair..." does not mention that SEM imports from non-CMC firms. Here "non-CMC" includes SEM and part suppliers.

2. Manufacturing Facilities

A. CMC is prepared, with respect to SEM's factory facilities including manufacturing equipment necessary for the manufacture of SEM MOTOR VEHICLES, to render consulting services to SEM as it desires.
B. CMC agrees, upon request in writing and insofar as SEM deems necessary to do so after consulted with SEM, to sell to the latter such machineries as tools, jigs, gauges, dies.

3. Technical and Manufacturing Information
   When requested to do so by SEM, CMC will furnish SEM with the following technical and manufacturing information related to SEM MOTOR VEHICLES:
   Engineering Parts List
   Production Parts List

4. Engineering Personnel
   A. CMC will dispatch its qualified engineering and production personnel to SEM's works to assist SEM for the purpose of instructing and training its employees who are engaged in the manufacturing of SEM MOTOR VEHICLES.
   B. CMC agrees to admit SEM's qualified engineering and production personnel to the workshops and departments concerned in CMC's works in Taiwan in which SEM MOTOR VEHICLES are manufactured, for the purpose of receiving instruction and training in every aspect of technical knowledge connected with the manufacture of SEM MOTOR VEHICLES.

The content of the above mentioned articles: manufacturing facilities, technical and manufacturing information, engineering personnel, are a standard form and there has been no any defective. The important thing is that how to exercise the contents of the articles. The exercise is a kind of art.

3.3.2 Car Manufacturer and Part Suppliers System

The vertical integration of raw material, parts and car firms is referred to as the "Car Manufacturer and Part Suppliers System" in the automobile industry. In order to control quality, cost and delivery on one hand, and also meet the Chinese government's requirement of localization on the other hand, SEM requires more than 61 parts suppliers. Among them 30 suppliers (Table 13–3) which came from Taiwan are concentrated in a district very close to the car manufacturer assembly plant (Figure 13–2). These Taiwanese suppliers are building modern plants which are larger with much more automation than the mother plants in Taiwan. They also transfer engineering technology and management skills to their own firm in China.

The Taiwanese suppliers accept the car manufacturer's directions concerning quality assurance, cost minimization and exact delivery etc.. They are also royal to

Table 13–3. Taiwanese Suppliers in Fujian (Chin–kou) Province

	Co. Name in China	Co. Name in Taiwan	Products
1	Lien-Hon	Yo-Lien	Seat,
2	Shia-Tzon	Shia-Shang	Muffler Ass'y, Tank, Pulley,
3	Spicer	ROC-Spicer	Real Axel,
		Shia-Shin	
4	Don-Nan	Jui-li	Body Parts press,
		China Motor Co	
5	Fu-Shan	Wu-Shan	Chasis Frame Ass'y, Panels, (Dies&Jigs,)
6	Mei-Shen	Mei-Shen	Air Condition System
7	Chung–Tuan	Chung-Tuan	Electric Cluster Ass'y, Combination Switch,
8	Ta-I	Ta-I	Lock Ass'y,
9	Shu-Zue-Shin	Shu-Zue-Shin	Clutch, Speed Cable,
10	Tai-Chuan	Tai-Chuan	Starter Motor, Generator, Instrument Meter,
11	Tong-Ing	Chon-Zu	Panel Press,
12	Shan-E	Shan-E	Brake Pump, Water Pump,
13	Yuan-Shien	Yuan-Hon	Al. Wheel, Steel Wheel,
14	Shin-Yu	Tai-Yu Elect.	Cable, Harness,
15	Chang-Yu	Yin-Shie	Door Trim,
16	Yin-Shie	Yin-Shie	Door Trim,
17	Shuan-Yu	Shuan-Yu	Press (small and medium),
18	Ho-Shin	Ho-Shin	Brake Parts, Brake Oil Pipe,
19	Right-Way	Right-Way	Piston, Connecting Rod,
20	Yin-Ming	Yin-Ming	Nut, Screw, Bolt,
21	Fu-Rubber-Plastic	Chung-Kuang	Rubber Products,
22	Zu-Shin	Zu-Chan	Engine Mounting, Fusible Insulator, Packings,
23	Fu-Yu (Rubber)	Tai-Yu (Rubber)	Rubber Horse, Sponge Extruded Products,
24	Fu-Chuan	Fu-Pen	Rubber Parts,
25	Ho-Shen	Ho-Shen	Hold Carpet, Held Lining, Rear Packing Trim,
26	Ta-E	Ta-E	Lamp, Bulb,
27	Tung-Yang	Tung-Yang	Bumper, Fender, Hood, Instrument Meter,
28	Chon-Zu&ChuChan	Tung-Chan	Engine Mounting, Sponge Extruded Products,
29	Chuan-Shin	Chuan-Shin	Seat & Accessory Parts, Steering Column,
30	Ming-Fang	Shin-Chang	Safety Belt, Door Lock, Window Regultor,
	Xia-Men Shih-Lin	Shih-Lin	Starter Motor, Wiper Motor,
	Proton Electronic	Taiwan Proton	Horn, Music Instrument,
	Chien Sung	Taiwan Matsushita	SPK, Radio, Motor,
	Xia-Men Kai-Fa	Kai-Fa	Shock Absorber,
	Xia-Men Shin-Yuan	Shin-Tung	Air Cleaner, Oil Filter,
	Xia-Men Lee-Yen	Taiwan-Lee-Yen	Piston, Piston Ring,
	Xia-Men Chien-Hong	Hong-Li	Nut, Screw, Bolt, Press Parts,
	Xia-Men Chien-Show	Chien-Shen	Back Mirrors,
	Xia-Men Cheng-Shin	Cheng-Shin	Tire,

Source: CMC (1997), Yulon Enterprise Group, Don-Nan (SEM) Automobile Case (Apr. 23, 1997), p.31. Companies from 1 through 30 are by SEM area in Chin-Kou.

the car manufacturer in terms of long-term business contact. Therefore these suppliers are not only vendors, but also partners who share the same destiny as the car manufacturer. These Taiwanese suppliers in China and SEM come together to form a so called "Car Manufacturer and Part Suppliers System."

Aside from the above mentioned 30 suppliers, there is also 31 suppliers coming from Taiwan which are distributed in the Xiamen area (Figure 13–2) · Shanghai city, Chiangsu and Tzechiang provinces. These 61 suppliers together are the basic suppliers to SEM.

The above mentioned pattern we can also find in Japan and Korea. But in the SEM case, it is worth noting the following three points which are different from those in Japan and Korea:

1. A Taiwanese car manufacturer (CMC) and 30 Taiwanese suppliers went to China simultaneously in the same year.
2. The 30 suppliers are concentrated in a district very close to the car manufacturer assembly plant (SEM).
3. Both car manufacturer and the suppliers share the same destiny, therefore they work together very closely.

Figure 13–2. SEM and Its Suppliers' Plant Distribution

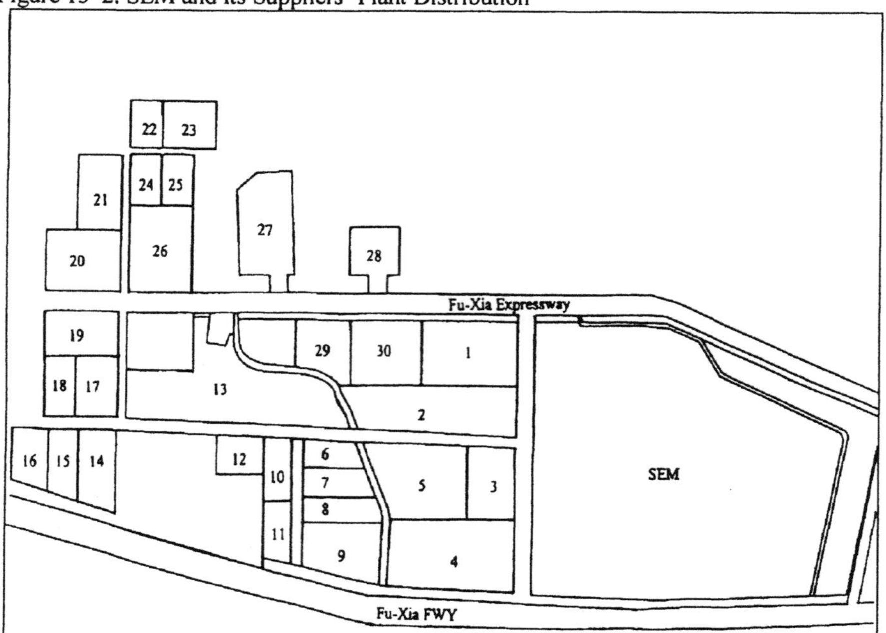

3.3.3 "Q.C.D.S." and localization

To meet the requirements of satisfactory quality (Q), minimized cost (C), just in time delivery (D) and speedy development (S) are the precondition of survival in the automobile industry. SEM and the suppliers are devoted to doing that in terms of technology transfer.

For the purposes of raising up the level of engineering, attracting foreign capital, transferring high skill management and creating employment etc., the Chinese government asks car manufacturers to localize car manufacture and sets the minimum rate of local content (RLC) to be 80%, that is, 80% of parts and components must be manufactured in China.

The RLC of a vehicle is defined in China as follows:

$$\text{RLC} = \frac{\text{total price of the full set of import parts - price of imported parts}}{\text{total price of the full set of import parts}}$$

Here the price is based on CIF.

Due to the requirement to manufacture locally parts and components, SEM has a localization schedule (Table 13–4). A manufactured part shares even a small percentage of RLC, but each part should be locally manufactured. Adding together many small percentage of RLC will become a big percentage of RLC. The schedule consists of 3 years from 1997 to 1999, and each year is divided into 4 quarters. In each quarter a list of parts and components which will be localized have been given and the RLC of each part and component also has been shown. For instance in Spring (Q_1) 1997, the RLC of weather strips is 0.59%. In each year we have 4 subtotals for RLC which corresponds to each quarter. Each year has a total and a cumulative RLC. For instance, in 1997 the subtotals of RLC are 6.098%, 28.46%, 6.098% and 3.751% respectively. The total and the cumulative RLC are 44.477% and 44.477% respectively in 1997, and 23% and 78.772% respectively in 1999.

Three years have gone, by end the car manufacturer and the suppliers have constructed their plants, and the car and parts are manufactured respectively. At the end of 1999, the RLC is over the scheduled 78.772% in 1999 and reaches 81.97%.

We should reemphasize here that due to a Taiwanese car manufacturer (CMC) and the Taiwanese suppliers going to China together, the technology transfer has been simultaneously given, therefore the requirements of "Q.C.D.S." and RLC was reached.

Table 13–4. Localization Schedule of Delica

	1997		1998		1999	
	Item	RLC	Item	RLC	Item	RLC
Q1	Weather strip	59	Front beam	1.184	Engine assembly and Relative parts	23.00
	Clutch cable	0.08	FrontPanelAssembly	0.20		
	Glass	0.97	RearPanel Assembly	0.419		
	Mirror	0.41	Rear axle	2.20		
	Battery	0.17	Fuel tank	0.39		
	Tool, (Garage) jack	0.18	WeatherStrip,FronDoor	0.053		
	Floor covering	0.09	Central door slide	0.249		
	Air cleaner	0.20	Floor board liner	0.031		
	Oil Filter	0.01	Window washer	0.14		
	Tyre	1.29	Boost pumps	0.44		
	Radio	0.65	Combination switch	0.18		
	Loudspeaker	0.14	Bracket seat	0.069		
	Grooved strip (window glass)	0.028	Battery head	0.214		
			M			
	Standardized parts	0.28				
	Safety belt	0.21				
	M					
Sub. T.		6.098		7.171		23
Q2	Lamp	1.70	Front beam	02		
	Wire harness	1.01	FrontFloorPanelAssembly			
	Steering wheel	0.16	Rear floor panel assy	0.148		
	Air-conditioning parts	8.33		0.008		
	DoorLock,InteriorHandle	0.22				
	Brake oil piping	0.12				
	Brakes	1.25				
	Trim brake	0.45				
	Hand brake	0.04				
	Lock	0.31				
	Seat, Trimming	7.15				
	Rubber parts	0.77				
	Wheel	0.487				
	Floor carpet	1.09				
	Door lock hinge	0.284				
	Drive shaft	0.41				
	Steering gear	2.93				
	Instrument product	0.46				
	Wheel hub	0.21				
	Radiator	0.43				
	Brake drum	0.51				
	M					
Sub T.		28.46		0.158		0

	Regulator	0.31				
Q3	Front exhaust pipe	0.098				
	Locking control	0.21				
	Pedal	0.172				
	Muffler	0.381				
	Oil filter	0.078				
	Shift lever	0.095				
	Engine support	0.452				
	Slide	0.065				
	Electric horn	0.03				
	Switches	0.29				
	Absorber	0.26				
	Door handle	0.09				
	Steel plate	0.35				
	Rubber&Plastics part	0.57				
	Wiper motor	0.16				
	Standardized parts	0.47				
	Drip	0.120				
	Drip Seal rid	0.075				
	M					
Sub T.		6.098		0		0
	Stabilizer	0.1	Front floor assembly	0.215		
Q4	Auto bumper	1.04	Rear floor assembly	0.539		
	MasterBrakeCylinder	0.14	Front roof assembly	0.089		
	Rear frame assembly	1.479	Front side panel Assy	0.203		
	Torsion	0.25	Rear Side Panel Assembly	1.008		
	Rear bumper	0.052	Front door assembly			
	M		Central Door Assy	1.067		
			Guard	0.681		
			Guard(Front Bumper)	0.081		
	Sub Total	3.751		3.967		0
	All	44.477		11.295		23
	Cumulative	44.477 (44%)		55.772 (56%)		78.772 (79%)

Source: CMC (1997), Yulon Enterprise Group, Don-Nan (SEM) Automobile Case (Apr. 23, 1997) p.30.

3.4 Part Suppliers

The 61 Taiwanese suppliers are going to China in the form of either 100% self–own capital, or joint ventures or only in the form of technical cooperation. In any form the Taiwanese and the counterpart Chinese suppliers signed a technical agreement and then Taiwanese suppliers transfer their technology to the firm in

China. I shall discuss the content of the technical agreement and the technology which has been transferred.

3.4.1 The Agreement

I am going to raise 3 points which are argued by both licensor and licencee.

1. Conclusiveness and nonconclusiveness

The licencee includes the nonconclusiveness right to manufacture and assembly the product in Chinese territory, and the licensor has the right to distribute the product himself or have it distributed by third parties under licence in China territory. In other words, the Chinese licencee can not assume the conclusive right of manufacturing and distributing the licenced product.

2. Territory

It is stated:

A. The territory is restricted to China. The licencee is not allowed to manufacture the product under licence in other countries.

B. The licencee is only entitled to distribute the product under licence as a single item (not as a part of another item) within the territory.

C. The product under licence is installed as original equipment in complete motor vehicles or is part of a "completely knocked down (CKD)" set for the assembly of vehicles built within the territory. There are no export restriction.

D. The licencee, however, shall not export the product under licence beyond the above-mentioned scope without the prior written consent of the licensor. In other words, the licenced product as a single item can not be exported without the prior written consent of the Taiwanese licensor.

3. Responsibility of Claims

It is stated:

A. The Taiwanese licensor is not liable for manufacturing and distributing. In fact, only if the licenced know-how and technical documentation are essentially defective, the licensor ought to bear the responsibility.

B. Furthermore, the Taiwanese licensor is not liable for infringement of the licence right by third parties who have rights that pre-date the Agreement even if known or not known through negligence by the licensor.

3.4.2 The Technology Transferred

The technology transferred consists of engineering and management. It can be described briefly as follows:

1. Engineering

A. Set of drawings for contract products.

B. The private firms internal standards; JIS. DIN.A, standards.

C. Material sheets.

D. Operation equipment.

E. Operation schedules.

F. Working instructions giving details for several operations.
G. Quality assurance.
H. Manufacturing and control.

2. Management
   A. Product strategy.
   B. Administrative management.
   C. Personal training.

Concerning the above-described technology transfer, I would like to point out 2 points:

- The Chinese part suppliers are all medium and small firms. They use no any modern technology. The counterpart Taiwanese part suppliers' technology transfer is essentially beneficial to the Chinese.In other words, the Chinese parts suppliers' standard (especially Fujian province) rises from zero into the positive range.
- The 61 Taiwanese suppliers came to China altogether in a short period. They caused a big impact within the parts industry in China.

3.5 Taiwanese Hybrid Technology

3.5.1 Definition

Since 1965, and even earlier during the period of Taiwanese history in which it was colonized by Japan from 1895 to 1945, Japanese technology has been transferred to Taiwan and has widely influenced Taiwanese industries. Taiwan industries mingled the Japanese technology with the Taiwanese native culture, and through digestion of the technology, built up a new hybrid technology. We call this hybrid technology "Taiwanese Hybrid Technology." The Hybrid Technology has three important characters:

3.5.1.1 Taiwanese technology with Japanese blood

You may *f*eel that the technology is not 100% Taiwanese, but you know that it is not equal to the Japanese. The software of management has especially this character.

3.5.1.2 With the capability of flexible manufacturing system (FMS)

In the early stage of economic development, Taiwan's commodity demand was quite small but consumer's demand had a great variety. In order to satisfy this kind of market, the Taiwanese firm introduced Japanese FMS on one hand, and has also developed a new FMS on other hand.

3.5.1.3 Applicable in China

Within the human race, languages, culture and personal relationships, make Taiwan and China a family. It is believed that Taiwanese hybrid technology which has been developed and used in Taiwan could be applied in China. For instance, Western and Japanese car makers may join with the Taiwanese car maker to approach China , but not other countries.

3.5.2 Diffusion of Japanese Technology

From 1985, many Taiwanese industries with their hybrid technology have been investing capital in China. In one sense, this means that the Japanese technology has been indirectly transferred to China since the Japanese technology has diffused into China.

In the case of the car manufacturer, the Japanese "Mitsubishi Motor Corporation" transfers technology to the Taiwanese "China Motor Corporation (CMC)," and CMC transfers technology to the Chinese "Fujian Southeast Motor Corporation (SEM)." In the case of part suppliers, most of the Taiwanese part suppliers have a technical agreement with the Japanese part suppliers. The Japanese part suppliers transfer technology to the Taiwanese, and after digestion the Taiwanese part suppliers transfer technology to the Chinese part suppliers (or their own) in China.

In the short run, over the next ten years, the Taiwanese hybrid technology will be continuously transferred to China and the Japanese technology, in one sense, will be diffused into China. In the long run, over 20 to 30 years, the Japanese technology will be directly transferred to China.

4 Conclusion

1.A Taiwanese car manufacturer (CMC) and 30 Taiwanese suppliers went to China simultaneously, and are concentrated in a district very close to the car manufacturer assembly plant (SEM).
2.These Taiwanese suppliers in China and SEM come together to form a so called "Car Manufacturer and Part Suppliers System." Both car manufacturer and the suppliers share the same destiny, and work together very closely.
3. Since the Taiwanese car manufacturer (CMC) and the Taiwanese suppliers have gone to China together, the requirements of "Q.C.D.S." and RLC have been reached.
4. Since 1985 the Taiwanese Hybrid Technology has been transferred to China. In one sense, this means that the Japanese technology has diffused into China.

References

Automobile Technical Development Center (1997) *Project Proposal*, Fujian Province and Southeast Motor Co., China.

Chen, C. C. (1983) A Study of Autoparts Industry in Taiwan, *Quarterly Journal of Bank of Taiwan*, 34 (2), 27–62.

Chen, C. C. (1986) Auslaendische Investitionen in Kraftfahrzeugbau in Taiwan, *Ifo–Studien*, 32 (1–3), 155–170.

Chen, C. C. (1994) The Local Content Strategy of Chinese Automobile Industrial Policy: A Case Study of Shanghai Volkswagen, The Journal of Social Science (Tokyo Univ.), 56 (2), 103–173.

Chen, C. C. (1995) Technology Transfer: Changes in the Performance Paradigm, *Social Science Japan* (Tokyo Univ.), 3, 24–25.

Chen, C. C. (1999) *Growth or Disappearance: A Managerial Economic Approach to Industries,* Taipei: Hwa-Tai Publishing Co..

Chen, C. C. (1999) *Taiwanese Investment in China: Don-Nan Automobile Company,* in M. Taube and A. Gaelli eds., Chinas Wirtshaft in Wandel, Muenchen: Weltforum Verlag, 189–223.

Chen, C. C. (2000) Automobile Industrial Policy and WTO Agreements: China and Taiwan, in K. Hamada, M. Matsushita and C. Komura eds., *Dreams and Dilemmas,* Singapore: Institute of Southeast Asian Studies, 134–165.

China Automotive Technical Research Center (1999) *1999 China Automotive Industry Yearbok.*

(Taiwanese) China Motor Co., Ltd. (CMC) (1995) *A Guide Book of China Motor Co.,* Taipei, Taiwan.

(Taiwanese) China Motor Co., Ltd. (CMC) (1995) *China Motor Co.'s Light Commercial Car Plan in China:* A Statement.

(Taiwanese) China Motor Co., Ltd. (CMC) (1997) *Yulon Enterprise Group: Don–Nan Automobile Case.*

(Taiwanese) China Motor Co., Ltd. (CMC) (2000) *The Outline of China Motor Co.'s China Investment.*

Chinese National Planning Committee (1994) *Chinese Automobile Industrial Policy,* Beijing, China.

Dept. of State, China (1999) *Implementation for the Investment Protection Law for Taiwanese*, Beijing, China.

Fujian Southeast Motor Co. (1999) *A Guide Book of Fujian Southeast Motor Co., Fuzhou,* China.

Fujian Southeast Motor Co. (1999) *Fujian Southeast Motor Co. – Its Current Management and Future Development, Fuzhou,* China.

Yulon Motor Co., Ltd (1994) *Guide Book of Yulon Motor*, Taipei, Taiwan.

14 Technology Transfer of the Toyota Production System in China*

Chunli Lee
Aichi University

1 Introduction

This chapter examines the impact made by the Japanese-style production method on the dynamic evolutionary process of production systems in China, with a view to adding the Chinese experience to the discussion on the evolution of manufacturing systems that has become so prevalent in recent years on an international scale.[1] Specifically, I shall go back to the first introduction of the Toyota production system (TPS) into China and the process of technology transfer, by focusing on the case of First Automotive Works (Diyi Qiche Jituan Gongsi; hereafter abbreviated to FAW), the representative Chinese automobile manufacturer.

We can trace the introduction of the Toyota production system into China to two instalments of technical guidance offered at FAW in 1977 and 1981 directly by Taiichi Ohno, a representative proponent of this system. Indirectly, also, the system was further adopted in a real sense from the late 1980s when FAW took the opportunity of building a transmission plant with technological assistance from the Hino Motor Company to begin introducing the so-called "lean production system" on a full scale.[2] FAW's transmission plant integrated the disparate

---

* Originally published as "Origin of the Adoption of the Toyota Production System" in *Japanese Yearbook on Business History*, vol.14, 1997. This article was translated by Edmund R. SKRZYPCZAK of Nanzan University, Nagoya, Japan.

[1] For more on the formation and evolution of production systems, see Takahiro Fujimoto, "Iwayuru Toyotateki jidosha kaihatsu/seisan Shisutemu no kyoso noryoku to sono shinka–Kega no komyo to jigoteki gorisei" (The competitive capability of the so–called Toyota–style automobile development and production systems, and their evolution: "Flukes" and ex post facto rationality), parts 1 & 2, Keizaigaku ronshu 61, nos. 2 & 3, 1995: and H. Shiomi and K. Wada, eds., Fordism Transformed: The development of Production Methods in the Automobile Industry (Oxford University Press 1995).

[2] "Lean production system" is a term proposed by the Massachusetts Institute of Technology / International Motor Vehicle Program (IMVP). Basically it is an idealized form of the Toyota

elements of the Toyota system that had been introduced separately in earlier years and established, for the first time in China on a plant level, a comparatively systematic Toyota system that had as its core the just-in-time method. This is why it occupies such an important place in Chinese manufacturing industry.

As far as I know, there have as yet been no studies, either in China or overseas, that set out to investigate the introduction of the Toyota production system into China, particularly into the automobile industry. Despite the inclusion of the automobile industry among the number of studies on the international spread of the Japanese-style production system and on the overseas penetration of Japanese firms – two popular topics of discussion in resent years – most of the studies deal with the United States, NIES in Asia, or the ASEAN countries, and there still are plenty of blanks to fill when it comes to studies on China.[3] One of the merits of this study lies in its greater three-dimensional elucidation of the process of introducing the Toyota system into China by including within its perspectives the "Japanization" presently unfolding on an international scale. At the same time, it could provide another frame of reference to which other studies on the international transfer of the Japanese-style production system can be compared.

As early as the late 1970s Chinese firm had paid more attention to the revolutionary efficiency of the Toyota production system and had begun to introduce this system earlier than American and European firms. This is a historical fact, noteworthy in itself. Nerveless, it cannot be denied that, under the double inertial force of the old enterprise system – a management system under a planned economy and the conventional Ford mass – production system – reform of the production system and a turnabout of the enterprise system in Chinese firms (especially state-owned enterprises) are more difficult to achieve than in American and European firms.

With these issues kept in mind, in part 2 this chapter will discuss the concrete technical guidance provided by Taiichi Ohno on his two visits to FAW. This was

---

production system. For more details, see J. Womack, D. Roos, and D. Jones, The Machine That Changed the World (New York: Rawson Associates 1990).

[3] The work by Womack et al. and one by Tetsuo Abo et al., Amerika ni ikiru Nihonteki seisan Shisutemu (The Japanese-style production system alive in America) (Tokyo: Toyo Keizai Shinposha 1991) are examples of the coverage given to other countries. For the few works on China's automobile industry, see Toshio Tajima, "Chugoku Jidosha sangyo no tenkai to sangyo soshiki" (The development of China's automobile industry and industrial organization), Shakaikagaku Kenkyu 42, no. 5, 1991; Guowuyuan jingji Jishu Shehui Fazhan Yanjiu Zhongxin (The State Council Research Center for Economic, Technological, and Social Development), eds., Yiqi zai gaige kaifang shiqi de jishu gaizao-laizi shengchan diyixian de diaocha baogao (Technological innovation at FAW in the period of reform and openness: Report from the front line of production) (Beijing: Zhongguo Caizheng Jingji Chubanshe (Chines Public Financial Economy Press), 1988; and Chunli Lee, Gendai Chugoku no jidosha sangyo – kigyo shisutemu no shinka to keiei senryaku (The Chinese automobile industry: Manufacturing system and technological strategy) (Tokyo: Shinzansha Publishing House 1997).

also the first introduction of the Toyota production system into China. In part 3 it will investigate the case of the FAW transmission plant, the representative Toyota-style plant within the FAW organization, to elucidate the process of technology transfer from Hino, the overcoming of the conflict between old and new systems, and the production management and quality control systems in this plant. I hope, by proceeding in this manner, that I can put China into the bigger picture of the worldwide dissemination of the Toyota production system. [4]

2 Introduction of the TOYOTA Production System at Faw

With technical assistance from the former Soviet Union, First Automotive Works was established in 1953 in Changchun City, thus becoming China's first automaker. Its production system was known for being a coherent, mature Ford production system based on a highly vertical integration incorporating casting, forging, machining, and final assembly processes.[5] Figure 14–1 on the next page shows the production logistics and organizational structure of FAW as of 1992. Except for amalgamated automakers and parts makers, the key parts of the internal organization roughly correspond with FAW's longstanding production logistics. [6] This traditional mass-production system of FAW was destined in the late 1970s to encounter the Toyota system and undergo a subsequent reform.

2.1 Ohno Raises Issues

The earliest introduction of the Toyota production system at FAW can be traced back to the direct guidance given by its originator, Taiichi Ohno, in 1981. His advice stirred up interest in the Toyota production system among the executive officials and the middle-management stratum of the company.

[4] The research for this study was based primarily on field surveys. I have visited FAW three times to conduct surveys there on 17–19 February 1992, 5–7 September 1994, and 21–24 December 1994 (including an interview with Professor Takahiro Fujimoto, the University of Tokyo). I have also conducted surveys of Toyota six times (January 1991, August 1992, November 1994 and 1996, July and November 1997) and of Hino one time (February 1996).

[5] For material on FAW's acceptance of and changes to the Ford system see Chunli Lee, "Adoption of the Ford System and Evolution of the Production System in the Chinese Automobile Industry, 1953–93", in Shiomi and Wada, eds., Fordism Transformed, and Chunli Lee, "Chugoku jidosha sangyo ni okeru kigyo shisutemu no keisei to shinka ni kansuru kenkyu" (Formation and evolution of the enterprise system in the Chinese automobile industry) (unpublished Ph. D. dissertation, Division of Economics, Graduate School of the University of Tokyo, 1996).

[6] In regard to the expansion of FAW's business organization from the late 1980s on, see Lee, op. cit. in Fordism Transformed. Figure 14–1 was compiled by the author from FAW publicity materials and Qiche Gongye Jiben Qingkuang 1991 (Basic state of the automobile industry 1991), vol. 2, pp.124–25.

Figure 14–1 Organizational Structure and Production Logistics of the First Automobile Co. Group

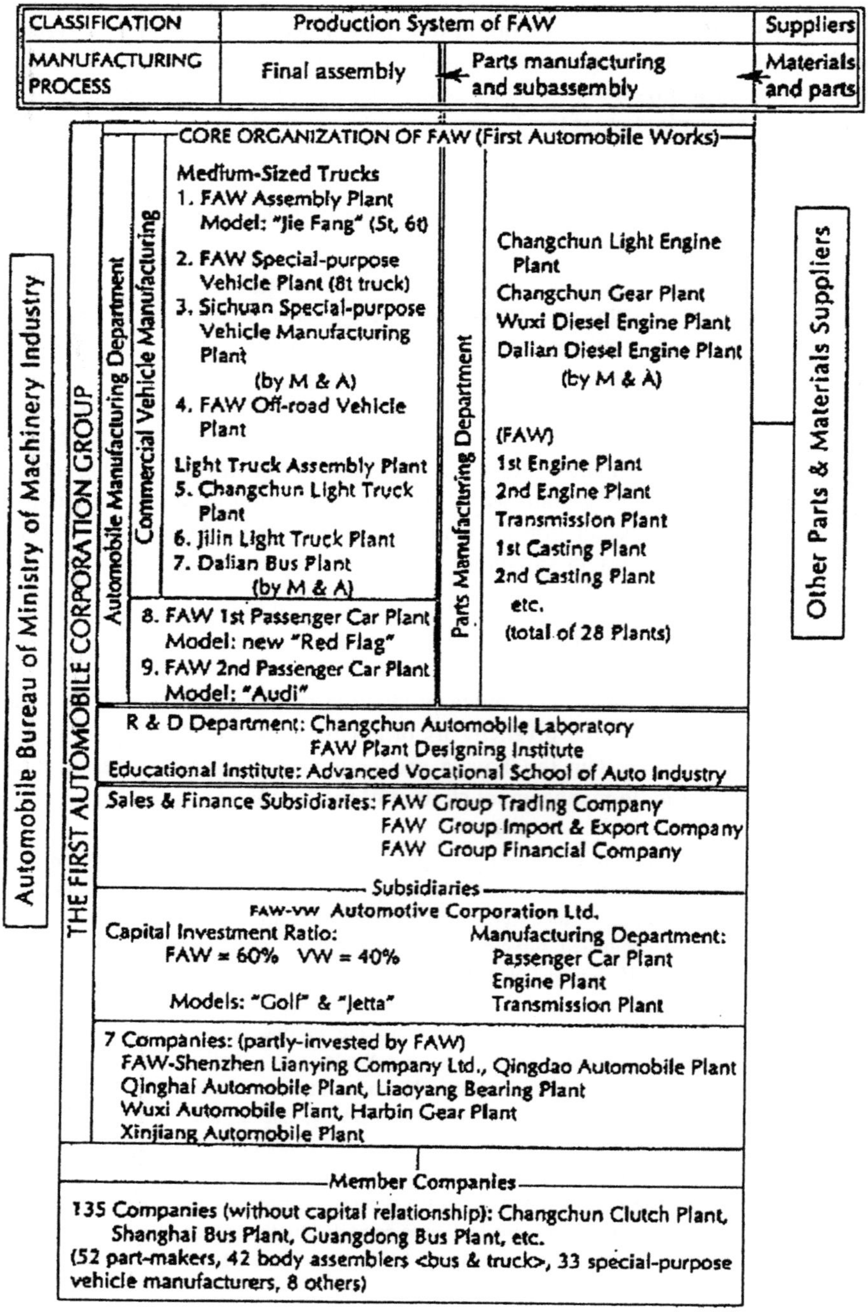

Ohno's first visit to China came in September 1977, when he visited FAW and other automakers. His impressions are recorded briefly in his famous work, i.e., Toyota seisan hoshiki (The Toyota production system):

> Recently (15–28 September 1977) I had a look at China's manufacturing industry. They are enthusiastic in their efforts to modernize. I believe that, underlying everything, from the time of Henry Ford I, through our first use of the Toyota production system after the war and right up to the present, and now in the manufacturing industry that China is aiming at anew, here is the universal element of the true "efficiency that Ford made mention of... between fifty years ago and the present, huge changes have arisen. The situation in China is changing enormously.[7]

Still, what were those changes that Ohno, who had been born in Dalian City in China, saw during his visit ? They have till recently been completely shrouded in the darkness of history. No 1977 accounts remain of what he said and did at FAW. Two facts, however, shed some indirect light.

The first is the fact that the first edition of Ohno's best-known work, Toyota seisan hoshiki, came out in May 1978, and a Chinese translation (unpublished) by the Technological Information Section of the FAW Department of Manufacturing Technology also appeared around the same time.[8] It is inconceivable that a translation could have been made so rapidly without the cooperation of the author.

The second is the fact that Ohno's words and movements on his second trip to FAW (14–21 June 1981) – at FAW's invitation – are faithfully recorded in FAW accounts.[9]

The general report prepared after the event by the FAW Department of Production Management, whose role it was to show Ohno and his group around the factories, records Ohno's concrete views regarding the problems existing in FAW's production system. They are trenchant criticisms delivered in Ohno's style, with no mincing of words.

He inspected all of the subfactories and summarized his impressions of the gravity of management problems in the following four comments on such things as quality, operations management, and safety.

Quality: Seems all of the factories are producing defective items.

---

[7] Taiichi Ohno, *Toyota Seisan Hoshiki* (The Toyota production system) (Tokyo: Daiyamondosha 1978), p. 199

[8] Zhiguo Li, Jingyi shengchan fangshi yu qiye jingji xiaoyi (Lean production system and its economic performance) (Beijing: Beijing Kexue Jishu Chubanshe (Beijing Science and Technology Press) 1994), p. 239, the bibliography

[9] The work cited in the preceding note by Zhiguo Li, vice president in charge of production, contains the first publication of notes taken during Ohno's lectures at FAW over ten years earlier. Unless noted otherwise, the material that follows is based on this work by Li and on an interview with Li on 6 September 1994. I would note passing that Li was the person responsible for inviting Ohno to FAW in 1981

Operations: They are accelerating the destruction of machines and equipment.
In-process items: Causing huge amounts of capital to lie idle.
Safety: if it were us (factories in Japan) we'd be too afraid to work. I have to admire the fact that there no accidents in these conditions. (What he really means is that it's unbelievable there aren't accidents!)

We admit that management in the factories has problems, but we hadn't raised them as seriously, with as much acuity, as Ohno did. The gravity of the problems is still not felt by our executive officials or the general workers. We are deeply stirred by the sharpness with which this one foreigner has pointed out problems to our company. [10]

Let us now look at two other accounts written down at the time of Ohno's inspection of FAW subfactories and manufacturing processes.

Quality control: In the general assembly plant we showed him two front axles that had been rejected and taken down from the line and were in the process of being repaired. They (Ohno and his group) expressed the opinion that rejected parts should be replaced in the line, and that removing from the line items with reject parts attached to them or with parts missing was inexcusable. He (Ohno) explained as follows:

This was the American way of doing things, but we don't agree with it. It's true that it's necessary to stop the line when you carry out replacements of parts in the line, but even so it's faster than taking things down from the line to repair them. One other thing: the supplementary painting process that comes later should be eliminate. It only encourages operators not to be concerned about quality control. [11]

Process control: Operations throughout the company are not producing items to fit in with the takt time of the final assembly line; instead, every process and every production line is operating at its own pace, without any control. There is a lot of in-process stock, but the workers keep on pushing right ahead, unconcerned about the quality of the products or about keeping the machine in good condition, because they want to work fast so they can get off work early. As a result they hasten the wear and tear of the equipment and shorten the lives of the machines. Situations like this they (Ohno and his group) found extremely incomprehensible... [12]

According to Ohno, assembly on the final assembly line should be synchronized with all the various chain conveyors, and at most there should be a

---

[10] FAW Department of Production Management, "Fengtian Qiche Gongsi daibiaotuan lai Yiqi fangwen qingkuang de huibao" (Report on the visit to FAW of the Toyota Motor Company delegation), appendix 3 in Zhiguo Li's work, p. 232.

[11] Ibid., pp. 233–34.

[12] Ibid., pp. 234–36

stock of two or three items-large numbers were not to be stockpiled beside the assembly line. Nor were tires to be brought over and left piled by the side of the road. If the tempo was out of kilter, it was preferable to stop the chain conveyors....As a general rule it is better not to stop the chain conveyors, but when the need arises it was all right to stop them.

As can be seen from the above, Ohno had some trenchant criticism and scathing remarks to direct at FAW. For a company that considered itself Number One in China's machinery industry, these came as an enormous shock.

2.2 On-the-Spot Guidance by Ohno

Ohno also provided direct technical guidance in the FAW engine and chassis plants. One of the things he did was to take the chassis plant's machining line for the final pinion carrier (zhoucheng zuo) of the rear axle as a sample, and he gave concrete technical guidance for it, even going so far as to change the layout of the line. These were the only cases of direct guidance provided by him in China, and represented the first experiment at introducing the Toyota production system. In order to compare the situation as it stood before kaizen and then after kaizen, let me briefly summarize what Ohno's guidance comprised. [13]

2.2.1 The Situation before Kaizen

There were seven pieces of equipment or machinery in the line, six of them being four different types of cutters, the other a machine for washing. There were five operators, each working alone at their respective processes. The processes were linked by roller conveyors, the average number of in-process stock in each process was 110, and of finished stock was 360; in-process items for which there was no room on the roller conveyor were placed on the floor.

2.2.2 The Kind of Kaizen Carried Out

1. First of all a takt time for the line was calculated on the basis of amount of production, and a figure of 2.6 minutes was arrived at. [14]
2. A relay switch was installed in the first machine tool so that a green light would go one very 2.6 minutes. It was fixed so that, when the light went on, the machine's electric power would be connected and it would go on. In this way, the operator in the first process was unable to begin working earlier – or later – than every 2.6 minutes.

---

[13] This is based on pp. 52–55 of Zhiguo Li's work cited above and an article by Kimitoshi Sato, "Xianchang shiyandian zongje baogao" (Complete report on workplace testings) , on pp. 214–18 of the same work by Li.

[14] The formula for calculating takt time is to divide the total amount of working time per day by the number of vehicles per day needed to fill orders.

3. The washing process was removed from the end of the first 5-man 7-process operation and replaced with a 1-man 6-process operation. The order of operations and distribution of time for this operation was shown on a standardized work chart.
4. The layout of the equipment was changed, the line shortened, the number of roller conveyors reduced. The way the washing machine was lined up was changed, and the parts that had been washed were sent to the subassembly of the immediately subsequent process.
5. Breakdown signal devices were attached to the processing lines, so that operators could at any time send a signal to the equipment maintenance section.
6. A "Get ready! Start!" system was put in place; in accordance with this starting signal, processing parts would be sent to the line and operations begun.

2.2.3 Post-Kaizen Results

1. One-man multimachine handling led to four fewer workers. Also, it became possible to produce at the same takt time as the rear axle subassembly line process that followed later, and synchronization was realized.
2. Wasteful labor was eliminated and costs could be reduced. In-process stock fell from 110 items to the 8 items being worked on, and the number of finished stock from 360 to 160. In-process stock funds were reduced by 30%.
3. The quality of parts improved, responsibilities became clear, and self-inspection was enhanced.
4. The exercise was useful for bringing problems to the surface and solving them at an early stage. Since the whole line stopped when a problem arose in the process, it contributed to preventing reoccurrences.

Several basic elements of Toyota-style process management are contained in the above summary: the reduction of worker numbers through multimachine handling; the realization of synchronization between earlier and later processes; the resultant reduction in in-process stock; the building in of quality; the automatic surfacing of problems. FAW officials were impressed, so great were the differences between the production line before and after kaizen. The direct results of Ohno's technical guidance were that it brought to light problems in the mass production system at the worksites themselves and with reference to specific things, and it made the FAW top management more attentive to production methods.

Evidence of this is contained in numerous reports, mostly produced by the Production Management Department, detailing aspects of Ohno's FAW visit and his technical guidance. Some examples, all of them appearing in June 1981, are:

- "Riben Fengtian Qiche Gongsi daibiaotuan Daye Naiyi xiansheng yu chang lingdao zuotan gui (jiluzhaiyao)" (Round-table discussion between Mr.

Taiichi Ohno of Japan's Toyota Motor Company delegation and top FAW managers (summary));

- "Daye Naiyi xiansheng fengwen Diyi Qiche Zhizao-Chang de baogao" (Report on Mr. Taiichi Ohno's visit to FAW);
- "Daye Naiyi xiansheng zai Diyi Qiche Zhizao-Chang zuotanhui de jilu zhaiyao" (Summary of a round-table discussion with Mr. Taiichi Ohno at FAW);
- Taiichi Ohno, "Yiqi tuixing Fengtian shengchan fangshi zhi wojian" (My views on promoting the Toyota production system at FAW);
- Kimitoshi Sato, "Xianchang shiyiandian zongje baogao (Changchun)" (Complete report on worksite testings (Changchun)).

Over a year and a half later, the most enthusiastic proponent of the introduction of the Toyota production system, Mr. Zhiguo Li, collected his explanations of the Toyota system as it would work in the FAW context in a book entitled *Shengchan guanli kexue fangfa yu yingyong* (The scientific methods and applications of production management, FAW 1983). This book was given the new title Xiandai shengchan guanli jichu (Foundations of modern production management) and published throughout the country in 1986.

The writings of Ohno, the records of his lectures, and the relevant reports were put to good use first of all for the education of personnel throughout the whole of the company, especially in regard to the area of production management. Ohno had delivered a severe shock to FAW's production system – the prototype mass production system in the country of his birth – through the technical guidance he provided.

2.3 FAW'S Own Introduction of the TOYOTA Production System

FAW's own moves to introduce the Toyota production system began in 1979.[15] Much earlier, in September 1972, the first postwar Chinese "Automobile Industry Observation Delegation" visited Japan, at the same time as the normalization of Sino–Japanese relations. Mr. Zhiguo Li, later to become an FAW vice president, was a member of the observation delegation that visited Toyota and nine other Japanese automakers and a small number of parts makers. This marked the first direct exchange between automobile industry circles in new china and their counterparts in Japan.[16] Later, in 1978, FAW sent twenty of its top management

[15] See Yiqi Biansuxiang-Chang (FAW transmission plant), "Tuixing zhunshihua shengchan fangshi, shixian qiye guanli zhengti yuhau-zai Yiqi Biansuxiang-Chang zhunshihua shengchan fangshi xianchang jingyian jiaoliuhui shang de huibao" (Promoting just-in-time production to achieve optimal management: A report presented for a worksite symposium at the FAW transmission plant on just-in-time production), Yiqi Gongzuo Qingkuang (FAW Review), No. 5, 1992, p. 38.

[16] See Zhiguo Li, Lean Production System, p. 241.

team, including the president of the company, to Japan. The group, known as the Qiye Guanli Xuexi Tuan (Enterprise management study team), spent five months visiting plants at Toyota, Nissan, Mitsubishi, Hino, and other companies. They are reported to have experienced one shock after another at seeing how advanced Japan's management system was. When this delegation returned to china its members produced, on the basis of there study notes, twenty-two instructional booklets on all the specialized areas they were responsible for. These instructional booklets, called "Yellow Books," were used in seminars for all the executives and technicians in the company. These stirred up the first Toyota study boom at FAW.[17]

> Beginning in 1979 FAW conducted early experiments with scientific management methods selected from among the advanced management systems of Japan and other countries to fit in with our company's actual conditions. These included kanban delivery, leveled production, the production of different model variations on the same line, quality control measures, control by visual inspection, target costs, value engineering, and system engineering. This was a trial that delivered the first shock to the conventional management thought and practices that FAW had introduced from the Soviet Union in the 1950s and had followed for twenty years. Control through the use of the kanban delivery that lay at the heart of the Toyota production system brought a stop to in-process inventory, and the method of supplying castings and external purchased parts directly into the process produced a golden age of production at FAW from 1979 to 1984.[18]

It is a historical fact, and one that should be accorded its due, that as early as the end of 1970s Chinese enterprises had adverted to the revolutionary efficiency of the Toyota production system and had begun to introduce this system even before European and American enterprises had done so. As a result, FAW, for example, was able to nearly halve the cost of in-process stock in 1983, when the kanban was introduced, from the 50 million yuan it spent the year before, to 26 million yuan.[19] At this stage, however, FAW's understanding of the Toyota system is thought to have still been at conceptual level, and it could not be described as fully developed. FAW's full-scale deployment of the Toyota production system did not take place until after the completion of its transmission plant with the technological assistance of Hino Motor Company.

---

[17] Shaojie Geng, "Yiqi tuixing jingyi shengchan fangshi de shijian he renshi" (FAW implementation of, and lessons from, promoting lean production) , in Quanguo Jijie Gonye Qiye Guanli Gongzuo Huiyi Jingyan Cailiao (Proceedings of the national machine industries conference on management practices) (1995), p. 49.

[18] "Promoting Just-in-time Production to Achieve Optimal Management", p. 38.

[19] Zhiguo Li, Lean Production System, p. 165.

3 Technology Transfer from HINO: The FAW Transmission Plant

The new transmission plant built under technological assistance provided by Hino integrated all the constituent elements of the Toyota system that had been introduced in bits and pieces until that time.[20] As an entity that established a comparatively systemic Toyota production system revolving around the just-in-time system, this factory is very significant. By the birth of a model factory at FAW, understanding of the Toyota system changed from a conceptual thing to something visible and concrete, and this served to instill in the employees a common value system.

3.1 The Production System at the Transmission Plant

The introduction of product technology and production management know-how from Hino was a deliberately intended technology transfer on FAW's part. FAW management saw the introduction of technology from Hino as an opportunity to learn about Japan's production management methods at the same time. Construction on the new plant was started in September 1985, and full production began in August 1990. During this period 23 technicians (57 man-months in total) were sent from Hino, and 49 people (66 man-months in total) were sent on eight separate occasions from FAW to Hino, where they visited factories, attended lectures, and received technical training.[21]

At the time of the survey I conducted in September 1994, the new plant was employing 1,900 people and running on a continuous two-shift system. It had 79 processing lines. Of its 960 machine tools, 900 were of Chinese make, with 60 Japanese-made machines in only the key processes. It was following just-in-time principles, and it acted as FAW's model factory. The following statement appeared on a notice board found at the entrance to the plant.

> In this factory we have replaced the conventional earlier-processes-push-later-processes system by a later-processes-pull-earlier-processes system. We pursue cost reduction, and we have introduced a one-at-a-time processing system, a stock supplementation between all the production lines, and the kanban delivery method for production control. On-site operators follow the wuwei yiti (5-in-1) quality control method of sanzi yikong (3 selfs and 1 control) , Shenhua gongyi (deepening manufacturing technology) , gongcheng luhua (process greening) , wubuliu (the 5 nonflows) , and product optimization activities. Operations management adopts the methods of multimachine handling and multiprocess handling; tool management involves collection and

[20] The materials I present in this section are based on interviews I conducted on 6 and 7 September 1994 and on the results of an inspection tour of the transmission plant.

[21] Zhiguo Li, Lean Production System, pp. 171–72.

> delivery at fixed locations, follow-up checks, and regularreplacement; while equipment management involves both repair of breakdowns and preventative maintenance. For shopfloor management we have introduced an ongoing campaign involving the five "-nesses" (5S): orderliness, tidiness, cleanliness, spotlessness, and professionalness.[22]

Every workshop has a notice board with a printed checklist of the separate elements that go into the just-in-time system. This list, shown in Table 14–1 on the facing page, gives the items to be inspected, the point standards, and the points gained by each line. These points gained are linked with the "management bonus" explained later. Let us look at the production management and quality control sections shown in Table 14–1.[23]

3.1.1 Production Management

1. One-at-a-time (ikko nagashi): This refers to the idea that the number of in-process items in the middle of every process in the production line must be one, and only one; this is the main feature distinguishing this process from the early-processes-push-later-processes system seen in the mass-production system. One-at-a-time is the key element in the just-in-time system that eliminates large in-process inventories, demands synchronizing production with line takt times, and synchronizes and parallels the flow of items from an earlier to a later process and the flow of information from a later to an earlier process. In this plant one-at-a-time was actualized on the whole production line in 1992.

2 Kanban delivery method: In this plant everything is so arranged that, unless kanban is sighted, no casting from the warehouse will be delivered, and the production line will not begin production. At one end of every line are located kanban boxes, divided into production instruction kanbans, finished-product inventory kanbans, and parts-withdrawal kanbans. One this last type (the parts-withdrawal kanbans) are recorded such items as the part name, part number, quantity, and so on. The inventory standard for externally purchased parts is one or two days.

---

[22] This is according to notes I took when I visited the plant on 7 September 1994. The terms that appear in the description of the quality control method will shortly be explained in the text.

[23] Unless I indicate otherwise, this account of production management and quality control is based on "Promoting Just-in-time Production to Achieve Optimal Management", pp. 39–42. Note that the inspection criteria and standard points for the preliminary line are not known. The Table is based on notes taken by the author during an inspection tour of the transmission plant on 7 September 1994.

Table 14–1 "Just-in-Time" System at
FAW Transmission Plant & Inspection Criteria

Inspection Items	Elementary Line (100 points)	Standard Line (80 points)	Point gain (minus points)
I. Production management			
1. In-process items between processes	≤ no. of jigs in earlier process	≤ no. of jigs in earlier process	X
2. On-line in-process items	≤ fixed number	≤ fixed number	
3. Finished goods stock	≤ max. stock rules	≤ max. stock rules	
4. Placement of parts on floor	Not allowed	Not allowed	
5. Input-output ratio	≥ 99%	≥ 99.6%	
6. Levelization ratio	≥ 90%	≥ 98%	
7. Kanban production	Execution by rules	Execution by rules	
II. Quality control			
1. Quality problems, by lot (criteria based on feedback information)	Not allowed	Not allowed	X
2. Process greening rate	≥ 90%	100%	
3. Work rules execution rate	≥ 90%	100%	
4. No. of parts awaiting processing	≤ 10	≤ 5	
5. Nonexecution of "3 selfs 1 control"	≤ 1 person/time	≤ 1 person/time	
6. Consignment of defective goods	≤ 1 person/time	≤ 1 person/time	
III. Tool management			
1. Replacement at fixed time not done	≤ 1 person/time	≤ 1 person/time	X
2. Infringement of requirement for collection/delivery at fixed locations	≤ 1 person/time	≤ 1 person/time	
3. Infringement of follow-up control of costly tools	≤ 1 person/time	≤ 1 person/time	
IV. Equipment management			
1. Extent of lubrication	≥ 99%	100%	X
2. Degree of cleanliness	≤ 0.5 (minus-pts. permissible range)	Attained standard	
V. Operations management			
1. Average work load ratio (per person)	≥ 65%	≥ 70%	X
2. Work configuration	Same as on standardized work chart	Same as on standardized work chart	
VI. "5-ness" (5S) shopfloor management			
1. Fixation ratio	≤ 95%	100%	X
2. Implementation of "5-nesses" at workplace.	≤ 0.5% (minus-pts. permissible range)	≤ 0.2% (minus-pts. permissible range)	

3. Control by visual inspection: Andon lamps are located on the transmission assembly line; these indicate the present working state of the line, the times for line stoppage, and so on. To indicate work standards there also is the "one chart, one manual, one card." The "one chart" refers to the Toyota-style standardized work instructions chart; "one card" refers to the work instructions card; "one manual" refers to the manual containing the various work standards for all the different production personnel. Also, the parts boxes are standardized in order to ensure quantities are uniform.

4. Multimachine handling: This means that, on average, one worker handles three machines (this may at times be as much as five machines). The production line is laid out in a U-shape. Process design and plant design were the result of a joint design by Hino and FAW.

3.1.2 Quality Control

In the transmission plant, quality control is carried out in two ways: by building quality into the production process (through zizhu jiancha, or self-imposed inspection) and by final inspection. In the concrete this means that they use the quality control method called "5-in-1" (Table 14–1): "3 selfs and 1 control," "deepening manufacturing technology," "process greening," "process greening," "the 5 nonflows," and product optimization.

1. "Three self and 1 control" (sanzi yikong): The "3 self" refers to SELF-imposed inspection, SELF-scoring, and filling out the "quality follow-up card" by oneSELF, and the "one control" refers to self-CONTROL (ziji kongzhi) activities.

2. "Deepening manufacturing technology" (shenhua gongyi) signifies the improvement and deepening of manufacturing techniques; in the concrete, it refers to mechanisms, known as pokayoke, or "faithsafe features," set up to prevent the production of defective articles.

3. "Process greening" (gongcheng luhua): one of the means for attaining quality control. The process inspection group carries out an inspection of a process on the basis of a checklist called "the criteria for process acceptability" and hand down a decision as to whether the process passes or fails the criteria. They make known the results by means of a round board hung onto a notice board. The front surface is green, which means Pass; the back is red, and it indicated Fail. The more green there is showing the higher the acceptability rate. This explains why this method of encouraging quality improvement is called "process greening."

4. "The 5 nonflows" (wubuliu): During a quality inspection, items that pass inspection are given five types of marks, including a Pass mark, a production date, a shift number and an item number, etc.. An item lacking any one of these five marks is not to be sent on to the next process. Hence the name, "the 5 nonflows."

5. Product optimization activities: These are consider to be the goals of thepreceding four items.

Whereas the introduction of the kanban delivery method at the plant was suggested by FAW, total quality control (TQC) was suggested by Hino at technological assistance stage, but not adopted. Inspection of the products is done by an inspection of all items. In addition, from 1991 a German variation of a quantified inspection Audit System was introduced by the joint venture partner, Volkswagen. In this system, one vehicle a day undergoes a sample inspection, with a score given by a minus-points system on the basis of a checklist covering several thousand items. Inspection results are published once a week on the notice board; once a month an inspection assessment review committee meets, and the lowest scores are called upon explain the results. The FAW television channel televises the results of the review committee every month.

The other control areas are shown in Table 14–1 and need no further explanation.

The introduction of the Toyota production system at FAW was reported in the Renmin Ribao (People's Daily) as following:

> As a breakthrough in production management FAW has carried out a revolution against the conventional mass-production management system. Replacing the past system of earlier processes pushing later processes along, by a system in which later processes pull earlier processes, it has managed, by implementing the pull system of one-at-a-time production, greatly to reduce inventories of in-process goods between processes, diminish revolving funds, achieve improvement in manufacturing quality, and greatly lower the rate of defects.
> By changing from having one worker operate one machine, as in the past, to one worker operating several machines, it has reduced the number of workers, started operating on a full rotation basis, and greatly lifted its production efficiency.
> By changing from the large-lot production of the past to small-lot production, it has become able to carry out multimodel production, cut back on storage space, and reduce work loads.
> By changing from the parts delivery system based on a storage system, as in the past, to a parts delivery system based on kanban matched with production takt

> times, it has been able to realize leveled production and has improved control standards on shopfloors... [24]

Judging from what we see here, we are able to conclude that the pull system, the production of multiple models in small volumes, multimachine handling, and the kanban system were key introductions, and the basic elements connected with the Toyota system of production management were in general outline part of FAW's production scheme. Nevertheless, the process of its attaining a solid foothold was also a process of repeated clashes between the conventional mass-production concept and a Chinese-style production management philosophy within the context of a planned economy system, on the one hand, and the concept of the Toyota system with the "just-in-time" system at its core. On the other hand, it was a process of overcoming conflicts between old and new systems at the same time. The section that follows will investigate the process by which the Toyota system was introduced and reflect on FAW's capability to learn.

3.2 Learning Capability: Overcoming Conflicts Between Old and New Systems

3.2.1 A Change of Cognition: Chinese Management Methods Out of Kilter with Japanese Production Sites

In 1987, when trial production was carried out at FAW after its new transmission plant was completed, Japanese specialists arrived to offer guidance.[25] The factory side was shackled by conventional management ideas, however, and opinions among the plant's executive officials were divided, with the result that the Japanese management system could not be implemented. Consequently, even though the management model for the production sites had been designed on the basis of Japan's management system, the management methods followed continued to be the conventional Chinese way of thinking. This crossing of wires threw the management of new transmission plant completely out of kilter. Product quality was reported as not coming up to expectations, and output as falling short of demand.[26]

Thus it was reported that, in the early days after the introduction of the Toyota system:

---

[24] "Xiang chuantong de daliang shengchan guanli moshi tiaozhan: Yiqi quanmian tuixing Jingyi shengchan fangshi" (Challenging the conventional mass-production system: FAW promotes lean production system companywide) , Renmin Ribao , 29 May 1994.

[25] Unless otherwise indicated, the Account given in this subsection is based on "Promoting Just-in-time Production to Achieve Optimal Management", pp. 45–46.

[26] Ibid., p. 45.

> After quality control graphs quality control process charts were handed over to FAW, they were displayed on the worksite notice boards, but only as a formality, not being taken very seriously (the way they were at Hino) in practice. When asked their impressions, people working on-site shrugged apologetically that "They're too detailed and there's just too many of them to get through."[27]

On the other hand, representatives from the Japanese side who had gone to FAW to offer technical guidance did what they could to explain the "5-nesses" (5S) idea (beginning with a "5-nesses" study meeting directed at middle-level managers from worksite supervisors up) by making use of every possible site, but to little effect, and the "bottom-up" approach did not work.[28] Similarly, with regard to the quantities in in-process storage, the Chinese side was reluctant to have line stops and preferred having large numbers on hand, whereas the Japanese side suggested reducing the numbers so that problems could be brought to the surface and kaizen effected, but their suggestions fell on deaf ears.[29]

In 1991 the factory's new executive officials started work; reassessing the Toyota system as the company's greatest strength, they decided to introduce it in earnest. From that time on the Toyota system gradually permeated the production setup, and rationalization results kept improving. Eventually it was this change in the executive officials' awareness that, through a top-down approach, effected a turnabout in the production system.

3.2.2 Modifying the Chinese Approach: A Bonus-Centered Incentive System

The most hotly debated item in the process of introducing the just-in-time system was the fact that multiprocess handling and increased work intensity was not linked to wages. Instead of the one-worker-per-one-machine that was the norm in the plant, multimachine handling was introduced, and one worker operated three machines. There was opposition on the worksite. Work intensity was being increased, but wages did not keep pace. As a result, even though the machine were laid out in a U-shape, workers continued as before to operate only one machine each. In addition, though an effort was made to cut down on workers and to remove surplus personnel from the lines and transfer them to subfactories elsewhere, personnel planning was determined by the central government, which considered originality in employment procedures to be undesirable.

---

[27] Li Song, "Chugoku Daiichi Jidosha no moderu chenji ni okeru gijutsu donyu oyobi sono kyushu shoka purosesu ni tsuite no kosatsu – Hino Jidosha to no transmission gijutsu teikei o chushin ni" (Study on the introduction of transmission technology in FAW's model changes and of the process of absorbing and digesting that technology) , Master's thesis, General Culture Division, the University of Tokyo, 1990, p. 42.

[28] Ibid., p. 48.

[29] Based on interviews I conducted on & September 1994. So is the next paragraph.

When a delegation from FAW visited Hino's Nitta plant and saw how Hino employees worked, they were astounded. They are reported to have been deeply impressed, saying that "It's unlikely that in our factory people would work this way for us, no matter how much we paid them."[30]

The solution to the problem was held over until after 1991. Officials came to realize "the need to use appropriate economic policies and effective incentive measures as backups" in order to promote the just-in-time system. As multimachine handling and multiprocess handling become more widespread, work loads increased and work intensified, so unless pay also increased proportionately, employees would lose the desire to go along with plans. This led to the introd

The "post wages" system that was introduced among on-site operators ranked the posts of operators on four levels, depending on such indices as the percentage of manual operations involved, work intensity, and technical complexity. The "post wage" of the highest post was three times that of the lowest, and the highest bonus for a direct operator was set at ten times that of an assistant operator[31]. The amount of wages and bonuses paid out was pitched to the production site and to multimachine handling.

The newly established "management bonus" was paid out to workers on the basis of the number of criteria points they had attained every month on their just-in-time production line, which had been divided into three types – preliminary line, elementary line, and standard line – each with its own target criteria (see Table 14–1). The six items checked were production management, quality control, tool management, equipment management, operations management, and "5-ness" (5S) shopfloor management. The checking was done by a process inspection group that deducted points as they went down a detailed checklist.

This typically Chinese modification in the form of an incentive system revolving around wages and bonuses reflected how things are done in Chinese enterprises. Even the process of implementing the new wage and bonus system had to on a visible form in a scoring system based on inspection criteria, and objectivity was demanded. The problem of wages was a problem facing state-owned enterprises in general, and it was the most sensitive part of the old management system.

[30] Song's master thesis, p. 48.

[31] It is probably appropriate to consider this "post wage" (a term coined by China's Department of Labor and Personnel) a form of position-linked pay peculiar to China. For more details, see Yo Nakanishi and Xin Geng, "Chugoku Daini Kisha Seizo-Sho 'Daini Jidosha Kojo' no 'koshi meisai hyo' – 'kyuryobukuro' no kokusai hikaku, sono 7" (Itemized account of salaries, Second Automotive Works of China: An international comparison of pay envelopes, part 7), Discussion Paper 91-J-14, Faculty of Economics, the University of Tokyo, 1991.

3.2.3 Results and Diffusion

By 1992 the just-in-time system had been introduced into the whole production line at FAW's transmission plant. The average work load rate per operator had risen from the old 27.7% plant average to 65%, machine stoppage time had become 80% shorter, and a total of 468 production personnel had been retrenched. Labor productivity rose from 129,000 yuan per person in 1991 to 303,000 yuan per person in 1994, and the number of transmissions produced per worker rose from 27.7 units in 1991 to 68.5 units in 1994 – in both cases, the increase being more than double.[32]

In addition, by the introduction of one-at-a-time processing at all stages of the production line, revolving funds for in-process stock was slashed by 50% (from 7 million yuan to 3.5 million yuan), defective item rates went down by 35%, and the rate of items passing inspection the first time round rose from 70% the previous year to 92% in 1994. Commenting on these results, specialists from the Japanese side were favorable in their assessment: "The present transmission plant was less of a worry than we expected. Its production output exceeded planned capacity, kaizen was well advanced, and it has become an outstanding factory."[33]

FAW widened the transmission plant experience and pushed for the idealized form of the Toyota production system, the lean production system (Jingyi shengchan fangshi), for the whole of the company. Renmin Ribao informed its readers of the effects of FAW's kaizen and how the system was being spread over the whole company.

3.3 Challenging the Conventional Mass-Production System: FAW Promotes Lean Production system Companywide

> FAW began to promoting the lean production system in 1992. The company began by selecting five factories, nine workshops, and three production lines within the company that all had different technological systems, processing methods, and production takt times, to serve as a trial. In the transmission plant, within one year of introducing the lean production system, production output doubled and labor productivity almost doubled. In the Changchun gear plant, a year after the lean production system was introduced production output had increased by 44% over the previous year, labor productivity by 37%, and profits per person by 25%.[34]

---

[32] Shaojie Geng, "FAW Implementation of, and Lessons from, Promoting Lean Production," p.54.

[33] "Promoting Just-in-time Production to Achieve Optimal Management", p. 31. Afterwards FAW learned cost management methods from Hino and set up a cost management department.

[34] "Challenging the Conventional Mass-Production System," 29 May 1994.

The same article goes on to describe the early results of FAW's kaizen and the diffusion of the lean production system.

> As a result of FAW's promotion of the lean production system, the company has already seen definite results, with economic results being especially notable. In 1993 sales rose by 45% over the previous year, and profits and tax payments increased by 53%; in addition, other economic and technological indices reached the highest levels ever. The lean system has also, in combination with three institutional reforms in labor and personnel, wages, and social insurance, brought about a shrinking of the management structure and minus growth in personnel. The enterprise has started to "get lean." At present both management and workers in the FAW group attach great importance to the lean system, and there is a boom in "creating a lean factory" by doing all work the lean way.

It is interesting to note that every FAW manager of section-head level and above was given a copy of the Chinese translation of *The Machine that Changed the World*, source of the concept of "the lean production system." In addition, from 1993 to 1995 FAW has assembled all those in charge of factories to thirteen specialized seminars focused on "the lean production system" held at FAW's Academy of the Communist Party (in Hewanzi).[35]

In view of the process by which the just-in-time system was introduced into the new transmission plant, it is safe to say that, in transplanting a new system, making it take root there after the addition of modifications, and beginning to spread it throughout the company, FAW shows it has both the organizational learning capabilities and the capacities to absorb technology. The production system that Ohno once so roundly criticized was dislodged from this plant, and the system he had hoped for was able to become a reality ten years later when a new factory was constructed with the technological assistant of a member of the Toyota group, Hino Motor Company.

Now, the problem really lies, if I may say so, in the technological transfer through construction of a new factory. What I mean is, in the case of building a new factory, a transplanted new production system will lead to a comparatively large impact, whereas in the case of trying to bring improvements into an old factory or kaizen into old manufacturing processes, the inertial force of the old established ways will act as a great restraint. Because no mechanism for technological transfer between factories has been built into the system, old and new systems come to coexist within one and the same enterprise and huge differences arise between factories. This is not a problem only at FAW, it is a phenomenon that can be seen often on a national level. FAW is struggling hard to overcome this problem, but how far it can introduce the ideas of the lean

---

[35] Shaojie Geng, "FAW Implementation of, and Lessons from, Promoting Lean Production," p. 55.

production system in a coherent form into the whole company will be the biggest touchstone of FAW's evolutionary capability.

4 Conclusion

We have seen the process by which FAW introduced, in stages, the Toyota production system and made it take root – from first introduction of this system through Taiichi Ohno's direct guidance in 1981, then via the construction of a transmission plant on the basis of technological assistant from Hino in later years. Ohno's raising of issues and the systematic introduction of a new management system at the transmission plant are no doubt the two epoch-making events in the evolutionary process of FAW's production system. The introduction of Japan's production management methods contributed to overcoming the rigidity of the old single-medel-mass-production system and increasing flexibility in the production system at FAW, and it provided a good opportunity for the production system to evolve from the Ford system to the Toyota system. In this sense, then, this study has added to the discussion about the international transfer of the Japanese-style production system; a case in point from China.

On the other hand, the case of FAW also has facets that put it beyond the range of the normal approach to the international transfer of the Japanese-style production system. The reason I say this is that, while FAW is a pioneer in introducing the Toyota production system into China, at the same time it is also the prototype of the Ford mass-production system in China.[36] The introduction of the Toyota system in only one aspect within the evolutionary process of FAW's production system. It seems to me, therefore, that the case of FAW has a wider range of application to international comparisons of the formation and evolution of production systems. Perhaps it occupies a place as a unique pattern in the world when it comes to the replacement of the old Ford mass-production system by the new Toyota production system and the latter's diffusion.

Furthermore, Chinese enterprises, especially the state-owned manufacturing enterprises, are facing the acute real problems of deterioration in present operating efficiencies and of breaking away from the old management system under a planned economy regime and the conventional mass-production system. With this double inertial force of the old enterprise system weighing upon everything, reforming the management system of Chinese enterprises and switching to a new production system are more difficult than in European or American enterprises. I

[36] For material on FAW's acceptance of and changes to the Ford system see Chunli Lee, "Adoption of the Ford System and Evolution of the Production System in the Chinese Automobile Industry, 1953–93," in H. Shiomi and K. Wada, eds., Fordism Transformed: The development of Production Methods in the Automobile Industry (Oxford University Press, 1995).

can only hope that FAW's challenge might provide some hints for ways in which China's state-owned enterprises can revive their competitiveness.

Note

This study represents a portion of the research findings from an International Academic Research project, supported by a Japanese Ministry of Education research subsidy and conducted in 1994–96 jointly with the Industrial and Technological Economics Research Institute of the Chinese State Planning Committee, identified as "Strategies for Transferring to China of Contemporary Japanese Diesel Engine Technology for Commercial Vehicles." I have also benefited from comments from the editorial committee of Japanese Yearbook on business History in the preparation of this study. This article is republished here with the permission of the editorial committee. For all the above assistance, I wish to record my profound gratitude. Also, the original Japanese version of this study, published in Keieishigaku (vol. 31 no. 2, July 1996) under the title "Chugoku ni okeru Toyota seisan hoshiki donyu no genryu," was awarded A Prize by the Business History Society of Japan in October 1997.

15 Hybrid Factory in Asia: A Case of Mitsubishi Motors Corporation

Hiroshi Kumon
Hosei University

1 Introduction

The theme of this chapter is the transfer of Japanese business and production systems to Asian countries, with particular reference to the subsidiary plants of Mitsubishi Motors Corporation (MMC). Japanese manufacturing industries have a 20-year track record actively expanding their production activities overseas. As a result, the feasibility of the overseas transferability of these Japanese systems has become widely accepted. Not only the subsidiaries of Japanese companies, but foreign companies themselves have introduced the Japanese system at their local enterprises. However, this does not mean that the system that Japanese and other companies introduce at the local overseas plants is necessarily the same as the system as it exists in Japan. Research has examined, in detail, the twin aspects of the application of the Japanese system as it developed in Japan, and the adaptation of this same system to the business environment of local overseas operations (Abo 1994, Itagaki 1997). The key elements of the Japanese production system are small-lot production, just-in-time (JIT) parts delivery, quality built into the manufacturing process, and multi-skilled workers, which are a requisite condition for implementing the necessary production and quality control into the local operations. Another important element is the long-term relationship between auto assemblers and parts suppliers, particularly in terms of the participation of parts suppliers, right from the early stage of product development, as well as the assurance of JIT parts supply. Finally, there is also the utilization of *kaizen* activities to bring the skills and know-how within the organization to bear on everything from common, everyday problems to changes that occur in the external environment. Japanese multinationals must decide whether to apply these elements to their local operations in order to display the superior competitive strength of their system, or whether to take into consideration the characteristics of the existing, local business environment. The consequent application or adaptation of these elements then gives rise to hybridization.

Factors underlying hybridization include the overseas expansion strategies of the individual companies concerned, characteristics of the industry, and the local overseas business environment.

Firstly, regarding individual companies, while it goes without saying that the character of a particular enterprise will vary in accordance with the character of its founder as well as the history of its growth and development, so too will its competitiveness. Then when it comes to expanding its operations overseas, the strategies that the company will adopt in order to exploit the competitiveness that it has built up domestically are also bound to vary. Factors that comprise its strategy for overseas expansion will include the extent to which it considers its home grown technological and organizational strengths as assets on the international playing field, the manner in which it plans to employ these strengths overseas, whether it should employ a joint venture approach or to go it alone, or whether to establish a knockdown (KD) assembly plant or an integrated production facility.

Secondly, industrial characteristics such as whether the manufacturing process involves numerous parts and manual operations or only relatively simple processes, or whether the product life-cycle is long or short, will determine plant management priorities.

Thirdly, the various local overseas business environments may differ considerably. If the environment is similar to that in Japan, particularly in terms of those elements that support the Japanese system, then there will not be any problems, however, that is seldom the case. If there are systemic differences between the overseas and Japanese environments, and if those differences are obstacles to the successful functioning of the Japanese company, then it will be necessary for the company to radically change those elements and create an entirely new system. However, since this may become the cause of friction between the company and its local environment, another option is to adapt to the local environment in order to avoid these difficulties. In other cases, although the local and Japanese systems differ, it may be found that the local system offers some functional equivalent. Although the systems may essentially differ, if functions of the local system can utilized, then it may be possible to make the Japanese system operate successfully within that environment.

These are the sorts of business environments that Japanese enterprises encounter among the industrially advanced countries. Whether the enterprises choose to vigorously change the local system or create an entirely new system in its place, to adapt to the local environment, or to make use of those elements that are functionally similar, will depend upon the whether these systemic differences are large or small. On the other hand, among the developing countries, particular those in Asia, there are cases where the overseas and Japanese systems have common elements. Even if there are no such common points, in most cases the Asian countries do not have the same kind of deeply rooted and firmly established systems as are seen among the industrially advanced countries. Since these countries have only been industrialized relatively recently, their environmental factors may include a shortage of skilled workers or business managers, poorly developed materials or parts industries, as well as an inadequate infrastructure. In addition, their governments may seek to regulate or to invite the influx of foreign capital.

As a result, when the Japanese system, whose competitive strengths are widely acknowledged, is transferred overseas, it will undergo hybridization. The hybridization theory has also won much support internationally (Boyer et al. 1998 Liker et al. 1999). Future research will focus on issues such as explaining hybridization patterns in terms of regions or enterprises and may, on that basis, suggest optimal hybridization patterns. This chapter will present an analysis of hybridization shown by individual enterprises in Asia. The characteristics of MMC hybrid plants in the Asian region will be the subject of the following discussion.

2 The History and Overseas Expansion of MMC

2.1 The Development Path of MMC

Mitsubishi Motors Corporation (MMC) originated as the auto manufacturing division of Mitsubishi Heavy Industries Ltd. (MHI). Two special characteristics of MMC are relevant to the present discussion. The first characteristic is that MMC inherited a sophisticated level of engine design and production technology from MHI, which the latter had developed and built up even from before World War II. This led directly to a wide range of products that MMC could develop in addition to passenger cars, including commercial vehicles and buses. The auto manufacturing history of MMC stretches back to before World War II. It is believed that the roots of the business lie in the Mitsubishi Model A, which was patterned after the Fiat, and which was produced by Mitsubishi Zosen K.K. at its Kobe shipyards in 1917 and then followed by the production of buses and commercial vehicles. After the war, MHI reactivated the production of commercial vehicles, however in 1950 the company was split into three entities, of which East Japan Heavy Industries and Central Japan Heavy Industries continued to carry out auto manufacturing. Both companies separated their auto making divisions into bus, commercial vehicle, three-wheeler and passenger car operations, and so there was a certain amount of production overlap.

In 1951, East Japan Heavy Industries entered into a tie-up with an American firm to run a KD plant at its Kawasaki plant, however it did not begin its own full-fledged production until New Mitsubishi Heavy Industries started to produce the small Mitsubishi 500 at its plant in Nagoya, in 1960. As the Japanese economy began to boom and was freed of its post-war restraints, the three former MHI companies amalgamated in 1964 and inaugurated the auto manufacturing division as one of five separate divisions which manufactured automobiles, ships, heavy equipment, machinery, and airplanes & special vehicles. From the outset, this auto manufacturing division carried out everything from development through to manufacturing, and it had a wide variety of products including trucks, buses, passenger cars, compact cars, tractors, jeeps, and scooters. While other auto makers began with the manufacture of commercial vehicles, two wheelers and three wheelers and only later expanded to the production of passenger cars, MMC inherited the entire vehicle manufacturing business from MHI, including auto manufacturing, giving it a large product fleet from the very outset.

The second notable characteristic is MMC's tendency to enter into tie-ups with foreign auto manufacturers. In the days when the motorization trend was just beginning to be established, MHI decided to set up its auto manufacturing operations as an independent division in an effort to help expand that business. The company made its auto manufacturing division a specialized and independent operation; it strengthened the division's ability to develop and market popular automobile models; it promoted a policy of reinforcing operating performance through tie-ups and affiliations (Mitsubishi Motors 1993: 232). Internally, MHI organized the "Auto Division Separation Committee" and promoted the independence of its auto manufacturing division. This also involved capital participation on the part of Chrysler Motors and in 1970 the division's independence from MHI and tie-up with Chrysler resulted in the creation of Mitsubishi Motors Corporation. The tie-up with Chrysler helped to introduce American technology, however at the same it also had some negative repercussions, as will be explained below, regarding the development of its overseas market.

In this way, the foreign tie-up, unusual for a Japanese enterprise, was a characteristic of MMC from its very inauguration. This was also in line with the overseas business development strategies of MMC's major shareholders such as MHI and Mitsubishi Corporation. In addition to the Chrysler tie-up, MMC also entered into a marketing agreement with Mercedes Benz in 1987 and received capital participation from Daimler–Chrysler in 2000. Other arrangements included capital participation in the management of a Nedcar plant in 1991 as well as a business tie-up for trucks and buses in 1999, both with Volvo. Undeniably, however, these various tie-ups between MMC and foreign businesses lacked a certain coherence. A complicated set of affiliations that saw its commercial vehicles division tie up with Volvo and its passenger car division tie up with Daimler–Chrysler can only be considered the result of unforeseeable circumstances. This bold strategy of forming alliances with major foreign automakers was also seen in MMC's push into Asia.

Moreover, in the 1990s, MMC successfully entered the new SUV market and at first it was able to expand its market share, however, the company was too slow in responding to the deterioration of the domestic market and ended up accepting a tie-up with Daimler–Chrysler and embarking upon the path of managerial restructuring.

2.2 The Overseas Expansion of MMC: Asian Priorities

A distinctive feature of MMC is its early advance into Asia. As did other companies, MMC focused initially on exports as its strategy for internationalization but after becoming independent from Mitsubishi Heavy Industries it turned to Asia to establish local overseas production. It has many subsidiaries in Asia, especially in ASEAN countries, producing not only vehicles but also carrying out the local production of parts to supply its local auto assembly operations. It operates eight assembly plants and two engine plants in eight East Asian and Southeast Asian countries. These foreign subsidiaries are located in Korea, Taiwan, the Philippines, Vietnam, Thailand, Malaysia, Indonesia and China (Table 15–1) .

Table 15–1. Profile of the MMC's Asian Plants

Plant	Location	Start-up	Equity	Employees (Japanese)	Products
MSC	Thailand	1987	MMC 46.23% MHTC 52.04% Local 1.73%	2,760 (31)	Car 2, Com.V 2
MMPC	Philippines1	1987	MMC 51% Nissho 49%	1,346 (10)	Car2, Com.V7, Bus 1
ATC	Philippines2	1973	MMC 5.3% Nissho 5.3% MMPC 89.4%	487 (5)	Transmission, Engine, Axle
MKM	Indonesia	1973	MMC 32.30% MC 32.30% Local 35.40%	853 (9)	Stamped parts, Engines
VSM	Vietnam	1994	MMC 25% MC 25% Proton 25% Local 25%	192 (6)	Com.V 4, Car 1
HMC	Korea	1979	MMC 4.10% MC 5.28% Local 90.68%	50,984 (0)	Car 10, Com. V 16 Buses 5
CMC	Taiwan	1986	MMC 15.40% MC 5.28% Local 79.32%	2,700 (4)	ComV 8, Car 2
Proton	Malaysia	1883	MMC 8.0% MC 8.0% Local 84.0%	5,662 (17)	Car 3, Engine
CFA	China	1996	MMC 21.3% Local 78.7%	1,300 (6)	Com.V 1

Source: Facts & Figures; Mitsubishi Motors Corporation 2000

Notes: (1) Car = Passenger Car

(2) Com.V = Commercial Vehicle

In contrast, MMC advanced into the USA and Europe later than the other Japanese auto producers. It was unable to develop its own internationalization policy freely because its agreement with the Chrysler Corporation, which was concluded when it gained its independence from Mitsubishi Heavy Industries, imposed restrictions on vehicle exports.

When MMC concluded a tie-up with Chrysler it also entered into a United States Distribution Agreement (USDA) with the same company, according to which the sale of Mitsubishi cars in the US and Mexican markets had to be conducted through the Chrysler sales network. A similar agreement was worked out with Chrysler Canada. Regarding sales outside of North America, it signed a Minor Market Distribution Agreement (MMDA) with Chrysler International SA (CISA) which had exclusive marketing rights to Chrysler cars. This agreement granted CISA the right to supply Mitsubishi cars to markets in Europe, the Middle East, Africa, Central and South America. As a result of these agreements, the only countries where MMC had the right to market its own cars either directly or through a trading company were 17 countries in Asia including Korea, Taiwan, the Philippines, Thailand and Indonesia. It was not until 1982 that these International Distribution Agreements (IDA) were finally dissolved and MMC received the right to set up its own sales network to market autos in Europe and North America. These were the circumstances that led MMC to emphasize exports to the Asian market. Then, after having secured a certain share of the Asian market through direct exports, it embarked on local production in Asian countries, placing its priorities concerning overseas production on plants located in Asia. This is the reason that MMC has a higher proportion of its local overseas production facilities located in Asia than average among other Japanese enterprises (Table 15–2).

In the 1970s, following its independence from Mitsubishi Heavy Industries, MMC pursued two different strategies regarding overseas markets: for developed countries, its strategy was to export, but in East and Southeast Asia, it decided to rely on a combination of exports and local production through joint ventures or technical tie-ups with local partners. Taking a closer look at its activities in Asia, it can be observed that in 1970, MMC's first technical tie-up was with China Motor in Taiwan. In 1972, it obtained a 15% equity in Chrysler Philippines. This company is now owned by MMC and a Japanese trading firm. In 1973, MMC established an auto parts company as a joint venture with local capital in Indonesia. Thereafter, the company turned to auto assembly by producing 4WD vehicles with added investment by MMC. In the same year, MMC concluded a technical tie-up with Hyundai Motors of Korea that resulted in Hyundai developing the first Korean automobile, the Pony, for which MMC supplied assistance in various ways, including supplying the engine. In 1975, MMC entered into a technical tie-up with a Thai auto assembly company.

In the 1980s, MMC implemented further internationalization by actively engaging in local production. At first, it directed most of its attention to Asia. Later, then in the second half of the 1980's it began to advance into the developed

Table 15–2. MMC's Overseas Production

(1,000units; %)

Year	Japan					MMC				
	Domes-tic	Over-seas	Asia			Domes-tic	Over-seas	Asia		
	A	B	C	B/A	C/B	D	E	F	E/D	F/E
1980	11,043	353	20	3.2	5.7	1,105	54	-	4.9	-
1981	11,180	376	20	3.4	5.3	1,095	56	-	5.1	-
1982	10,732	388	10	3.6	2.6	969	52	-	5.4	-
1983	11,112	456	15	4.1	3.3	975	50	-	5.1	-
1984	11,465	654	42	5.7	6.4	1,095	50	-	4.6	-
1985	12,271	956	209	7.8	21.9	1,153	80	31	6.9	38.8
1986	12,260	1,317	283	10.7	21.5	1,178	84	49	7.1	58.3
1987	12,249	1,572	356	12.8	22.6	1,232	101	55	8.2	54.5
1988	12,700	1,809	466	14.2	25.8	1,261	189	132	15.0	69.8
1989	13,026	2,453	612	18.8	24.9	1,230	275	166	22.4	60.4
1990	13,487	3,507	966	26.0	27.5	1,333	422	224	31.7	53.1
1991	13,245	3,696	1,056	27.9	28.6	1,406	444	251	31.6	56.5
1992	12,499	4,051	1,161	32.4	28.7	1,396	452	260	32.4	57.5
1993	11,228	4,668	1,383	41.6	29.6	1,362	508	317	37.3	62.4
1994	10,554	5,318	1,642	50.4	30.9	1,306	612	382	46.9	62.4
1995	10,063	5,901	1,991	58.6	33.7	1,328	695	408	52.3	58.7
1996	10,346	6,138	2,020	59.3	32.9	1,200	755	448	62.9	59.3
1997	10,976	6,331	2,113	57.7	33.4	1,240	845	493	68.1	58.3
1998	10,050	5,867	1,521	58.4	25.9	1,081	606	303	56.1	50.0

Source: Japan Automobile Manufacturing Association, Inc.

countries. Its first local operations were in Korea and Taiwan. In 1982, it obtained equity in Korea's Hyundai Motors through an arrangement with the Mitsubishi Corporation. The following year, when Malaysia established its national auto company, Proton (Persahaan Otomobil Nasional Berhad), MMC participated in the form of investment with Mitsubishi Corporation. In this way, MMC came to hold equity in the largest Asian auto producer outside Japan, namely Hyundai Motors, and also in the company with the largest production capacity among ASEAN countries, namely Proton. In 1986, after the Taiwanese government began to approve joint ventures with foreign firms, MMC also obtained a share of equity in China Motor. The next year, it set up an auto assembly plant with a local partner in Thailand. MMC has also taken advantage of its relationship with Proton to facilitate its advance into the communist countries of Vietnam and China. It has gained permission to begin local production of vehicles in Vietnam and also in China.

3 Overseas Management by MMC: Joint Ventures and Technical Guidance

Two distinctive features characterize overseas plant management by MMC. The first of these is the predominance of joint ventures as the form of engagement, and in particular those in which a local partner takes the upper hand in plant management. MMC's plants in Asia can be classified into those where MMC has managerial control and those where the local partner has control. The former include plants in Thailand, the Philippines, and Vietnam, and the latter include plants in Korea, Taiwan, and Malaysia. In every case of the latter, the joint venture has become the largest local manufacturer in that country, with the help of powerful partners or managers. The second major characteristic is that in those joint ventures where MMC has the managerial authority, the tendency is for MMC to provide production technology guidance. As previously discussed, one aspect of the Japanese-style production system involves production or quality management which relate directly to production, and another aspect are those features that relate to human organization. In the case of MMC, what its local operations all have in common is that plant management is unfailingly characterized by the vigorous application of the Japanese system in terms of those aspects directly related with production. In terms of the human organizational aspects, however, the application of the Japanese system is by no means universal, as indeed there are cases where management adapts to the local system.

3.1 MMC Sittipol in Thailand

MMC established its local operation, MMC Sittipol Co. Ltd., in Thailand in 1987. It retains managerial authority and holds a majority share of the equity in that company. MMC has dispatched 31 Japanese personnel to the company (about 1 per cent of the total workforce) who fill the positions of president, vice-presidents, and other main positions. The company operates two medium-scale plants, the Lardkrabang plant, which produces commercial vehicles such as trucks and buses, and the Leamchabang plant, which produces both passenger cars and pick-up trucks. It is also the first company within the ASEAN countries to succeed in the export of fully assembled vehicles and the first to produce trucks exclusively for export.

The company has attempted to apply the Japanese production system through the initiative of Japanese management, but functioning of the system must be improved. It has adopted the same employment qualification system as in Japan, a system which determines basic wages and the promotion route. It has also introduced individual performance evaluations for all employees. This evaluation partly determines the skill wages, and points accumulated thereby have an effect on promotion. Other elements of the Japanese system, such as multifunctional skills, quality control, small group activities, and a labor-management consultation system, have also been adopted. Some of these elements differ from the way they are applied in Japan and the Japanese managers are not happy about this. Some first-line supervisors do not play a sufficient role in administration; job standard practices are not prescribed by them but by staff members.

3.2 Two Plants in the Philippines

MMC owns two auto plants in the Philippines. One of these is an auto assembly plant and the other is a transmission and engine assembly plant. These plants contrast in their application of the Japanese production system. In other words, the auto assembly plant reflects an adaptation pattern, while the transmission and engine assembly plant demonstrates the application pattern.

In 1972, MMC began capital participation in Chrysler's Philippine plant, Chrysler Philippine Corporation (CPC) and effectively took charge of plant management. Then in 1985, MMC and Nissho Iwai purchased 100% of the company's stock, which is now Mitsubishi Motor Philippine Corporation (MMPC). MMC has transferred 10 Japanese personnel to this plant, including the company's president and vice-president.

In accordance with the local parts procurement policy of the Philippine government, MMC established the Asian Transmission Corporation (ATC) in 1973. This company assembles transmissions and engines and supplies them to CPC. In due course ATC also began to supply transmissions to Thailand, Taiwan, and Indonesia, in line with policies for the reciprocal supply of auto parts among the countries of ASEAN. There are five Japanese personnel at this plant occupying top positions including those of president and vice-president. From the outside, therefore, both enterprises seem very similar, however, they differ in terms of their actual plant management, particularly their labor relations.

As mentioned above, these two enterprises are contrasting examples of how the Japanese system is applied, and they contrast most sharply in regard to wages, job promotion, and labor relations. Turning first to the auto assembly plant, it should be noted that MMPC had difficult relations with its labor union for a long time. Regulations concerning union input on wages and union interference in the job promotion system hindered the type of manufacturing process management that emphasizes quality or to the training of multi-skilled workers. The same labor union, which has represented the workers since Chrysler was in charge, still calls itself the Chrysler labor union and it adopts a confrontational posture towards management in terms of labor relations. Regarding workers' wages, the most common wage system in the Philippine auto industry is the rank-based wages system that is seen in the American electrical assembly industry or in continental

Europe. The wage system at MMPC is quite similar to the traditional US style wage system. In other words, the hourly wage classifications are ranked from 1 to 4. Promotion along this scale is automatic according to seniority, and 95% of the workers are at rank 4. The wage is composed of the minimum wage and annual increase. Although there is also an additional individual evaluation assessment which is 100 pesos, this is small in comparison to the standard wages and it is difficult to determine whether this functions as an effective incentive. Promotion to supervisor involves an interview with the personnel department, however, when it comes to management at the shop floor, the authority of the union executives is too powerful and undermines the authority of the supervisor. For this reason the supervisors have lost their enthusiasm and a situation of inadequate production management has persisted for a long time.

The determination of job standard practices and the method of production control are very similar to those reported at some traditional plants in the US. In other words, the supervisors lack the ability to write up the job standard practices, and this function therefore falls to a staff member who then submits the job standard practices to the shop floor. The deployment of shop floor workers is determined according to peak production conditions. Quality control emphasizes inspection and repair at the final stage of production, so as to maintain a fixed level of quality at the point of shipping. In this way, Japanese managers struggled in the face of confrontational labor relations until a thirteen-day strike occurred in 1998. Since then, management has gradually won back some of its shop floor authority and there are apparently plans to improve the wage system. In addition to recovering shop floor authority from the union and normalizing the role of the supervisor, the company is also striving to increase the amount of the wages based on individual evaluation.

At ATC, on the other hand, the company has achieved harmonious labor relations and it has introduced a Japanese-style management system that takes local customs and practices into consideration. The wage system is one of rank-based wages, reflecting 10 different wage ranks, in addition to which seniority as well as job performance evaluation are factored in to determine the final wage. The supervisor carries out the evaluations that function as the means of determining wages. For example, even if a worker rises from rank 3 to rank 4, this does not automatically guarantee that his wages will increase accordingly. His wages will only rise to rank 4 if his job skills are commensurate with that level. Job evaluations are given on a 5-grade scale. Harmonious labor relations are being maintained, and regular labor-management council conferences are held. Although there was a strike in 1986, the experience has taught everyone the value of talking things out, and this has resulted in conferences. Representatives from each of four groups, namely, management, each of two different labor unions, and the supervisors' group, meet once every two months to discuss matters at a meeting that is chaired by the Japanese president. Below the labor-management council there are seven sub-committees made up of representatives from each work area in the plant. Each conference addresses the issues of safety, employee welfare, hygiene, quality & productivity, improvement of working conditions, and sports. With the company president chairing these conferences and making a visible effort to create and maintain harmonious labor relations, this system is showing results. In fact, even in regard to job management, the job standard practices, which are originally drafted by an engineer, are then re-arranged and amended by the shop floor supervisor, and later improved upon by workers as a *kaizen* activity (small group activities). Shop floor workers achieve quality control by building quality into the manufacturing process at each line. Out of 18 lines, 8 lines are carrying out ppm quality control. Although the defectives ratio is not as low as in Japan, in the case of machine processing operations, a very low level of 0.2% is achieved.

4 Hybrid Evaluation of MMC's Plants in Asia

The hybrid evaluation model developed by the JMNESG (Japan Multinational Enterprise Study Group) may be used to analyze application of the Japanese production system in the case of MMC's Asian plants. This model was developed specifically to assist in evaluating the international transfer of the Japanese system. It assumes that there are 23 items, or features of the Japanese production system, that when fully applied would reflect the total transfer of the Japanese production system to a given local environment. Each of these 23 items is evaluated on a five-point scale, from the perspective of application of the Japanese production system to the local environment. A specific evaluation standard was determined for each item. The framework for the five-point grading system is as follows: If the local plant applies the item in the same way as the parent company does in Japan, then it receives 5 points. However, if the local plant totally adapts by conforming completely to the local environment, then it receives only 1 point. Accordingly, if its production system reflects an intermediate position between full application and full adaptation, then it receives 3 points. This is the basic concept underlying the five-point grading system. By the same token, 4 points or 2 points are awarded if the local plant's production system more closely resembles the Japanese system or the local system, than an intermediate position, respectively (Abo 1994). This model makes it easy to identify the application characteristics of a given local production system. Furthermore, it is possible to derive more useful data by simplifying these results. By classifying the 23 items into certain categories and then calculating the average application points for the items in each category, it is possible to distinguish certain types of application patterns. For example, 22 of the 23 items can be usefully grouped into the following four categories or aspects: human-method, human-result, material-method and material-result. "Method" items refer to the actual processes underlying the Japanese management/production processes, while "result" items refer to the necessary physical resources (human or material) such as production equipment, local content, or the number of Japanese expatriates.

Table 15–3. Hybrid Evaluation for 3 Regions

	Human		Material		Average
	Method	Result	Method	Result	
USA	3.1	3.7	2.9	3.6	3.3
Asia	3.4	2.4	3.3	3.6	3.3
UK	3.4	2.8	3.3	2.7	3.2

Sources: Abo (1994), Itagaki (1997), and field research by author.

As Table 15–3 indicates, and as suggested above, the 22 items of the hybrid analysis are grouped into four categories: (1) Human–Method, (2) Human–Result, (3) Material–Method, and (4) Material–Result. The hybrid evaluation model makes it possible to derive hybrid patterns for technology/organization transfer.

The hybridization pattern seen in Japanese-affiliated manufacturing plants located in the UK display the "method-application, result-adaptation" pattern. This means that "method" items recorded an average of more than 3 points, which reflects an application orientation; human method is 3.3 points and material method is 3.4 points. On the other hand, "result" items recorded an average of less than 3 points, indicating an adaptation orientation. This pattern suggests that the plants apply the Japanese system and use local resources in human and material aspects. Positive application of the Japanese system assures efficiency and quality. Also, since the plants do not depend to a high degree upon their Japanese parent companies for material and human resources, this reduces the expenses otherwise associated with transport, and special allowances for local life, etc. Therefore, this pattern minimizes costs while maximizing the benefits to be obtained from application of the Japanese system; it is the ideal type of technology transfer for the activities of the multinational enterprises.

The companies studied in the US show a "method-application, result-application" pattern. Moreover, the degree of application for results is higher than that for method; the average degree of application for method is about 3 points (human-method 3.1 points, material-method 2.9 points) while application for result is quite high at 3.7 for human-result and 3.6 for material-result. In their transfer of the Japanese system they apply Japanese methods while relying heavily upon Japanese results.

The Asian pattern shows a "method-application, material result-application" pattern. Application is higher than 3 points for both human and material methods, however when it comes to results, the degree of application is high for material-result but not for human result; material-result is high at 3.6, but human-result is low at 2.4 points. Asian plants take advantage of the similarity between Japan and other Asian countries in the human resource aspect. For this reason, Japanese companies do not expatriate many managers from the parent companies to the local plants in Asian countries. On the other hand, Asian countries rely heavily on Japan for equipment and parts because they have not fully developed their own

Table 15–4. Four Aspect Evaluation for MMC's Asian Plants

	Human		Material		Average
	Method	Result	Method	Result	
Korea	2.5	1.0	3.5	1.3	2.3
Taiwan	3.8	1.0	3.8	2.3	3.3
Malaysia	3.5	2.0	2.8	3.0	3.1
Thailand	3.2	2.5	3.0	3.7	3.1
Philippines 1	2.1	2.0	2.0	2.8	2.2
Philippines 2	3.3	2.0	2.8	3.3	3.1
Vietnum	2.5	2.5	1.5	5.0	2.7
Austrailia	2.7	1.0	2.8	1.8	2.4

Source: Culculation by author

Notes: (1) Human Method = Work Organization + Group Consciousness + Labour Relations

(2) Human Result = Ratio of Japanese Expatriates + Position of Local managers

(3) Material Method = Maintenance + Quality Control + Process Management + Procurement Method

(4) Material Result = Equipment + Local Content + Suppliers

industries to supply machinery and other supportive materials. For this reason, there is a high degree of application in material result.

Table 15–4 shows hybrid patterns for each of the MMC plants in Asia. Two factors that determine the type of hybrid patterns are the enterprise's strategy in regard to applying the Japanese system, and the overseas business environment at the local plant. The surveys that were carried out in the process of our research revealed that among Asian countries, it was Taiwan that offered a business environment most suitable for the application of the Japanese system. The business environment in Taiwan has many aspects in common with that in Japan partly due to the fact that the level of economic development is also very similar to Japan's. This is reflected in conditions at the MMC plant in Taiwan. The hybrid pattern of China Motor was method-application, result-adaptation, and the application of the Japanese production system is promoted through the initiative of local managers.

The Philippines is unusual among Asian countries in its tendency towards confrontational labor relations. In the area of work organization, the wage system has rank-based job wages and workers are called "hourlies." MMC has two plants in the Philippines which are fundamentally different in character. The vehicle assembly plant has fairly confrontational labor relations, even by local standards, and the level of application of the Japanese production system is quite low. The hybrid pattern for this plant is method-, result - adaptation. On the other hand, the transmission plant has harmonious labor relations and it has a mixture of application elements of the Japanese system. For the human aspect it shows a method-application, results-adaptation pattern, while in the material aspect it is method-adaptation, results-application. Thus, in the Philippines, where labor relations can easily become confrontational, a division in the type of hybrid patterns is apparent.

The plant in Thailand revealed a hybrid pattern that was fairly similar to the transmission plant in the Philippines.

5 Conclusion

This chapter has discussed the overseas expansion of MMC and the hybrid patterns of its local production plants in Asia. The first notable feature about MMC's overseas production is its conspicuous concentration in Asia. In terms of changes in the overall ratio of overseas to domestic production, the trend for MMC is very close to the average ratio for Japanese auto manufacturers. In regard to production in Asia, however, the ratio is very high. Whereas the average ratio of overseas production in Asia versus overall for the Japan auto manufacturers is 30%, in the case of MMC this ratio stands at 60%. In general, the order for internationalization in the auto industry is from exports to overseas production. Since the international sales agreements that MMC entered into with Chrysler restricted its ability to sell automobiles overseas, MMC had to concentrate its attention on Asian markets, which were not subject to those agreements. This is the reason that MMC focused its overseas production efforts on Asia, an effort that was assisted by the diversity of its product fleet, which included trucks and buses.

Secondly, MMC adopted a variety of forms for its overseas production. Due to the presence of governmental regulations, it is fair to say that the joint venture is the most common form of overseas production in Asian countries. Moreover, in forming these joint ventures MMC chose strong companies as its business partners in Korea, Taiwan, and Malaysia. Its energetic pursuit of tie-ups with foreign partners, and the cooperation it received from other companies in the Mitsubishi group no doubt helped to account for the variety of forms the company adopted in its foreign ventures.

The third notable characteristic about MMC's overseas expansion is that since the company originated as a division of MHI it enjoyed a high level of production technology. While this can certainly be used to advantage in the management of an overseas production plant, there are limitations to the international transfer of that technology. A particular example is the human organization aspect of the system, whose transfer is constrained by the local business environment. In other words, in the transfer of the production system, certain elements of the system adapt to the local environment. This was apparent in the plants located in the Philippines. Although it was not a subject of this paper, even at MMC's plant in Australia, where MMC has complete managerial authority, the opinions of local managers who have been at the plant since its Chrysler days are respected, and human organizational aspects of the Japanese system are not always transferred. Thus, adaptation to the local environment is seen even at plants where the company has full managerial control. When Japanese auto manufacturing enterprises enjoy managerial authority they generally try to apply the Japanese production system in a comprehensive manner. MMC, however, places priority on the transfer of those system elements directly related to production, and will adapt to the local environment on those aspects related to human organization.

References:

Abo, T. ed., (1994) *Hybrid Factory: The Japanese Production System in the United States*, Y: Oxford.

Boyer, R., et al., eds. (1998) *Between Imitation and Innovation: The Transfer and Hybridization of Productive Models in the International Automobile Industry*, NY: Oxford University Press.

Itagaki, T. ed. (1997) *The Japanese Production System: Hybrid Factories in East Asia*, London: Macmillan.

Kumon, H., (1994) "International Transferability of the Japanese Production System: Japanese-affiliated Auto Plants in the USA, the UK, and Taiwan," Hosei University, *Journal of International Economic Studies*, No.8.

Kumon, H., (1997) "The Japanese Production System and Its International Transferability," Universiti Utara Malaysia, *Malaysian Management Journal*, Vol.2, No.2.

Kumon, H., et al., eds. (2000) *Mirroring Consensus: Decision-Making in Japanese-Dutch Business*, Utrecht: Lemma.

Liker, J.K., et al., eds. (1999) *Remade in America: Transplanting and Transforming Japanese Management Systems*, NY: Oxford University Press.

Mirza, H. ed. (1998) *Global Competitive Strategies in the New World Economy: Multinationalism, Regionalization and the Transnational Firm*, Cheltenham: Edward Elgar.

Schutte, H. ed. (1994) *The Global Competitiveness of the Asian Firm*, NY: St. Martin's Press.

Japan Automobile Manufactures Association, Inc, *The Motor Industry of Japan*.

Mitsubishi Motors, *Facts and Figures*; Mitsubishi Motors Corporation 2000.

Mitsubishi Motors, *Mitsubishi Jidosha-kogyo Kabushi Kaishashi* (History of Mitsubishi Motors Corporation), 1993.

Subject Index

Author and Company Index

MIX
Papier aus verantwortungsvollen Quellen
Paper from responsible sources
FSC® C105338
FSC
www.fsc.org

If you have any concerns about our products,
you can contact us on
ProductSafety@springernature.com

In case Publisher is established outside the EU,
the EU authorized representative is:
Springer Nature Customer Service Center GmbH
Europaplatz 3, 69115 Heidelberg, Germany

Printed by Libri Plureos GmbH
in Hamburg, Germany